Introduction to Behavioural Science

Martin O'Grady

Gill & Macmillan

Gill & Macmillan Ltd
Hume Avenue
Park West
Dublin 12
with associated companies throughout the world
www.gillmacmillan.ie

© 2001 Martin O'Grady
0 7171 3127 0
Index compiled by Kate Duffy
Print origination in Ireland by Carole Lynch

A catalogue record is available for this book
from the British Library.

Contents

Chapter 3 Perception

Chapter 4 Learning

Chapter 5 Intelligence

Chapter 6 Personality

Chapter 7 Attitudes

Chapter 8 Motivation

Chapter 9 Groups and Leadership

Chapter 10 Organisational Design and Culture

Chapter 11 Society, Culture and Work

A Message to the Reader

At present you are most probably taking a third-level course which you expect will equip you for a role in the workplace. A great proportion of human endeavour occurs in the workplace. Workers built the pyramids; workers put men on the moon; workers developed and ran the economies that made such events possible. With the exception of the forming of relationships, child rearing and the pursuit of leisure, virtually every significant human activity is carried out principally in the workplace. Virtually all workplaces require constant co-operation among employees. Understanding people, their capacities and limitations, their tendencies and ways of thinking, is surely a step towards better co-operation. That is what this book is about – helping you to better understand others.

The potential benefits of understanding others are not, of course, limited to the workplace. Three major aspects of life – relationships, child rearing and leisure – were mentioned above as generally taking place outside of this context. One can hardly doubt the equal relevance of insight into human behaviour to those realms of daily life.

Human behaviour can be explored from a number of complementary standpoints. Firstly, there are key characteristics in respect of which people show striking variations. These include the following:

'Perceptual Processes' – the way information about the world is initially processed and stored in the brain.

'Learning' – relatively enduring changes or potential changes in behaviour that result from experience.

'Intelligence' – variations in mental capacity to process information and solve problems.

'Personality' – relatively permanent tendencies to think, feel and behave in particular ways over time and across situations.

xiv   Introduction to Behavioural Science

'Attitudes' – emotional, cognitive and behavioural responses to people, objects, issues and events encountered in life.

'Motivation' – the factors and circumstances that drive or encourage
individuals to apply effort in the pursuit of particular goals.

Those six characteristics provide the subject matter for Chapters 3-8.
Though nobody is fixed inevitably for life in respect of any of the factors
discussed, we all carry around our own unique blueprint for each characteristic, which we stamp upon reality as we encounter it. Day to day, you
remain the same person in terms of your personality, attitudes, intelligence, ability to learn and so on. You are more predictable and understandable to others to the extent that they grasp these essential features
of your make-up.

A second approach to understanding human behaviour is to explore
the effects of human interaction. While you remain essentially the same
person in terms of your individual characteristics, you will inevitably
change behaviour in response to those you engage with. If you view
someone as well-meaning and co-operative, you are likely to ignore the
many little ways in which he or she may cause you inconvenience. If you
view him or her as selfish and unhelpful, you are likely to react with some
hostility to the same inconveniences. Our actions are the products of
those with whom we deal as much as of our own individual selves. This
leads to an exploration of group effects with which Chapter 9 is concerned. It looks at the processes by which we are drawn into interdependent relationships and how those relationships impact upon us.

A third approach to explaining behaviour involves a focus on a specific context within which a great deal of action, in particular action that
is work-related, takes place. This context is the 'Organisation', which is
dealt with in Chapter 10. All organisations are designed in order to control the actions of the people operating within them, and they vary in
the way they are designed so as to effect this control. Organisations can
be designed to restrict freedom and initiative or alternatively to promote
individual responsibility and autonomy. Whatever their intended effects
and ultimate outcomes, an understanding of organisational design and
culture is essential to a full exploration of human behaviour.

Finally, all of us grow up within a framework of generally accepted values, norms, rules and expectations emanating from the culture of our own society. Whether, for example, we live to work or work to live is largely a product of our culture. Culture changes over time along with other defining features of society such as its economy and political arrangements. Ireland has gone through a period of radical change in the last 40 years or so, and these changes have had profound effects on our culture and behaviour, not least in the context of work. Chapter 11 explores the broad influences of society and culture on behaviour with particular emphasis on the Irish context.

Whether we are seeking to understand individual human characteristics, group processes, organisational influences or the impact of the broader society within which we live, we are reliant on the work of innumerable behavioural scientists – psychologists, sociologists and others. It is essential at the outset to understand how they explore their topics and arrive at conclusions. Chapters 1 and 2 are devoted to explaining what exactly is meant by the term 'behavioural science' and how such scientists conduct what we call research.

It is intended that this book will shed light on much that is familiar and yet may pass daily without question or understanding. Why are advertisements designed as they are? Why do employers take such different approaches to the management of staff? What do intelligence tests tell or fail to tell us? Can personality be measured objectively? Why do organisations feel as if they have personalities of their own?

The reader is advised to consider the structure of each chapter. It is designed to encourage active rather than passive reading, an approach that is far better for learning and retention. Active reading involves reading with certain questions in your mind. You actively interrogate the text. Use the learning objectives and the story or illustrative case in the introduction to each chapter to identify the questions you should seek to answer. Constantly check your understanding by mentally summarising the answers the text gives you. As you read the material, ask yourself if the answers to the questions are becoming clear. If you have difficulty understanding some issue, don't just skip it, read back on the relevant paragraphs and see if you have missed any crucial point. Research shows that a key difference between better and weaker students is that while the better ones engage with material they find hard to understand, the weaker ones jump impatiently ahead. It is in your power to be a better student. If you still do not understand a particular point, read on and see if things become clearer as you complete the chapter.

Don't forget that a textbook is not a course in itself. It is one of several learning sources you should draw on. Your behavioural science lecturer is a key resource. Help him or her to help you by asking about anything that you find confusing. As you read through each chapter you will encounter text boxes. They are examples and further elaborations on points made in the body of the text. Read them! They should help make important issues clearer. At the end of each chapter read carefully through the summary asking yourself if you now understand each point. If not, read the relevant part of the chapter again. The references scattered everywhere throughout the text and listed in full at the end of each chapter indicate the original material from which the information is drawn. It is good practice to read some of this original material if you can lay your hands on it. Your college library should have a range of the books and journal articles listed.

If you adopt the more active approach described here to reading this text book, not only will you learn more and make more productive use of the time spent on it but you will also find the whole process much more rewarding. Enjoy the read.

Martin O'Grady

Chapter 1

What is Behavioural Science?

LEARNING OBJECTIVES

When you have read this chapter you should be able to explain:

- the alternative pathways to arriving at knowledge and their associated limitations;
- how the scientific method attempts to overcome the difficulties involved in knowing what is true;
- what the main characteristics of the scientific approach are; and
- how the scientific approach is applied to the study of human behaviour.

INTRODUCTION

At the start of the third millennium it is a generally accepted fact that all the matter in the universe, including our own bodies, is made up of 105 basic elements such as carbon, nitrogen and oxygen. Within the human body as in all living things the elements form molecules which are built up into different kinds of cells. There are many different kinds of cells corresponding to the different kinds of tissue in the body such as skin, bone and brain tissue. It is accepted that the brain is a very complex organ comprising billions of cells known as neurones intricately linked up together in a complex network. It is this organ that physically controls our behaviour – everything from our breathing to our personalities, learning and memories. In the chapters that follow we will explore the factors that influence the brain so as to produce the individual pattern of behaviour that we witness in each person.

Our current understanding of matter in general, the human brain and human behaviour was not shared by the majority of people throughout history. Learned scholars proposed what became widely accepted views of human behaviour that to us now seem ridiculous. Aristotle (384-322 BC), a Greek scholar who influenced the whole of western philosophy, believed that the function of the brain was only to cool down the blood. The heart was the seat of the human soul and responsible for human behaviour. We still talk about people being soft-hearted or hard-hearted, though we know that the heart has nothing to do with how people behave.

Another great Greek scholar, Hippocrates (c.460-370 BC), explained that human personality was a function of the makeup of one's body. He, together with other learned men of his time, believed that the body was made up of four substances: blood; bile; black bile; and phlegm. The substances, or *humours* as they were known, were understood to exist in differing proportions in different people. The one that dominated, according to Hippocrates, dictated one's personality type. Those high on blood were held to be hopeful, optimistic types, those high on phlegm, slow and apathetic. A predominance of bile produced an ill-tempered individual and a high level of black bile resulted in depression and fearfulness. This view of the human body and its effect on human personality endured right up to the seventeenth century.

The issue of interest to us in this chapter is how did we eventually come to discover that such ideas were totally in error? How have we come to know what we now know? What makes the information expressed in this textbook any different to the views of Aristotle and Hippocrates, doubtless men of far greater intellect in their day than the present author? The answer lies within an understanding of science.

To most people 'science' is a thoroughly familiar word. It is impossible to progress through the school system without significant exposure to subjects that are all part of this concept called 'science'. Physics, chemistry and biology will immediately come to mind. Indeed, you may well have been left with the impression that science is a kind of collective term to describe the study of those three subjects because that is what 'science' in school largely deals with. This, however, is not an accurate picture. The term 'science' does not refer to the subject matter being studied at all. It refers instead to the way it is studied or investigated, to the way knowledge about any particular subject is obtained.

Physics, chemistry and biology are just three areas to which a common method called 'science' is applied to uncover knowledge. In physics, for example, this method is used to discover how the universe was created and what laws govern the matter of which it consists. In biology it is used to explain the makeup and functioning of living organisms. This same method can be used to explore almost any topic of interest, from UFOs to how economies function. Of more direct interest to us here, it can be used to explore human nature and human behaviour.

Behavioural science is the use of the scientific method to understand human behaviour. To appreciate what this means it is necessary to understand what the scientific method involves and how it works. Firstly, however, you will need to grasp what problem the scientific method is designed to overcome. Put simply, it is the problem that has faced humankind from its primeval origins on the plains of Africa: how to know what is true from what is false; and how to know, for example, whether Hippocrates' theory of personality is correct.

SOURCES OF KNOWLEDGE

If you think for a moment about how you 'know' anything is true, you will find that you rely on a limited number of sources of information.

Sources of information can be described as falling under the following three headings:

Personal experience channelled through your five senses – e.g. you can *see* that a person is behaving angrily or that the sun is shining.

Reputable reports or authoritative sources – reports by others, whom you trust, that something is true, e.g. your doctor tells you that you have an inflamed appendix, your lecturer tells you that personality is partly inherited through the genes or you read in the newspaper that five people died in a fire in Dublin.

Logical thought – putting together information you already have in a new way to arrive at a fresh piece of knowledge. For example, if you accept that personality is partly a product of genetic inheritance and that identical twins have exactly the same genes while fraternal twins share on average only 50 per cent of their genes, it should logically follow that identical twins can be expected to have more similar personalities than fraternal twins (see Chapter 6 for a discussion of this example).

If you discount divine, magical or supernatural inspiration (see Box 1.1 below), these are the only three routes to finding out what is true about any topic. You experience it yourself, you are told it by someone else or you can work it out from information you already have.

BOX 1.1

DIVINE, MAGICAL OR SUPERNATURAL INSPIRATION

For most of human history in all parts of the world divine or magical inspiration was an unquestioned route to knowledge. It was assumed that certain chosen individuals, variously called shamen, druids, oracles or religious teachers, had direct links with the supernatural where it was assumed true knowledge resided. Ordinary folk depended on them not just for knowledge of the afterlife but for information on everyday material issues. When will the rains come? What causes thunder and lightning? When is a good time to wage war? How will my illness be cured? Those were the kinds of questions which could only be answered by such special members of the community, by those who could tap into a great fount of knowledge beyond normal human access.

What is the status today of this historically well-trodden path to 'knowledge'? Do so many people read their horoscopes or seek the advice of fortune-tellers about their futures just to poke fun at those quaint relics of our pre-scientific, superstitious past? Not so. A straw poll among your friends or classmates will doubtless reveal that there is a widespread lingering conviction that 'mystics' may know more than the ordinary mortal.

From a scientific standpoint should we dismiss all claims to magical or supernatural insight as nonsense and the work of crackpots and charlatans? It is tempting to do so and in the vast majority of cases we would be right. A true application of the scientific method, however, demands that we keep an open mind but subject such claims to rigorous scrutiny.

Even a superficial scrutiny will reveal the hollowness of most supernatural 'insights'. However, it is not beyond the bounds of possibility that certain humans possess unusual and as yet unexplained powers. Whether any individual does or does not possess a peculiar route to knowledge is amenable to being tested. Even if such powers are demonstrated and have no explanation known to science, it does not follow that we must accept them as supernatural. Just as dogs can detect smells and sights entirely outside the scope of the human senses, it may be the case that some individuals have special sensory capacities, which in time may be fully understood.

Indeed, evidence from the field of cognitive psychology (see Chapter 3) suggests that we all have abilities of which we are largely unconscious. In the past it has often been suggested that powers of intuition (knowing things without any obvious source of knowledge) in individuals have some kind of supernatural basis. Psychologists now suspect that intuition may be due to the fact that much of our information processing is unconscious. They have even been able to demonstrate experimentally that people can act on visual information presented for such a brief period that they have no awareness of having seen anything (see Claxton, 1998, for a brief review of relevant research).

What once seemed supernatural may, with adequate scientific scrutiny, be shown to be natural enough, though none the less fascinating for that.

THE PROBLEM OF RELIABLE KNOWLEDGE

Each of the three approaches to discovering accurate information described above has its own in-built flaws or problems. Let's consider each in turn:

Personal experience – There are a number of reasons why one's own experience is a limited and unreliable route to knowledge. Firstly, our system for processing information is highly selective in what it brings to our notice. We are much more likely, for example, to notice things that stand out in some way. Changes in lighting or colour, movement and unusual shapes capture our attention (see Folk, Remington and Wright, 1994). Conversely, we are likely to remain unaware of a great many other sights and sounds, which were available to be seen and heard, simply because we cannot process a great deal of information at the one time. A further problem with information detected through the senses is that we build up an understanding of what we have seen, heard etc., that is significantly based on our existing knowledge, needs and expectations (e.g. Hastorf and Cantrill, 1954). Hastorf and Cantril asked students from two schools to watch a video of a football match between their school teams and to record the number of fouls committed by members of each team. Both groups of students detected more fouls committed by the opposing side. Their partisanship dictated what they actually noticed. The processes of selection and organisation inherent in our perception system will be discussed in more detail in Chapter 3.

Then there is the problem of memory. Any knowledge that we obtain through our senses is necessarily a memory of what we have experienced. Memory, as we all know when studying for exams, deteriorates over time. You may have witnessed five raiders entering a bank but months later, when asked in court for the number, you may have forgotten and say there were four or six. Court cases frequently reveal serious mistakes and misidentifications in eyewitness reports (see: Wells, 1993; Cutler and Penrod, 1995). Part of the eyewitness accuracy problem has to do with the selective and constructive way humans initially perceive information, as discussed in the last paragraph. The problem also derives from the way in which memory operates. Researchers have demonstrated that our memories are affected by later information. Memories from different occasions may become conflated or suggestions after the event may take on the dimensions of actual memories (see: Loftus, 1979; Loftus and Hoffman, 1989).

A further problem with personal experience is that it confines one to a limited sample of events that may be unrepresentative. If I were to visit

Paris on three occasions and each time it was raining heavily, I might come away with the conviction that it has a particularly wet climate – which would be wrong. If one's total knowledge of Limerick City was derived from either the feature film or the novel, *Angela's Ashes* (McCourt, 1996), imagine how inaccurate a picture of contemporary Limerick would result.

In many areas where each of us has personal experience, our sample of the total picture is very limited. The laws of probability, therefore, dictate that we are likely to be presented with an unrepresentative impression. Finally, to add to all those basic flaws, just discussed, there is the following obvious limitation of gaining information through one's senses: it limits you to knowledge that you have had the opportunity to witness. The whole of history and much of the world would remain unknown if we had to rely for knowledge solely on our experience.

Reputable reports or authoritative sources – Throughout history most people have relied mainly on this source of knowledge, whether the reports of what was true came from one's parents, from wise elders, from religious leaders, from journalists or from scientists. The big problem concerns how to know if a source is trustworthy – that it knows and is willing to tell you what the truth is. Generally, leaps of faith were made in regard to authoritative sources. Religious leaders or those supposed to have supernatural powers were heavily relied on for knowledge. When the Christian Church taught that the earth was flat and at the centre of the universe, it was taken to be the truth. People accepted that the church was an authoritative source. Now we know that all this was wrong, as was a great deal of what was said by authoritative sources in the past (see Box 1.2 below for a discussion on the relationship between science and religion). Yet we still rely heavily on authoritative sources. If I have a headache, I may take a paracetamol or an aspirin tablet. Its manufacturers advertise that it will relieve pain and cause no harm in the process. How am I to know that this latter claim is true, that paracetamol or aspirin are indeed harmless substances to take?

I may suspect that watching a lot of violent TV causes a child to act more violently in the playground. But how am I to know for sure? Who can I trust to tell me and how did he/she establish the truth in the first place? This is where science comes in. Science is a method (or more properly a collection of methods) developed and refined over time to solve the problem of how we can decide whom to trust. How it works will be described in simple terms later in this chapter.

Logical thought – In classical Greece this was thought to be a superior pathway to knowledge, somehow purer and less tainted than personal experience. Yet, quite obviously it is dogged by the problems of the other two approaches. To work anything out logically one must begin with some information from which to draw inferences. Anything worked out logically from available information will only be true if the information on which it is based is true. That clearly brings us back to the problems associated with personal experience and reputable reports.

BOX 1.2

ARE RELIGION AND SCIENCE COMPATIBLE?

In the US the ancient battle lines between science and religion are drawn up once again. Perhaps they have never been stood down in some parts. In 1632 in Italy the issue was whether or not the earth lay at the centre of the universe. Following careful astronomical observation, Gallileo published the view that it was not. He was forced by the Inquisition to retract. The Church held that his views were heretical. In 1999, in Kansas, the issue was whether life evolved over millions of years or was created in six days as stated in Genesis. The Kansas Board of Education, under pressure from religious fundamentalists, did not go so far as to ban the teaching of Darwin's Theory of Evolution but did declare it not to be examinable information in schools in the state. Kansas is the latest of several states to curtail in some way the teaching of evolution as an explanation for life on earth.

If Darwin, as most scientists hold, was correct, does it follow that the Bible was wrong on this most fundamental of all issues? If humans evolved from lower organisms, where is the need for God and why should anyone pay any attention to the Bible? Most devout Christians do not take the Bible literally. They see it as more of a parable. The Genesis story is a simple timeless way of putting across the general idea that there is a Divine author of all reality. How the material world unfolds and to what plan is unknowable to mortals. The key teachings of the Bible do not concern explanations for material reality, which is the province of science, but rather matters of morality or right and wrong, areas that are not the direct concern of scientific exploration.

Does it follow then that science can tell us nothing about morality, about what actions are right or wrong? Not entirely. While science cannot decide the basis on which we declare an action to be right or wrong, once the criteria for the morality of an act is agreed on religious or philosophical grounds, it can tell us whether the action meets those criteria. A widely accepted criterion (though by no means the only one) for defining any given action as 'right' or 'wrong' is whether it harms or injures those affected by the action. The scientific method can easily be harnessed in this context. Take, for example, the controversy over human cloning. Behavioural, medical and biological scientists can attempt to predict the consequences for the health, life expectancy and quality of life of the product of a human cloning in a given set of circumstances. If it were to be shown that a human clone might reasonably expect to suffer serious adverse psychological consequences – say through feeling himself or herself to be a 'freak' – then the morality of human cloning could be questioned on a scientific basis.

A further problem is that not everyone is terribly good at using logic. It is quite common for individuals to draw conclusions from information that do not stand the test of logic. Prejudices are a good example of this. Racist individuals when faced even with lots of real live members of the disliked race, who evidently are quite nice persons, commonly do not revise their view of the race (see Kunda and Oleson, 1997). They simply, without any particular evidence, assume that the cases they have met are unrepresentative. Another example of where people commonly fail in their use of logic is to assume that the first or the most obvious conclusion drawn from the available information must be the truth. Whether a conclusion is obvious to any individual is to a large extent based on assumptions applied to that situation, assumptions that may or may not be true.

A striking study carried out by Rosenhan (1973) revealed the extent to which normal assumptions can lead even highly trained professionals into serious error. Rosenhan and a number of colleagues showed up at psychiatric hospitals complaining of hearing voices. They were all admitted and in the main diagnosed as having schizophrenia. After admission they made no further effort to seem in any way abnormal. Yet staff saw ample evidence of abnormal behaviour. As part of their research into how psychiatric patients are treated they all kept diaries. This was interpreted as abnormal behaviour. Simply, it never occurred to the staff that ordinary psychiatric patients would keep detailed diaries for some useful purpose. This was, therefore, further evidence of abnormality fitting in with the diagnosis already made.

All of us are severely limited in what we can find out through personal experience (and even then our perception and memory of what we experience is highly unreliable). We are also frequently limited in our logical powers. As a result, we constantly rely on others to give us the knowledge to make all kinds of important decisions. We need to have some way of knowing when to trust a source. That is the intended contribution of science.

HOW SCIENCE WORKS

In simple terms, science is a collection of methods and approaches designed to establish with as much confidence as possible what is true about any subject. It relies heavily on rigorous cross-checking of work. The saying that 'two heads are better than one' is true, only much more so, of science. In science, it is 'many heads are better than one'. In the practice of science there are a variety of detailed procedures for investigating any question. They are called 'research designs'. The most powerful of these is called the 'experiment'. Research designs and experiments will be discussed in more detail in Chapter 2. The objective of the precise procedures or research designs is to make it clear to all how the scientist came to the conclusions he or she arrived at after investigating a subject.

Even then, the work of one scientist is never trusted. It must be carefully analysed and even repeated or 'replicated' by others to see if there are any flaws in the methods and to see if the same results emerge again.

While science has roots in western civilisation dating back over 2000 years, it is only in the last few centuries that it has taken on anything like its current status as a route to knowledge. A brief overview of the development of science is given in Box 1.3 below.

Let's look now in some more detail at what makes science work – what its essential characteristics are. Remember, it is a method that can be applied to almost any subject. On this course we are concerned with its application to human behaviour.

THE CHARACTERISTICS OF SCIENCE

Specialisation – There is simply so great a volume of information that no scientist, no human, could be expert in anything other than a very narrow field. If scientists did not specialise, no progress would be made, as they would spend all their time trying to gain a grasp on existing knowledge and would have no time to explore anything new. Nowadays, different areas of scientific enquiry are highly specialised because of this. A scientist who specialises in biology will normally specialise in some very precise area within that field such as the study of a particular species of fresh-water snail or a particular type of bacterium. A psychologist will not study human behaviour in general but will specialise in an area like human memory or the behaviour of humans in small groups.

A large and widespread community of experts – If every scientist deals with only a narrow area of study, it is essential that there are lots of scientists to study related areas so that a bigger picture can be built up. It is essential also that there are sufficient experts in individual areas to cross-check and replicate each other's work. This greatly helps to prevent errors from going unnoticed. It also prevents fraud. Unfortunately, both individual scientists and institutions have in the past attempted to mislead the public about important matters. Would you trust a pharmaceutical company to tell you about the risks and side effects of a drug, if there were no way of checking the truth of what they said?

You can probably appreciate now why a large number of experts in each area is desirable – but why widespread? This is to ensure that under all circumstances there are experts in each field who are free to tell the truth. Imagine if all the experts on the study of intelligence were resident in Nazi Germany during the 1930s. They would not have been free to publish any research which disagreed with the government's view that certain races such as Jews and Slavs were intellectually inferior. If all the experts were in Germany there would have been no one of scientific standing to say that this was rubbish.

It is easy to imagine a similar situation if all the world experts in a field, say nuclear energy, were employed by the same employer or even industry – the nuclear power industry. The public would be right to feel sceptical about what they said about the safety of nuclear power. The important thing is that scientists who are free from pressure should always exist, so that they can publish what they believe to be the truth. Even the most honest scientist may be a bit reticent in criticising the work of a friend or work colleague. Those who are far apart and with no personal relationships are likely to be less inhibited in speaking out. In this way, where criticism is merited, it will emerge.

A communication system – You will have noticed that a '*community*' of experts was referred to above. A community is only a community if there is some facility for communication among the members. We normally think of communities as living closely together and meeting each other regularly. However communication need not be face to face. It can be over the telephone, through the internet, etc. The most important vehicle for communication among scientists is through publications. Having carried out their research, scientists have available to them specialist journals in which to publish the details of their work and findings. These journals are available to other experts in the field world-wide, who can then examine, criticise or replicate the work, publishing their views and findings in turn. Scientists also communicate through conferences where they meet and discuss their work in detail and, of course, through the internet, on the telephone, face-to-face and so on. Clearly, if scientists were not able to communicate easily with each other they would be greatly hampered by not being able to avail of the insights and discoveries made by others.

In addition, it would not be possible for scientists to critically appraise each other's work. Errors and downright attempts to mislead would go undetected. Science as we know it would come to a halt.

Conventions of scientific behaviour – Conventions are unwritten rules. All scientists develop an understanding of what it is to behave in a scientific way. It is not all that easy to explain in a complete sense what this involves, but the list of conventions which follow make up the principal features of scientific behaviour. Taken together, they add up to a recipe for ensuring that whatever is studied is examined in a highly systematic way, that the findings and how they are arrived at are clear to those who have expertise in that area and that it is possible for others to check if the findings and conclusions are correct.

CONVENTIONS OF SCIENTIFIC BEHAVIOUR

Systematic observation and measurement of variables – Ordinary individuals who are interested in human behaviour may pay more attention than average to what they can see or hear other people doing as they go about their day to day business. In this way they may build up impressions of how others behave. If they happen to work in a shop they might notice that shoppers tend to take the first few steps inside the door quite quickly without looking around them and then slow down and begin to examine the goods on display. This may suggest that it is better not to display goods too close to the door. We all make observations like these. Scientists cannot depend on this kind of random observation. They need to establish if such observations hold true generally or only under certain conditions.

Scientists also need to quantify any effects – how many steps are taken quickly before the shopper slows down? To establish the facts in this kind of detail requires a systematic approach to observing whatever variables are of interest. *Variables*, incidentally, are simply any characteristics that vary or change from person to person, time to time or place to place. Behavioural scientists observe a great many human variables like personality, motivation, intelligence, behaviour in particular situations and so on. Any characteristic of humans that never varies – if such exists – is hardly of interest to study.

'Systematic observation' means the observation of variables of interest under precisely defined and perhaps even controlled circumstances. Following the shopping behaviour example mentioned above, before a behavioural scientist could draw conclusions that shoppers take a number of steps inside the shop door before they slow down, the conclusion would have to be based on, say, video evidence of a great many shoppers in a wide variety of shops. Simple casual observation in one or two settings would not be enough. One or two persons' impressions are not sufficient.

BOX 1.3

THE HISTORY OF SCIENCE

The origins of science can be traced back to classical Greece during the 5th and 6th centuries BC. The teachings of philosophers such as Thales, Empedocles, Pythagoras, Zeno, Hippocrates and the more famous Plato and Aristotle from this era form the logical foundations of scientific thought. Their contribution was mainly to break with the tradition of invoking magical and mythological causes to explain natural effects and to look to nature itself for understanding; an approach essential to the development of science.

After the decline of the Grecian civilisation, the impetus towards modern science offered by the classical philosophers stalled almost entirely for a whole millennium. For the most part European civilisation, such as it was, reverted to a religion- and superstition-dominated view of the world, frequently hostile towards any reflection on natural causes and effects.

The 12th and 13th centuries saw a rebirth in learning and interest in scientific issues. This was in part due to contact with the Islamic world, which had kept alive some residue of classical insights, and partly due to the development of urban centres with well-off, literate upper-classes. In the 13th century universities were founded throughout Europe. Scientific thinking was still, however, very seriously confused with religious and superstitious concepts. Learned men thought of all understanding as emanating from God and all events as having an ultimately divine or demonic origin.

The break with a religion-dominated world view took place in the 17th century during what became known as the Scientific Revolution. The key development was the conviction that science should be based on the search for natural causes and consequences and not on an exploration of the Divine Will. An English scholar, John Locke (1632-1704), initiated a widely popular philosophical system known as empiricism, which emphasised observation and experience as the route to knowledge. This was the essential intellectual underpinning of science as a method. Among the notable scientific figures from this period were Galileo (1564-1642) in Italy, Francis Bacon (1561-1626), an English philosopher and statesman, and, most notable of all, Isaac Newton, English mathematician, astronomer and physicist (1643-1727).

The ideas of Locke and the discoveries of Newton were seized on by a group of French writers known as the Philosophes, the best known of whom were Voltaire (1694-1778) and Diderot (1713-1784). They popularised throughout Europe the idea that knowledge was to be obtained through observation and critical rational thought and rejected all religious and superstitious explanations for reality. This movement became known as the Enlightenment and was particularly important for the development of a scientific approach towards human behaviour in all its forms.

Though not without setbacks, the scientific approach gradually took on prestige and received a great deal of state and royal patronage throughout Europe. Societies to bring scientists together, to aid the advancement of science and to disseminate its discoveries were founded, firstly in Britain and France and later in other countries. This marked the first recognition of science as a collective endeavour, a key feature of its modern success. Previously and indeed in the main up to the 19th century, science tended to be practised in isolation by well-off amateurs of great ability. Growth in the body of existing knowledge necessitated an increased specialisation on the part of practitioners which in turn required a system to co-ordinate their efforts.

In the 19th century there was a growing democratisation and urbanisation of society throughout Europe, trends that favoured scientific exploration. The practice of science became more specialised and professionalised with the growth of a sophisticated university system and a well-developed network of journals and other publications facilitating communication among scientists. Charles Darwin (1809-1882) moved biology to the forefront of research with the publication of his theory of evolution in 1859. The application of the scientific approach to human behaviour followed in the late decades of the 19th century. The history of scientific psychology, for example, is usually traced back to the establishment by Wilhelm Wundt in 1879 of a laboratory at the University of Leipzig in Germany for the experimental study of human behaviour.

In the 20th century the main changes were not in the nature of scientific enquiry but in its scale and in its status. In simple terms, the amount of money devoted to science, the number of professional scientists and the number and variety of institutions involved in scientific research grew enormously. The US, particularly after the influx of scientists in the 1930s and 1940s from Nazi Germany, became more and more important. Today, on account of its size and resources, it dominates in many fields of scientific enquiry, not least in the behavioural sciences.

The challenge facing science in the 21st century is how to decide what questions science should seek to answer and how to harness its power for the wellbeing of humanity as a whole. Developments in fields such as nuclear physics, and, more recently, biochemistry and genetics, have raised the spectre of science unleashing forces that may ultimately destroy our planet. The pressing questions are no longer about how to investigate but what to investigate and what to do with what we discover, questions that science alone can not answer. In many respects we are back once more to philosophy, from which science originally originated, to help us answer those most difficult but truly essential questions.

Measurement of variables involves their quantification. It is not enough for scientists to use vague terms like 'often' or 'a lot' or 'seldom'. They need to be quite precise and develop methods of measuring variables. In behavioural science this may be something as simple as a count of particular behaviours in a certain time period. A measure of the outward signs of stress shown by a public speaker might be drawn from a careful count of hand and body movements during the speech. Measurements may also be highly complex, such as intelligence and personality tests that are based on extensive research.

Use of research designs – Research designs are detailed plans for investigating and answering questions. A scientist does not launch into a piece of research. First a detailed plan is drawn up as to how best – given the available resources – to answer the question at hand. There are a number of standard designs commonly used by scientists such as experiments and surveys. These will be dealt with in greater detail in Chapter 2. For now it is enough to remember that a research design is a detailed plan of how the research is to be carried out.

Use of statistics – This refers to a branch of mathematics which is essential to research. All scientists need to summarise and make sense of their findings. Don't forget that they will typically be measuring variables of one kind or another so they will end up with figures that need to be understood. Let's say we were curious to find out if the typical IQ of males and females differ in this college. Because the overall IQ of males and females in the general population does not differ, we would expect to find no difference in the college population. Let's say we measured the IQ of every student using a standard test and listed the IQ of all the males down one column and of the females down another; we would be left with two long lists to compare. Before we decided that there is no difference between males and females we would have to summarise the figures in some way to help compare them. The obvious thing to do is to get the 'mean' or 'average' of each – to add up each column of figures and divide by the number of figures in the column. A mean or average is a simple statistic – a simple formula or calculation that helps us to summarise and understand numerical information.

There are a great many other such formulas or procedures. Among the decisions statistics can help with are: (1) deciding if two groups differ on some variable – more than you would expect by chance; and (2) deciding if variables are correlated – as one increases does the other increase or fall?

One very important contribution of statistics is in deciding whether the findings made in a particular piece of research are likely to happen by chance. If we return again to the IQ example mentioned above, it would be very time consuming and expensive to measure the IQ of every student in the college. Normally what scientists will do in such circumstances is take a random sample of the overall group of interest. This overall group they refer to as the 'population' of interest.

Clearly, the bigger a random sample is, the more likely it is to be representative of the population from which it is drawn. A random sample of three males and three females might happen to include one or two very unusual cases – say individuals with unusually high or low IQs. This could be very misleading. However if the sample were to be 100 males and 100 females, then the average of each should be more like the average of the overall population of students. Having chosen a sample and carried out the measurements, statistics can tell us if the findings are likely to have occurred by chance. Say, with the 100 randomly sampled male students and 100 randomly sampled female students, we found an average IQ difference of ten points between the sexes. Our statistics would almost certainly tell us that this difference is too big to be a chance outcome, whereas with an IQ difference of two points, we might be told that this difference is likely to occur by chance and we should put no faith in it.

Recording of methods and findings – Science thrives on a lack of trust. Nothing is taken for granted. When a piece of research is carried out and results produced, it must subsequently be possible for other scientists to know precisely how the work was done. They must know how the sample was obtained, how the variables were measured and so on. Ideally it should be possible for one researcher in a distant part of the world to read the research report of another and do the exact same piece of research with no detail changed except for the sample studied. Sometimes it may be possible to use the exact same sample.

Of course, if this is possible, it is also possible to find any errors or omissions in the original piece of research. If I read a piece of research which just said that '*a random sample of 100 students at a particular college was used*' I would not be satisfied, because I would need to be told how it was ensured that the sample was really random (i.e. every student at the college had the same chance of ending up in the sample) and not biased in some way. Let's say the research report also stated the following: '*a random sample of 100 students was obtained by asking for volunteers in the college canteen*'. I would immediately detect a flaw in the research design. Students who volunteer may be unusual in some way – perhaps more outgoing or more interested in research, maybe even more intelligent than average. Furthermore, those who use the canteen may not be representative of the student population as a whole. Perhaps students who live away from home are more likely to visit the canteen. Only if the researcher records all the details of how the research is carried out is it possible to spot flaws like this. There is a duty on scientists to record in great detail every aspect of their research work.

Publishing methods and findings – It is not enough to record what was done, it is essential that it be published. In a world where every scientist had only the best interests of science at heart, every discovery would be published in full detail immediately. In that way others could use whatever breakthrough was made to further advance their work and to advance the overall knowledge of the subject. However, unfortunately, this is not always possible. Scientists have to concern themselves with funding for their research. A drug like Viagra, the world-wide selling drug launched by Pfizer in Ireland in 1998 for the cure of male sexual impotence, might have been developed long ago if the scientists working on it could have shared their knowledge with other experts elsewhere at every stage of its development. However, if this were done no organisation or corporation could ever patent and make a large profit from such a discovery. They would then have no motivation to invest the very large sums of money necessary to carry out the development. When we take account of the fact that in 1998 alone Pfizer's Annual Report shows that it spent $2,594 million on research and development, one gets a sense of the money they need to recoup.

Scientists themselves also have a motivation to keep work secret. They wish to have the honour and the status of making some great discovery. Every scientist dreams of being a Pasteur, a Marie Curie or an

Albert Einstein. If they share too much too early, someone else may have the honour of making the big breakthrough. That was essentially the fate of Alfred Russel Wallace (1823-1913), who had arrived at the theory of evolution at the same time and perhaps before Charles Darwin. Uninterested in fame, he passed on his findings to Darwin. Darwin became a household name after he published his famous book, *On the Origin of Species by Means of Natural Selection* (Darwin, 1859) and Wallace faded into obscurity.

Nevertheless, if scientists did not regularly share their work by publishing it in a detailed form, the progress of knowledge would be seriously hindered. Teams of individuals would be doing the exact same work in different parts of the world. Far better to know about each other's work so as not to waste time reinventing the wheel. At the end of the day, all important findings and how they were found must be published so their accuracy can be established. It is more a matter of when to publish rather than whether.

Critical evaluation and replication – As suggested above, science thrives on scepticism. It is the duty of those who practice it to always retain a questioning mind. Every flaw must be rooted out, every error uncovered. In this way, the process is almost the opposite of normal human relations. If in our daily lives, we spent our energies finding fault with the work of others we would have no friends and nobody would work with us. Yet this is exactly what scientists must do. They do it in the pages of scientific journals – very publicly. Naturally, egos get bruised and feelings hurt, but that is far better than mistakes going undetected. In a thousand different ways in our daily lives, we rely on this critical eye which experts cast on each other's work. We rely on it to know that the food we eat is safe, the air we breath is unpolluted, the medicines we take do their job, the houses we live in will not fall down and so on. One person can easily err or even seek to cover up or mislead. Hundreds or thousands of experts are not so likely to miss something important. Small groups who work together might be too loyal to each other to engage in very public criticism. Through publications the opportunity is given to experts world-wide to critically evaluate research. In this way personal loyalties, collusion and the like should not be a problem.

Having said all that, nothing human is perfect. Scientists have, in the past, fallen below acceptable standards of critical analysis. Sometimes the views of renowned experts are taken as gospel when they are in error (see Box 1.4 below) and the views of unknown scientists dismissed when they are correct. The latter is especially true when something very unusual or unexpected is being suggested. In 1982 a young medical researcher from Australia called Barry Marshall proposed just such an unexpected idea. He provided convincing evidence that, contrary to long prevailing medical wisdom, stomach ulcers were not primarily caused by stress and poor diet but by infection with a bacterium called *H.pylori* (Reville, 1998). He and another scientist called Robin Warren had isolated the bacterium from the stomach tissue of ulcer victims. Marshall had then deliberately infected himself with the bacteria, which caused him acute stomach inflammation, nausea and vomiting. At this point he cured himself completely with antibiotic drugs. Soon it became clear that even long term chronic ulcer sufferers could be cured in the same way. Despite this major discovery, several years later there remained a great many doctors around the world who continued to treat ulcers in the old, less successful, way. So radical was the shift in thinking required that it took many medical practitioners a long time to be convinced, despite the scientific evidence.

While critical evaluation is essential to science, replication is just as important. No discovery is taken to be 'for real' until the research has been replicated a number of times. This means doing the research again and again to see if the same findings are obtained. In 1989 two scientists at the University of Utah, Stanley Pons and Martin Fleischmann, caused a major stir when they claimed in a highly publicised press conference to have successfully carried out a process known as 'cold fusion' (Close, 1991). Fusion involves the joining together of atoms – which if it were carried out would release enormous amounts of energy without any radiation. This would represent a safe and infinite source of power for the world, a tremendously exciting prospect. It is the opposite of fission – the splitting of atoms – from which nuclear energy now comes. Physicists had always believed that fusion could only happen if the temperature was enormously high – something like the heat at the core of a nuclear explosion. The difficulty lies in controlling such heat. No practical method has been found.

Pons and Fleischmann claimed to have demonstrated fusion in an ordinary test tube at ordinary temperatures. Enormous international publicity followed. Immediately, teams of excited, if somewhat incredulous, scientists around the world set out to replicate their experiment. It was at this point that the wheels began to come off the 'cold fusion' wagon. Scientists at some of the best equipped research institutions in the world, such as the Harwell laboratories in Britain, failed entirely to show any evidence of the remarkable effects described by Pons and Fleischmann. The findings could not be replicated with any degree of reliability. Gradually the whole episode faded from popular consciousness. There are still scientists who claim to demonstrate evidence of cold fusion but their claims are hotly contested by other experts as based on misinterpretation of data or sloppy research design (Kestenbaum, 1997).

In one way the cold fusion affair represents the normal process of science. A piece of research is carried out and a discovery claimed. The methods and findings are made known to the broader scientific community. Other scientists critically evaluate and attempt to replicate the research. If the research approach is sound and findings are reliably replicable, credence is lent to the original discovery. If faults are found in the research or others fail to replicate the results, doubt is cast on the value of the 'discovery'. Where the cold fusion affair differs from the norm is that the cart was put before the horse. The international publicity preceded the process of critical evaluation and replication. In the words of one scientific commentator, writing in New Scientist:

'The general public assumes that when researchers claim to have made a major discovery it has been thoroughly and carefully researched. Parts of the test-tube fusion episode failed sadly on this score.'

(Close, 1991)

The principal area in which it failed was that Pons and Fleischmann held a press conference to announce their discovery before the critical evaluation and replication phase. This caused the international press to treat their announcement as if it were already a fact and not an unreplicated experimental finding in one laboratory. It was really a case of the press and public failing to understand how science works. But why had Pons and Fleischmann taken such a risk in going public before their findings had been checked in the normal way? The answer lies in what they had to gain. By going public when they did, if their discovery had indeed been real, they would have guaranteed that their names would have been ever after synonymous with one of the most important scientific breakthroughs of all time – a means of harnessing a safe, cheap and limitless energy supply.

We should never forget that scientists are just as human as everyone else.

SCIENTIFIC PROOF

Research is at the core of all the sciences, including behavioural science. It is through research that information regarded as true or reliable is discovered. This is not to say that scientists are never wrong in what they say. They frequently are. There is an argument in science (Popper, 1986) that research can only prove something to be untrue or false: it can never fully prove something to be true. This is particularly so of general rules or laws about anything. It may be a generally accepted rule that all objects – big and small – in the universe are drawn towards each other by the force of gravity. It would only take a single observation of one object not being pulled by the force of gravity to disprove this law. No matter how long a general fact like this is taken to be true and no matter how many observations have shown it to be so, there may yet be some case waiting to be found which disproves the rule.

Only an infinite amount of observations can prove in an absolute sense the truth of any general statement. Since this is not possible, it can be said that no absolute proof of truth exists. (It is of interest that recently astronomers have had reason to doubt the truth of our understanding of gravity – observations of distant objects in the universe strongly suggest that gravity may also push apart as well as pull together objects, at least under certain circumstances.) Proof, in practice, amounts to a sufficient body of research findings leading to the scientific community being convinced beyond reasonable doubt that a particular theory is indeed true. Of course, even when the weight of evidence is very great there may still be dissenters who remain for some reason unconvinced. There are still a small number of scientists largely associated with religious fundamentalism in the US who regard the core propositions of Darwin's theory of evolution as unproven despite a wealth of supporting evidence, which has put the matter beyond doubt for the majority. In the words of Isaac Asimov:

> '... no reputable biologist feels any doubt about the validity of the evolutionary concept.'

> (Asimov, 1987, p. 713)

BOX 1.4

THE CASE OF CYRIL BURT

On 24 October 1976 the Sunday Times in Britain published a dramatic article by a writer called Oliver Gillie entitled 'Crucial Data Faked by Eminent Psychologist'. The psychologist in question, Sir Cyril Burt, who died at the ripe old age of 88 in 1971, had indeed been eminent. He was widely regarded as one of the leading British psychologists, if not the leading British psychologist, in the first half of the 20th century. His work demonstrating the inheritability of personality and intelligence was most influential and his findings were little questioned during his lifetime. How could such a pillar of academic pre-eminence and respectability be exposed as a fraud? What exactly had Oliver Gillie to report?

The first academic to openly question the honesty of Burt's work was Leon Kamin, an American psychologist. He brought attention to the fact that during Burt's retirement he had published two important articles, in 1955 and 1966, reporting what were highly improbable research findings when the two articles were looked at together (Kamin, 1974). Both articles reported studies he carried out (or said he carried out) on the relationship between the IQs of identical twins raised together and raised apart. The importance of such studies is that, since identical twins have identical genes, differences in their IQs cannot be due to inheritance but must be due to some aspect of their life experiences. If identical twins, who are raised apart (adopted by different foster parents shortly after their births), still maintain very high similarities in their IQs – as you would expect if IQ were an inheritable characteristic – then it shows that life experience does not have much influence on IQ and it is mainly down to inheritance through the genes. This is precisely the finding that Burt claimed from his two separate studies.

The odd thing that Kamin noted about his two studies is that Burt did not simply report similar findings for each but reported mathematically and precisely the same findings. In one article he reported findings from a study of 83 identical twins raised together and 21 pairs raised apart. In the second article he reported results of a study on 95 identical twins raised together and 53 raised apart. In each of the two studies the correlation (correlation refers to a statistical summary of relationship between a number of pairs of figures – in this case twins' IQ scores) for twins raised together was .944 and for those raised apart was .771. The chances of getting identical findings such as this in two separate studies with two separate groups of twin pairs is virtually nil. Similar findings would be fine but exactly the same down to the third place of the decimal in each case is simply not credible. Kamin concluded that the figures must have been made up.

After Kamin had published his sensational claim the floodgates opened and many psychologists came forward to cast doubt on the scientific honesty of Burt's work. Obvious flaws in his methods and his analysis were pointed out. Efforts to discover the origin of his samples of identical twins proved fruitless. Even research assistants that were supposed to have worked with him seemed never to have existed or at least could not be traced. In different articles Burt had made contradictory claims about how many identical twins brought up in separate homes he had been able to find and about how common a phenomenon this is (Butler and Petrulis, 1999).

What Kamin had originally brought to the attention of the academic community, Gillie brought to the attention of the public at large. The most respected of scientists had been unmasked as breaching the cardinal rule of good science. He had invented research to bear out his assumptions. He believed that intelligence was largely a genetically inherited human characteristic and in the absence of adequate scientific proof he had set to inventing some. Why or how exactly Burt came to do this remains a mystery. In his defence he was getting old at the time and perhaps his faculties were deteriorating. Nobody will ever know for sure. A much more pressing question, however, is why the flaws in his publications, evident after his death, were not highlighted by psychologists while he was alive. Why had there been a widespread failure of the expected standards of critical evaluation by his peers? William Reville in his *Science Today* feature in the Irish Times on 27 November 1995 offered a disturbing answer to this question. 'In science,' he asserts, 'if you are deemed to be an eminent researcher and your publications confirm existing popular theories, your work is accepted relatively uncritically'. This is a worrying possibility. For the protection of us all, science must not fall prey to this all too human error.

An ironic footnote to this saga is that Burt's conclusions about the inheritability of IQ and personality have since been strongly supported by actual research – see Chapters 5 and 6.

THE BEHAVIOURAL SCIENCES

The main challenge in answering the question posed by the title of this chapter lay in understanding the concept of science. Now that this issue has been addressed in some detail the reader may be able to fully understand if we say that *behavioural science is the application of the scientific approach to the understanding of human behaviour in all its forms*.

In keeping with the general scientific trend of specialisation there is not one but several contributory behavioural sciences, the principle ones being psychology and sociology. The focus of psychology is on individual human behaviour and characteristics such as personality and intelligence. Sociology focuses on the behaviour of aggregates, groups or collections of individuals such as the urban working class, the population of late 20th century Ireland or the workers in a particular organisation. Other behavioural sciences include: anthropology (the study of technologically primitive societies); and linguistics (the study of language development). Economics is also taken to be a behavioural science in that it involves the study of human behaviour in albeit a limited but crucial sphere of existence – that of production and consumption of material goods and services.

The behavioural sciences throw up a number of challenges to scientists, which, though shared to some degree with other areas of research, are particularly acute when carrying out research on human behaviour.

The first obvious issue is the thorny one of ethics, and the question of what actions are acceptable to carry out on humans for the purposes of research. There is general agreement that any actions likely to result in pain, stress or harm of any kind to the research participants have to be engaged in with great caution. A general rule of thumb is that any research involving any appreciable risk of enduring harm to participants cannot be justified. Another generally accepted rule is that where temporary pain or discomfort may result the participants should be aware of this and should not be under pressure at any point to continue against their wills. Adults, who for any reason may have a problem understanding or making decisions about what they are getting involved in, and, of course, children, require special protection.

The great problem thrown up by these ethical considerations is that it is in identifying the causes of long term harm to humans that behavioural sciences such as psychology and sociology can make one of their more valuable contributions to humanity. Does a lack of stimulation in early childhood result in a lowered intellect? Does regular exposure to violence on TV cause children to behave more aggressively? Does stress in the workplace result in diminished productivity? As we will see in Chapter 2, the only certain way to answer such questions involves carrying out experiments where these potentially harmful conditions are imposed on selected individuals. It is an ethical problem that prevents behavioural scientists from carrying out the precise pieces of research which would lead to the most valuable and convincing results. The ingenuity of behavioural scientists is particularly challenged to find alternative safer ways to answer research questions. It may also strike the reader when considering some of the research examples described in this text that some researchers have sailed very close to the wind in ethical terms in their desire to answer important questions.

Another major problem in the behavioural sciences is that human behaviour and responses to the environment are not only a function of being human but are also impacted upon a great deal by environmental circum-stances. The last three chapters of this book deal specifically with external circumstances: the groups, organisations and societies to which one belongs. Inevitably, the way we respond to the world is influenced by the way we were raised by our families which in turn reflects the culture of our own society. The problem this presents is that findings in one society may not hold true in another. The response of Irish workers, for example, may be very different to that of, say, Japanese or Brazilian workers to a particular style of manage-ment. This issue of cultural differences is raised at different points through-out this text. Indeed, significant cultural differences involving norms of behaviour and response to circumstances may exist within the one society. Rural people may differ in important ways from urban dwellers, women from men, old from young and middle class from working class, travellers from members of the settled community. All of this makes generalisations more problematic. The only solution is replication of research with differing samples of participants to establish if the findings hold true. This is another compelling reason for a large and widespread community of scientists.

Perhaps the most crucial difference between the behavioural and all other sciences is the fact that the subject matter of the former possesses insight and intelligence. Humans are not simply objects acted upon by outside forces but act in accordance with their own understanding of external events. Knowing why individuals behave as they do from their own standpoint, therefore, becomes as important as knowing the external circumstances that influence their behaviour. This leads many behavioural scientists to focus more on exploring through communication the personal perspectives of their subjects than on the measurement of objective behaviour. This contrast in approach will be discussed in Chapter 6 when the exploration of human personality is discussed. It is the contrast that lies between quantitative research approaches and qualitative research, which is discussed in Chapter 2. The challenge facing behavioural scientists is to rely as little as possible on subjective interpretation when exploring human behaviour and yet not leave the personal perspective or phenomenology of the individual, which is at the heart of the human state, off limits to research scrutiny.

In Chapter 2 the challenges involved in research methodology will be explored in greater detail.

SUMMARY

One of the great challenges that has always faced humankind is how to distinguish what is true from what is false or what is established from what is just a theory.

The challenge arises from the flaws inherent in the limited routes to knowledge, which we all possess. We must discover what we know through our own experience, through logical deduction or from the reports of others in whom we place our trust. Our own experience is hampered by the fact that it can allow us to gain information of events only when we are personally present. Even then it has been amply demonstrated that the way in which humans process and remember information results in a great deal of error. Logical thought suffers from twin deficiencies. On the one hand, the conclusions reached can not be correct unless the premises from which they have been drawn are correct, simply moving the problem back a stage. On the other hand, the use of logical thought is an intellectual skill at which by no means everyone is proficient. As regards accepting the reports of others, the immediate problem presenting is how to decide whom to believe. What is to stop the source from lying or being in error?

In reality we are largely dependent on this latter source, the word of others, for most important information about the world. The function of science is to furnish us with a means by which we can place our confidence in certain sources of information knowing that the information has been arrived at in a manner that minimises the possibility of error. Behavioural science is the application of the scientific approach to gaining knowledge about human behaviour.

Science consists of a series of methods involving agreed conventions as to how information is to be established and rigorously cross-checked by many experts. Science may be described as having the following characteristics: specialisation by individuals in relatively narrow areas of study, the existence of a large and widespread community of individuals studying each area, a system of world-wide communication among scientists and a common adherence to a set of principles of scientific behaviour. Specialisation is necessary to ensure the development of expertise in a world where the amount of established knowledge is enormous.

A large and widespread community of experts with a world-wide communication system ensures complementary and cumulative work. It also ensures the existence of experts willing and in a position to criticise and identify the flaws in the work of others. Operating within a framework of behavioural conventions guarantees accuracy and accountability in relation to scientific work.

The conventions of scientific behaviour may be summarised as follows: an emphasis on systematically observing and measuring variables of interest, the use of research designs, the application of statistical methods to interpret findings, careful and comprehensive recording of methodology and results, willing communication of the detail of one's work to other scientists through publications and the critical appraisal and replication of the work of others. Through this approach, while one or even many scientists may fall into error, there should always be others in a position to identify their mistakes. Equally importantly, this approach maximises the cumulative impact of scientists operating in many different parts of the world so that there is no reinvention of the wheel.

Behavioural science involves the application of the scientific approach to the understanding of human behaviour in all its forms. Research, which is at the core of science, presents certain particularly acute challenges to behavioural scientists. There are serious ethical considerations involved in carrying out research on human beings. Research which may in any way harm or hurt a participant has to be questioned in terms of its morality. This acts as a major obstacle to the exploration of important factors that are harmful to individuals. Another problem in conducting research on humans has to do with the great variability in human circumstances. Findings based on studies carried out in one culture or society may not apply to differing cultures and societies. There is a particular onus, therefore, on behavioural scientists to carry out cross-cultural studies to establish the generalisability of findings. Probably the greatest challenge of all facing scientists in the study of human behaviour is that humans are intelligent creatures who act in accordance with their own personal interpretations of external events. Behavioural scientists must, therefore, try to maintain objectivity while at the same time exploring the unique subjective insights of those they study.

Science can and does result in errors. It is not perfect. Indeed, a perfectly logical case has been advanced that it can only ever prove something to be wrong, never that a rule is true in all circumstances. If even one accurate observation runs contrary to a rule, then that rule must be found false. No amount of observations can absolutely prove a rule to be true. Science can not furnish us with absolute truths. That said, it is the best approach developed by human kind to provide information which, as a matter of probability, is likely to be correct.

REVIEW QUESTIONS

1. Referring to the problems that exist in arriving at trustworthy information, explain the contribution of science to humankind.
2. Describe the characteristics of science and the conventions of scientific behaviour, emphasising their contribution to establishing accurate knowledge.
3. Discuss the unique problems facing scientists who study the behaviour of human beings.
4. Explain:
    (a) the three approaches to obtaining knowledge;
    (b) how science contributes to the solution of the problems associated with those approaches.

REFERENCES

Asimov, I., (1987), *Asimov's New Guide to Science*, Aylesbury, England: Penguin.
Butler, B.E. and Petrulis, J., (1999), *British Journal of Psychology*, February, v.90, 155-160.
Claxton, G., (1998), 'Knowing Without Knowing Why', *The Psychologist*, May.
Close, F., (1991), 'Cold Fusion I: The Discovery That Never Was', *New Scientist*, 19 January.
Cutler, B.L. and Penrod, S.D., (1995), *Mistaken Identification: The Eyewitness, Psychology and the Law*, New York: Cambridge University Press.
Darwin, C., (1859), *On the Origin of Species by Means of Natural Selection*, London: John Murray.
Folk, C.L., Remington, R.W. and Wright, J.H., (1994), 'The Structure of Attentional Control: Contingent Attentional Capture by Apparent

Motion, Abrupt Onset and Color', *Journal of Experimental Psychology: Human Perception and Performance*, 20, 317-329.

Gillie, O., (1976), 'Crucial Data Faked by Eminent Psychologist', *Sunday Times*, 24 October.

Hastorf, A. and Cantrill, H., (1954), 'They Saw a Game: A Case Study', *Journal of Abnormal and Social Psychology*, 49, 129-134.

Kamin, L., (1974), *The Science and Politics of IQ*, London: Wiley.

Kestenbaum, D., (1997), *Cold Fusion: Science or Religion*, R&D, April, 39, 5, 51-54.

Kunda, Z. and Oleson, K., (1997), 'When Exceptions Prove the Rule: How Extremity of Deviance Determines the Impact of Deviant Examples on Stereotypes', *Journal of Personality and Social Psychology*, 72, 965-979.

Loftus, E.F., (1979), *Eyewitness Testimony*, Cambridge MA: Harvard University Press.

Loftus, E.F. and Hoffman, H.G., (1989), 'Misinformation and Memory: The Creation of New Memories', *Journal of Experimental Psychology: General*, 118, 100-104.

McCourt, F., (1996), *Angela's Ashes: A Memoir of a Childhood*, London: Harper Collins.

Popper, K., (1986) *The Poverty of Historicism*, London: Ark.

Reville, W., (1995), Science Today, *Irish Times*, 27 November.

Reville, W., (1998), Science Today, *Irish Times*, 1 May.

Rosenhan, D.L., (1973), 'On Being Sane in Insane Places', *Science* 179, 250-258.

Wells, G.L., (1993), 'What Do We Know About Eyewitness Identification?', *American Psychologist*, 48, 553-571.

Chapter 2

Research Methodology

LEARNING OBJECTIVES

Having completed this chapter you should be able to:

- explain how research questions are identified and formulated as hypotheses;
- distinguish between a theory and a hypothesis;
- distinguish between observational, correlational and experimental research designs;
- explain the limitations of observational and correlational designs;
- explain how researchers distinguish 'chance' from real findings;
- explain what is meant by 'internal validity' and 'external validity' of research designs;
- distinguish between nominal, ordinal, interval and ratio scales of measurement;
- distinguish between tests of typical performance and tests of maximum performance;
- distinguish between 'norm', 'domain' and 'criterion' referenced tests; and
- explain what is meant by reliability and validity of measurement.

INTRODUCTION

The following is the text of an article printed in *The Examiner* newspaper, which describes the findings of a research study (Flanagan, Moriarty and Daly, 1999) on stress in Irish workplaces:

'Being young and single is damaging to your health: age, children and education can affect your stress levels

Nurses are among the most stressed members of the community and are in danger of burn-out because of the demanding nature of their work.

That is the warning from a study on stress levels in the workplace, which says that workers who deal regularly with people suffer the greatest levels of stress.

The study, which included a survey of almost 2,000 people, found that stressed workers are more likely to be young and single with a high standard of education.

Nurses, teachers, supervisors and health workers top the stress league, while shift workers who alternate between day and night shifts are also prone to dangerous stress levels. However, age, number of children and hours worked also impact on stress levels. The report found:

Workers over the age of 40 are significantly less stressed than younger workers, with employees in the 26 to 36 age-group topping the stress league. Those over the age of 56 are the most easy-going of all workers.

Married and single employees suffer from similar stress levels, but the number of children workers have can affect on (sic.) stress levels. The more children parents have, the less likely they are to be suffering from stress, with parents who have six or more children suffering the least amount of stress.

Stress levels increase in relation to the number of hours worked, with part-time workers clocking up far less stress than full-time employees.

Level of education has an impact on stress, with levels increasing according to the number of qualifications they have secured. Workers who have obtained post-graduate qualifications score the highest in the stress league tables.

The results, published in *Administration*, the journal of the Institute of Public Administration, note the quality of life for increasing numbers of workers is affected by their failure to cope well with stress.

Just 1 per cent of workers reported no stress at all.

High stress levels can cause low job satisfaction, anxiety, emotional exhaustion and depression. If gone untreated it can result in disorders such as migraine, ulcers and heart disease.

For employers it can also affect employees' performance and lead to high levels of absenteeism.'

Written by Carl O'Brien, in The Examiner, *23 February 2000. Published with permission of the author and* The Irish Examiner *newspaper.*

For the ordinary citizen this article is a typical source of scientific information. Unless you are a professional scientist or have some particular motivation, you are unlikely to read the journals in which researchers publish their work. You have, therefore, to rely on reports such as the one reprinted above. Journalists and indeed scientists talking to the media have to summarise. They cannot describe every detail of the research. Newspaper articles must be readable and accessible to the average reader. The problem is that in the process it is very easy for misunderstandings to arise as to what was actually scientifically established by the research. The difficulty lies in the potential for false interpretation based on an insufficient understanding of research methodology. Often the amount of information presented in media reports is not adequate to verify whether a particular interpretation is justified. What should one watch out for?

Take the above article. What is one to make, for example, of the finding that workers with more children suffer less stress and that those with six or more children suffer the least stress of all? The seeming implication is that having lots of children causes parents to experience less stress at work.

Though the article does not say so, one might also be forgiven for coming away with the conclusion that education is a cause of stress.

A further message, which seems clear from the report, is that certain professions, such as nursing, teaching and supervisory management, are exceptionally stressful occupations.

It may come as a surprise that while the article is in no way inaccurate in reporting the actual study findings, none of the above conclusions can be safely drawn. What the study has actually shown is that stress is related to a number of other factors such as occupation, number of children and educational qualifications. It does not tell us (nor indeed did the newspaper report reprinted above) the causes of the relationships found.

Having learned to cope with lots of children might conceivably (though it seems unlikely) teach one to experience less stress in all aspects of one's life including at work. In this sense it is possible that having more children reduces workplace stress. A more probable explanation for the finding that those with six or more children report less stress in the workplace is that those who choose to have that many children do so partly because they are not prone to stress. The anticipated stress of caring for and supporting such a large family dissuades the majority of the working population from going beyond three or four children at most. A further possible explanation of the relationship between stress and family size is that having a low stress job facilitates individuals to have more children because it allows them to have more energy and mental resources left over for their care. Yet one more possibility is that those with more children may be older since family size has decreased dramatically in Ireland in recent decades. Age or career stage may then be the relevant variable.

Similarly, alternative explanations can be put forward for the other relationships found in the study. Conceivably (though improbably), for example, a high proportion of nurses or teachers may experience stress without the professions being in any way especially stressful. This could be so if, for some reason, those professions attracted an above average proportion of individuals with stress-prone personalities. As for the relationship between stress and qualifications, having more educational qualifications tends to lead to higher level jobs with more responsibility. More responsibility may result in more stress.

We have been considering here the contrast between 'correlation' and 'causality'. This is a key issue in understanding research. It is a common misunderstanding to assume that because two variables, such as stress and number of children, are related or correlated, then one must cause the other. A study such as the one reported in the *Examiner* article reprinted above falls short of being able to tell us which variables cause which effect.

Any reader with an inclination towards scepticism might also wonder how the variable 'stress' was measured. Did individuals simply report whether or not they felt stressed and, if so, would this have been an accurate measure of stress? Perhaps different individuals might interpret the concept stress in different ways. Another question that might spring to mind concerns those who were studied. How were they chosen? How can we be confident that they represent workers at large? If a different sample had been studied would the results have been the same?

The only way to grasp what conclusions can reasonably be drawn from a given piece of research and to estimate the confidence we should place in its findings is to understand the basic principles of research methodology.

Research methodology concerns all the details of how research is conducted. It deals with how the research question is formulated, who or what the research is to be conducted on, what activities are involved, how variables are measured, how the findings are to be interpreted and whether findings can be generalised beyond the immediate context of the study. It is with those issues that this chapter is concerned.

At the end of the chapter, armed with its information, we will return to the research study reported above, examine its research methodology in more detail and comment on its conclusions.

HOW SCIENTISTS CHOOSE THEIR RESEARCH

Scientists do not work in a vacuum. In the first place their world is full of the existing knowledge about their subject areas that has already been generated by other researchers. That is why your typical scientist spends a long time studying the subject before doing any serious research. Scientists have to know where to begin. There is no value in reinventing the wheel. Knowing the subject area well gives a good idea about what is *not* known about it – about what the obvious questions are that research might answer. Researchers must also know how to state a question so that a piece of research can be designed to provide the answer. At this point there are two words of particular importance to scientists: *theory*; and *hypothesis*. An understanding of them will help us to understand how researchers think and work.

THEORIES AND HYPOTHESES

A theory is an explanation for existing observations or findings, which has not yet been proven to the satisfaction of the scientific community.

A hypothesis is a prediction that can be tested in a particular piece of research.

Think back again to the conventions of scientific behaviour described in Chapter 1. The first convention had to do with systematic observation and measurement of variables. Scientists must observe in as precise a way as they can. Astronomers may use telescopes to help them observe the stars. Behavioural scientists may use video cameras to help them observe human behaviour. Often observations are made which present a real challenge to scientists to explain them. Behavioural scientists may observe that public speakers do many things that seem to be of no obvious assistance in delivering a speech. They may observe speakers putting their hands up to their faces, taking off and putting on their spectacles, shuffling their feet, waving their hands in front of them and so on. An explanation for this may be that these behaviours help to reduce stress is correct. This would be, however, simply a *theory* – an explanation for observations which has not yet been proven.

Let's now think about how we might look for evidence to support this theory. Obviously the best kind of evidence would be the kind we can check out. This is where the word *hypothesis* comes in. Remember that a hypothesis is a prediction, which can be tested. If our theory about reducing stress is correct, what kind of predictions would we expect to hold true? An obvious prediction is that speakers who feel more stressed produce more of the observed behaviours – shuffling their feet, waving their hands, etc., when speaking. If we could show that to be true, it would give weight to our theory.

Another possible prediction or hypothesis we might derive from our theory is that the observed behaviours actually reduce the signs of stress in the body. In other words, an attempt to reduce stress, by feet shuffling and so on, works as intended. From the standpoint of science the two hypotheses are useful only if we can design research to test them. If they are not testable they are of no help. Take note at this point that a theory such as the one being used in this example can give rise to several different hypotheses. Theories can not normally be tested by a single piece of research. The job of the scientist is to think up all the hypotheses that should be true if the theory is true and then test them all. If any one of them is found to be false the theory may have to be revised. A theory can stand for many years until eventually someone disproves a single hypothesis that should have held true. The theory has then to be rethought.

Now that we understand the role of theories and hypotheses, let's consider how a hypothesis might be tested in research.

RESEARCH DESIGNS

Broadly speaking there are two general categories of research design: *experimental*; and *non-experimental*.

They differ mainly in how much the researcher seeks to exert control over or interfere with the variables being studied. Experimental involves a lot of interference, non-experimental much less so.

Experimental research designs

In an experimental research design or an experiment, the researcher tries to identify if one variable is the cause of another. Taking the first hypothesis from our public speaking example above: 'speakers who feel more stressed produce more bodily movements when speaking'. This can be put another way: 'stress causes public speakers to produce movements'. In this hypothesis there are two key variables of interest. There is the supposed cause: stress. And there is the supposed effect: bodily movements. In an experimental design these variables are called the *independent* and the *dependent* variables.

Independent and dependent variables

The *independent variable* in an experiment is the variable that is thought to cause the effect.

The *dependent variable* is the variable which is thought to be effected or caused by the independent variable. In other words, it is dependent on the independent variable.

If one hypothesised that lack of exercise causes obesity, then amount of exercise becomes the independent variable and level of obesity becomes the dependent variable. To take another example, if it is predicted that increasing workers' level of responsibility for how they carry out tasks increases their job motivation, then level of responsibility is the independent variable and job motivation the dependent variable.

The objective of an experiment is to impose the independent variable, eliminate the influence of all other variables and see if it causes the effect expected on the dependent variable. Thus, to return to our body movements in public speakers example, if stress causes the hand waving or other movements observed, we have to impose the stress on a number of speakers, eliminate all other possible causes of hand waving and see if the stress produces the hand waving. Immediately you can see that this is not an easy task. How can we ensure that stress is imposed? And how can we eliminate all other possible causes of hand waving?

Let's start with producing stress in public speakers. Personal experience and casual observation would suggest that certain events in a public speech increase stress – suddenly finding, for example, that some of your notes are missing or being required to talk about something about which you are not confident or realising that your audience is likely to be critical. These events can be manipulated to produce stress in an experiment. Let's say we get volunteers to give a lecture to a large audience and ensure that they do not discover until they have begun to speak that their notes are partially illegible. It is a fair guess that they will find the lecture more stressful as a result. If we want to be sure that stress is induced we could always have a small heart monitor attached to them during the lecture. Stress should produce an increase in heart rate, which will be readily detectable and even measurable by the monitor. The subjects or participants who gave the lectures can also report afterwards how stressed they felt. So much for the independent variable.

How about the dependent variable? Let's say we concentrate only on hand movements. We need to be able to say with accuracy how much movement there was. This can be tricky. Certainly the subjects can be video-taped, but we still have to record the degree of hand movement. To do this we might categorise movements into say, face touches, head scratches, finger pointing, right hand waves, left hand waves, fist clenching and unclenching. A count of each might then be made using several observers. In this way an overall count of hand movements can be used. Alternatively, the proportion of the time that each hand is still or in motion can be measured from a videotape. Now we have some measures of the dependent variable.

Controlling other variables

The next challenge is to show a causal relationship between the independent and dependent variables – to show that the stress actually causes the hand movements in the current example. This involves eliminating other explanations for the hand movements. It helps a lot here to have some idea of what other explanations there might be. One obvious possibility is personality or individual differences. Some people may naturally wave their hands around more than others when they speak. Another possibility is that the audience is the key factor. Perhaps speakers use more hand movements when they are attempting to get through to larger audiences. Alternatively it might be something as simple as the temperature of the room. Maybe the movements are an unconscious attempt to keep warm. The more one thinks, the more possibilities there are. Intuitively we may feel that some are more likely than others – based on our own experience. However, science needs to be objective and consider all possibilities.

It may have occurred to you that there seems to be a simple answer to our problem here. If we have experimented on several individuals giving a lecture and taken a measure (using heart beat or self report or whatever) of each individual's level of stress and then also measured their hand movements, surely we can see if those who experienced more stress showed more movement. If they did is that not the answer? Have we not shown that stress causes hand movements? It is tempting but dangerous to assume so. All we have actually shown is that stress and hand movements tend to go together (or correlate, as scientists put it). It doesn't have to follow that the stress causes the hand movements. Why not? The reason is that something else may be the cause of both. Personality might be a candidate here. Those with certain types of personalities may be inclined both to feel more stress and quite independently to move their hands more when they speak in public. A lot of variables tend to correlate without one being the cause of the other. A famous example is from the US where it was once shown that cases of violent crime tend to correlate with the level of ice cream sales. Additives, driving people to violence? Nothing of the sort! The weather is at the root of both. When the weather is hot, more ice cream is sold and, for various reasons, when the weather is hot there are more cases of violent crime. *Correlation does not prove causation.* This is one of the more important lessons of science.

So, back to our stress and hand movements experiment – how are we to eliminate all the other possible causes of hand movements? One technique is to subject the same sample of individuals to two different conditions – a high stress lecture and a low stress lecture. It has been suggested above how stress might be manipulated: making notes illegible and so on. Using the same sample in both the high and low stress lecturers eliminates the influence of all individual differences such as personality. Of course, the two lectures for each person have to be made as alike as possible in all other ways – same room, same temperature, same audience, same furniture, and same length of lecture. Ideally the only difference should be the degree of stress imposed. Then if we find that there is appreciably more hand movement in the high stress situation, we can state with some confidence that stress causes public speakers to move their hands more.

Interpreting the findings

As you think through this example it should also serve as an illustration of how difficult it is to cover every possibility. Maybe, for example, it is only stress caused by a particular factor, which results in increased hand movements. Maybe we missed some other crucial difference between the two experimental conditions – the low stress and the high stress lecture. That is why no theory is proven or taken to be true following a single piece of research. Research needs to be replicated – to see if it works using a different sample or at a different time. Refinements of the design – perhaps using other methods of inducing stress in our example – need to be tried out. And in the end proving one hypothesis true does not normally prove a theory true. Remember our theory in this case was that bodily movements are an attempt to reduce stress. Just showing that stressed speakers move their hands more does not show that the movements have anything to do with reducing the stress. More research and more experiments are needed to explore that aspect of the theory.

Recap on experimental design

At this point you should have some idea of how experimental designs operate. Firstly, there is a hypothesis which proposes that one variable (the independent variable) causes changes in another (the dependent variable). Then a research design is put together to manipulate or impose the independent variable on a group of subjects or participants. The affects of all other variables are eliminated in so far as possible and the dependent variable is measured to see how it has been affected – to see if changes are indeed caused by the independent variable. You can see now why experimental designs involve a lot of interference with the variables being studied – particularly the independent variable.

Naturally occurring experiments

The level of interference with subjects involved in an experiment is not always possible to carry out – often for ethical reasons. You cannot harm individuals just to study the effects. Sometimes by accident, however, circumstances arise that allow for what is known as a *'naturally occurring experiment'*. This might occur where it is possible to predict some event which it is expected will have important influences on individuals. Let's say we were aware that the occupants of a village were to be relocated because their valley was being flooded to create a hydroelectric dam. This would present the opportunity to examine the psychological effects on the villagers of being uprooted. While nobody would suggest that you could relocate a village just to study the effect on its population, the fact that it was happening in any event would allow for such a study – otherwise impossible – to be carried out.

Non-experimental research designs

While experiments are the most powerful methods of carrying out research, as mentioned above, they often involve a lot of interference with and imposition on the subjects or participants. Experiments are also frequently quite costly to carry out. Often experiments are not possible or even desirable. Then scientists may have to use non-experimental research designs. Two general types of non-experimental design – the *observational* study and the *correlational* study – will now be described.

Observational research designs

Discussion of this research approach takes us to a debate that exists within the behavioural sciences, that between 'qualitative' and 'quantitative' approaches to research. Observational research differs from both correlational and experimental in that they are both quantitative approaches while it is qualitative. Quantitative research is based on measuring the variables of interest in the most refined and accurate way possible. Its exponents, following in the mainstream scientific tradition as described in Chapter 1, seek to minimise subjectivity and scope for the researcher to impose his or her own prejudices on what is found. Its opponents in the behavioural sciences counter that such an emphasis on measurement leads researchers to ignore a great deal about the human condition that is essential to any proper understanding. They particularly point to the fact that human behaviour is a function of individual experience and understanding, which needs a qualitative approach for its exploration. The qualitative approach involves such activities as the careful observation of behaviour and its recording in notes and diaries. It may also involve detailed discussion or in-depth interviews with individuals so as to explore how they interpret their environment, experiences and behaviour from their own standpoint.

Silverman (1998) argues that it is a mistake to argue in favour or against either quantitative or qualitative approaches and that such a dichotomy is open to question. He suggests that objectivity should be the aim of all researchers and that there is no reason why the two research approaches can not be used together. One should use whatever approach or combination of approaches is likely to be most valid for the purpose. If the objective of one's research is, for example, to gain insights into how psychiatric hospitals are experienced from the perspective of patients, then it is difficult to see how one can begin with a quantitative approach. How is one to even make a choice of which variables to measure (even assuming one has the means to measure them) unless one has some prior insight into variables which are of relevance to the issue? If, however, one adopted a qualitative approach and obtained employment in a psychiatric facility (as did Goffman, 1961) so as to observe, gain the confidence of and discuss their perceptions with patients over an extended period, one should have a much clearer picture of hypotheses that might be testable by a less subjective quantitative approach so as to cross-check the accuracy of conclusions reached in the observational phase.

Sociologists (behavioural scientists who study the behaviour of large sections of society like 'the urban working class' or the 'rural poor') make significant use of the observational approach, as do anthropologists (behavioural scientists who study behaviour in technologically un-developed societies.)

Arguably the purest of qualitative approaches to research is the Participant Observation Study where the researcher deliberately becomes immersed in the circumstances being studied so as to observe from the inside, so to speak, and be able to interpret actions and events more accurately. Goffman's study of a psychiatric facility, mentioned above, is a classic example of such a study (Goffman, 1961). *Inishkillane: Change and Decline in the West of Ireland,* by the English sociologist, Hugh Brody, is another typical example of this approach (Brody, 1973). Brody spent extended periods living in two rural communities in the west of Ireland so as to observe and interpret the attitudes and lifestyles of their popu-lations. He concluded that their traditional, patriarchal lifestyle, based on subsistence farming, was in terminal decline.

Psychologists (interested primarily in individual human behaviour) also sometimes use observational studies, particularly where there may be difficulties carrying out quantitative research.

A good example of an observational study in the field of psychology was that by Elizabeth Kubler-Ross (1969) who observed the behaviour of 200 terminally ill patients up to the point of their deaths. From her observations and in-depth interviews with those patients she published a stage theory of human response to dying. She proposed that all humans when faced with the prospect of their own deaths react in similar ways, going through a series of adjustment changes: first disbelief, then anger, followed by bargaining, depression and finally acceptance. Since its publication many health professionals around the world have been pre-sented with the stage theory as if it had been proven. It is important to recognise that an observational study such as that by Kubler-Ross cannot prove a theory. It is also important to realise that such a theory can never be tested experimentally. Think of what would have to be done to test the stage theory of dying through an experiment; consider also what would be involved in a Participant Observation Study of dying.

Another famous observational study – this time in the field of industrial psychology – formed part of the Hawthorne Studies, a series of studies on the performance of employees at the Hawthorne plant (near Chicago) of the General Electric Company. One of those studies, carried out in 1931-32 by a team of researchers headed by Fritz Roethlisberger and William Dickson, became known as the Bank Wiring Room Observation study (Roethlisberger and Dickson, 1964). This involved the careful observation of a number of workers in a particular room in the plant over an extended period of time. The observations revealed that their productivity was largely a function of informal rules that developed within informal groups of workers. In effect, workers tended to naturally develop into cohesive loyal groups independent of the formal groups to which they were assigned. The informal groups had a rule structure of their own development as well as informal leaders. The rules effectively prevented individuals from working too fast or too slowly. The overall objective was to reduce pressure from the management on employees. Apart from the fact that the observation was extended over a long period of time, this piece of research was very basic from a scientific standpoint. Yet it was most influential in drawing attention to the role of informal groups in determining worker productivity.

The risks of observational studies

On account of the high level of dependence on the observers' subjective judgments and conclusions, it is risky to place too much faith in the findings of purely observational studies. There is a powerful tendency for individuals to see what they expect to see and to find evidence supporting existing convictions. In addition there is a real danger, one magnified in Participant Observation Studies, that the presence of the observer will interfere in some crucial way with the events being studied possibly in the direction of prejudices and preconceptions.

There is a humorous story told of an observer unwittingly interfering with the subject matter under observation. An English scholar observing the way of life of the Blasket Islanders expressed a wish to see a funeral wake. A group of islanders anxious to oblige and at the same time capitalise on the situation decided to stage an event. They mentioned to him that there had been a death on the island but that the man had been very poor and there would not be enough money to buy the drink and tobacco essential to a proper wake. As anticipated, the unsuspecting scholar immediately offered to subsidise the entertainment. All went well at the wake until the volunteer 'corpse' lying motionless under a sheet realised that the bargain he had struck was being reneged on by the others. They were drinking his share of the porter that was to have been laid aside for him. Unable to control his anger, he jumped up, to the great consternation of the scholar who ran from the house in terror.

A much subtler example of the power of expectations to bring about their own reality is that of the experiment carried out by Rosenthal and Jacobson (1968). They led teachers to believe that they had used tests to identify specific children who showed particular academic ability. After a year, it was found that the majority of children randomly assigned as superior had shown improvements in real performance well beyond the remaining children. The teachers had somehow reacted to their expectations of the children so as to fulfil their own prophecies. In any study where the observer interacts with the subject matter under scrutiny, the danger of self-fulfilling prophecies is always present.

As Silverman points out, when research methodologies are described in opposition to each other, such as in the qualitative-quantitative debate we have at best 'pedagogic [teaching] devices for students to obtain a first grip on a difficult field' (Silverman, 1998, p. 80). Methodologies should be thought of as complementary, to be used together as appropriate. If, for example, one is carrying out an observational study of behaviour there is often no reason why some quantitative rigour cannot be introduced through observers' counts of specific behaviours. Likewise with interview recordings, 'impressionistic' reports of their contents can be augmented by identifying content categories of relevance and having several 'judges' rate the reports according to those categories. Inevitably a degree of subjectivity will always remain in the outcome due to decisions about which behaviours to count and how to interpret what those behaviours mean. Even in the most rigorous experimental research using a quantitative approach, some degree of subjectivity remains. It is through the process of replication and cross-checking, as outlined in Chapter 1, that confidence in all research findings is built up.

Correlational studies

This differs from observational research in that the objective here is to measure at least two variables and identify the degree of relationship between them. In behavioural science a simple example might be to measure, say, income and intelligence in a sample of individuals and compute the relationship between the two in an effort to test the hypothesis that those with higher IQs tend to earn more. Note that to carry out this study you do not have to interfere with the variables in any way other than to measure what already is the case. Think about how this differs from an experimental design.

The obvious limitation of this approach is that, even if you find a clear relationship between the variables measured – even if you find that those with higher IQs earn more money – it tells you nothing about why that is the case. It may be that being clever helps people to earn more money. It may be that those born into affluent families tend to have higher IQs (which research has demonstrated internationally; see for example Murthy and Panda, 1987; Fergusson et al, 1991). Then, quite independent of their IQs, they may go on to earn higher incomes because they inherit family businesses and get better jobs through family connections and so on. *Correlation simply does not prove causation.*

This example of the relationship between income and IQ serves as a good illustration of the difficulties behavioural scientists regularly face when studying human variables. For obvious reasons they often cannot carry out the kind of experiments that would test hypotheses of interest.

Think about the experiment you would have to carry out to check if a higher IQ causes individuals to earn higher incomes. Ideally you would have to take two large random samples of the population at birth (or before) and somehow cause one group to develop higher IQs than the other while at the same time interfering with no other aspect of their development that could possibly have a bearing on their potential to earn. Then you could trace their subsequent incomes as adults and, if the higher IQ group earned appreciably more on average, you could put that down to their superior intellects since they would *on average* differ in no other way from the low intellect group. That they would differ on average in no other way is ensured by the two groups being large random samples of the same population – thus ending up with the same mixture of social classes, personalities and so on.

Even if IQ could be manipulated without affecting any other aspect of an individual's development (which is not possible) it would clearly be a wholly unethical study to carry out. Fortunately there is at least a partial answer to this problem. More sophisticated correlational studies can be used to achieve some of the results of an experimental study.

Tracing causation through correlational designs

The trick is to exclude the other likely causes of whatever effect is of interest. In our example there may be a number of obvious reasons (other than intelligence) why those with higher IQs tend to earn higher incomes. Say, you suspect that social class or income of parents may be the real cause – both causing higher IQ scores and higher income. In this case you can examine the relationship between IQ and income within groups where parental income and social class is the same. If, for example, you identify a large sample of individuals of varying IQ whose parents earned the same level of income and discovered that those with higher IQ still earned more income, you could exclude parental income as the cause. This process can be repeated to exclude other possible causes of higher income. Of course, at the end of the day there may always be some important variable that you don't know about and have not thought to exclude. Nevertheless, this correlational study approach goes some way to identifying cause and effect even if only by being capable of ruling out certain causes. Often it is the best type of research that behavioural scientists can do because of ethical or resource considerations.

Detecting chance research findings

Whatever the nature of the research design, at the end the researcher is faced with the question of whether or not the results are simply a 'fluke' – a pure chance outcome. Two factors are involved in resolving this issue. One concerns the sample on which the research was carried out and the other the size of the actual finding. In simple terms the bigger both are the less likely it is that the finding is a result of chance alone. Why is this so? The answer lies in the nature of probability or chance.

Let's consider sample size first. Human characteristics tend to vary in the general population in a predictable way. A high proportion of individuals lies close to the average and the further from the average one goes the fewer individuals one will find. Take height in women as a simple example. Lots of women measure in at around five foot three, four and five inches, which is close to the average. With each inch one goes up or down, the proportion of women gets progressively smaller. You are not likely to come across very many women who are six foot or taller. The very same kind of distribution applies to men with a higher average.

However, if you picked a very small sample of individuals for a piece of research the chances of them being unrepresentative of the population or of individuals in general are high. The smallest sample one can take is a single person. If you randomly chose a single person to represent your class at college the chances of the tallest person in the class being picked are equal to the chances of anyone else being picked. However if you chose a random sample of, say, 10 per cent of the class, it is very unlikely that you would end up with the 10 per cent who are the tallest class members. You would most probably find that the average of your sample is close to the class average. The greater your sample the more assured you could be that this would be the case. In fact, sample sizes do not have to be very large to be representative so long as there is no bias in the selection of individuals. A few thousand individuals picked at random can fairly safely be assumed to be representative of the complete adult population of Ireland.

The point is that if the research sample is too small or there is some bias in how individuals are chosen the sample may not be representative and any findings may have to be discounted as chance outcomes.

The other factor concerns the magnitude or size of the finding made. If one is, for example, examining the difference between two groups on some variable, the larger the difference found the less likely it is to be a product of chance. Imagine for a moment that you are interested in the performance difference in the Leaving Certificate examination between males and females. Let us say that you took a random sample of 1 per cent of all those who sat the examination in a particular year and dis-covered a difference of 3 CAO points between the average of the sexes in favour of females. You would naturally wonder if that represented any real or significant performance difference. A second entirely independent sample of 1 per cent might well produce a similar difference in favour of males. However if your original finding were a 30 points difference, then it would be extremely unlikely that a difference of such magnitude could result from chance alone. All other things being equal, the larger the finding the more probable it is that it represents something real.

Fortunately there are a variety of statistical calculations that can be carried out based on the sample size and the magnitude of findings to estimate the probability that the finding is a result of chance. It is a general convention that if the probability of the finding being a result of chance is less than 5 per cent or five chances in a hundred, then the result is reported as *statistically significant*. It is taken to be a finding worthy of attention.

MEASUREMENT OF VARIABLES

Finding ways of measuring variables of interest is a challenge to all researchers. Irrespective of which branch of science one is involved with, measures boil down to simply turning variables into numbers. If you meas-ure temperature, you end up with a number of degrees. If you measure intelligence you get a number of IQ points. Even personality can be turned into numbers known as standard scores – measures of how like or unlike the average an individual is with respect to a given personality trait.

Because the numbers generated by any measure of any variable are usually summarised and made sense of using mathematical calculations it is important to know the true nature of the numbers your measuring instrument has produced. As a very simple illustration of this fact, it is common to find questionnaires where individuals are asked to categorise themselves on some variables such as, say, nationality, as follows:

1. Irish;
2. Other EU national;
3. Non-EU national.

When questionnaires are analysed by computer it is common to enter data such as this as 1, 2 or 3 depending on the individual response. Of course, averaging those figures would make no sense whatsoever – though computer programmes will happily do that if asked! This is because the figures just stand for categories – they are just convenient labels. This is the most basic type of measurement – nominal measurement. There are three other types as well. The four types or scales of measurement will now be explained.

TYPES OR SCALES OF MEASUREMENT

The four types are: (1) *nominal*; (2) *ordinal*; (3) *interval*; and (4) *ratio*. They rise in that order in level of sophistication. Let's look at each in turn.

Nominal measurement

This is where if numbers are used at all, they simply stand for categories. A measure of gender or sex will result in two categories: male and female. All that is being done is dividing individuals or cases into discrete categories. Numbers are just a convenient shorthand. No mathematics such as addition, averaging and so on can be done on such numbers.

Ordinal measurement

This involves a rank ordering of the individuals or cases. In this case the numbers do stand for something – the relative positioning of individuals or cases along some measured dimension. An example would be the place positioning in a horse race or the rank order of achievement in a class test. The numbers tell us the order in which cases come but do not tell us how far apart they lie from each other. In the rank ordering of a class on some test, the person at rank one might have attained 95 per cent but the person at rank two may have only attained 60 per cent and the one at rank three, 59 per cent. This leaves the person at rank one way ahead of the field, a fact that is not apparent when only the ranks are known. Researchers, particularly in the behavioural sciences, often use ranks where they do not have great confidence in the precise accuracy of their measuring tools. A certain amount of statistical analysis using various mathematical calculations can be carried out on ordinal data.

As discussed below in the section on interval measurement, a great many measures used in the behavioural sciences are ordinal measures. See also Box 2.1 below for information on some measuring scales often quoted in news bulletins which are often mistakenly assumed to be interval scales.

BOX 2.1

MEASURING WIND SPEED AND THE STRENGTH OF EARTHQUAKES

When there is a gale warning or a report of a hurricane somewhere in the world we frequently hear weather forecasters refer to force 9 gales or force 12 winds. Likewise reports of earthquakes are usually accompanied with descriptive figures such as 'measuring 7 on the Richter scale'.

It may come as a surprise that neither of those scales have equal intervals.

Wind strength is measured on the Beaufort scale. It consists of 13 rank-ordered categories. Each category refers to a particular zone of wind speed. At the bottom of the scale zero refers to wind speeds of less than 1 mile per hour (mph). One refers to speeds of 1-3 mph. Further up the scale, however, the zones increase in span. For example, 7 describes wind speeds of 32-38 mph, a span of 6 mph, while 11 refers to 64-73 mph, a span of 9 mph. Thus wind speed does not increase in even or equal intervals across the scale.

The Richter scale for measuring the strength of earthquakes operates in such a way that each step up the scale represents a 10-fold increase in the size of the shock waves released by the earthquake. Translated into energy released or the level of tremor felt causing damage to buildings, etc., each step up the scale represents roughly a 30-fold increase. This means that an earthquake measuring 7 on the Richter scale releases about 30 times more energy than one measuring 6, and 900 (30 by 30) times more energy than a tremor measuring 5. The interval between the Richter scale points is far from equal.

Both the Beaufort and the Richter scales are ordinal but not interval scales.

Interval measurement

This occurs when our measuring tool is capable of measuring the variable into equal intervals. When you get a measure of temperature using a thermometer you know that each degree is the same as each other one. In other words the distance between 10 degrees and 12 degrees is the same as that between 17 and 19 degrees. That is because a degree on the centigrade scale always has the same meaning. The scale does not in any way mask the distance between neighbouring points like a rank order scale can do.

Ratio measurement

Here we have both an interval scale and a true zero point. On the dimension being measured the figure 0 represents the complete absence of whatever the characteristic is. Height in centimetres or inches, for example, is measured on a ratio scale. Weight is measured on a ratio scale. Where such a scale exists, all mathematical operations can be carried out on the figures. This is the most accurate form of measurement.

There is some controversy in the field of psychology about whether many measures of mental variables produce a true interval scale. Attitude surveys are a good example. Here numbers are used to reflect the strength of an attitude, where perhaps a person is asked to agree or disagree with a statement on a scale of 1 (Strongly Agree) – 5 (Strongly Disagree). It is debatable whether the intervals on such a scale are really equal. Respondents to such a questionnaire may answer as if there is a greater attitude difference between, say, 4 and 5 than between 3 and 4. Despite this problem it is common (if questionable) practice to treat such scales as if they were interval scales. Note that if the intervals are in fact unequal an average or mean score for a group gives a misleading impression. Sidney Siegel discusses this issue in some detail in Chapter 3 of his widely used text, *Non-parametric Statistics for the Behavioural Sciences*. He states:

> 'Many personality inventories and tests of ability or aptitude result in scores, which have the strength of ranks. Although the scores may appear to be more precise than ranks, generally these scales do not meet

*the requirements for any higher level of measurement and may properly
be viewed as ordinal ...'*

(Siegel, 1956, p. 24)

Chisnall (1975) makes the same point about certain attitude measurement scales (see chapter 7).

The crucial feature missing from an interval scale is a true zero point.
When you measure height in centimetres, zero means no height.
However, when you measure temperature on either the Celsius or
Fahrenheit scales, zero does not mean no temperature. On the Celsius
scale it just means the temperature at which water freezes – many other
substances such as alcohol do not freeze until much colder. On the
Fahrenheit scale zero has no precise meaning at all, 32 degrees being the
freezing point of water. Even the Kelvin scale does not have a true zero,
in that –273C is only a theoretical absolute zero. It has never been
reached and, seemingly, cannot be reached.

The effect of there not being a true zero is that you cannot meaning-
fully say that any point on the scale is half or twice (or any other multiple or fraction of) any other point. A day which is 80F degrees is not
twice as hot as one which is 40F degrees. This can be demonstrated by
converting to the Celsius scale. If 80F degrees really was twice 40F
degrees, then the conversion should not change the mathematical relationship between the two points. In fact the conversion does change the
relationship. See Box 2.2 below for conversion data.

ACCURACY OF MEASURES

Whatever instrument or tool is used to measure a research variable and
irrespective of the scale of measurement that results, it is crucial for the
success of research that the measure has the qualities of *reliability* and
validity. Indeed, the same two characteristics are essential in any measure
for any purpose.

BOX 2.2

TEMPERATURE SCALES AND THE ABSENCE OF A TRUE ZERO

The formula for converting Fahrenheit to Celsius is:

$C = \frac{5}{9} (F - 32)$ where C = degrees in Celsius and F = degrees in Fahrenheit

Some examples of conversions are as follows:

Fahrenheit	0	32	40	80	212
Celsius	−17.7	0	4.4	26.7	100

A 40F day is not half as hot as an 80F day. Take note in real life of two days that correspond to those two measures. One you will find is a very hot day in summer, the other a cold day in winter. It makes neither mathematical nor intuitive sense to say that one is half as hot or twice as hot as the other. Temperature scales, lacking a true zero point, do not lend themselves to this kind of calculation.

Reliability of measurement

Reliability refers to the consistency with which the measuring instrument (be it a thermometer or an IQ test) does its job, in so far as returning scores is concerned. There are two approaches to measuring reliability: *test-retest* and *internal*.

Test-retest reliability

A bathroom weighing scales that indicated you were seven stone one day and eight stone the next would immediately be discarded as unreliable – failing to measure consistently. This kind of check on reliability is called *test-retest* reliability. It is expected that a personality or an IQ test will be high on test-retest reliability, that they will give much the same results on different presentations of the test to the same person. This, of course, is based on the assumption that personality and intelligence do not change to any appreciable degree over time (see Chapters 5 and 6 for an analysis of this assumption).

A measure of learning such as an examination in behavioural science, on the other hand, cannot be expected to return the same results for the same individuals on two occasions if those taking the test have had an opportunity to either learn or forget some relevant material. An exam should demonstrate test-retest reliability over a short time interval where the examinees are not allowed to avail of any learning opportunities in the meantime. Imagine that you sat a one-hour paper in the morning and obtained a mark of 72 per cent. In the afternoon you were given a second opportunity to sit the paper which you did with equal vigour to the morning effort, only to find that your second attempt resulted in a mark of 54 per cent. Clearly it would give rise to concerns about the accuracy of the examination as a measure of your true knowledge of the subject. One or both results would have to be unrepresentative of your learning.

Internal reliability

Where psychological tests of various kinds, (including assessments of performance, achievement or ability) are concerned, there is another kind of reliability sought – *internal reliability*. This is a measure of the degree to which the test is measuring a single variable as opposed to measuring other unwanted variables as well. A test intended to measure knowledge of behavioural science might also be partially a test of English language comprehension if some of the questions or items included unusual words or phrases. In other words, to answer certain questions on the test you might need both a knowledge of behavioural science and an unusually high standard of English. This would diminish the internal reliability of the test. In other word the test would not consistently throughout all the questions measure just knowledge of behavioural science. A common check for a lack of internal reliability is to check performance on individual questions or items against overall performance on the test. If good performers on the test seem no better or even worse than poor performers on certain items, then those items may be measuring something different to the test as a whole.

Validity of measurement

Validity is a simple concept. A measure is valid if it measures what it is supposed to measure. Thus a personality test is valid if it is actually a measure of personality. There is only one general way to establish the validity of any measure and that is to compare the results obtained with some other measure or indicator of that variable.

If there already exists a well proven measure of the variable then the results obtained using a new measure can be validated by checking them against results on the established measure. This may arise where a cheaper, shorter or simpler test of a variable is being devised. If a ten minute test of mathematical aptitude produced results matching very closely those of a well established measure that takes, say, an hour to complete, then the shorter measure can safely be used in its place.

A bigger challenge faces researchers when trying to show the validity of a measure for which there is no existing alternative. The approach then is to see if the measure is capable of doing what you would reasonably expect such a measure to do.

If, for example, a personality test is supposed to measure sociability, one way of checking its validity would be to find a group of individuals among whom there is reason to expect a high level of sociability and a group where there is reason to suppose they may not be sociable. An indicator of sociability may be the jobs people choose. It is reasonable to expect air cabin crew to be sociable – particularly if they claim to like the job. It is reasonable to expect data entry clerks who enjoy their work not to be particularly sociable. If the test can differentiate between the two groups, finding higher sociability scores among the air cabin crew, then that is evidence of its validity.

Another approach to establishing the validity of a new measure is to set up an experimental situation. Take a measure of sociability again as an example. Researchers might organise a waiting room situation where individuals with known scores on the sociability measure are obliged to wait, one at a time, for a period in a room with a stranger or group of strangers – colleagues of the experimenter's. The room would be monitored using a closed circuit TV link or with a one-way mirror by observers who are unaware of the personality test scores. Their job would be to rate the subjects on evidence of sociability such as speaking to the others in the room and initiating conversation. The sociability ratings would later be compared with the personality test scores. If there was a reasonable match, that would stand as evidence of the validity of the test.

The validity of any test or measure used in the behavioural sciences is rarely, if ever, established through a single piece of research. Checks on validity go on and on. Some personality tests have many hundreds, even thousands, of pieces of research checking out their validity. Researchers will generally be happy to use a measure only if its validity for that purpose has been adequately demonstrated.

How do you know that your bathroom scales is a reliable and valid measure of weight?

VALIDITY OF RESEARCH DESIGNS

The word validity is also used when discussing how adequate a research design is for its purpose.

Here there are two recognised types of validity – *internal validity* and *external validity*.

Internal validity refers to the degree to which a research design is capable of demonstrating what it is claimed to demonstrate in relation to the sample studied. Failures of internal validity could result, for example,

from poor variable measures or flaws in the way the research was conducted. In relation to experimental designs where the objective is to
show that one variable (the independent variable) causes changes
in another variable (the dependent variable), the design is said to be
internally valid if it is capable of showing such a relationship. The big
challenge is to eliminate the effects of all other possible causes of change
in the dependent variable other than the independent variable. How
this is achieved was discussed above under the heading *Experimental
research designs*.

External validity refers to the extent to which it is possible to generalise the findings from the sample on which the research was carried out
to the overall population of interest. The more confident we are that the
sample is representative of the population, the more externally valid we
can deem the piece of research. The larger the sample and the more
random the selection of its members (every member of the population
having the same chance of appearing in the sample) the more likely the
research is to have external validity. A sample of 1000 adults taken
randomly from the overall electoral register is much more likely to be
representative of the adult population of Ireland than a sample of 100
adults stopped at random on the streets of Dublin.

An important external validity concern in the field of behavioural
science is whether findings generated in one culture can be generalised
more broadly. It is often dangerous to assume that they can. A great proportion of published research in the behavioural sciences emanates from
the United States and it is often assumed that the results are applicable
world-wide. However, the population of other countries (even technologically developed countries such as Ireland) may have different
habits, values or ways of viewing the world that result in different
responses under similar circumstances. The only way to know whether a
finding in one country corresponds to findings in others is to carry out
similar research on samples from those countries.

In summary then, it can be said that just as the validity of research
measures refers to how well they do their jobs, so also the validity of
research designs refers to how well they do their jobs. Both are about
achieving their purpose.

TESTS OF MENTAL VARIABLES: TESTS OF MAXIMUM AND TYPICAL PERFORMANCE

The word test is used in two ways in the field of psychology. It is important not to confuse the two. The most common use of the word test – with which we are most familiar because of their use in education – is to refer to *tests of maximum performance*. A test of maximum performance is one where the test taker is challenged to do his/her best, where one can do better or worse than others on the test and where the effort applied can be expected to have a bearing on the outcome. The Leaving Certificate consists of such tests. IQ tests also fall into this category.

The other use of the word test is with reference to *tests of typical performance*. Though the word test is often used, such measures are not tests in the commonly understood meaning of the term. On such a test it is not possible to do better or worse. There is no basis for competition with others. Effort will not change one's scores. What is required is simply honesty. Personality tests fall into this class. The objective is to represent oneself as one typically or usually is. You cannot perform well or poorly on a personality test. You are simply asked questions about yourself and you can answer honestly or not – in other words represent yourself as you typically are or alternatively misrepresent yourself.

UNDERSTANDING TEST SCORES

Test scores only have meaning when you understand how the test was constructed and what it is designed to achieve. If you were told that you had scored an overall total of 131 on a standard IQ test, this may or may not mean anything to you. If, however, you are told that only around 2 per cent of the overall population score above 130, you can immediately grasp the meaning of your test score. You are an unusually bright individual.

To understand what test scores mean you need to understand how the test was designed. There are three different ways in which a test can be designed. In each case the scores refer or are *referenced* to different sources. The three are: *norm referenced, criterion referenced* and *domain referenced tests*. Sometimes domain referenced tests are described as specific types of criterion referenced tests. This will be discussed below.

Norm referenced tests

This is a test where the scores are understood by comparison with the scores of other takers of the test. Your absolute performance (how exactly you answered) is not the important outcome – what is important is how your scores compare with those of others. One common way of reporting the results of such a test is to assign each individual who took the test to categories called *percentiles*. The categories run from 1-99. If a person's score is better than, say, 27 per cent of those who took the test, then that score puts the individual in the 27th percentile. A percentile is defined by the percentage of individuals who scored below that score. If you are told after taking such a test that you scored in the 78th percentile, then you know that you have performed better than 78 per cent of test takers. Dividing the scores into percentiles in this way is just one approach to reporting norm referenced test results.

The most common approach taken to reporting norm referenced tests is to use what are known as *standard scores*. This involves mathematically transforming the actual scores in a way that shows how far from the average each score is and at the same time what proportion of individuals taking the test scored as well or as poorly as that.

The key to understanding the scores in each case is to know what proportion of test takers score at or below any particular reported score.

Of course, with a norm referenced test, it is important to know who the other test takers were or what group the 'norms' are based on. Norm based tests such as IQ tests are based on representative samples of whole countries' populations. IQ scores have meaning only because it is already known what proportion of the population can be expected to get any particular score. For example, a score above 130 can be expected in only $2\frac{1}{4}$ per cent of the population, whereas half the population can be expected to score above 100.

Personality tests are norm referenced tests of typical performance. Their objective is to describe an individual in terms of important dimensions or characteristics of personality and to indicate how like or unlike the average an individual is.

Criterion referenced tests

A test of this kind is designed so that it predicts performance on some activity or skill. A test constructed so that it is known that good performers on the test will be suitable for some specific type of job or can be expected to perform well on a training course would be an example.

Normally the test is researched using participants who have had the opportunity to display their performance on the criterion (the job or course or whatever). Only items distinguishing between good and poor performers on the criterion are included in the test. You can appreciate that if a job required a lot of work with figures – carrying out mathematical calculations – then a good criterion referenced test for predicting performance on the job would be based on numeracy or mathematics questions. If a job required a lot of report writing, the appropriate test might concentrate on English.

Norm referenced tests such as intelligence tests (and also domain referenced tests, described below) can be used as criterion referenced tests, if appropriate research has shown that they predict the criterion in question.

Domain referenced tests

Such a test acts as a measure of the proportion or percentage of a body of knowledge or skill of which an individual shows a command. School and college examinations are tests of this kind. There is a syllabus for a subject (the domain or body of knowledge taught on the course) and the examination is a measure of how much of this syllabus or domain of knowledge each student can demonstrate a command of at the end of the course. Such tests are usually based on questions, which are random samples of the domain. The mark awarded corresponds to the proportion of the full knowledge relevant to those questions which the student is able to show. The fact that not everything covered on the course (i.e. the full domain) is examined does not matter since the students do not know in advance which parts of the domain will be examined. In this way a sample is likely to be as accurate as a test of all the knowledge covered on the course. Inevitably, if anything about the sample to be examined is revealed in advance, then the test is no longer a *valid* (see above) test of the domain.

BOX 2.3

THE LEAVING CERTIFICATE AS A CRITERION REFERENCED TEST OF SUCCESS IN THIRD LEVEL COURSES

In June 1999 a Commission appointed by the Minister for Education reported on the relationship between Leaving Certificate points and success in third level courses (Lynch et al, 1999).

Their study was based on a representative sample of all 1992 third level entrants to a total of 27 higher education colleges.

It was found that there is

'a strong correlation between an individual's performance at the Leaving Certificate and higher education performance generally ... However, the correlation is not a perfect one ... The study shows that several factors – higher education sector, field of study and gender – mediate the relationship between Leaving Certificate and higher education performance.'

(Commission on the Points System, Final Report, 1999)

Some specific findings were that:

The relationship between Leaving Certificate and third level performance was generally similar within the University and the Institutes of Technology sectors. Such differences as were found seem largely to be due to the different mix of Certificate, Diploma and Degree courses within the two sectors.

Comparing students with equivalent points, a much higher proportion failed in the sciences than in the humanities.

Although females enter third level with better Leaving Certificates than males, they do not perform as well. This trend is most striking in the humanities. In the University sector men are 1.8 times more likely to obtain a first class or upper second in those courses despite marginally poorer Leaving Certificates. In business degrees only 66 per cent of females obtained a second or first class honour while 93 per cent of males achieved that level (Lynch et al, 1999).

Sometimes domain referenced tests are described as criterion referenced tests with the domain of knowledge being the criterion measured.

As indicated earlier, domain referenced tests can also be used as criterion referenced tests in the sense described here. Thus, domain referenced tests may be used to predict some other independent criterion so long as they have been shown to do so successfully. It is quite sensible, for example, to use the Leaving Certificate (domain referenced test) to make up the CAO points system which is then used to select the more suitable candidates for limited places on third level courses so long as the points act as a predictor of success at third level. If they were ever shown not to do so at all, then the Leaving Certificate exam would not be a suitable criterion referenced test for this purpose. See Box 2.3 for a discussion of the validity of the Leaving Certificate as a criterion referenced test for entry to third level courses.

STRESS IN THE WORKPLACE REVISITED

Knowing what we hopefully do now about the various issues that are important in research methodology, what judgments should we arrive at in relation to the Flanagan, Moriarty and Daly (1999) study discussed at the beginning of this chapter?

The study needs to be appraised in terms of the following:

(1) Research design employed: was it observational, correlational or experimental and what conclusions may be drawn from the findings?
(2) Were the findings analysed in such a manner that chance outcomes have been eliminated in so far as is reasonable?
(3) The validity and reliability of the variable measures employed: is evidence presented that the measures were capable of returning consistent and accurate accounts of the variables under study?
(4) The internal and external validity of the study: was the methodology sound and can we safely generalise from its findings to a broader population?

A close examination of the original study reveals a number of important details that enables us to come to some conclusions.

The research design was correlational, studying the relationship between measures of stress and mental wellbeing and a variety of bio-graphical and work related factors such as occupation, age, marital status, number of children and educational qualifications. It is not possible therefore to arrive at the conclusion that the relationships found are of a causal nature. Indeed the authors of the study recognise this at a number of points. For example, on the finding that those with higher educational qualifications reported higher levels of stress, the authors point out that 'it is unlikely that these findings reveal an inherent stressor in education or qualifications' and go on to offer an alternative explanation for the findings: 'It is more likely that the higher qualifications of some staff have led them into careers with greater responsibilities and/or supervisory roles which may be the root of the higher stress levels' (Flanagan, Moriarty and Daly, 1999, p. 86).

Elsewhere, they suggest an explanation for the lower stress levels reported by workers with larger families: 'This has probably got more to do with the lower levels of stress experienced by older staff and the less stress generated by older children than any stress-reducing characteristics of children per se' (p. 86).

The editor of the newspaper article, in search of an eye-catching title, fell into the very common trap of treating correlation and causality as one and the same. The study, as we now see, did not in fact show nor claim to show that 'children and education can affect your stress levels'.

On the question of whether or not findings reported could be chance relationships, the research report shows that appropriate statistical tests were carried out to identify whether this was the case. These tests take account of the number of subjects used in a particular piece of analysis and the size of the relationships or differences found on the measures used. The evidence is that the authors avoided presenting any chance relationships as real.

As regards the validity and reliability of the measures used, some con-clusions can be reached through a reading of the research report though the more concerned researcher would have to explore further to reach firm conclusions. Three measures were used: a biographical survey to collect data on variables such as occupation, marital/family status and hours of work, a standardised questionnaire known as the General Health

Questionnaire to measure general health and coping and a Stress Scale specially developed by the research team.

No detailed information was given on the biographical survey from which it might be deduced whether or not it contained any possible sources of error. Sources of error in biographical questionnaires can arise where respondents are either not sure themselves of the correct answers to the questions asked or might be motivated to conceal certain information. Some of the data sought through the questionnaire can safely be assumed to be error-free such as, for example, marital/parental status, occupation and hours of work. One might have some doubts, however, about questions on sick leave and exercise, biographical details that might be prone to errors of memory or exaggeration.

No data on the validity and reliability evidence shown for the General Health Questionnaire is presented in the report. A reference for the origins of the measure (Goldberg, 1978), is provided, however. Through this it would be possible to obtain the relevant information. Ideally, however, a summary of the available validity and reliability data would have been given in the report, enabling the reader to come to immediate conclusions about how accurately the answers given by respondents to the questions contained in the measure represent their real state of health.

Little or no data was presented to indicate the validity of the Stress Scale, which was developed by the team carrying out the research, other than the fact that it correlated with the General Health Questionnaire. Given that there is a wealth of research supporting the relationship between stress and health failure, the correlation may be taken as a kind of validation of both measures. No information on the test-retest reliability of the stress scale was offered. However, data is given which supports the internal reliability of the scale showing a strong relationship between ten sub-scales (each a measure of stress from a particular source such as workload or client-related) and the overall scale.

The absence of adequate evidence on the validity and reliability of the measures used leaves one somewhat less confident than would otherwise be the case about the internal validity of the study.

If one accepts the accuracy of the findings, the remaining issue concerns their generalisability – the external validity of the research study.

This depends on the participant or subject sample size and how it was drawn. The sample consisted of 684 employees of what was described as 'an Irish human services organisation' providing services in the areas of psychiatry and learning disabilities. Originally 1,786 employees – the full staff complement – were included but only 38 per cent (n = 684) returned the completed measures. The response rate varied from occupation to occupation being as low as 22 per cent for catering/housekeeping and as high as 70 per cent for administration.

One problem with lower response rates is that it allows for the possibility of those responding not being representative of the group as a whole. It is possible, for example, that those who experience higher levels of stress are more likely to respond, perhaps hoping that the survey will alert the organisation to problems in the workplace they perceive as causing them stress. If this were to happen it would distort the picture obtained. Differing response rates across occupations (reported) and across other biographical variables such as gender (not reported) could also distort comparisons. The problem with the sample being drawn entirely from the staff of one organisation is that the results may be peculiar to that organisation. The manner in which the organisation is managed, its recruitment practices or its internal culture (see chapter 10 for discussion on organisational culture) may be responsible to some degree for the results, which might not be found elsewhere. Before comparing the results of this study with those of similar studies carried out in other workplaces, one would need to be hesitant in generalising from the findings.

Those new to the concept of behavioural research might be forgiven for interpreting the above list of reservations about this study as reason to ignore it entirely. This would, however, be a serious mistake. It is in the nature of behavioural research that rarely will a study not be amenable to criticism. While some flaws such as the use of entirely invalid measures or extremely small samples may render a study useless from a scientific standpoint, often a far from perfect study is useful when compared with results obtained through similar studies elsewhere.

Of course, the reader must interpret research findings with caution and identify shortcomings but one must also be mindful that important information is normally obtained not from a single study but from an accumulation of different pieces of research over time. While one might reasonably question the generalisability of findings from a sample drawn from within one organisation, the discovery of a further study obtaining similar findings in a totally different organisation by a different research team would lend considerable weight to the study just discussed.

SUMMARY

Researchers do not work in a vacuum. They decide to explore certain questions because they are aware of gaps which exist in the current knowledge of their subject area.

Scientists begin by developing theories, which are explanations for observations or findings. They then seek to obtain evidence to support those theories. To do this they develop hypotheses. These are statements or predictions that can be tested through a piece of research. When all the hypotheses that can reasonably be derived from a theory have been found true then the theory is taken to be a correct explanation. If a hypothesis can not be proven then the theory has to be revised or rejected.

A research design is a detailed plan for testing a hypothesis or carrying out a particular piece of research. There are two broad types of research design: experimental and non-experimental.

An experimental design seeks to demonstrate that one variable (called the independent variable) is the cause of change on another variable (called the dependent variable). This research design involves manipulating the independent variable while holding all other variables constant or unchanging except the dependent variable to see if the independent variable is capable on its own of producing change in the dependent.

Non-experimental designs are not so capable of showing cause and effect relationships. They may be divided into two types: observational and correlational.

Observational research simply involves observing carefully and often conducting discussions and interviews with individuals of interest. Conclusions are then drawn by the researcher. There is always the risk that the conclusions are influenced by the observer and would not be reached by another researcher. It is a 'qualitative' research approach in contrast to experimental and correlational designs which are 'quantitative'. In practice it is best to treat research methodologies as complementary with choices being made on the basis of what approach will answer the research questions posed with as much objectivity as possible without losing sight of the purpose of the research.

Correlational design involves measuring the variables of interest and computing relationships between them. It is not possible to infer causality from relationships found. It is possible to eliminate possible causes of effects on variables using a correlational design. This is achieved by studying relationships between variables within samples that are known not to differ on variables that might be responsible for the effect of interest.

Findings based on larger samples drawn at random and findings of greater magnitude are less likely to occur by chance. There are statistical calculations that can estimate the probability of a given result occurring through chance alone. Where the probability of a finding being the result of chance alone is estimated to be less than 5 per cent it is taken to be a significant result.

The validity of a research design refers to how well it is capable of doing its job. Internal validity concerns how capable the design is of showing what it has claimed to show with respect to the sample studied. External validity refers to how generalisable the findings are to the wider population of interest. External validity depends on the sample being representative of the wider population from which it was drawn.

Research measures result in figures or numbers reflecting the variables studied. The meaning of those numbers and the way they can be analysed depends on the nature of the measuring scale used. Research measures, depending on how they work, result in either nominal, ordinal, interval or ratio measurement.

Nominal measurement means that any figures used are just labels for discrete categories. Ordinal measurement results in figures that indicate the rank ordering of the cases along the dimension measured. Interval measurement not only places the cases in order but indicates the interval between each case. Ratio measurement achieves all that interval measurement does but, in addition, uses a scale where zero means the absence of any quantity on the dimension measured.

Research in the behavioural sciences uses a wide variety of tests of human variables. It is important to distinguish between 'tests of maximum performance' and tests of 'typical performance'. The former accord more with everyday use of the word test in that it involves a measure where effort can be expected to produce better results and where it is possible to compare results on a best to worst dimension. The latter involve measures such as personality tests where the objective is not to do well but to represent oneself honestly as one typically is.

The scores produced by tests, whether maximum or typical performance, have different meanings depending on what those scores are designed to refer to. Norm referenced tests produce scores that indicate where a result lies with respect to those obtained by a group the scores for which are known. Criterion referenced test scores predict or indicate performance with respect to some skill or activity such as ability to do a job. Domain referenced test scores indicate the proportion of a set body of skill or knowledge over which the testee has a command.

Ideally, all measures of variables used in research should have high 'reliability' and 'validity'. Reliability is the consistency with which measuring instruments result in scores. Test-retest reliability is assessed by repeated measures of the same testees when the factor being measured ought not to have changed in the interval. Internal reliability refers to the consistency with which a multi-item measure measures the same factor throughout all the items. It is checked by finding the relationship between scores on items and scores on the measure as a whole. Validity cannot exist without reliability but the opposite is not the case. Validity refers to the extent to which a measure has been shown to measure what is intended. It is checked by comparisons with other measures of the same variable and by establishing if results yielded by the instrument accord with logical predictions.

REVIEW QUESTIONS

1. Describe the main factors that need to be taken into account in designing a sound piece of research.
2. Explain the defects that could result in a research design having poor internal and external validity.
3. Explain each of the following briefly, using examples as appropriate:
   (a) interval measurement;

(b) experimental research design;

(c) internal reliability of measurement;

(d) hypothesis;

(e) norm referenced test.

4. Distinguish between experimental and correlational research design, explaining the advantages and disadvantages of each approach.

5. Describe in as much detail as possible how it might be shown that hunger results in poor exam performance.

REFERENCES

Brody, H., (1973), *Inishkillane: Change and Decline in the West of Ireland*, London: Allen Lane.

Chisnall, P.M., (1975), *Marketing: A Behavioural Analysis*, UK: McGraw-Hill.

Commission on the Points System, (1999), *Final Report and Recommendations*, November, Dublin: Stationery Office.

Fergusson, D.M., Lloyd, M. and Horwood, L.J., (1991), 'Family Ethnicity, Social Background and Scholastic Achievement: An Eleven Year Longitudinal Study', *New Zealand Journal of Educational Studies*, 26, 49-63.

Flanagan, N., Moriarty, T. and Daly, A., (1999), 'Who is Stressed and Why? Occupational Specific Stress among Staff in an Irish Human Service Organisation', *Administration*, 47, 4, 70-90.

Goffman, E., (1961), *Asylums: Essays on the Social Situation of Mental Patients and Other Inmates*, Harmondsworth: Penguin.

Goldberg, D., (1978), *General Health Questionnaire – 12*, UK: NFER Nelson.

Kubler-Ross, E., (1969), *On Death and Dying*, New York: Macmillan.

Lynch, K., Brannick, T., Clancy, P. and Drudy, S., (1999), *Commission on the Points System Research Paper No. 4, Points and Performance in Higher Education: A Study of the Predictive Validity of the Points System*, Dublin: The Stationery Office.

Murthy and Panda, (1987), 'A Study of Intelligence, Socio-economic Status and Birth Order Among Children Belonging to SC-ST and Non-SC-ST Groups', *Indian Journal of Behaviour*, 11, 25-30.

Roethlisberger, F.J. and Dickson, W.J., (1964), *Management and the Worker*, Cambridge MA: Harvard University Press.

Rosenthal, R.R. and Jacobson, L., (1968), *Pygmalion in the Classroom*, New York: Holt, Reinhartand Winston.

Siegel, S., (1956), *Non-parametric Statistics for the Behavioural Sciences*, McGraw-Hill.

Silverman, D., (1998), 'Qualitative/Quantitative', in Jenkins, C (Ed.), *Core Sociological Dichotomies*, London: Sage.

Chapter 3

Perception

LEARNING OBJECTIVES

On completion of this chapter you should be able to:

- define 'sensation' and 'perception';
- distinguish the key characteristics of perception from those of sensation;
- describe how optical illusions and the process of depth perception illustrate the active nature of perception;
- explain the process of 'perceptual selection';
- explain the experimental evidence that demonstrates unconscious processing of stimulus information, a necessary requirement for subjective influences on perceptual selection;
- explain the process of perceptual organisation referring to categorisation, schemata and prototypes;
- describe the errors of social perception that follow from the active selective nature of the perceptual system; and
- explain how errors of social perception can be minimised.

INTRODUCTION

On 18 May 1999, Jill Dando, the widely popular and high profile BBC presenter, was assassinated by an unknown assailant. It was 11.30 am and she had just walked out of her home in the affluent southwest London suburb of Fulham. She died instantly from a single bullet to the head fired at close range from a 9mm automatic pistol. There was widespread shock and amazement throughout Britain. No motive for the killing could be identified.

Almost a year later the police were no nearer to identifying the killer. On 18 April 2000, Crimewatch, a BBC programme (which, ironically, Jill Dando had presented before her death), broadcast a new appeal for information based on specific clues.

Chief Inspector Hamish Campbell, leading the police investigation into the murder, explained that a dozen witnesses said that they saw a man in his 30s or 40s hanging around her home. All agreed that he wore a dark suit and appeared agitated. However, three of them described his suit as too big for him. Three said he wore a trilby hat and several said that he had a mobile phone.

Despite the differences in description the police believed that this was the same man and that he may have been a psychologically disturbed stalker who had developed a morbid obsession with the attractive and stylish TV presenter.

Jill Dando

The question of interest to us here is why different witnesses who walked close by this individual and noticed something odd about his behaviour, which drew their attention, still came away with quite vague and conflicting information about him. Did he or did he not wear a hat? Was his suit too big for him? Did he or did he not have a mobile phone? And what about other details of his appearance? Some of the differences in appearance are easily explained. He may have been using a mobile phone when one witness saw him but not when seen by another. The hat, how-ever, suggests different individuals – or does it? Perhaps he took off his hat at some point and witnesses failed to notice him holding it in his hand. Perhaps he had disposed of it somewhere? Why then was it not found later? What of the over-sized suit? That could not have been changed. Were the witnesses, after all, describing different individuals?

Unfortunately, this kind of conflict in witness evidence is common-place. Police, lawyers and the judiciary are confronted with contradictory descriptions of evidence every day. It is not necessarily that witnesses have seen different things. The problem is that humans are just not particularly good at forming and retaining an accurate impression of the objective world. Some of the problem is down to memory. For example, people sometimes add to their memories of one scene items witnessed in another (Loftus, Miller and Burns, 1978). Also, as we are all aware when sitting an examination, memory for detail deteriorates with the passage of time and a very high proportion of this memory loss occurs in the hours imme-diately after the event (Thompson, 1982). Much of the difficulty lies, however, in forming the initial impressions. Humans are not like video recorders. VCRs record what is there. Humans confronted with the same scene are quite capable of literally 'seeing' different things. This is due to the peculiar way in which we process information coming in through our senses. The processing of sensory information is called 'perception'.

After exploring how our perceptual system works in this chapter it should be much clearer why some witnesses saw the man in Fulham as having a hat when others did not and why in the eyes of some he was wearing an over-sized suit, a detail not apparent to others. It should also be clearer why they failed to pick up a more detailed impression of the man such as the exact colour of his suit, whether he was wearing a tie and, if so, what colour and so on. It will become apparent that to a large extent we each live in our own subjective perceptual world, creating our own images of what we encounter. This has far reaching implications not least for how we deal with others. After all, if we are disposed to create our own personal impressions of others that may well be at odds with what they are really like, it is small wonder that our social worlds involve a fair share of misunderstanding and conflict.

While this chapter is primarily concerned with the whole process of turning sensory information into conscious awareness – the process of perception – it will be necessary to first focus on the initial detection by the sensory organs of the information. This is the process of sensation.

SENSATION

Before our brains can arrive at any conscious awareness of the outside world (or for that matter, anything happening in our own bodies) our senses have to respond to some aspect of this world.

The five senses are: sight; hearing; taste; smell; and touch. Together they provide us with the raw material from which to be aware of and understand the world around us. It is important to emphasise, again, that the senses only provide the raw material. Meaning is made of this material in the brain. Each of the sense organs, such as the eyes and ears, respond to specific *stimuli*.

Stimuli are features of the environment, which our sense organs are capable of detecting.

Sensation involves physical responses of the sense organ tissues to the appropriate stimuli.

The eyes respond to light – usually reflected off objects. The ears respond to sound waves, usually vibrations of the air (but can be of other media such as water – you can hear a certain amount under water). What do you think the nose responds to? The response in each case is essentially a biological response, i.e. a change in the tissues that can be measured in a physical sense. An example is the way the ear drum vibrates in response to sound waves causing the movement of bones inside the inner ear and ultimately causing changes in the nerves leading to the brain. The changes in the nerves are chemical changes. The eyes have cells within them that respond to different kinds of light, shade and colour in different ways.

Many stimuli are produced within our environment which the human senses are not equipped to detect. Our ears make no response to a wide range of high pitch and low pitch sounds. The ears of dogs, on the other hand, can detect high pitches, which for us do not exist at all. The same is true of low pitch sounds for whales. Likewise, our eyes do not detect infra-red or ultra-violet light. Certain insects like flies and bees are able to detect light of such wavelengths. They see a very different world to us. While it is important to appreciate that the world detected by our senses is only a portion of the real world of stimulus information that is out there, this point is of limited concern here. That is because, broadly speaking, with a few exceptions such as congenital limitations in colour vision experienced by a small proportion of people, all humans are equipped to detect the same range of stimuli. Thus, to that extent, we are all capable of experiencing the same world.

Two important points need to be appreciated about the sense organs. They are *passive* and they are understandable in *biological* terms.

Being understandable in biological terms means that the process can be explained through the analysis of physical changes in the components and tissues of the sense organs. Take hearing as an example. In response to sound waves the ear drum vibrates causing movement of bones in the inner ear, ultimately leading to chemical changes in nerve cells which transmit messages to the brain.

Being passive means that the sense organs have no choice about responding when exposed to the appropriate stimuli. Once light reflected from an object in the field of vision falls upon the eye, it inevitably responds with changes in certain cells. Likewise, the ear drum inevitably vibrates in response to a range of sound waves. This happens continuously. Our senses are responding to a barrage of stimuli all the time. It does not follow, however, that we ever become aware of all those stimuli. In fact, we only become aware of a small proportion. If our senses are passive and continue to receive the stimulus information, why do we fail to become aware of much of it? More interestingly, how is the choice made between what we become aware of and what not? The answers to those questions lie in the process of perception.

THE PROCESS OF PERCEPTION

Perception can be defined as:

the psychological process of actively selecting and organising stimulus information detected by the sensory organs so as to create conscious awareness.

In contrast to sensation, perception is an active process, which must be understood in psychological terms. There is no way to understand perception through an analysis of tissue or nerve cell responses. We must rely on psychological terms such as interpretation, understanding and memory. While we are passive recipients of sensations, we are active creators of perceptions. Perception involves each of us making our own personal sense or interpretation of the sensory information detected by our sense organs.

In the definition above, 'selecting' and 'organising' summarise the active nature of the perceptual process. The implication is that not all of the stimulus information detected by the sense organs is used to create conscious awareness and such information as is used gets organised in some way. Organising inevitably involves some kind of transformation or change. It is becoming clear that what we become aware of is at some remove from what is actually out there.

To understand the process of perception it is best to deal separately with its two sub-processes: *selection*; and *organisation*, though in practice, as we will see later, they depend on each other.

THE PROCESS OF PERCEPTUAL SELECTION

Our senses are from moment to moment bombarded with stimuli such as sights, sounds and smells. Our sense organs have no choice but to respond (biologically – by changes in cells and tissues) to all those stimuli. Our brains, however, are not fast enough to cope with all this material. We simply do not have enough time to think about it and consciously make sense of it. If we had to think about all the information coming in through our senses we would take forever to take any action. Crossing a busy street our eyes can still detect the colour of cars, the names on shops, the architecture of buildings and so on. None of this helps us to safely cross the street. What is relevant is the position and speed of cars. If we had to think about what is relevant and what is not, we would never be able to cross a street. Fortunately, humans have developed a remarkable ability – the ability to unconsciously process a great quantity of stimulus information and select relevant information for detailed conscious processing. This is the process of *perceptual selection*.

Crossing a busy street we are able to process all the incoming information – colour, speed etc. of cars – at very high speed and, without our becoming aware of the process, pick out the material that is relevant – speed of cars, for example – which we then consciously think about and use.

Meeting a stream of people on a busy street you are unlikely to be aware of their details. Yet you will have no difficulty identifying someone you know well. How do you do that?

But, if we are never consciously aware of the information, which has not been selected for use, how do we know it was ever processed in some unconscious way?

Proof of the ability of humans to process information of which they are entirely unaware has been obtained through a number of clever experiments such as 'dichotic listening tests' and 'subliminal exposure experiments'.

Dichotic listening tests

The example described here is an experiment carried out by Mac Kay (1973) based on a method described initially by Cherry and Taylor

(1954). It uses information coming into the ears as opposed to the eyes but it is safe to assume that the same general principles apply to all sensory information.

The test participants were fitted out with headphones. Each ear was linked to a separate tape recorder. Into one ear was played a list of sentences and into the other a list of words – one word for each sentence. The participants were asked to listen carefully to the ear into which the sentences were being played while ignoring the other ear and to either repeat aloud or write down the sentence as it was being played. A check was carried out to see if subjects became aware of the words being played into the unattended ear. This involved a trial where immediately after a sentence and word had been played participants were asked to write down what the word was. Only one subject out of 36 correctly reported the unattended word. Attending to the sentences prevented them from shifting their attention to and processing the words.

The sentences which they listened to were vague in terms of meaning. An example was: 'They threw stones towards the bank yesterday'. This might mean the bank of a river or it might mean a financial institution. The sentences were the same for all participants. The words played into the unattended ear to match the sentences were varied from person to person. However, in every case, the words were picked so that they might (had they been heard) suggest a meaning for the matching sentence. To match the sentence: 'They threw stones towards the bank yesterday', the word 'money' or the word 'river' was used.

Afterwards, for each sentence actually heard, the participants were asked to choose between two sentences as to which one matched the heard sentence most closely in meaning.

Thus, for the sentence, 'They threw stones towards the bank yesterday', subjects were asked to choose between 'They threw stones towards the side of the river yesterday' and 'They threw stones towards the savings and loan association yesterday'.

Participants who had the word 'river' played to their unattended ear were significantly more inclined to opt for the first sentence, while those who had been played 'money' were more inclined to opt for the second.

It is clear that, though the participants were unaware of the words, they were using them to give meaning to the sentences. For this to be possible the participants had to be unconsciously processing the words (auditory stimuli).

Subliminal exposure experiments

This type of experiment involves flashing a word or picture on a screen for such a brief period that viewers are unaware that any stimulus has been presented. Despite the viewers' lack of conscious awareness several researchers have demonstrated unconscious processing of the stimuli (e.g. Murphy and Zajonc, 1993; Bornstein and Pittman, 1992; Baldwin, Carrell and Lopez, 1990).

The Murphy and Zajonc (1993) study will serve as an illustrative example. They presented participants on a screen a number of characters from the Chinese alphabet and asked them to rate how much they liked the look of each one. Each character was shown for two seconds. What the participants were wholly unaware of was that, just before each character was presented, another visual stimulus was flashed on screen for just four milliseconds. Three different stimuli were used: a picture of a smiling face; a picture of an angry face; or a geometrical shape. The participants showed a significant preference for the characters preceded by the happy face, with least preference for characters preceded by the angry face.

Again, as in the case of the 'dichotic listening tests', the evidence is that stimulus information outside of conscious awareness can be processed.

OBJECTIVE AND SUBJECTIVE INFLUENCES ON PERCEPTUAL SELECTION

It is the capacity to unconsciously process at a very rapid pace a great deal of stimulus information that enables us to cope with the great volume of information from our environment pouring in each moment through the senses. The next question concerns what governs our choice or selection of this information. On what basis do we unconsciously decide to consciously process certain sights, sounds, etc., in a more detailed way? Both objective and subjective factors play a part. Objective factors are characteristics of the stimuli that do not depend on who is experiencing them. Subjective factors are those that depend on the evaluation of the stimulus by the person involved. It is the latter case that involves the unconscious processing.

Subjective factors include:

1. knowledge;
2. personality;
3. motivation and needs;
4. attitudes and interests;
5. intelligence and ability.

Imagine that you are making your way through the Amazonian jungle with a local native. Which of you, do you think, would notice the deadly tree snake camouflaged against a branch lying across your track at eye level just a few feet ahead? Your eyes may be just as acute as his and you may even briefly scan that very branch, but without knowledge and experience of what exactly to expect, you will be unlikely to select the relevant stimulus. The native, with a body of relevant knowledge and experience to draw on, will become aware of the danger much more quickly. Now change your location and imagine that you are both crossing a busy city street. Which of you will be best equipped to select from the cacophony of sounds entering your ears the sound of a car suddenly accelerating across your path? Both of you will doubtless 'hear' the sound at a sensory level but it is you, now in the role of native, who will have a lifetime of experience and knowledge of traffic sounds to draw on. It is this that will cause your unconscious selection system to push the sound into awareness and allow you to respond accordingly.

It is not just your knowledge but also your immediate needs and motivation that dictates what your perceptual system selects as you cross a busy street. Standing at the kerb without any intention of crossing the street, you will inevitably select very different stimulus information for conscious awareness. Safe from the hazards of traffic, you may become aware of the faces of people walking by on the other side or the type of shops visible along the street.

Personality attributes, attitudes and interests and even gender also have major effects. Sociable individuals, for example, become aware of more information about people. A botanist or an avid gardener will inevitably select different information for conscious processing when looking into somebody's garden than will a person who has no knowledge of plants. Women typically notice more about colour than men do. It is not that men are unable to see what colour shirt someone was wearing. They are simply less likely to select that stimulus information for conscious processing. Interestingly, research has shown that women accumulate far more adjectives describing colour than men do.

Referring back to the murder of Jill Dando, what factors might have caused witnesses to notice the over-sized suit while others missed that detail? A greater interest in and appreciation of fashion could easily result in a detail like this being noticed. This applies also to the possibility that the suspect wore a hat. Hats may have more importance in the perceptual worlds of some individuals, resulting in their being selected for conscious processing. Others may well have seen the hat in a sensory fashion, but because hats were of no interest to them this detail was not selected. If, by good fortune, a fashion expert had been one of the witnesses, the police might now have a much more detailed description of the suspect's apparel: exact colour, pattern and design of suit; colour of shirt and tie; etc.

Which information is selected and which not is decided on external grounds as well. Certain characteristics of stimuli – particularly those that cause stimuli to contrast with background information – make them more likely to be selected for attention. Had the Jill Dando suspect been wearing a canary yellow track-suit, there would certainly have been less discrepancy in witness descriptions. Stimulus characteristics that lead to selection include:

1. loudness;
2. brightness;
3. colour;
4. movement;
5. repetition;
6. novelty;
7. strength.

In other words, even when we have no immediate motivation to hear certain sounds or notice certain smells or sights, they intrude on our notice if they occur in sufficient contrast to the background stimuli already there. Advertisers use contrast – flashing neon signs in cities, for example – to make people attend to their advertisements over the barrage of stimuli being experienced at the same time. Likewise, a loud explosion would intrude on your awareness even in the middle of your attempts to cross the busiest street. Engrossed in study you might not seem to hear the first few peals of a distant church bell but as the peals keep coming chances are they will eventually insinuate themselves into your awareness. Their volume or tone will not have altered but the repetition eventually scales the selection barrier. You only become conscious of a mouse, that has all the while been sitting quietly by a dark skirting board at the periphery of your vision, when it darts from one position to another. The mouse is visible to the eye all along, but it requires the contrast of movement to raise such a small stimulus to consciousness.

Take a moment to think about the variety of ways in which advertisers capitalise on these objective characteristics of stimuli to make us notice their advertisements!

Now that we understand the process of perceptual selection, we can see that we are each likely to come away with a different picture of any experience to which we are exposed. It all depends on what we select for conscious processing. While certain contrasting stimuli, such as very loud noises or distant bells that ring repeatedly, will probably be noticed by everyone, the remaining stimuli will be selected or not depending on our knowledge, interests, personalities and so on.

Perceptual selection causes us all to experience our own version of the world, which is not exactly the same as that experienced by anyone else. We are not like cameras or tape recorders. They simply take a record based on the sights and sounds that are there. They do it unselectively. We take a record of the world that is highly selective.

In the next section it will become clear that it is not only the process of perceptual selection that causes us to live in our own unique versions of the world. We each organise the stimulus information which we select in our own way. It is a wonder that we can communicate with each other at all about the worlds we live in! We will now go on to examine the process of making sense of the selected information – the process of perceptual organisation.

THE PROCESS OF PERCEPTUAL ORGANISATION

In one sense, the world as we experience it, even after screening out a lot of stimulus information through perceptual selection, is still much too complex to deal with in detail. Paradoxically, in another sense, the information provided by our senses is too basic to represent the rich world of our conscious awareness.

The stimulus information that makes up a common sight like a chair is in fact very complex and varies each time we see a chair from a slightly different angle and each time we see a new chair. Yet, on detecting the sight of a chair, we need to be able to respond without delay in an appropriate manner. Each fresh sighting of a chair is a new unique experience. Yet we have not got the time to think this information through. The same applies to every other sight, sound, smell, taste and feeling.

To add to the challenge we face, the visual world as detected in our eyes does not consist of clear discrete objects in three-dimensional space as we experience it. Our eyes have no direct system of detecting depth. What the eyes actually see is a flat world consisting of contours and variations in light, dark and colour. From this our brains have to extract at a remarkable speed the nature of the visual world we experience.

It is clear that this can only be achieved by a system of short cuts. How our mechanism of perceptual organisation works in detail is still the subject of much debate and disagreement. An analysis of this debate is beyond the scope of this text. It is agreed, however, that certain general features apply.

UNDERLYING PRINCIPLES OF PERCEPTUAL ORGANISATION

The first challenge facing our process of perceptual organisation is how to distinguish one stimulus from all the others around it.

Every visible object and audible sound occurs against a complex background of other objects and sounds. But what is the background and what is the object? Which parts of a visual scene go together to make up a particular object? Which sounds occurring over time belong to each other and which are from totally separate sources and therefore unrelated? Because our brains are so good at answering those questions we remain largely unaware that the problem exists.

Only when the challenge is particularly difficult do we have any sense of what we so effortlessly achieve all the time. The camouflage evolved by many insects and other creatures provides us with a good example. Even when staring closely at a leaf insect or a stick insect sitting on a plant it is extremely difficult to figure out which bits are insect and which are plant. Object and background are virtually indistinguishable. The same problem exists to a lesser or greater extent all the time. It is perhaps easier to appreciate that the problem exists for auditory stimuli. Think of holding a conversation with several people at once, something we all do with relative ease. The voices are all intermixed in time in a most complex way, yet we have little difficulty following the gist of what each person is saying.

Much of the explanation for how we accomplish such feats of information analysis lie within three deceptively simple principles of perceptual organisation first described by a group of German psychologists known as the Gestalt School in the early part of the 20th century. The school included such notables as Max Wertheimer, Kurt Koffka and Wolfgang Kohler. The word 'gestalt' means 'whole' in German and was applied to them because they demonstrated how humans organise the elements of sensory experience into something greater than the parts, into the 'gestalt' or whole that constitutes our conscious awareness of the world.

The three principles are those of :

1. proximity;
2. similarity; and
3. closure.

The principle of proximity

The principle of proximity states that humans have a strong tendency to group together or categorise objects or experiences that occur in close proximity. Thus, a row of desks in a classroom are seen as if they in some way belong to each other. We automatically see the rows of desks in a room as separate groups of desks. We automatically see the following array of six dots as comprising three groups based on their proximity:

Proximity is a good, if by no means perfect, clue as to which sensory experiences belong together. One does not have to scan the environment as a whole to locate the parts of an object – they will be proximate or close to each other. Having located one part of a stick insect, one can be assured that only plant-like formations close to that are part of the creature. The same applies to sounds. If a series of honks from a car horn outside your window seem to come from the same location, you assume it to be from the same car, perhaps someone trying to catch your attention. If the honks come from different locations, then they are taken to have nothing to do with each other. If the members of a group with whom you are conversing could change locations as if by magic, making sense of the conversation would suddenly present a greater challenge, in that elements of conversation that were proximate could not be used as a clue for source.

Proximity is, of course, no guarantee that things belong together. Similarity is a further clue as to what goes with what.

The principle of similarity

The principle of similarity states that humans have a strong tendency to group together objects or experiences that are similar. It is natural for us to categorise people based on their sex or age or physical appearance in general. We automatically see the following array of symbols as making up four separate groups. Despite the fact that the symbols are equidistant, we do not make categories of those that differ from each other.

A car horn honking and a bird singing are not assumed to be related, even if they come from the same general location. A series of similar bell peals from the same location is taken to be from the same bell, because of the similarity in sound. The similarity of individual voices is a major clue to help us distinguish who is saying what in a group conversation. Even, if as suggested above, the individuals in a group conversation were able to change places at will, the clue of similarity of voice would still remain, to help identify which utterances belonged to whom.

Insofar as the visual world is concerned, normally objects are in some way dissimilar from the background, giving us an immediate indication of where the object ends and the background begins. It is the undermining of this reality through the evolution of colours and shapes similar to background habitats that provide camouflage for so many living creatures. One of the principal clues is missing, making it difficult for us, and more importantly for predators, to identify the creature.

The principle of closure

A further obstacle to us making sense of our sensory world is that the stimuli coming from any one source are frequently only a partial representation of what the source actually is. Look around the room you are in at this moment and see how many specific objects are partially obscured by others. Yet this presents you with no particular difficulties in identifying what you are looking at because most objects are familiar. You do not see a chair partly obscured by a table as a part chair – you mentally fill in the missing parts to 'close' the image or make it whole. It is perfectly feasible to watch a TV programme and follow a conversation taking place nearby without losing the gist of either. In reality one rapidly switches attention back and forth between the two and mentally fills in the parts missed in both. This is due to the principle of closure.

The principle of closure states that humans automatically fill in missing parts where they detect that a stimulus or an experience is incomplete. Even though most objects we view in the real world can only be partly seen at any one time, being obscured by other intervening objects, we see them as if the full image is available to the eye. When beginners paint landscape scenes they tend to paint what they know to be there – not what they can actually see. The distant red object they know to be a hay barn is painted as a hay barn in detail. In actual fact all the eye can see is a distant red blob in the landscape. More accomplished painters avoid 'closing' or completing images they see and paint them as they see them. Examine a good landscape painting closely to see this. A distant building may be painted by only a few rough brush strokes. The painter leaves it to the viewers to complete the image in their minds, as they would have to do if they viewed the scene for real.

EVIDENCE OF THE ACTIVE NATURE OF PERCEPTION

The effect of the three principles for organising perceptions is that we each organise the basic stimulus information coming in through our senses in our own unique way. Thus, not only do we each select different stimuli for processing, we also organise the selected information in our own way. This means that we actively create in our minds the world we are conscious of, using the sensory information we have selected as basic building blocks. This becomes most evident when we consider visual illusions, such as:

1. the Muller-Lyer illusion; and
2. the figure-ground illusion.

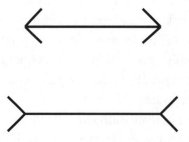

The Muller-Lyer illusion.

In the Muller-Lyer illusion, individuals commonly see the line with the outward facing fins as being longer than that with the inward facing fins. This is an illusion. The two lines are exactly the same lengths. They throw exactly the same image on the eye. It is our active perceptual organisation that makes them seem different.

The figure-ground illusion.

In the figure-ground illusion, observers detect different images at different times. One moment the image appears to be a chalice, the next moment it appears to be two faces staring at each other. Again, the change is not in the real image. It depends entirely on how we actively organise the image in our minds at any given moment.

In an illusion, we find that we are forced to see things contrary to how they are or, alternatively, we create different understandings of an image at different times. The image is not wrong or changing from moment to moment. It is our active organisation of the image that is changing or is at variance with what is actually there. This is clear evidence of the fact that perceptual organisation is an active process.

Another powerful source of evidence that perceptual organisation is an active process comes from how we see distance or depth in our visual world. In fact careful study of the eyes have revealed that the eyes have no direct detectors for depth or distance. We make up the appearance of depth in our visual world from clues that our eyes can detect.

The clues for depth fall into two categories: (1) clues detectable with one eye (monocular clues); and (2) those only detectable through the use of both eyes (binocular clues). Among the monocular clues are the following:

Lens accommodation – to focus the image of an object on the retina of the eye the lens must change shape depending on the distance of the object. The actions of the eye muscles achieving this change in shape give feedback to the brain, furnishing it with a distance clue.

Relative size – objects throwing a large image on the eye are taken to be nearer than objects throwing a smaller image. This, of course, is not perfect evidence. Out at sea it is very hard to tell whether the small craft one can see is actually a large craft far away or a small one that is much nearer.

Superposition – when one object is partially concealed or obscured from view by another, it is generally assumed to be further away.

Height in the visual field – the higher up one has to look the further away an object is assumed to be. One can see this clearly when looking across a flat plane towards the horizon. To see the ground close by, you have to look down towards your shoes. To see progressively further away, you have to go on raising your glance until your line of sight is at the horizon.

Texture gradient – the further away you look the less texture or detail you can see in the environment. Standing at the edge of a ripe field of corn, you can see the individual ears close by but the detail fades and fades as you look further out the field until all you can see is a golden wash of colour.

Linear perspective – parallel lines seem to converge with greater distance. A long straight railway line or road offers a good illustration of this phenomenon.

It is interesting to note that monocular clues are the means by which painters or artists create the appearance of depth on a canvas. The foreground is closer to the bottom, background to the top (height in visual field). A mountain partially concealed by another is assumed to be further away (superposition). Distant objects are made smaller on the canvas (relative size).

Less detail is painted in objects that are further away (texture gradient). Roads and railway lines are made narrower to indicate distance (linear perspective). Artists simply use the fact that our eyes have no direct means of seeing depth and that depth is created in the brain. The human brain is ready to respond to the same clues on canvas as are used in the real world to see depth.

Binocular clues, however, are of no use to the painter whose canvas really is flat. The same applies to the monocular clue derived from lens accommodation. The eyes do not change shape when moving focus from the foreground to the background of a painting. Binocular clues derive from the fact that our two eyes, being some distance apart in the face, see all objects from a slightly different angle.

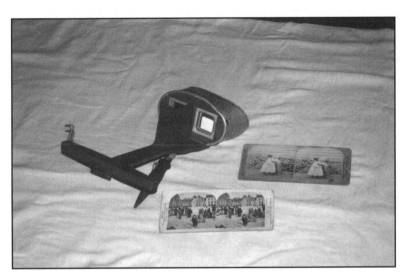

A stereoscope (above) capitalises on binocular disparity. The twin photographs on the cards are taken from slightly differing angles and when looked at through the stereoscope a single strikingly three-dimensional picture is seen.

We, in effect, see two slightly different versions of everything and the two are composed into a single image in the brain. The binocular clue as to depth comes from the fact that the difference in the angle of view of the two eyes (binocular disparity) varies depending on how far away an object is. Up close the difference is greatest. The difference in angle of view grows smaller as the object gets further away.

Another clue deriving from two eyes is that to focus on nearer objects the eyes have to be drawn closer together and rolled further apart to focus on objects further away. We can feel the eye control muscles making the adjustments and derive some information as to the distance of the object being focused on. While binocular clues are very useful for perceiving depth in the real world (with one eye, you cannot judge depth so well but can cope using monocular clues) they are of no value to create the illusion of depth on canvas. One's eyes are at the same distance apart looking at the foreground and the background in a painting.

Were it not for the highly active, constructive nature of our perceptual systems we would be unable to detect distance in our visual environment. That our visual world is so effortlessly three-dimensional is testimony to the power and speed of our brains in organising sensory information.

THE PROBLEM OF NOVELTY

To make sense out of the world of sensory experience it is not enough simply to distinguish specific objects, sounds, smells etc. from the background stimuli. We must also decide what each object or sound is and then respond appropriately. All this must be done at a speed faster than conscious thought. Otherwise we would be immediately overwhelmed. Imagine what it would be like to walk along the street and not be able to instantly recognise, without thought, what each familiar object is. Imagine if you had to pause to think about a lamp-post or a car or a person coming towards you on the footpath so as to decide what they were and how you should respond to them. Your world would be so full of hesitation that normal progress would be impossible.

Right now you are probably thinking that there is no need for hesitation because most of the sights, sounds and smells that you encounter every day are familiar. You have encountered them before so you have already learned what they are and how to respond to them. Though this seems obvious, it is only partially true. Certainly there is a lot of familiarity in our worlds but it is to some degree an illusion of familiarity. In reality a great deal that we encounter is novel. Take all the cars that you have seen today. How many of them have you seen before? Ask the same question about the people you have seen. Of course cars and people are familiar but cars and people are categories of visual objects. Each specific instance of the category differs from every other instance. No two cars are the same objects and definitely no two people are the same. This reality holds for every class of experience you can imagine, from church bell peals to the smell of roses. If, however, we were to respond to each specific instance of a category as novel, giving as much thought to each new car we see as a native of the Amazon jungle might give her first sighting of a motor-car, our progress through daily life would slow to a halt. Our solution is to respond to all of reality in terms of categories or classes of experience and not as specific cases.

PERCEPTUAL CATEGORISATION

Each new experience is assigned to one or more of a set of categories we have built up in our memories. Each new car and each new sighting of the same car is responded to by assigning the experience to the category of 'car' and possibly into a number of sub-categories such as 'sports car' or 'Ford Mondeo' and so on. Similarly, each new person we meet is categorised as, for example, 'man', 'woman', 'stranger', 'foreigner', 'lecturer' or 'student'. An experience is usually assigned to several categories at once. The point is that we do not respond to experiences as unique. We respond having assigned them to the appropriate categories. We then know already how to make sense of them.

You would become particularly aware of the value of your categories if you saw something that did not belong to any specific category you held in memory. Think for a moment what it would feel like to look out into your garden and see a furry animal about the size of a cat, which did not look like any animal you had ever even seen in a photograph. Initially you would scan all the categories for animal you held in memory and, having failed to find a match, you would have no idea what to make of the creature or how to deal with it. You would not know whether it was safe to approach it or whether it would attack or scamper away if you tried. You would wonder if it had escaped from someplace and whether you should report the sighting, perhaps to the Gardaí. At least you would have the general category, 'animal', which would help you make some sense of what you saw.

The same problem would arise to some extent if you detected a totally unfamiliar sound or smell, say within your own house. You would at least be able to categorise it in a very general sense, whether for example it sounded like an animal cry or a machine sound or whatever. But if it failed to fit into any specific category, you would be at a loss to know what to do about it or whether anything should be done. By being able to immediately categorise sensory experiences we know immediately how to respond to them or know whether any response is called for. The more precise the category to which we are able to assign the experience the less we have to think about how to respond. This saves an enormous amount of time, which would otherwise have to be spent in mental effort attempting to decide how to deal with everyday experiences.

CATEGORY SCHEMATA

For each category, we hold in our memories a list of rules as to what belongs to it and a clear outline of how the category is to be responded to. This is called the '*schema*' for the category (Bartlett, 1932). If we fear spiders, anything going into that category is responded to with fear. While a crane fly ('daddy-long-legs') has many of the features of certain spiders, those who fear spiders do not necessarily respond to the sight of such an insect with fear. That is because it has not been assigned to the category 'spider', where the rules say to respond with fear. You can probably recognise at this point how this is likely to impact on our understanding of new people we meet, an issue discussed in detail below.

CATEGORY PROTOTYPES

Because it is a slow process going through the full schema for a category or a set of categories to identify where a new experience should be assigned, we use a shortcut. For each category we appear to possess a '*prototype*' (Eysenck and Keane, 1995, pp. 242-247). This is a mental representation of our own best example of that category. It is a mental template we apply to new experiences. If there is a reasonable fit, then we apply that category to the experience.

This is easy to understand in relation to categories of physical experiences. For the category 'cat' you have a kind of mental image of what a 'cat' is like – a kind of ideal cat. It is probably of average size in terms of cats you have encountered. Chances are it has reasonably thick fur, is fairly rounded in shape and it has four legs, a tail and whiskers. Confronted with a Manx cat without a long tail, you are likely to take a moment to decide what it is because it conflicts with your prototype. Confronted with an extraordinarily large cat, or one without fur (such a breed exists), you are likely to hesitate, also for the same reason.

The same approach is adopted for experiences coming through the other senses. We each have a prototype for categories like 'door bell sounds', 'human voice', 'engine sounds' and so on. If you are visiting some distant relatives for the first time and you hear a sound that reasonably approximates to your prototype for a door bell, you will have no difficulty deciding what it is, even if it is not a door bell sound that you have actually heard before. If, however, your relatives' door bell is a novel variety designed to produce, say, a rapid tapping sound, the difference from your prototype will most likely result in you failing to recognise what it is you are hearing.

Many experiences that we need to categorise are not simply of a physical nature. This is particularly so in our understanding of other people. Categorising someone's behaviour as unfriendly, just, foolish, clever, envious or selfless involves abstract dimensions of reality. We have prototypes for such categories also, but of course they cannot be simply physical images like one might have for the category 'cat'. For abstract categories, prototypes may be more like simple rules of thumb. For one person the category 'unfriendly' might have a prototype that consists of the following dimensions: coldness in tone of voice; unwillingness to communicate; and avoidance of eye contact. For each of the dimensions, the individual will have a mental image of what their own best example is (a mental image of 'coldness in tone' perhaps). Of course another person may have the exact same prototype for 'shyness', thus categorising the same behaviour in a different way. It is important to recognise that prototypes are based on learning and will therefore vary from person to person.

RECAP ON HOW OUR PERCEPTION SYSTEM WORKS

To recap then, we 'select' some aspects of sensory experience for conscious processing. In doing this we need to immediately distinguish individual sights, sounds and smells from background stimuli. This is achieved by organising the world of sensory experience in terms of the principles of proximity, similarity and closure. This, together with the use of prototypes, enables us to quickly assign experiences to appropriate categories. Our understanding of the experience (be it a sight, sound or whatever) and our responses to it, depends on the 'schema' for each category to which the experience has been assigned. Schemata (plural of schema) include all kinds of information about a category. A simple element typically to be found in a schema concerns the dimension of 'like-dislike'. Another example would be 'interesting-uninteresting'. Some individuals will have 'interesting' as part of their schema for the category 'motor cars'. This will affect their responses when they detect an object to be assigned to that category. They will respond with interest, therefore paying more attention. This is essentially the reason why some individuals remember much more (make, model etc.) about a motor car they have seen. It is also one more reason why we all come away with different memories of a scene.

You may wonder about the order of perceptual selection and organisation. Which comes first? Inevitably some measure of organisation must take place before selection, otherwise we would not be able to make any sensible decisions on what to give our attention to and what to ignore. It is probable that the system of organisation works at a number of levels. The level of organisation achieved before selection is probably quite basic but sufficient to get us by. A more detailed level of organisation involving more precise categorisation is carried out on stimuli that rise above the threshold of consciousness, i.e. selected stimuli. Walking in the countryside in summer, one's eyes pick up many stimuli representing such objects as flying insects. They are unconsciously categorised as familiar insects and are not processed further into specific categories such as wasp, fly, etc. If, however, an insect comes very close, it may be bumped into consciousness and recognised as, say, a bluebottle, with whatever implications are contained in our schemata for that category – perhaps disgust.

The main implication of how we organise our perceptual experiences is that we respond to everything as members of categories, not as individual, unique experiences. We need to act this way so as to keep up with the world of sensory experience bombarding us all the time. However, responding to things in terms of categories inevitably reduces the accuracy of our responses, because all objects categorised together will not be exactly the same. We trade off accuracy for speed. Next we will examine how this trade-off has major implications for our processing of information about people.

SOCIAL PERCEPTION – ERRORS AND BIASES

You probably agree that every person is a unique individual. It would follow then that the best way of responding to other persons is as individuals. Yet this is just what our processes of perception prevent us from doing. So as to be able to process information quickly, we have a powerful tendency to categorise first and then respond in terms of the category. Added to this is the fact that we constantly select and screen out stimulus information. Inevitably all of this leads to problems in our dealings with others. Let's now consider what kind of problems result.

Stereotyping

This is the most obvious effect of treating individuals as members of categories. A stereotype involves an assumption that a group (or category) of individuals possesses common traits or characteristics. Usually we think of stereotypes as negative as, for example, in racist stereotypes. They can just as easily be positive, where a group is assumed to have some positive traits in common. The assumed traits are part of an individual's schema for the category. Thus an individual might have a category for 'French' and as part of the schema for that category they might have the notion 'romantic'. It would cause them to be more inclined to assume that the behaviour of a given individual assigned to that category was in fact romantic. If the person had been assigned to another category – say

German – where no assumption of 'romantic' existed in the schema, they would interpret the same behaviour differently. Categories can cause us to see what we expect. That is essentially the effect of a stereotype.

Social psychologists point to the fact that some degree of stereotyping may be inevitable due to the complexity of the social world and the limited amount of time available to us to make decisions about it (Hamilton and Sherman, 1994). However, we should be conscious that stereotyping is very closely wrapped up with forms of prejudice such as racism and sexism. Immediately a person is responded to as a member of a category, the content and justification for one's schema for that category becomes all-important. We should be aware of very common errors. One such error is an illusory correlation. If we observe one or two members of a given group behaving in a particular way, let's say dishonestly, we are likely to come to the assumption that all members of the group are like them (Hamilton and Sherman, 1994). It is in the nature of schemata to cause us to select and remember information that confirms the given schema (Olson et al, 1996; Stangor and Macmillan, 1992).

This may have profound effects in Ireland at the moment on how people perceive 'asylum seekers'. There is ample evidence that a significant proportion of the population have negative schemata for what is widely dealt with as an undifferentiated social group in terms of popular understanding and media discussion. All it will take is for one single asylum seeker to commit a serious crime such as murder or rape for those negative schemata to be powerfully and in many cases irreversibly confirmed. Amongst such a growing and doubtless very heterogeneous group the chances of a single criminal act must be statistically high. If it happens, it will say absolutely nothing about all the other asylum seekers but it is one unfortunate consequence of the human perceptual system that it will convince a great many of the unacceptability of the group as a whole.

Halo effects

A *halo effect* arises when we assume that some prominent positive characteristic of an individual – say good looks or a good dress sense – implies that the person has other deeper positive characteristics – say, good personality or that they are careful and methodical. When the same assumption is made about a negative characteristic, it is said to be a *horns effect*. Both effects are potential sources of error when evaluating an unfamiliar person, as happens in a job interview.

Interviewers tend to make up their minds in the first four or five minutes of an interview (Webster, 1982). Their overall judgments of the candidate's suitability are influenced significantly by superficial factors such as appearance, attractiveness and gender (Kinicki and Lockwood, 1985). Of course, actual suitability for a job depends on a complex array of much less accessible characteristics but, as in all social interactions where we need to judge others, we have limited time and information available, and we therefore tend to overemphasise information easily obtained. First impressions really do count.

Priming

This is the tendency to use the most available – often the most recently arrived – information in memory to make sense of an experience. In effect, we can be primed or set up to interpret an experience in a particular way. Imagine you are travelling on a bus and on entry you have a dispute with the bus driver about the validity of your student travel card. Then, a stranger sits into the seat beside you and makes some comments to you. Having been primed to think negatively by your recent experience, you will be more likely to interpret the stranger's overtures to conversation in a negative way. This may happen to us all the time without our knowing it. It arises out of our need to structure or make sense of our experiences as quickly as possible. It is easier to make sense of an experience by using ideas that are present in our minds rather than to have to dig deeper.

It might strike you that the bus example used above may lend itself to an alternative explanation, i.e. that one's emotions at a given moment can dictate evaluation. The bus driver made you feel negatively so you are likely to evaluate a subsequent event in a negative manner while still feeling unhappy. Goleman (1996) discusses in detail the impact of emotions on behaviour and thought (see Chapter 5, Box 5.1). Even if the emotional explanation applies, it is still a form of priming – being biased by one's emotions to evaluate a new situation in a particular way.

Consider the following research example. Higgins et al (1977) asked research subjects to participate in two separate studies. In one they were required to identify colours while at the same time committing words to memory. In the second they were asked to read a description of an individual named Donald and then evaluate him. The description was of an individual who went to extremes in his quest for excitement – shooting rapids, piloting a jet-powered boat, thinking of sailing across the Atlantic. The same description was given to all participants. Unknown to the participants, an attempt had been made to prime their thinking in different ways in the first task. Participants were randomly divided into different groups. Some were asked to remember words appropriate to Donald's description that could be used in a negative evaluation of his behaviour. Others were given words that could be used to positively evaluate him, while more participants were required to memorise positive or negative words that would not be relevant to the information given about Donald.

An analysis of the descriptions or evaluations of Donald given by participants in the second study revealed a very striking trend. Among those asked to memorise words potentially relevant to Donald's behaviour, 70 per cent who had memorised positive words evaluated him positively in contrast to only ten per cent of those memorising negative words. No such difference was found between participants who had memorised irrelevant negative or positive words.

It is more than a little disturbing to think that our evaluations of social reality could be so prone to random priming at any time.

Anchoring

This is a tendency with many similarities to priming. Anchoring involves having a difficulty in taking on board the impact of new information – effectively being anchored in existing ideas to make sense of our experiences. An experiment by Ross, Lepper and Hubbard (1975) illustrated this tendency. A group of individuals were given the task to judge whether suicide notes were real or fake. They were given feedback indicating whether they had been more or less successful than average on the task. In fact all the feedback was given at random and participants were afterwards informed of this fact and told that the experiment had actually been to study the effect of success and failure on physiological responses. Nevertheless, when asked to rate themselves on how accurately they thought they actually had distinguished real from fake suicide notes and how well they would do on a new set of notes, the ones who had been given positive feedback rated themselves more positively than those who had been given negative feedback. Though they had been told that the feedback had no meaning, they still remained anchored in the impression that they were good or bad at the task.

Again, it is faster and demands less effort to make sense of the world through existing knowledge than to revise our views in the light of new information. The implication of this tendency is to limit the power of rational argument. Just as a law of physics declares that matter possesses inertia, it also seems to take a strong push to dislodge individuals from their current understanding of the world. If one has developed a negative stereotype of a group or a negative attitude towards an individual, then, even when new evidence discredits the attitude, it is likely to be adhered to even in the face of common sense.

Use of overly simple prototypes

The personal prototypes or mental images we use to help us categorise experiences are often quite simplistic. This is hardly surprising since categories of reality are frequently complex and include cases that differ significantly from each other along many dimensions. Prototypes by their nature must be relatively simple to function as a rapid system of assigning experiences to categories. Mistakes are inevitable.

Most individuals' prototype for a 'German' probably includes fair hair, blue eyes and tall stature. Many Germans, of course, are none of those. Aronson, Wilson and Akert (1999) discuss the case of an abstract category: 'randomness'. They point out that individuals tend to believe that in a number of tosses of a coin a sequence of heads and tails that looks random (e.g. HTTHTH) is more likely to occur than a sequence that seems to have a definite pattern (e.g. HHHTTT). Despite the fact that both have the same statistical chance of occurring, prototypes for randomness seem to involve variety rather than pattern, leading to a mistaken conviction that the latter sequence is somehow not random.

This, of course, leads Lotto players to assume that a sequence of numbers like 4, 7, 21, 26, 32, 33 is more likely to come up than the sequence 1, 2, 3, 4, 5, 6, which, unfortunately for Lotto players, is not the case. It also leads us to assume that individuals who have had a string of accidents on the road or in the workplace must be somehow responsible, since the pile-up of accidents on one person conflicts with our simple notion of 'randomness'. This, again, is not necessarily the case, since random events do not distribute evenly with everyone having the same level of 'fortune' or 'misfortune' (McCormick and Ilgen, 1987, pp. 426-427). There is simply nothing to stop random events from showing striking patterns, just as there is nothing to stop the clouds from forming shapes that look like animals or faces.

Box 3.1 below uses a particular example to explore another abstract prototype, that of 'justice', a category or concept which has a considerable bearing on our dealings with others in all areas of life.

BOX 3.1

PROTOTYPES FOR JUSTICE – THE CONTROVERSIAL CASE OF PHILIP SHEEDY

All kinds of implications for our evaluation of others and their behaviours flow from the use of prototypes. Take the concept of 'justice', a fundamental expectation in our dealings with others. Justice is a very complex category and the application of any kind of prototype will inevitably eliminate a lot of situational and contextual information relevant to the categorisation of any individual action as 'justified'.

Take the highly publicised case of Philip Sheedy. On 15 March 1996 he left a pub in which he had been drinking and drove off at speed in his recently purchased sports car. He lost control of the car, which literally flew into the air and landed on another car at a round-about. A young mother was killed instantly, her husband seriously injured and her two children injured also. He was sentenced to four years imprisonment as a result. Was he treated justly? In the media furore which later ensued, a great many seemed to think he was. Others seemed to think otherwise. They included two senior members of the judiciary, both later forced to resign over their involvement in the case. For those who categorised Sheedy's sentence as 'justice', one presumes that 'harm done' figured largely in their prototype for 'justice'. In this case the harm done – the killing of a young mother – was grievous by any standards.

An interesting insight into the prototype of justice applied at least by two commentators on the incident can be gleaned from a passage by journalists Gene Kerrigan and Pat Brennan in their book, *This Great Little Nation* (Kerrigan and Brennan, 1999). They compare Sheedy's four-year sentence to those meted out to three teenagers who had broken into the historic crypt of St Michan's church in Dublin (famous for preserving corpses in a mummified state) and smashed open 300-year old coffins, desecrating the remains and accidentally starting a fire. One received a six-year prison term and the other two three years' probation each. Kerrigan and Brennan make the following comment: 'One might conclude from these sentences that destroying old bones was considered six times more serious than killing a woman in front of her children'. The multiple of six comes from the comparison between the actual six-year sentence given to one of the teenagers and the statement by the sentencing judge in Sheedy's case that the original trial judge had suggested to him that a prison sentence was not appropriate in the case. The trial judge in the Sheedy case was the same one who sentenced the teenager. Six years, then, for desecrating the remains in a historic vault and no prison sentence for killing a young mother. If harm done is central to one's prototype of justice, as clearly it is with Kerrigan and Brennan, then this is not justice.

There is no doubt that an infinitely greater harm resulted from the actions of Philip Sheedy. However, this simple and intuitively appealing 'punishment equalling harm done' prototype for justice fails to address the important issue of responsibility. Is not degree of responsibility much more important than harm done when deciding punishment? To be responsible for an outcome, one must have some intention, or at least some foresight, of that outcome. The teenagers very deliberately set out to break into the vault and smash open the coffins. One even used a skull as a football. Sheedy can hardly be said to be responsible in the same way for where his car landed. He is not like someone who is responsible for where a bullet arrives as a result of shooting a gun at that target. He did not cause death and injury as a wilful act. He had no intention, desire or forethought of killing anyone. What he was guilty of doing was driving a car, while intoxicated, in a manner likely to endanger others. Where his car ended up was the consequence of a particular misfortune – a few feet either way and no one might have been injured. This puts him in the same position as all intoxicated or reckless drivers. That a tragedy ensued from his irresponsible actions makes him no different to all those who act in a similarly irresponsible manner but by good fortune escape such singular tragedy. They can all be reasonably said to be acting with a level of 'wickedness' equal to Philip Sheedy.

Should all convicted drunk or reckless drivers be sentenced to four years imprisonment? Perhaps they should, but that would hardly fit the prototype for justice that seems to be applied by many such as Kerrigan and Brennan in the case of Philip Sheedy, where the ultimate outcome was emphasised above all other elements of the case. It is highly unlikely that those who viewed his sentence as just would view a mandatory four-year sentence as just in the case of all drivers who are found by the Gardaí to be driving dangerously even while under the influence of alcohol, though not involved in any accident.

The point is that prototypes are simplifications of reality. Used unthinkingly, they can lead to serious errors in categorisation and serious errors in how we understand others and their actions.

Inadequate selection of content information in 'script' situations

Much of the perceptual information we use to appraise other people comes through the process of communication.

When we communicate verbally, whether through speech or writing, there are two distinct aspects to the communication. There is the content of our message, what we intend to convey. There is also the structure: how the message is phrased. We can cope with great variety in structure and still grasp the meaning of a message. Thus, we often take no particular notice of structure. However, if the structure of a message is degraded to a particular point we begin to notice, because it interferes with our understanding of the content. This will become apparent if you are trying to understand someone who has a very poor grasp of the English language. You may have to pause for a moment to understand the message, 'Please to tell me toilet ... way to', before grasping that you are being asked for directions to the nearest toilet.

Structure, it would seem, is easier to process than content, and, with certain messages at least, we take a short-cut to understanding content by assuming that if the structure is of a familiar format then the content of the message is the one that usually goes with that structure. Of course, this is fine so long as your prediction is correct. Have you ever been distracted while talking to someone and relied on the general sound of what they were saying to enable you to make responses that mask your absence of mind? You may have been embarrassed when you said something like 'I know' or 'I'm sure' in the wrong place, producing a puzzled look on the face of the person talking to you.

It is possible that quite a lot of the time we are operating in social interactions in a somewhat mindless or distracted state similar to that just described and that we rely for guidance on our familiarity with the general features of the situation. Abeslon (1976) described situations where the general features have such familiarity to us that we can operate on a kind of auto-pilot without much thought. When you physically bump against someone on a crowded street and say 'excuse me' or 'sorry' you are probably responding without any real thought or intentionality. It is as if you are saying your piece from a script. The word 'script' was in fact used by Abeslon to describe this kind of situation.

An experiment by Langer, Blank and Chanowitz (1978) identified a script situation and illustrated how individuals may respond to communications from others in such situations by analysing their structure and assuming that the familiar content is present.

They hypothesised that individuals in an office environment might treat certain requests as scripts, being so used to them as to feel able to respond automatically without fully analysing their contents. They suggested that requests that have become 'scripts' may be heard only in terms of structure with an assumption made that the contents are as usual. A request usually has three parts in its structure: an *apology*, the *request* and a *reason* for the request. Their experiment was conducted on 120 unwitting office staff who were about to use a photocopier or xerox machine. The request was to be allowed to step in and make a number of copies. They hypothesised that so long as the request was relatively small, office staff would agree to the request if it followed the expected three-part structure and would not be affected by any lack of content. In the experiment three forms of the request were used with different office staff:

1. Adequate structure and content: 'Excuse me (*the apology*). I have five (or 20) pages. May I use the xerox machine (*the request*), because I am in a rush (*the reason for the request*)'.
2. Adequate structure and inadequate content: 'Excuse me (*the apology*). I have five (or 20) pages. May I use the xerox machine (*the request*), because I have to make copies (*meaningless reason for request*)'.
3. Inadequate structure and inadequate content: 'Excuse me (*the apology*). I have five (or 20) pages. May I use the xerox machine (*the request*) (*no reason for the request included*)'.

Request 1 is a normal request, which the subjects expected. Requests 2 and 3 are deficient but in different ways. The second request has some words included to fit all the expected parts but the words offered as a reason for the request in fact offer no reason at all. The third offers no reason either, but does not include any kind of meaningless reason in its place.

Subjects were asked to allow the experimenters to copy either five or 20 pages. In each case if the number of pages the experimenter wished to copy exceeded the number the subject was about to copy the favour was defined as 'big'. If the subject's number of pages exceeded that of the experimenters, the favour was defined as 'small'.

The researchers hypothesised that if the recipients of the request – the subjects about to use the Xerox machines – were not processing the requests at the level of content but only at that of structure, then requests 1 and 2 would be just as successful. Request 3, however, was expected to be less successful, since they would detect the lack of structure – no words to fill up the reason section. They further predicted that this would be the case only for small favours, because for large favours there would be sufficient motivation to attend to content.

They were proved right on all counts. For the small favour, subjects acted as if they had not noticed that there was really no more content in request 2 than in request 3. 'Because I have to make copies' is not a reason at all – what else would they be doing but making copies? Yet request 2 obtained as much compliance as request 1. In the 'big' favour situation this was not the case. Requests 2 and 3 resulted in similar levels of compliance, which were significantly lower than request 1. The greater demand caused subjects to turn up their level of attentiveness and select for content information as well as structure.

This phenomenon results directly from the need described above to process information selectively. Such processing of communications in familiar contexts (script situations) frees up thinking space for other activities without too much danger of getting it seriously wrong. Now and again, however, this is bound to get us into hot water when we do or say something inappropriate through not processing the content of what is being said to us.

THE CONSEQUENCES OF OUR PERCEPTUAL SYSTEM FOR SOCIAL INTERACTION

What all the above errors and biases in social perception have in common is the attempt on the part of the individual to process information more quickly. The problem is that with sources as complex and unpredictable as other humans, mistakes and misunderstandings are inevitable.

Let us summarise the kinds of errors we are led into in our dealings with others:

1. selectively noticing and failing to notice information about others, due to our own assumptions, expectations, interests, needs and personalities;

2. categorising individuals on the basis of highly limited prototypes;
3. responding to individuals on the basis of their group membership or assumed group membership;
4. assuming common traits and characteristics among those we group together;
5. overly emphasising salient characteristics, such as the outward appearance of others;
6. thoughtlessly categorising and interpreting the behaviour of others in accordance with limited prototypes and easily accessed information in memory;
7. lazily adhering to earlier views or impressions rather than revising them in accordance with new information or evidence;
8. responding in familiar social interactions without adequate analysis of communication content.

All in all we can readily see that this is hardly a recipe for good social relations based on thoughtful understanding. Are we doomed irrevocably to be lazy and biased in our perception of others, gripped by prejudice, slaves to stereotypes? The answer, unfortunately, is that we are – unless we make special efforts not to be. The ubiquity of racism and prejudice is a disturbing testimony to this.

Fortunately we are all granted some measure of self-determination. We can set out to mould ourselves. Having digested the contents of this chapter, what steps can you take to improve your perceptual response to others? Here are a few practical suggestions:

1. Be wary of first impressions. Take no serious action in response to others without allowing some time to pass that allows for the collection of further information. Give everyone a chance. You will frequently be pleasantly surprised. The opposite is also true. Those about whom you initially have a good feeling may with further exposure turn out to be disappointing.
2. Do not assume that your emotional reactions are inevitably correct. Emotional reactions are often based on very selective processing of information.

3. Watch out for the effects of stereotypes, which inevitably you possess, about social classes, religious groups, occupations and races; they will lead you wrong a high proportion of the time.

4. Try to deal consciously with others and not mindlessly on the basis of habit.

5. Reflect on how you make judgments about the actions of others. Are you using simple prototypes to categorise their behaviour as 'friendly' or 'unfriendly', 'envious' or 'supportive', 'just' or 'fair', 'selfish' or 'helpful? – the list goes on. Evaluative concepts like these are complex categories of reality. Thoughtless application of simple rules of thumb will not suffice for a fair analysis of any behaviour.

6. Allow your views to remain open to change. There is no view formed which cannot justify some measure of change in the light of new information. Try not to discount facts, views and evidence that conflict with your current understanding. This does not make you a straw in the wind. It just means that you allow for the possibility of being wrong.

7. Always remember that others are labouring under the same system of perceptual selection and organisation. Do not be too dismissive of them when they dismiss you as a member of one of their least favoured groups or as having some superficial negative characteristics that they overly emphasise. Reacting with hostility will only confirm them in their prejudices. One should never take offence at not being initially liked or accepted. It is certainly no moral judgment on you as a person.

SUMMARY

Sensation is the response made by sensory organs of the body to environmental stimuli. Perception may be defined as the psychological process of actively selecting and organising stimulus information detected by the sensory organs so as to create conscious awareness.

Sensation is a passive process in that one's sensory organs are unable to choose not to respond to relevant stimuli. It is also best described as a biological process in that it involves changes in physical tissue in the body, not thoughts or understanding. Perception, on the other hand, is an active and psychological process. It involves the selection and organisation of stimulus information and cannot be understood solely in terms of biological concepts. Psychological concepts such as awareness, understanding, interpretation and memory are essential to understand perception.

Perception involves two distinct processes: selection; and organisation. Of all the stimuli which impact on our sensory organs, we actively process only a fraction. Stimuli are selected on objective and subjective grounds. The objective grounds are those which cause stimuli to contrast or stand out from the background. The subjective grounds concern such factors as existing knowledge and current motivation. To employ subjective criteria for the selection of stimuli to consciously process requires an initial stage of broad-based unconscious screening or processing of stimuli. That we are capable of making use of stimuli of which we remain unconscious is illustrated through dichotic listening tests and subliminal exposure experiments.

The process of perceptual organisation involves assembling the basic raw data of sensory experiences, which have been selected, into a meaningful whole. There are three fundamental organising principles involved. These are the principles of proximity, similarity and closure. These, respectively, are the tendencies to group together stimuli that occur close together in time or space, to group together stimuli with similar characteristics and to complete mentally stimuli that are objectively incomplete.

A further key element of the organising process is to assign new stimuli detected to categories which have been built up through experience. Each category is governed by a schema, which is our own personal understanding of that category. The assigning of an experience to a given category dictates that we understand and respond to that experience in accordance with our schema for that category.

Experiences are quickly assigned to one or more categories on the basis of their similarity with the prototypes for those categories. A prototype is one's personal idealised image of what a 'best' example of that category is like.

The process of perception can be shown to be active in nature through an exploration of visual illusions and depth perception. Visual images such as the Muller-Lyer and the figure-ground illusions do not change as they are observed, yet the observer can see essentially different images from moment to moment, illustrating how we actively organise our perceptions. The eyes lack a direct means of detecting depth or distance. Despite this we are all able to see a clear three-dimensional world through organising visual clues that are available to us concerning distance.

Social perception is the application of our perceptual processes to understanding other people. Because we are constantly confronted with such an enormous array of stimulus information and need to process the world of our experience very quickly to survive, we are driven to take a variety of information processing shortcuts. When applied to people these can lead to serious error.

Among the shortcuts we take in social perception are stereotyping, halo effects, priming, anchoring, use of simple prototypes and use of scripts. Stereotypes involve responding to all members of a category or group of individuals in an undifferentiated way by assuming that they all share a common personality profile. The *halo effect* arises when we base a generally positive appraisal of an individual from a superficial positive characteristic such as appearance or accent. Its opposite, basing a negative appraisal on a superficial, negative characteristic is known as the *horns effect*. Priming involves the selective use of information that is more accessible in memory to appraise a social situation. Anchoring refers to having difficulty in taking on board new information, which conflicts with an existing appraisal. Prototypes are one's own best mental example of a category, which in certain instances may be overly simple and result in a mistaken categorisation of experience. Scripts are situations that are so familiar that we respond within them as if by auto-pilot, failing to process the full information available. This can be a problem if something unexpected occurs and we respond 'by script', assuming that the situation is the same as usual.

The nature of our perceptual processes is that we are inevitably inclined to make errors when dealing with something as complex as social reality. The solution is to deliberately attempt to process information about others in a more conscious and controlled way so as to avoid mistakes and misunderstandings.

REVIEW QUESTIONS

1. Explain why perception may be described as an 'active' and 'psychological' process and describe the evidence supporting its active nature.
2. Describe the twin processes of perceptual selection and organisation.
3. Discuss the idea that humans are 'cognitive misers' who invest no more effort in processing information about the world than is absolutely necessary.
4. Explain the main varieties of error in social perception to which humans are prone.
5. Discuss the internal or subjective basis for perceptual selection and how it is known that humans unconsciously process sensory information.

REFERENCES

Abeslon, R.P., (1976), 'Script Processing in Attitude Formation and Decision-Making', in J.S. Carroll and J.W. Payne (eds), *Cognition and Social Behaviour*, Hillsdale, NJ: Erlbaum.

Aronson, E., Wilson, T.D. and Akert, R.M., (1999), *Social Psychology*, (3rd Edn), (p. 90), New York: Longman.

Baldwin, M.W., Carrell, S.E. and Lopez, D.F., (1990), 'Priming Relationship Schemas: My Advisor and the Pope are Watching Me From the Back of My Mind', *Journal of Experimental Social Psychology*, 26, 435-454.

Bartlett, D.C., (1932), *Remembering*, Cambridge: Cambridge University Press.

Bornstein, R.F. and Pittman, T.S. (eds), (1992), *Perception Without Awareness: Cognitive, Clinical and Social Perspectives*, New York: Guilford.

Cherry, C. and Taylor, W., (1954), 'Some Further Experiments on the Recognition of Speech With One and With Two Ears', *Journal of the Acoustical Society of America*, 26, 554-9.

Eysenck, M.W.,and Keane, M.T., (1995), *Cognitive Psychology: A Student's Handbook*, UK: Erlbaum (UK) Taylor and Francis.

Goleman, D., (1996), *Emotional Intelligence*, London: Bloomsbury.

Hamilton, D.L. and Sherman, S.J., (1994), 'Social Stereotypes', in R.S. Wyer and T.K. Srull (eds), *Handbook of Social Cognition*, (2nd Edn), Hillsdale, NJ: Lawrence Erlbaum Associates.

Higgins, E.T., Rholes, W.S. and Jones, C.R., (1977), 'Category Accessibility and Impression Formation', *Journal of Experimental Social Psychology*, 13, 141-154.

Kerrigan, G. and Brennan, P., (1999), *This Great Little Nation*, Dublin: Gill & Macmillan.

Kinicki, A.J. and Lockwood, C.A., (1985), 'The Interview Process: An Examination of Factors Recruiters Use in Evaluating Job Applicants', *Journal of Vocational Behaviour*, 26, 117-25.

Langer, E., Blank, A. and Chanowitz, B., (1978), 'The Mindlessness of Ostensibly Thoughtless Action: The Role of Placebic Information in Interpersonal Interaction', *Journal of Personality and Social Psychology*, 36, 635-42.

Loftus, E.F., Miller, D.G. and Burns, H.J., (1978), 'Semantic Integration of Verbal Information Into a Visual Memory', *Journal of Experimental Psychology: Human Learning and Memory*, 4, 19-31.

McCormick, E. and Ilgen, D., (1987), *Industrial and Organisational Psychology*, (8th Edn), London: Allen and Unwin.

McKay, D.G., (1973), 'Aspects of the Theory of Comprehension, Memory and Attention', *Quarterly Journal of Experimental Psychology*, 25, 22-44.

Murphy, S.T. and Zajonc, R.B., (1993), 'Affect, Cognition and Awareness: Affective Priming With Optimal and Suboptimal Stimulus Exposures', *Journal of Personality and Social Psychology*, 64, 723-729.

Olson, J.M., Roese, N.J. and Zanna, M.P., (1996), 'Expectancies', in E.T. Higgins and A.W. Kruglanski (eds) *Social Psychology, Handbook of Basic Principles* (pp. 211-238), New York: Guilford.

Ross, L.D., Lepper, M.R. and Hubbard, M., (1975), 'Perseverance in Self-Perception and Social Perception: Biased Attributional Processes in the Debriefing Paradigm', *Journal of Personality and Social Psychology*, 32, 880-92.

Stangor, C. and Macmillan, D., (1992), 'Memory for Expectancy-Congruent and Expectancy-Incongruent Information: A Review of the Social and Social Developmental Literatures', *Psychological Bulletin*, 111, 42-61.

Thompson, C.P., (1982), 'Memory for Unique Personal Events: The Roommate Study', *Memory and Cognition*, 10, 324-332.

Webster, (1982), *The Employment Interview*, Schonberg, Ontario, Canada: SIP Publications.

Chapter 4

Learning

LEARNING OBJECTIVES

On completion of this chapter you should be able to:

- describe the behaviourist approach to understanding learning;
- describe the social learning approach to understanding learning;
- describe the cognitive approach to understanding learning;
- explain the classical and operant conditioning processes using the correct terminology;
- explain why the behaviourist learning model is unable to account for insight and latent learning with reference to the work of Kohler and Tolman;
- explain the cognitive element in classical and operant conditioning;
- outline some of the main applications and insights derived from the behaviourist, social learning and cognitive approaches to understanding learning.

INTRODUCTION

Is it possible that Lauren, though just 24 hours in the outside world, has been learning for weeks or even months and that she can remember what she has learned?

To most people this must seem an unlikely proposition. After all, young infants even seem to forget that an object ever existed immediately it is out of their sight. Surely they do not have the equipment to learn before birth? That is not the way Dr. Peter Hepper, of Queen's University Belfast, looked at infants. There was evidence that newborn infants seemed to recognise very early on the sound of their own mother's voice. Perhaps they remembered it from having heard it while in the womb. A foetus is capable of hearing after only 16 weeks of development. After birth, very young infants seem to pay special attention to novel sights and sounds. He hypothesised that infants after birth might be able to remember sounds that they had only heard in the womb and not since. He set out to experimentally test this notion.

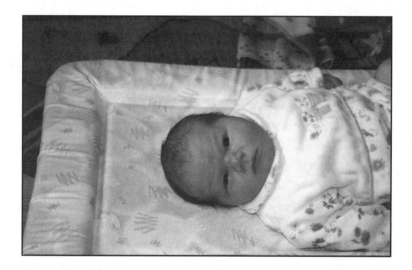

Immediately it may strike you that there seems to be a major problem here. How is one to know what infants recognise or remember? They can't tell anyone. Fortunately, Hepper was able to capitalise on an interesting behaviour displayed by infants from birth. They respond differently when they detect a novel stimulus, whether it is a sight or sound or whatever. For example, if you play a certain note repeatedly infants will show a decreased sucking rate on an artificial nipple, but if the note is then changed to a different one their sucking rate will speed up again. Similar changes happen in heart rate and body movements.

Hepper (1991) chose for his experiment 30 healthy newborn babies born at the Royal Maternity Hospital in Belfast. They had been deliberately chosen so that 15 of them had been exposed daily before their births to repeated renditions of a particular piece of music – the theme tune to the Australian soap series, *Neighbours*. Their mothers were avid viewers and it was estimated that the group would have heard the tune a minimum of 360 times during their pregnancy. The other 15 infants matched the '*Neighbours*' group on a variety of health and physiological scores but had no exposure to the theme tune. Their mothers did not watch the series. The hypothesis was simple, that the '*Neighbours*' group would show signs of recognising the tune when first played to them after their births while the control group would show no such signs.

The babies were tested two to four days after their births, before they had any opportunity to previously hear the *Neighbours* theme tune since they were born. Three measures to indicate recognition were used. Gross bodily movements – of the arms, legs and head – were carefully counted. Heart rate was recorded on a monitor producing a paper tracing and a categorisation of behavioural state was reached for each infant. The states were: sleep; drowsiness; alert; active; and crying.

The infants were undressed, linked to the heart rate monitor and left for three minutes. Then, a 30-second observation period followed to see if the two groups were behaving differently in any non-random way before hearing the tune. No significant difference was found between the two groups on any of the three measures. At this point a tape of the *Neighbours* theme tune was played for three minutes. The three measures were recorded again during the final 30 seconds of those three minutes.

The two groups showed significant differences on all three measures. The group exposed repeatedly to the *Neighbours* theme tune in the womb showed a decrease in heart rate, a decrease in bodily movements and tended to adopt the 'alert' state after hearing the music. All the changes were statistically significant, indicating that they were not just random differences. The control group comprising the 15 infants not exposed in the womb to the tune showed no statistically significant change on any of the measures after hearing the *Neighbours* theme tune for the first time.

The evidence strongly points towards the '*Neighbours*' infants having learned in the womb to recognise a tune to which they had been repeatedly exposed. If it was just the sound of the music – without it being familiar – that produced the changes in heart rate, movements and behavioural state, then both groups should have behaved the same.

To see how specific the nature of their recognition for the tune was (did they recognise the specific tune or just recognise music), Hepper (1991) conducted a further experiment using 20 other infants whose mothers had been avid *Neighbours* watchers. They were treated the same as the previous two groups, except, in their case, ten of them were played the theme tune to *Coronation Street,* which their mothers did not watch, and ten were played the *Neighbours* theme backwards. Using the same three measures, no evidence of recognition of those stimuli was found. It seems that the babies exposed to the *Neighbours* theme recognised that specific tune as familiar.

This study throws a light on the idea of learning that is rather different to our usual notion of what is involved. Typically we associate learning with a level of awareness and mental activity one hardly expects to be found in unborn infants. Because of our inevitable association of learning with education we are inclined to view learning as involving understanding and the deliberate commitment to memory of information. Learning, however, can take other forms. We do not have to understand what a sound is to learn that it is familiar and recognise it when we hear it again. But at least we know it is a sound, you may counter, which involves understanding. On the other hand, the babies in Hepper's study had no way of understanding anything about the tune they heard. They had no opportunity to learn what music is. Nevertheless, one cannot doubt that they had learned to recognise the tune as familiar.

Have you ever had the experience of suddenly feeling good when you heard a particular piece of music or detected a certain smell? On reflection, it might be a tune that reminds you of a happy episode in your life; or a smell might, for example, be the smell of furniture polish that pervaded your grandparents' home where you loved to visit when you were young. You have not learned that the smell or the music is objectively good in some sense. What you have learned is an association between one stimulus and another.

How then do psychologists define learning? The following definition seems robust enough to cover anything that we will discuss as learning in this chapter:

'The process of learning can be said to have occurred when a relatively permanent change in behaviour or behaviour potential has been produced by experience.'

(Zimbardo, McDermott and Metaal, 1995, p. 243).

Learning must be as a result of some experience. Experiences involve anything that has been processed by the senses and the perceptual system as described in Chapter 3. The effect must be to bring about a relatively enduring change or a potential change in behaviour. The route you take to college, the answer you give to a question and the manner in which you respond to another person are all possible examples of changes in behaviour. Fleeting changes are not described as learning. It would not make much sense to describe as learning a change in behaviour such as the act of raising one's hand to swat a fly that has landed on your forehead. It would, however, be meaningful to include as learning the decision never again to attempt to swat a wasp with your bare hand after it has stung you in the act.

The inclusion of potential changes in behaviour is to cover the common eventuality where the change in behaviour does not occur until some time after the learning. Having experienced serious delays going on a particular journey I may have learned that this is a route to be avoided but it may well be months or years before I have to go to the same destination and draw on my learning to choose an alternative route. Some theorists, as we will see below, are unwilling to define anything as having been learned unless it is given behavioural expression. Others view learning more in terms of the information stored in memory.

If we are to understand learning we must view the concept from quite a broad perspective, examining the various theoretical frameworks that have been advanced to explain what learning involves.

DIFFERENT APPROACHES TO UNDERSTANDING LEARNING

Broadly speaking, there are three approaches within the field of psychology to explain the learning process. One is called the *behaviourist* approach. The others are known as the *social learning* and the *cognitive* approaches.

They differ quite radically in their assumptions and how they view learning.

The behaviourist approach has its origins in a general theory or school of psychological thought that dominated the discipline in the 1930s, 1940s and 1950s. It is primarily associated with the work of Ivan Petrovich Pavlov (1849-1936), John B. Watson (1878-1958) and B.F. Skinner (1904-1990). It held that in trying to understand humans, psychology should limit itself to studying only variables that could be directly observed and accurately measured. All internal mental states or activities were treated as off-limits. Notions such as thought, memory, understanding and so on cannot be directly observed and should not therefore be considered. Nothing going on inside the head was to be studied. This left two sets of factors. One was the observable behaviour of the individual. The other was the environment and how it affected the individual.

It was assumed that the environment controlled human and indeed animal behaviour. It was assumed that behaviour mainly occurred in response to specific environmental stimuli. The job of psychologists was to explain behaviour by identifying the correct stimuli behind it and finding out how, for each person, the stimuli came to produce the behaviour. The behaviourist approach explained all behaviour as learned. Learning therefore was central to the whole theory. Learning in turn was explained as simply the forming of associations between specific environmental stimuli and specific behavioural responses.

The word 'learning' had connotations of mental activity about it, so it was replaced with the word 'conditioning'. Responses or behaviours that had been learned were described as 'conditioned responses' as opposed to 'learned responses'. Essentially the same thing was meant, however.

Behaviourist psychologists were convinced that many of the differences between humans – such as personality, motivation, ability, etc. – could be explained by this theory. People differed only because they had learned or had been conditioned to associate different responses with different stimuli. Because behaviour had been learned, it could be unlearned or relearned. 'Bad' behaviour was simply down to unfortunate associations having been learned. If the associations were changed, then the behaviour would change.

This approach to understanding the human condition could be viewed in a very positive or negative light. On the positive side, it suggested that people were not victims of their birth. Genetic inheritance was given little or no place in understanding why people acted as they did. It was all down to learning. This meant that great change could be brought about in anyone. A hardened criminal could learn to act as an honest and productive member of the community. On the negative side, there was little room for free will. Humans were seen as products of their environment. Whoever controlled the environment could control the person. All that was necessary was to ensure that a person developed associations between the right stimuli and the right responses. Once the criminal had begun to associate his dishonest actions or responses with unpleasant stimuli, such as captivity or the disapproval of society, he would terminate his dishonest behaviour. The idea that control of the environment meant control of the person gave rise in the minds of many to a frightening vista of 'total control worlds'. The idea that we could not or would not decide for ourselves how to behave, but were instead moulded by the environment, was a very unpleasant notion.

While the behaviourist theory seemed initially to many to offer an explanation for all human behaviour, eventually psychologists were able to identify learned behaviour that could not be explained in this way. Even some learned behaviour in animals could not be explained in terms of associations between responses and stimuli. We will examine below this evidence that a cognitive explanation was also necessary to fully explain learning. Contrary to the behaviourist approach the cognitive explanation would have to focus on what takes place inside the learner's head. It would have to look at how both humans and animals process information and learn from that. Cognitive psychology, exploring internal information processing, is now a major speciality within the general field of psychology.

As for the social learning approach, it arose out of the simple observation that, contrary to behaviourist assumptions, learning occurs in the absence of behaviour or at least in the absence of the learner having to do anything. It is perfectly possible to learn from watching the behaviour of others. A child does not have to figure out by trial and error how to fire an arrow from a bow, for example. He or she can see someone else perform the action and then go on to do it at the first attempt. In fairness to behaviourist theorists, there may be an argument here as to what learning actually is. A behaviourist may point out with some justification that just because the trial and error phase has been bypassed by observing another, it does not mean that the child will make firing an arrow from a bow part of his/her repertoire of behaviour. That will become the case only if the action is rewarded or reinforced in some way. This takes us back to the behaviourist explanation with the environment moulding behaviour through its effects. Nevertheless social learning – imitating others – is of interest to study, as it is at least a potential first step on the road to learning.

THE BEHAVIOURIST APPROACH

As already stated, the behaviourist explanation of learning focuses solely on environmental stimuli and learner responses or behaviours. Learning is taken to be the building up of associations between stimuli and responses. The associations are built up through two processes: *classical conditioning* and *operant conditioning*. Remember that 'conditioning' is the behaviourist word for 'learning'. We will now look at the two processes separately and see how they work.

Classical conditioning

Classical conditioning was so called because it was the first type of conditioning to be described.

This form of learning was initially described by Ivan Petrovich Pavlov (1927). He was a Russian physiologist (expert in bodily functioning) who at the time was investigating the digestive system of dogs. He observed – as do most pet owners – that dogs respond to the smell of food by salivating. More interestingly, he observed that if a bell were rung (or a light turned on) just before the food was presented to a dog and if this were repeated a number of times, the dog would respond to the sound of the bell (or the light) by salivating in the absence of any smell of food. He concluded that this was a learned response. The dog had learned or been conditioned to associate the response of salivating with the stimulus of the bell or the light.

Based on this kind of observation, Pavlov developed the general model of learning called classical conditioning. All classical conditioning begins with *an unconditioned stimulus*. This is a stimulus like the smell of food, which naturally produces some response. Dogs naturally salivate in response to the smell of food. Likewise, humans do not have to learn to respond with fear to a sudden loud noise. Even newborn babies will be startled at a sudden loud sound. Another example of an unconditioned stimulus would be the prick of a pin. We don't have to learn to jump away when pricked with a pin.

An unconditioned stimulus will produce what is known as *an unconditioned response*, a response that is not learned but occurs naturally. If the unconditioned stimulus occurs repeatedly at much the same time as another neutral stimulus (one which does not produce any response initially), that second stimulus will become a *conditioned stimulus*, which produces a *conditioned response*. In other words, the neutral stimulus will eventually gain the power to produce the same response as that originally caused by the unconditioned stimulus. The person or animal will in effect have been conditioned to associate the neutral stimulus (now called a conditioned stimulus) with the unconditioned stimulus so that a conditioned response is made. Though the response had already been shown by the learner, s/he has now demonstrated the learning of new behaviour. The new behaviour is the response in a new set of circumstances, that is, in response to a new stimulus, the conditioned stimulus.

Using Pavlov's example, the classical conditioning model can be illustrated as follows:

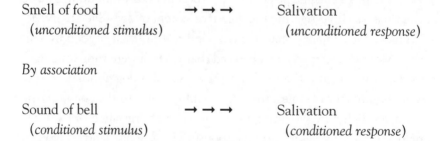

Smell of food   → → →   Salivation
  (*unconditioned stimulus*)   (*unconditioned response*)

By association

Sound of bell   → → →   Salivation
  (*conditioned stimulus*)   (*conditioned response*)

While Pavlov's illustrations were with animals, the same principles apply to humans. Many of our emotional responses are learned through classical conditioning. If on a visit to a city one had the unpleasant experience of being mugged, by association the very name of the city may be enough to later evoke a fear response. Similarly, the sound of a particular piece of music may be capable of making you feel happy if in the past that piece of music became associated with something good. Perhaps it was played a lot when you were on a particularly enjoyable holiday. Likewise, a piece of music can evoke the opposite response if you had learned in the past to associate it with an unhappy event or phase in your life. Many of our likes and dislikes may be learned in this way. Even political preferences are amenable to this form of conditioning. You can imagine that if a political leader bore a striking resemblance to Adolf Hitler, people might not respond well to him. Though logically they might be fully aware that the resemblance was only physical, nevertheless the association would produce a bad response. As a result, politicians are very concerned about their superficial images.

The advertising industry relies a lot on classical conditioning. Advertisers wish the public to associate their products with positive emotions. To do this they rely on unconditioned stimuli (dramatic scenery, music, figures oozing sex appeal or power) to evoke unconditioned responses (positive emotions). By designing advertisements, which allow the product, say, a particular model of car (initially a neutral stimulus) to be associated with the unconditioned stimulus, they hope that the car will take on some of the power to evoke the positive response. The car will then have become a conditioned stimulus.

It may occur to you that once a stimulus becomes a conditioned stimulus, it should be possible to associate it with a further neutral stimulus and classically condition the response to that stimulus also. A child may learn to fear a certain look on his mother's face because he associates it with her shouting at him, which he naturally fears. In turn, the child may associate the look with certain actions of his, which his mother disapproves of (such as pulling down objects from the kitchen table) so that he may begin to have a bad association with doing those things and learn to avoid them.

Focusing on another example, why do you think the shape of cars that is popular changes all the time? It is because marketing and advertising is capable of getting us to change our association every few years with what is modern and 'new'. The shape of car that today we associate with being modern will in a few years become dated and old-fashioned in our eyes. We have simply been conditioned to make those associations. That way, we are made to want to discard our old cars and buy new ones. That we feel 'modern' or 'new' to be good may be the product of previous conditioning. Not everyone has learned this association. Vintage car lovers clearly have the opposite association.

A further case of classically conditioned learning comes from the world of clinical psychology. Phobias may often be arrived at in this way. A phobia is an extreme fear reaction to something harmless. In Ireland we have no poisonous spiders. Yet many individuals respond to spiders with extreme fear (arachnophobia). This may be a conditioned response whereby the individual learned, probably in early childhood, to associate the stimulus 'spider' with fear. The original unconditioned stimulus may have been the sight of fear in a parent, which happened to occur when a spider was present. The parent's fear may or may not have been caused by the spider and indeed the fear may not have been real at all. The child may just have perceived a response as fear. The perception of fear in a parent usually results in a fear response in a child. (*Note here a weakness in the behaviourist model. Recall that the model focuses only on factors that are objective or observable: stimuli and responses. Stimuli may indeed have an objective reality but it is not that objective reality we, as humans, respond to. It is our own perception of that reality. Ghosts may have no objective reality but if a person believes that a particular stimulus [sight or sound] is a ghost, then there is no doubt that he or she will respond to that perception and not to the objective reality of the stimulus.*)

While clearly a wide variety of behaviours or responses – which politician to vote for, what car to buy, how to respond at the sight of a spider, which music to prefer – may be learned through classical conditioning, the process has one great limitation. Responses can only be learned if they are capable of being produced in the first place by an unconditioned stimulus. We all learn to do, say and write a great deal that is not produced in response to unconditioned stimuli. How can one hope to explain the process by which a child learns to talk through classical conditioning? What are the unconditioned stimuli that result in all the vocal sounds that go to make up a language? Clearly the behaviourist model needed a further mechanism to explain the vast bulk of learned responses. This mechanism was operant conditioning.

Operant conditioning

The main principles of operant conditioning were outlined by the American psychologists Watson (1930) and Skinner (1938).

An 'operant' is any action of a human or animal which is not produced by an unconditioned stimulus. We are, therefore, talking about literally anything at all that the human or animal happens to do – anything it is capable of doing. For any creature there are a virtually unlimited number of operants it can produce – limited only perhaps by its physical and mental capacities and by its instinctive nature. Animals are much more driven by instinct than humans. Each animal tends to have an instinctive drive to produce certain operants or behaviour, like nest building in birds and hunting in cats. Humans are much less predictable.

According to the behaviourist view of learning, both animals and humans are shaped or conditioned by the environment to behave in certain ways and to avoid other behaviours. In other words, out of all the things a creature can potentially do, the environment, through the process of operant conditioning, restricts behaviour to certain particular actions. This is achieved by a strikingly simple mechanism. Behaviours or operants that become associated with reinforcing stimuli (reward) in the environment tend to be repeated. Behaviours that do not become associated with reinforcing stimuli tend not to be repeated and ones that are associated with unpleasant stimuli are quickly eliminated.

Reinforcing stimuli are said to be either positive or negative, though in both cases the effect on behaviour is the same in that the repetition of some action or operant is encouraged or made more likely. The distinction is that positive reinforcement is the rewarding of behaviour that has the effect of continuing or commencing a desirable state of affairs for the creature involved. When a child presses the correct switch to turn on the TV successfully, she is positively reinforced by the desired appearance of the picture on the screen. When an individual at last finds and implements the correct action to turn off an ear-splitting house alarm, it is a case of negative reinforcement through the termination of an undesirable state of affairs. It is easy to become confused in this latter case, expecting that negative reinforcement must be an unpleasant experience or stimulus that discourages behaviour. Such a stimulus is known simply as punishment. The point to remember is that reinforcement, both negative and positive, encourages the repetition of the associated operant.

B.F. Skinner.

If humans (or indeed animals) associate their actions with reinforcing stimuli, then they learn to behave that way. We learn to do what brings reward and avoids unpleasant consequences. Behaviourist psychologists were convinced that this simple principle of learning would explain all behaviour that could not be explained through classical conditioning. They believed that the learning of even very complex material could be explained through operant conditioning. Take how a child learns to speak in the complex language of its own community. Behaviourists explained this as simply the stringing together of a great many very simple operants or behaviours. All languages are made up of a limited number of sounds. Initially a child simply makes random sounds. Of all the sounds it makes it receives more attention from adults (a reinforcing stimulus) for sounds that are more like words and less attention for unfamiliar sounds. Thus, it repeats sounds that are more like words. The closer to words the sounds are, the more attention they receive. The child, therefore, draws ever closer to making word sounds. Proper words when spoken win more reinforcement. Adults understand them and respond appropriately. This is reinforcing. Words can, of course, be strung together in any sequence but it is the meaningful sequences that gain reinforcement. In this way the child eventually learns to speak in grammatically correct sentences.

It should be pointed out at this stage that later studies of language development in children strongly suggested that language learning was not that simple. Careful observations of children from different cultures with different languages reveal a striking similarity in the process of language development. Children go through the same stages in learning their own language the world over. If language learning were achieved only through operant conditioning, there should be a great deal of variation in the steps leading to success. Also the rate at which language is learned – given how many words and grammatical structures have to be acquired – would seem to be much faster than could be learned by operant conditioning. Operant conditioning works on a kind of trial and error basis. There are simply too many possibilities for getting it wrong in speaking a language. If getting a sentence grammatically correct simply happened by accident, a child might have to wait forever to get it right and gain reinforcement. It is now generally accepted that the learning of language requires a more complex explanation.

Most of the experimental work to understand the details of how operant conditioning works was carried out on animals. The same principles apply to humans, however.

A typical experimental demonstration of operant conditioning from the work of Skinner would be the following. A hungry rat is placed in a cage. In the cage there is lever or handle which if pressed will cause a food pellet to be dropped into the cage. Initially, the rat can be observed producing a variety of operants. It runs back and forth, sniffs at the floor, nibbles at the bars and raises itself on its hind legs to sniff around higher up. Eventually, it noses around the lever and by accident leans on it with its front paws and presses it down. The food pellet drops into the cage. The rat eats the food pellet and returns to the kind of behaviour it was showing before. Eventually, again by accident, it presses the lever. The food pellet is dropped in once more. The rat eats the pellet. After this has happened a number of times, it is noticeable that the rat restricts its behaviour to the actions that press the lever. It now only produces the operant that results in the food being delivered. Other behaviours, like nibbling at the bars and so on, are forgotten for the time being.

The rat seems, very deliberately and intelligently, to do only those things that win it food. It concentrates on lever pressing. Behaviourists, of course, do not talk about intelligent behaviour. They explain the outcome in simple terms. The rat has been conditioned to associate a particular operant (lever pressing) with a reinforcing stimulus (food pellet). It repeats that operant, therefore, and only stops when it is no longer reinforcing, that is, when it is no longer hungry.

In this example we are dealing with a simplified world. In the restrictions of the cage the rat can only do a limited number of things. One particular action is always reinforced and the environment never changes. The lever is always in the same place and so on. In the real world, both for animals and humans, things are not so simple. Actions do not reliably result in reinforcement. Food cannot always be used as a reinforcing stimulus. The environment keeps changing and there are an unlimited number of possible behaviours. To understand how operant conditioning works in the real world, a number of details discovered through experimental work need to be grasped. These are described in the following four sections.

Primary and secondary reinforcers

Primary reinforcers are stimuli that will naturally be found rewarding. Food to the hungry, water to the thirsty, the presence of a parent to an infant: all are naturally rewarding. Clearly there are a limited number of stimuli, however, that are naturally reinforcing. Only things that directly satisfy basic instincts for food, water, maintenance of body temperature, security and so on can act as primary reinforcers. Humans typically experience a great many other things as reinforcing. They are secondary reinforcers. We have learned to find them reinforcing, presumably because they have become associated with primary reinforcers. Praise

BOX 4.1

SECONDARY REINFORCERS AND SOCIALISATION

Let us think for a moment in some detail about how verbal praise might become a secondary reinforcer and what would happen if it did not.

Consider a very young child without any grasp of language. Simply saying to her: 'You are a very good girl' will have no rewarding effect whatsoever. What will be rewarding for such a young infant? Being held closely, certain tones of voice, being rocked, being fed are all well known to be reinforcing for young infants. Parents are likely to accompany these physical reinforcers (say, when trying to comfort a crying baby) with praise-giving such as: 'You are a very good girl'. If we consider the physical reinforcers (being held close, etc.) as initially unconditioned stimuli, and the termination of crying or feeling happy and secure as the unconditioned response, it is easy to see how praise by long association with such unconditioned stimuli can take on the power of conditioned stimuli as the child grows older. In this way, praise will take on the power to act as a reward.

By a process of generalisation, praise or positive regard from others, such as teachers and other adults, will also take on reinforcing properties. Praise will, in other words, have become a learned or secondary reinforcer. Imagine then a child, perhaps raised in an over-crowded institution, who receives little or no physical comforting or accompanying praise when he is upset or under any other circumstances either. It is easy to see why this child may not learn that the praise of others is a reward and may in fact be highly insensitive to the responses of others and as such extremely difficult to socialise or teach the normal rules of good behaviour. Children who are insensitive to the social communication of negative and positive regard present a great challenge for teachers and others charged with their care and development. It is very difficult to mould their behaviour. They are on the very slippery slope to delinquency.

and the good opinion of others is a secondary reinforcer for most people. It only acts as a reinforcer, however, because originally the person as an infant learned to associate the praise and positive regard of parents and carers with security and the satisfaction of other basic needs. It is difficult to imagine a child being affected by the social responses of others if s/he has no regard at all for the praise of his or her primary carers.

The fact that we can learn to experience a very great variety of stimuli (praise, money, cars, clothes – to name but a few) as reinforcing means that there are lots of possible ways for operants to be reinforced. This increases the power of operant conditioning.

Partial reinforcement

In the real world no action will always predictably result in reinforcement. You may do all the right things to get a good mark in an exam, or win a match, and while normally your efforts result in the desired reward, occasionally through bad luck or whatever you may be denied your reward. If an operant is not always followed by a reinforcing stimulus, will the learner fail to repeat the operant? Experimental studies of this have revealed that the opposite occurs. When reinforcement is partial – less than every time – a stronger association is built up between the operant and the reinforcing stimulus (admittedly it may take longer to learn the association). Let's take the example of the rat and the lever again. If the rat were only rewarded after every third press of the lever, it would still learn to press the lever to gain the food pellet. And more interestingly, if the connection between the lever and the delivery of the pellets were broken, the partially reinforced rat would persist longer at the lever pressing before giving up than a rat that had been reinforced constantly.

If the rat had been on a partial reinforcement schedule that was random – a varying number of lever presses each time resulted in reinforcement – the strongest of all associations would be established. The rat would persist much longer in lever pressing after reinforcement was terminated before the operant would become extinct. Animals on random reinforcement schedules have been known to work to exhaustion to gain a reinforcement that is not going to come.

Random reinforcement schedules are common in the world of humans and indeed animals. If you watch wildlife programmes on TV you will have noticed that animals that hunt very frequently fail to catch a prey they are chasing. Yet they persist despite a very high proportion of failures to successes. They are on a partial reinforcement schedule that is random. Sometimes the first attempt will result in success, sometimes the tenth. This will cause them to persist. For humans also, effort will not always result in success every time but eventually many of our behaviours when repeated again and again gain reward. This causes us to persist, not always wisely.

The persistence of superstitious behaviours can be explained in this way. A group that practices rain dances will certainly not be rewarded all the time. But occasionally rain will fall by accident after a rain dance has been completed. This is a partial reinforcement schedule and will result in great persistence in the repetition of the operant. The rain dance superstition will continue. If rain had always fallen after every dance in the past and suddenly this time it did not, it would be assumed that the practice was failing to work. The rain dancers would be much less willing to go on doing the same thing.

Generalisation and discrimination

The effect of operant conditioning is, as we have seen, to encourage repetition of operants or behaviours previously associated with reinforcing stimuli. In fact, it goes a little further than that. Generally it causes the learner to generalise to other related operants or behaviours as well. Learners reinforced for a given behaviour tend to act as if they expect reinforcement to follow from a range of related behaviours as well. A child reinforced by praise for playing appropriately with the family pet dog may well expect to win reinforcement for playing in a similar way with other dogs, even the neighbour's fierce guard dog.

If reinforcement does not follow the related behaviours, the learner will, eventually, discriminate which specific operant or action is reinforced from those not reinforced. In a common experiment carried out to illustrate this, a pigeon is conditioned to peck at a red disk to gain reinforcement with food. The pigeon will normally generalise to other colour disks if they are introduced, expecting to get fed for pecking at those as well. If however, food only follows pecks at the red disk, the pigeon will quickly learn to discriminate and peck only when the disk is red. Even goldfish have been conditioned to discriminate on the basis of shape. In a T-shaped pipe they can be conditioned to swim to the left or right to win food reinforcement depending on whether the entrance to that side is square or triangular. If reinforcement is provided at the end of pipe only if the entrance at the T-junction to that side is square shaped, then they will learn to always swim through the square irrespective of whether it is on the right or left.

Experience is sufficient to learn discrimination. Sometimes, however, we may not wish the learner to suffer the harsh consequences of experience. You would not wish your child to learn from experience that it will 'not be reinforced' for playing with the neighbour's guard dog. Discrimination has to sometimes be assisted through punishment – in this case scolding the child for going towards the neighbour's dog.

Punishment must, however, be implemented with care. Leaving aside the risk of violating basic human rights associated, especially but not uniquely, with physical punishment, there are other attendant risks. Punishment may not only discourage the undesirable behaviour but a range of other behaviours as well. Too much disapproval of a young child's language errors can discourage not only the errors, but speech itself. Too much scolding, disapproval or criticism can lead to the victim developing a fear or dislike of and a determination to avoid a situation or a person. An excess of criticism for your mistakes when learning to drive may well cause you to drop the whole effort or find someone else to teach you. It should also be noted that punishment for undesirable behaviour does not in itself promote desirable behaviour. That requires reinforcement of the correct behaviour.

The general recommendation is to use punishment sparingly and, where it is necessary, ensure that it is accompanied by positive reinforcement of desired behaviour.

Shaping

This is a systematic application of conditioning principles to training difficult skills. It involves breaking down the skill into simple component behaviours, allowing or inducing the learner to practice those behaviours and initially reinforcing the learner for each component. Gradually the threshold for reinforcement is raised. This will mean that instead of each component being reinforced, reinforcement will only be given for a few components being put together. Later, reinforcement will only be given if lots of the components are practised in the right order, and, finally, reinforcement is given only if the total skill is implemented.

Babe: The behaviourally shaped pig.

Teaching someone to drive is significantly a process of shaping. Initially the learner should be reinforced with praise for practising any of the basic skills of driving even in a very imperfect manner. For example, getting the car into motion even after a number of stalled attempts should win praise to encourage persistence. Later, of course, only better attempts at driving should be reinforced. At the end of the learning process, only the kind of driving (proper implementation of all the component skills) that will pass the driving test should be reinforced.

A careful application of 'shaping' can result in remarkable feats of training. Circus animals are largely trained in this way. The tricks they perform in the ring are a long sequence of simple behaviours that have been conditioned through reinforcement. Anyone who watched the 1995 Universal Pictures feature film 'Babe' or its 1998 follow up 'Babe: Pig in the City' will have witnessed what can be achieved through the process of shaping.

APPLICATIONS OF THE BEHAVIOURIST MODEL OF LEARNING

As we will see below, the early expectation of behaviourist psychologists that all learning could be explained solely through this model proved overly optimistic. Nevertheless, the simple conditioning principles outlined above have a very significant bearing on our lives and on what we learn. We generally do repeat actions that bring reinforcement. If you wish to encourage some behaviour and have it repeated, reinforce it. If you want people to talk to you, reward them by being friendly and interested when they do. Sometimes attention, even seemingly negative attention, is reinforcing. If you want to discourage annoying behaviour, it may be necessary to completely ignore it. It is generally advised that temper tantrums in young children should receive as little attention as possible. Constant scolding, because it involves attention, may be reinforcing the behaviour.

Behaviourist learning principles have major applications in the fields of training and education. Learning is best achieved if the learner is active (behaviour) – in some way doing something with the material to be learned. If the learner asks questions, of him or herself or of someone else, and then seeks to find the answers to them from a book, from another person or from whatever source, then that is activity. This is better than passively reading or listening to a lecture. One can make a practice of mentally asking and answering questions to oneself even in the course of a lecture (e.g. 'Is this what he means?' 'Yes, I think it is, now that I have heard more'). The same can be done while reading a book. Discovering that you know the answers to the questions is reinforcing. This encourages you to persist and makes the whole process more rewarding. It also causes you to remember material much better – that, however, requires a cognitive explanation.

Behaviourist principles also apply to the habits of everyday living. Many of the difficulties of dieting or giving up smoking can be explained in terms of classical and operant conditioning. Classically conditioned associations between food or cigarettes and other environmental stimuli can make the process of cutting down or cutting out very difficult. Normally, having a cup of tea or coffee in one's hands should not make one want to smoke a cigarette. However, if the association between drinking tea and having a cigarette has been built up through practice, then having the tea will bring on the craving. Falling nicotine levels in the blood is the unconditioned stimulus. Need for a cigarette is the unconditioned response. Having a cup of tea in one's hands is a conditioned stimulus. It has no power in itself to induce the cigarette-craving response. By being paired for long enough with smoking, it takes on the power to induce the need. The victim in this case can resist the temptation to smoke each time he/she has a 'cuppa' and gradually the association will be broken – the response will become extinct. Alternatively, he/she can avoid having cups of tea or coffee. Of course, having a 'cuppa' at another time or in another place may not have such a strong association with smoking.

The use of cigarettes or food as positive reinforcements also makes trouble for the dieter or the person giving up smoking. Individuals often reward themselves with junk food or cigarettes for doing some boring work or when they have had a particularly bad day. Food and cigarettes then become part of an operant conditioning sequence. If the reinforcement is terminated, the motivation to carry out the boring job or whatever is diminished. The only solution may be to find alternative sources of positive reinforcement. The difficulty in finding alternative handy reinforcing stimuli is the great problem. The easy availability of cigarettes and fatty or sugary foods, such as crisps, sweets or bars, as snacks makes them ideal positive reinforcers. Hence the undeniable difficulty of avoiding them.

LIMITATIONS OF THE BEHAVIOURIST MODEL OF LEARNING – NEED FOR A COGNITIVE EXPLANATION

While it is not to be denied that classical and operant conditioning play a significant role in what we learn, the behaviourist model is not the full story. A great deal is learned, even in animals, but especially in humans that cannot be explained through associations between behaviours or responses and stimuli from the environment. Learning can occur without any response or without any direct impact of the environment on the learner. This is particularly true of what we call complex learning, for example, learning to understand how things work or how to solve a problem – the kind of learning to which educational institutions are devoted.

We have seen already how the acquisition of language cannot be explained as simply a process of responses being shaped by reinforcement. Likewise, learning has been demonstrated in animals, which cannot be explained by the behaviourist model.

Insight learning

Wolfgang Kohler, working in the 1920s (Kohler 1925), showed that apes could learn by a process of *insight*. Insight means in effect mentally manipulating the environment and drawing conclusions so as to solve a problem. Trying things out in the mind side-steps the process of trial and error involved in operant conditioning. Kohler worked with chimpanzees. He describes how one chimp called 'Sultan' solved a problem. Sultan was confined in a cage. Outside and beyond his reach was a piece of fruit. Naturally Sultan wanted to get the piece of fruit. Presumably he had previously been reinforced (nice taste) for eating such a piece of fruit. Having failed to reach it, Sultan eventually picked up a stick which was inside the cage and tried to reach it with the stick. In the wild chimpanzees are natural tool users. The attempt to use the stick to pull in the fruit may just have been an instinctive behaviour. As one would expect, based on an operant conditioning framework, Sultan quickly gave up his attempt to reach the fruit with the stick because it was not successful (termination of non-reinforced behaviour). He then carried out other behaviours such as tearing at a piece of wire projecting from the netting of the cage. Not being rewarded, he soon gave this up too. Then he looked about him and stared at a longer stick, which also lay outside the cage but nearer than the fruit. Without pausing any further, he used the short stick to pull in the longer one, and then used the longer stick to pull in the fruit.

This unbroken sequence of actions could not have been a result of operant conditioning. If it were, there should have been much more trial and error before success. For instance, having pulled in the longer stick, he might have again attempted to use the shorter stick to obtain the fruit or done anything else before, by accident, he used the long stick. The fact that the sequence was unbroken implies that the chimpanzee had some kind of image of the long stick working before he even had it in his paws. He had solved the problem in his head through insight.

This form of learning is, of course, very common in humans. Humans do not have to have their behaviour directly moulded by environmental stimuli. They can think about the relevant aspects of the world and come to conclusions as to the best way to behave in the circumstances. They often learn from their thoughts, not from associations with outside stimuli. They, of course, also learn from seeing what others do as opposed to having to do it initially themselves. This is called *social learning*, which will be discussed later in this chapter.

Latent learning

Edward C. Tolman (Tolman, 1932) also experimentally demonstrated learning of a complex nature in animals that defies explanation through conditioning principles. He showed that rats could learn a mental image of the geography of a maze, of which they made no immediate use and which the environment did not reinforce. This learning remained in their memories in a latent state (doing nothing) until the environment later reinforced its use. Remember that Kohler's chimpanzee was immediately reinforced for implementing the learned sequence of actions. Tolman's rats were not. Yet they maintained the learning for later use.

Tolman devised a complex maze with a start box and a box where a food reinforcement was available. He counted the average number of trials it took for a group of novice rats (no previous experience of the maze) to learn to find their way from the start box to the reinforcement at the other end of the maze. He then compared their performance with that of a group of rats (experienced rats) who had been previously allowed to wander around in the maze without reinforcement. The experienced rats learned the route to the reward more quickly. Presumably this was because they were making use of some mental route map of the maze they had built up when wandering around there before. Conditioning principles would dictate that learning would only take place when reinforced. Yet it was clear that the rats had latent learning, which did not result from any reinforcement. Again some kind of cognitive explanation is needed to throw further light on this kind of learning.

Humans do this all the time. We accumulate mental representations or memories of all kinds of information, which may not be used immediately and for which no obvious reinforcement is available. Have you ever been involved in a quiz? Of course there is a reward in this situation for coming up with answers to the various questions. At the time you learned the bits and pieces of relevant knowledge from TV, books, newspapers or wherever, it is doubtful if any reward existed to encourage learning.

THE COGNITIVE ELEMENT IN CONDITIONING

A careful scrutiny of the processes of conditioning reveals that for them to be fully understood reference to essentially cognitive concepts (mental activity) becomes necessary.

Research indicates that for classical conditioning to occur the learner must believe that the conditioned stimulus (CS) acts as a reliable predictor of the unconditioned stimulus (UCS). It has been shown that dogs exposed to electric shocks quickly learned to get away from the source of the shocks when they heard a tone. However, they learned to do this only if the tone reliably predicted the arrival of the shock (shock only came if tone had come just before). If they were exposed to shocks some of the time without the tone being played in advance, they did not learn to use the tone as a signal to avoid the shock (Rescorla, 1967).

Appreciating whether one thing predicts another is a cognitive notion. It is the interpretation of the learner – be it animal or human – that seems to matter. If the learner interprets a neutral stimulus as not being a reliable predictor of an unconditioned stimulus (even if in fact it is) then he, she or it will not learn to make the association.

The point was made earlier that it is not a stimulus so much as one's perception of the stimulus that is responded to. Perception is very much a cognitive phenomenon involving memory and interpretation. It was originally assumed that mental constructs such as memory, interpretation or beliefs had nothing to do with classical conditioning. It seems, however, that on the contrary there is a significant cognitive element (i.e. it involves thinking) in such conditioning.

The same applies to operant conditioning. Research evidence indicates that it is not sufficient for a reinforcing stimulus to follow an action for a learner to come to associate the two. The learner also has to believe that it is in fact his actions that control the reinforcement. If the learner thinks that the reinforcement is somehow independent of his actions, then the operant conditioning will not occur.

Dogs previously exposed to electric shocks, which they could not escape by any action of their own, could not subsequently learn to jump a low fence to escape the shocks (Maier and Seligman, 1976). Even when it was repeatedly demonstrated to them, by their being lifted over the fence, that all they had to do was get to the other side of the fence to escape the shocks, they could not learn the association. They simply would not learn to jump the fence. It seems their previous experience of unavoidable shocks had convinced them that escape from shocks (reinforcing stimulus) was not under their control. This is a cognitive explanation where we assume belief intervenes between the stimulus and the response in the learning sequence.

It is clear then that a full explanation of the behaviourist learning model requires a partly cognitive explanation. Thus behaviourist learning and cognitive learning (e.g. insight learning) are not entirely separate modes of learning. There is evidence, however, that they are to a significant extent separate learning systems involved in the learning of associations (through classical and operant conditioning) and in the kinds of complex learning, such as insight or latent learning, which we normally attempt to explain through the cognitive approach. Different parts of the brain seem to control the two modes of learning. The parts of the brain primarily associated with memory and understanding (key issues in

cognitive learning) do not seem to be required for the learning of associations between responses and stimuli. Animals that have had those parts
of their brains surgically removed, can still be classically and operantly
conditioned. Likewise, severely brain damaged (from birth or due to
accidents) humans, who do not have parts of the brain we know to be
used in complex learning, can still be conditioned.

THE SOCIAL LEARNING APPROACH

Before considering the cognitive element in learning, the social learning
explanation deserves some consideration, particularly as an extension on
the behaviourist explanation described above.

Psychologists such as Bandura (1977) have argued persuasively that a
great deal of learning (perhaps the bulk of learning in humans) is based
on imitating role models in one context or another. Whether this indis-
putable fact in some way undermines the behaviourist explanation of
learning is a matter of debate, as discussed earlier in this chapter. What is
hardly debatable is the importance of role models in the learning process.
It is clearly of great interest to know the conditions under which role
models are likely to be imitated. Are there certain characteristics which
role models may possess that can make them more attractive, more
noticeable and more likely to be copied by others? Are there certain
individuals who are more likely to imitate certain role models? Are there
certain types of behaviours that are somehow more attractive than
others for copying and are there certain circumstances that encourage or
discourage copying behaviour? These are all research questions that arise
out of the social learning perspective.

Much of the research attention has focused on social learning in children. It is of great interest to those concerned about the development
and welfare of children to know what link exists between role models
and learned behaviour. This is particularly true in an era when children
are exposed to a bewildering array of role models, many displaying the
most unacceptable behaviour, on television. In the absence of the TV
and VCR it would be a rare and unfortunate child who ever witnessed
homicidal or other extremely violent behaviour. Yet this is now standard
viewing fare for most children.

The question is, can TV characters act as role models for learning just like real live models and are they likely to possess the characteristics that will attract imitation?

The research attention here has mainly focused on violent role models. A large and growing body of both correlational and experimental research (for reviews of the literature see: Geen, 1994, 1998; Eron et al, 1996) indicates that there is indeed a relationship between watching violence on TV and behaving more violently towards others.

The correlational research can be questioned on the basis that it may well be the case that children who are more prone to violence tend to watch more violence on TV. However, the experimental evidence has shown that children randomly assigned to watching violent programmes display more violence in their subsequent play and interaction with others than control groups randomly assigned to watching similar amounts of non-violent programme material.

Critics of the studies point to the fact that the studies only demonstrate a short-term effect and that it has not been proven that watching violent TV has long-term consequences. This may not, however, be a very relevant point. Violence on TV or in videos is the daily viewing fare of many children. It is estimated that in the US the average child will have been exposed to 8,000 murders and 100,000 other violent acts on TV before even leaving elementary school (Huston at al, 1992; Kunkel et al, 1996). The situation is not as extreme in Ireland but it would be foolish to deny the growing parallels between what happens here and in the US. Even if the effects of televised violence are short-term, since the role modelling is daily, any tendency to imitate the modelled behaviour results in a daily escalation in violent or aggressive behaviour. If it were shown that a food additive, say one present in most breakfast cereals, had the effect of making children more aggressive in the hour after consumption, it is doubtful if the manufacturers could defend their product on the basis that the effect was short lived.

A behaviourist perspective on learning would suggest that it is not sufficient to see role models behaving violently for a child to adopt similar behaviour as part of his or her ordinary repertoire. In addition, the violent acts must be accompanied by some kind of reinforcement. The unfortunate fact is that violence will often bring at least short-term reinforcement. If two children are competing over who should play with a toy, the chances are that the more violent one will have his or her way. Under the close scrutiny of responsible carers violent behaviour may be curbed. Unfortunately, it is the very same children, who receive less supervision due to their parents or carers being overstretched, inadequate or uncaring, that are more likely to be allowed watch a great deal of unsuitable TV.

What then of TV acting as a source of positive role models? There is research evidence that TV can have a positive effect on children's behaviour in this way.

Whether children are more influenced by pro-social TV role models (Hearold, 1986) or by anti-social models (Eisenberg, 1992) is a source of disagreement among those who have reviewed the relevant research.

A tentative conclusion, however, about the motivation to imitate in young children reached by developmental psychologists (see Newcombe (1996) pp 195–6) gives rise for some concern. There is evidence that role models that arouse stronger emotions in a child are more likely to be attended to and to be imitated. Thus, children imitate their parents more than siblings and active outgoing two-year-olds are more likely to be copied by quiet two-year-olds than vice versa. Violent activity by its nature is loud, attention grabbing and emotionally arousing (presumably the reason why there is so much of it on TV). Loving, caring, gentle and sharing behaviour does not have the same capacity to arouse. Is it therefore less likely to be copied? Unfortunately the answer may well be yes.

THE COGNITIVE APPROACH TO LEARNING

In considering the question of what kind of behaviour is more capable of capturing attention and being copied, we have strayed into the arena of cognitive research. This concerns how humans detect, process, store and retrieve information about the world. Cognitive psychology is now a major speciality within the broad field of psychology, which produces a large body of research every year.

So extensive and complex is the field of cognitive psychology that we can only deal with it in brief in this chapter. We will, however, take a look at the kind of approach it takes and how it seeks to come to a better understanding of learning.

In direct opposition to the behaviourist approach, the cognitive approach attempts to get inside the head of the learner, to find out how information is processed, stored and accessed in the brain. It attempts to identify the rules governing these processes, much as a computer scientist might seek to figure out how a particular computer programme operates.

We already encountered some of the findings from cognitive research in Chapter 3 when we considered the process of human perception. Learning inevitably begins with perception, when information enters the senses and is processed by the brain. If we do not notice or process some available piece of information, we cannot learn from it.

We saw how there is evidence that a very great volume of stimulus information detected by the senses is unconsciously processed, most of it immediately discarded and some of it passed on for deeper, conscious processing. The rules governing this selection process are of obvious relevance to understanding learning. If one does not even become conscious of something one is unlikely to learn much from it.

It is generally agreed among cognitive psychologists that information selected at this early stage of processing is then held in a short-term or working memory store. Here it is further processed and either lost very quickly or else transferred to a long-term memory store where it remains open to recall for a shorter or longer period depending on a number of factors. Again, the mechanisms by which information is transferred to long-term memory and subsequently retained or lost are of great importance to knowing how we learn.

In summary then, some of the important questions to understanding the learning process that the cognitive approach attempts to answer are:

What dictates which aspects of the information detected by our senses will be selected for conscious processing?
Why is some information held in short-term memory forgotten immediately and other information transferred to long-term memory?
Why is information lost from long-term memory and what enhances our ability to retain and retrieve information over the long term?

While complete answers to those questions are not yet available, research has produced a rich body of evidence enabling us to make a reasonable guess at how the cognitive processes work.

THE ROLE OF PERCEPTION IN LEARNING

As we saw in Chapter 3, certain physical characteristics of stimuli, specifically ones that make them stand out from the background in some way, cause the stimuli to be noticed. Where there is change, attention is more likely to be captured. TV involves constantly changing stimuli, therefore is a powerful attention grabber. A lecture or a talk, which includes visual aids and a varying tone on the part of the presenter, holds the attention of an audience much better than a speech read out in a monotone.

It is not just the objective characteristics of given stimuli that command attention. We know that unconsciously humans constantly scan information available to them using their knowledge of the world stored in long-term memory. On this basis stimuli which have particular subjective relevance or meaning are also much more likely to be attended to and consciously processed. If a lecturer can use examples or explanations that fit in with knowledge students already have, their attention is more strongly held and learning is facilitated. If material being explained does not strike any chords with listeners, attention tends to wander.

THE ROLE OF MEMORY IN LEARNING

Of course, actually attending to information is only the beginning of learning. The information then has to be processed in some significant way to transfer it to long-term memory. Research evidence indicates that incoming information is first stored for a duration of up to 12 seconds in a kind of working or short-term memory store. This store can be thought of as 'present time' for all of us. It is the immediate reality in which we live. Numerous studies have demonstrated that it is only capable of holding around seven discrete items of information at any one time. Most people, briefly shown a sequence of numbers such as 26495198367, can only repeat the first seven numbers immediately afterwards. The same applies to a sequence of letters or words. There is one way, however, that far more information can be retained in short-term memory. That is, if the information can be 'chunked' together in some meaningful way. Imagine you are briefly shown the following array of letters and asked to repeat them immediately afterwards:

AI.....BFB.....IGA.....ABM.....WIF.....A

Imagine now you were shown the same letters presented as follows:

AIB....FBI.....GAA.....BMW.....IFA

Doubtless you will agree that following the second presentation, you will remember more of the letters. That is because you were able to immediately draw on knowledge in your long-term memory to make meaningful chunks out of what were previously separate letters.

The implication is clear. If incoming information can be rendered meaningful in some way, the short-term memory can store much more of it, greatly improving the chances that it will be transferred to long-term memory – that it will be learned, in other words.

Information in short-term memory will, as the name suggests, last only a short time, that is unless it is rehearsed in some way. There is research evidence indicating that visual material tends to be recoded as sounds in short-term memory. Thus if we are presented with a visual array of letters, words or numbers we mentally rehearse them as if we were saying them to ourselves. If we are prevented by the need to process other information from carrying out this rehearsal we forget the material and do not transfer it to long-term memory. It is probable that the act of rehearsal allows for some physical change in the brain through which the information is stored as a memory.

Research evidence indicates that visual and semantic codes can also operate in short-term or working memory (See Solso, 1995, pp. 193-201 for a discussion of coding in short-term memory).

The next question is: what causes us to remember some pieces of information forever and to soon forget other things that we learned? The brain stores information not as discrete or separate items but in some kind of meaningful network or structure. We saw previously, when we explored perceptual organisation in Chapter 3, how we make sense of our world. There the idea of categories was used to explain our approach. All new sights, sounds and so on are understood as belonging to existing categories of reality. Of course the categories are all related to each other in very complex ways. When you were taught in school about the 1916 Rising you may have categorised the event under 'History', which is a sub-category of 'subjects learned at school'. You may also have categorised it under 'Dublin', which is a sub-category of 'places in Ireland'. Some kind of connection is formed between 'History' and 'Dublin' in the process.

The fact that memories are based on connections can best be understood by the strategies you are likely to use if asked to remember what you were doing at 9.30 p.m. on 24 December last. To access this information you might go through a connection network such as:

HOLIDAYS – CHRISTMAS – CHRISTMAS EVE – AT HOME – RAINING HEAVILY – WATCHED TV.

Through a sequence of meaningful connections, you are able to access a clear memory of what you were doing at that particular time. The implication is that if information is connected up to a meaningful network it will remain accessible, but if not then it is likely that it will be forgotten. The more you already know (providing a rich framework for making connections) the more you will be able to remember. If you know very little about the geography of, say, Somalia it is very difficult to commit to long-term memory the name of a town or river there. If you are already familiar with the country it is much easier to integrate new information about it.

Another finding about long-term memory is that it is affected by emotion in a number of ways. Exciting or traumatic events and associated information often stick in memory particularly well. One reason is that we pay more attention to and are more likely to rehearse information associated with heightened emotions. Another interesting possibility is that there is a different biological mechanism involved in the memory of emotionally loaded information (Cahill et al, 1994). The role of emotion in memory takes us back to role models on television and why violence, being emotionally arousing, is probably more prone to imitation than many other more acceptable behaviours. If something is remembered better it stands a greater chance of influencing behaviour.

In recent years, advances in brain imaging techniques such as PET Scanning (a mechanism which actually allows computer images of areas of the brain which are active at any given time to show up in different colours to non-active areas) has allowed researchers to match up thinking with evidence of localised activity in the brain. This promises to further push forward our understanding of human thought and learning processes.

Memory, of course, is expressed as retrieval – accessing information stored in the brain. You must have had the tantalising experience of just not being able to access a name or a piece of information that you were convinced you really knew. Try as you might, it would not come back to you and then later it suddenly hopped into your mind. Something had prompted its retrieval. The issue here has to do with cues or hints that are available to you to help access the information in memory. The more links you have formed in your memory with a particular piece of information the more retrieval cues that exist to access it. When someone reminds you that the girl being talked about is the one with very short hair who spent a long time talking to your friend Jim at the party on Friday night last, you may be able to recall her using those cues if you have formed those links with her in memory.

The context in which one learns information is also a cue to retrieval. It is easier to retrieve information if one is in the same context as that in which it was learned. A striking experimental demonstration of this involved divers learning words under water or on the beach. They learned equally well in both situations but retrieval was much better in the same situation (Godden and Baddeley, 1975).

Context can consist of the environment or it can have to do with an emotional state. Evidence suggests that, for example, one is better able to remember happy events in the past when happy and unpleasant events when unhappy (Bower, 1981).

SUMMARY

'The process of learning can be said to have occurred when a relatively permanent change in behaviour or behaviour potential has been produced by experience.'

(Zimbardo, McDermott and Metaal, 1995, p. 243)

There are three main approaches to understanding the process of learning: the behaviourist theory; the social learning theory; and the cognitive theory. Each one adopts a different perspective on the process, and together they offer a comprehensive framework within which to understand how learning occurs.

The behaviourist approach concentrates entirely on events in the learning process that are accessible to observation. It views learning as the forming of associations between learner responses and environmental stimuli. It suggests that such associations are built up through the processes of classical and operant conditioning.

Classical conditioning occurs when a neutral stimulus becomes associated with an unconditioned stimulus and takes on the power to produce a response previously produced by the unconditioned stimulus. The neutral stimulus is then termed a conditioned stimulus and the response made to it a conditioned response. Classical conditioning has provided a useful explanation for the learning of emotional responses such as fears, likes and dislikes. It also explains the learning of habitual behaviours.

Operant conditioning occurs when a response becomes associated with a reinforcing stimulus resulting in the repetition of the response. Alternatively, it occurs when a response becomes associated with an unpleasant or punishing stimulus resulting in the extinction of that response. This learning process has extremely widespread applications from the socialisation of children to training in the workplace. The process has been extensively researched, revealing important insights into the development of secondary reinforcers, the implications of generalisation and discrimination and the application of operant conditioning in the shaping of complex behaviours.

Contrary to the claims of its original proponents, evidence indicates that the behaviourist learning process has a cognitive dimension.

Classical conditioning is only successful where the learner interprets the neutral or conditioned stimulus as being a reliable predictor of the unconditioned stimulus. Likewise, operant conditioning is only successful when the learner interprets the reinforcing stimulus as resulting from the operant response. The concept of interpretation is only understandable from a cognitive or information processing standpoint. It is not amenable to direct observation.

Contrary also to the beliefs of behaviourists, forms of learning have been demonstrated that cannot be explained from the behaviourist perspective. Insight and latent learning have been shown in animals. In contradiction to behaviourist theory both involve forms of learning that do not occur in direct response to environmental stimuli. It is clear, therefore, that further approaches to learning are necessary to achieve a complete picture.

The social learning approach suggests that much learning takes place through the observation of role models. Unlike the behaviourist approach it allows that the learner does not have to experience the environmental consequences of his or her actions. Learning can be achieved vicariously by capitalising on the experiences of others who are observed. Much research has focused on the characteristics of role models likely to be imitated and the conditions under which this will take place. A particular focus has been placed on the effect of TV role models on children. The evidence is that children are inclined to imitate both pro- and anti-social behaviours witnessed on TV. The emotionally arousing and attention-grabbing nature of violent TV role models may make them particularly prone to being copied by children. A great deal of evidence has been accumulated that watching violent behaviour on TV does indeed lead to more aggressive behaviour in real life among children.

The cognitive approach to learning focuses on the way information is perceived, processed and stored. Of all the stimuli impacting on the senses only a small proportion is consciously processed in working or short-term memory. The selection of this information is carried out at an unconscious level using both subjective and objective criteria.

To be learned, information has to be selected or attended to in the first instance. Selected information is processed in a short-term or working memory store, which is capable of holding approximately seven discrete bits of information at one time. The restrictive limits of this store are extended through the chunking of information. The capacity to chunk – based on existing knowledge – is a key to greater learning capacity. Information in working memory is stored for up to 12 seconds or so and either committed to long-term memory or lost. Coding in working memory is primarily but not uniquely auditory.

The process of rehearsal in working memory appears crucial to transferring information to long-term memory. A number of factors are known to be important in long-term retention and retrieval of information. The more information is associated with other information in memory, the better it is retained and subsequently retrieved. Information associated with heightened emotions is retained better partially due to better attention and rehearsal and partly due to the apparent existence of a specific biological mechanism associated with emotional memories. Retrieval of information is aided by relevant cues. Memory associations assist the cueing process. Retrieval is also enhanced by matching the retrieval context with that of the original learning. Further insights into the precise mechanisms of memory are likely to follow from research using PET scanning, which enables local areas of the brain active during cognitive activity to be visualised on screen.

REVIEW QUESTIONS

1. Explain, with the aid of appropriate examples, the processes of classical and operant conditioning.
2. Explain what is meant by 'insight' and 'latent' learning and why their existence suggests that the behaviourist approach is only a partial explanation for the learning process.
3. Discuss the cognitive approach to understanding learning and the lessons it offers on how to improve individual learning.
4. Discuss the relevance of television in the context of social learning.
5. Contrast the behaviourist, social learning and cognitive approaches to understanding learning.

REFERENCES

American Psychological Association, (1993), *Violence and Youth: Psychology's Response*, Washington DC.

Bandura, A., (1977), *Social Learning Theory*, N.J.: Prentice Hall.

Bower, G.H., (1981), 'Mood and Memory', *American Psychologist*, 6, 129-148.

Cahill, L., Prins, B., Weber, M. and McGaugh, J.L., (1994), 'Addrenergic Activation and Memory for Emotional Events', *Nature*, 371.

Eisenberg, N., (1992), *The Caring Child*, Cambridge, M.A.: Harvard University Press.

Eron, L.D., Huesmann, L.R., Lefkowitz, M.M. and Walder, L.O., (1996), 'Does Television Violence Cause Aggression?' in D.F. Greenberg (ed.), *Criminal Careers*, 2, 311-321, The International Library of Criminology, Criminal Justice and Penology, Aldershot, England: Dartmouth Publishing Company Ltd.

Geen, R., (1994), 'Television and Aggression: Recent Developments in Research and Theory', in D. Zillmann, J. Bryant, A.C. Huston (eds), *Media, Children and the Family: Social, Scientific, Psychodynamic and Clinical Perspectives* (pp. 151-162), Hillsdale NJ: Erlbaum.

Geen, R., (1998), 'Aggression and Anti-social Behaviour', in D. Gilbert, S. Fiske and G. Lindzey (eds), *The Handbook of Social Psychology* (4th edition, Vol. 2, pp. 317-356), New York: McGraw Hill.

Godden, D. and Baddeley, A.D., (1975), 'Context Dependent Memory in Two Natural Environments: On Land and Under Water', *British Journal of Psychology*, 66, 325-331.

Hearold, S., (1986), A synthesis of 1043 effects of television on social behaviour. In G. Comstock (ed.), *Public communication and behaviour* (Vol. 1, p. 66–133). New York: Academic Press.

Hepper, P.G., (1991), 'An Examination of Foetal Learning Before and After Birth', *Irish Journal of Psychology*, 12, 2, 95-107.

Huston, A.C., Donnerstein, E., Fairchild, H., Feshback, N., Katz, P.A., Murray, J.P., Rubinstein, E.A., Wilcox, B.L. and Zuckerman, D., (1992) *Big World, small screen: The role of television in American society*, Lincoln: University of Nebraska Press.

Kohler, W., (1925), *The Mentality of Apes*, New York: Harcourt Brace (Reprint Edn. 1976, New York, Liveright).

Kunkel, D., Wilson, B.J., Linz, D., Potter, J., Donnerstein, E., Smith, S.L., Blumenthal, E. and Gray, T. (1996), *The national television violence study*, Studio City, C.A.: Mediascope.

Maier, S.F. and Seligman, M.E.P., (1976), 'Learned Helplessness: Theory and Evidence', *Journal of Experimental Psychology: General*, 105, 3-46.

Newcombe, N. (1996), *Child Development, Change over Time*, N.Y.: Harper Collins.

Pavlov, I.P., (1927), *Conditioned Reflexes*, New York: Oxford University Press.

Reiss, A.J. and Roth, J.A., (1993), *Understanding and Preventing Violence*, Washington DC: National Academy Press.

Rescorla, (1967), 'Pavlovian Conditioning and Its Proper Control Procedures', *Psychological Review*, 74, 71-80.

Skinner, B.F., (1938), *The Behaviour of Organisms*, New York: Appleton-Century-Crofts.

Solso, R.L., (1995), *Cognitive Psychology*, Boston: Allen and Bacon.

Tolman, (1932), *Purposive Behaviour in Animals and Men*, New York: Appleton Century Crofts, (Reprint Edn. 1967, New York, Irvington).

Watson, J.B., (1930), *Behaviourism* (Rev. Edn.), New York: Norton.

Zimbardo, P., McDermott, J.J. and Metaal, N., (1995), *Psychology: A European Text*, UK: Harper Collins.

Chapter 5

Intelligence

LEARNING OBJECTIVES

Having read this chapter you should be able to:

- explain what intelligence is, including that:
  - it is normally defined in terms of its effects,
  - it consists of organic/brain factors and information processing skills;
- describe how intelligence is measured, showing an understanding of the following issues:
  - IQ test origin and design,
  - mental age,
  - Intelligence Quotient (IQ),
  - distribution of IQ,
  - standard scores and percentiles,
  - factor theory,
  - general intelligence (g),
  - limitations of intelligence measures,
  - alternatives for work,
  - requirements of a good test;
- explain what influences intelligence, including research evidence for:
  - genetic factors,
  - environment,
  - race.

INTRODUCTION

Imagine you are sitting across the table from a psychologist who asks you to respond to a series of questions and problems like the following:

1. What is steam made of?
2. What is pepper?
3. Why is copper often used in electrical wires?
4. Three women divided 18 golf balls equally among themselves. How many golf balls did each person receive?
5. In what way are a circle and a triangle alike?
6. Say the following list of digits backwards: 7–1–8–7.
7. Make the following design using the blocks provided:

8. In each line of symbols, are both of the two symbols on the left among the line of seven symbols at the right?

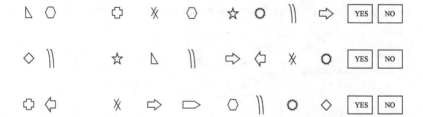

What kind of inferences do you think might be drawn from your answers? A few points may strike you immediately. Clearly, to answer questions 1-3, some level of knowledge or information is required. Also, a facility with language is necessary – the ability to understand words and to explain their meanings. Item 5 seems to test something similar. Item 4 requires a facility to carry out basic mathematics. Item 6 seems simply to involve short-term memory. Items 7 and 8 appear to test skills that are not formally learned and, once the requirements are understood, require no verbal or numerical skills to complete.

The issue is: what have all these questions in common? What they have in common is that they measure various intellectual abilities or skills that go together to make up what is usually referred to as intelligence. Of course, the items used above are just examples and quite simple ones at that. In reality much more demanding items are required to measure the full range of intelligence. Nevertheless they serve to illustrate the nature of standard intelligence tests. In this chapter we will see how such tests came about and what logic lies behind the choice of questions included. We will also see that not every expert agrees that intelligence tests measure the full range of mental skills that might reasonably be called intelligent activity. We will also examine the evidence as to where intelligence comes from. Is it something we learn or is it an innate ability inherited through the genes?

WHAT IS INTELLIGENCE?

'Intelligence' is a word frequently used in ordinary conversation to describe a person or explain an achievement or an action. When we use this term we assume that others know what we mean. We would say that it is a quality or characteristic that people have more or less of, which helps them to do certain things more or less easily. We would say that intelligence helps one to learn, to solve problems and to understand information. It is regarded as an essential prerequisite for educational success and for most careers and classes of employment. We judge other people by this yardstick all the time and more than any other quality it is rightly or wrongly seen as the essence of what it is to be human – what differentiates us from the lesser species.

However, if challenged as to what actually is this characteristic called intelligence that helps us to do those things and that is deemed so important, we would probably find it hard to say. We might suggest that it is 'brain power' or something vague like that. The truth is that 'intelligence' is not at all easy to define and most attempts to say what it is rely on saying what it does – what it helps us to do.

It is interesting to see how those scientists who have devoted much of their careers to the measurement of intelligence explain what it is they are measuring.

The first modern test of intelligence was developed in France by Alfred Binet and Theophile Simon in 1905. At the time they described as follows what they understood intelligence to mean:

> 'It seems to us that in intelligence there is a fundamental faculty, the alteration or lack of which is of the utmost importance for practical life. This faculty is called judgment, otherwise called good sense, practical sense, initiative, the faculty of adapting oneself to circumstances. To judge well, to comprehend well, to reason well, those are the essential activities of intelligence.'

(Binet and Simon, 1905)

This explanation of intelligence is very similar to that suggested by David Wechsler, another pioneer in the development of modern intelligence tests. Wechsler wrote that:

> 'Intelligence is the aggregate or global capacity of the individual to act purposefully, to think rationally, and to deal effectively with his environment.'

(Wechsler, 1958)

What is striking about both explanations is that they rely on describing what intelligence helps us to do in order to explain what it is. This still leaves us to wonder what it is that is doing the helping?

The question of what intelligence actually is can be asked in another way: in what ways do those who have more and those who have less intelligence differ? Clearly the differences must lie within the brain and nervous system. The nature of those differences must relate to either:

1. basic biological or organic differences, that is, differences in the structure or architecture of the brain/nervous system;
2. differences in some kind of basic skills for processing information stored in the brain;
3. a combination of both of the above.

The combination explanation is the explanation best fitted to current scientific information on the topic. As we will see later there is clear evidence that differences in measured intelligence are partially accounted for by genetic inheritance. Anything genetically inherited must have a biological basis. It must be expressed as physical differences of some kind between individuals. Thus, intelligence must in part be a function of how the brain/nervous system is structured or laid out. However, we also know that intelligence is also partially due to life experiences – particularly early childhood experiences (see below). This suggests that some kind of basic skills for processing information may be learned by individuals to a greater or lesser degree and that those skills also underpin intelligence.

Recently, careful research on brain development in babies has shown that at birth the brain is very undeveloped and that the manner in which the brain develops is strongly affected by the experiences of the individual baby. At birth the brain is made up of some 100 billion neurones or nerve cells. These are connected together with great complexity. At birth the pattern of connections is far from complete and it is experience that decides what the final network will be like. Evidence from both animals and humans reveal that infants deprived of a stimulating environment do not develop as many working connections as normal. The mechanism appears to be that initially, shortly after birth, the brain produces an enormous number of connections between nerve cells, but later many of these are lost again if they are not used.

'Each time a baby tries to touch a tantalising object or gazes intently at a face or listens to a lullaby, tiny bursts of electricity shoot through the brain, knitting neurones into circuits as well defined as those etched into silicon chips.'

(Nash, 1997)

In short, exposure to stimulation causes brain activity, without which the brain will not develop properly. Thus, learning and brain development go hand in hand. Learned skills and brain structure are not separate but instead are deeply intertwined factors. We all inherit a tendency to have our own unique brain structure but we all have unique experiences also in childhood, which in turn affect the development of our brains.

Intelligence then can best be seen as a complex interrelationship of brain structure and learning.

THE INFORMATION PROCESSING APPROACH TO RESEARCH ON INTELLIGENCE

While major strides forward are being made in the understanding of the development and structure of the brain and nervous system, which is throwing more light on the biological basis for intelligence, research is also ongoing into the skills through which intelligence is expressed. A particular branch of psychological research known as the *information processing approach* is seeking to identify the mental processes or skills that operate when we engage in intellectual activities demanding the use of intelligence. The idea is that there may be some common set of skills that underpin all intelligent activity, whether that activity has to do with solving math problems, for example, or trying to solve a murder mystery.

The work of Sternberg (1985) illustrates the information processing approach to understanding intelligence. He has chosen to examine what individuals do when trying to solve problems found in intelligence tests. One type of problem he has examined is an analogy problem. An example would involve the test taker being given a pair of words, which are related to each other in a particular way, e.g. *Lawyer: Client*. They are then given another word, e.g. *Doctor*, and asked to find a word that bears a similar relationship to it. The answer, of course, is *Patient*. Sternberg is interested to find out what the test taker does mentally between reading the problem and identifying the solution – during a lapse of what may be a second or less.

Sternberg has identified a number of mental skills or activities, which contribute to solving such problems. The important ones he calls 'Encoding' and 'Comparison'. Encoding involves drawing out from memory information as to what each word represents. About the word 'lawyer', a person may remember that a lawyer is college-educated, works in an office or the law courts and works for people who hire him. About the word 'client' they may immediately think that it refers to a person who is given a service by someone else. Comparison involves scanning the encoding for each word looking for some basis on which to match them. Having come up with the encoding for 'lawyer' and 'client' just given, a quick scan through the 'encodings' will arrive at a basis for comparison and a solution to the analogy: lawyers give a service to clients and doctors give a service to patients. 'Patient' is therefore the solution.

Sternberg has identified that individuals who are good at solving analogy problems spend more time carrying out the encoding and come up with a more complete idea of what the words stand for. For the word 'lawyer', a poor analogy problem solver might only come up with the notion that a lawyer is college educated and works in an office or in the law courts. Thus they would find it hard to solve the problem. Sternberg has also identified that good analogy solvers are faster at carrying out the comparison process. They can find matching aspects of the words at greater speed. Through this kind of work it may eventually be possible to identify what these very basic skills are, which make up all kinds of intelligent behaviour. It may even be possible to train people in such skills to make them more intelligent. It is easy to understand how someone brought up in a culture or environment where there is little emphasis on this kind of analytical approach to language might not develop very good encoding or comparison skills.

While learned skills and experiences in general have an effect on the brain and the structure of the brain is important in the learning of such skills, we are as yet unable to tell very much about a person's intelligence from the structure of the brain. To understand and measure intelligence we are entirely reliant on inferring it from the behaviour of the individual –

from the skills and abilities they can display. While the work of Sternberg and others is trying to pin down which skills and activities we should infer intelligence from, as yet there is no totally foolproof way of deciding which skills we should concentrate on. We will discuss this problem below when dealing with the measurement of intelligence.

MEASUREMENT OF INTELLIGENCE

The modern scientific approach to the measurement of intelligence had its origins in France in 1905. It emerged from the work of two psychologists, Alfred Binet and Theophile Simon. Binet had been asked by the French government to develop a test that would identify children who were too slow intellectually to cope with normal schooling. The impetus for this development came from the fact that a law had been passed in 1881 making school attendance compulsory for all children.

In 1905 Binet and Simon published a test which is regarded as the forerunner of all modern intelligence tests. It was based on reasoning and problem-solving tasks which Binet and Simon assumed to be at the core of intelligence (see section entitled **What is intelligence?** above). They also assumed that among children ability should rise with age. In light of this they included a range of items of increasing difficulty to suit various ages. Through testing samples of children of various ages they established what the average performance was at any given age. Let's say, for example, children of age eight got 50 items on average correct. This score of 50 would then be taken to represent the mental age (MA) of an eight-year old. In other words, no matter what the actual chronological age (CA) of a child was, if s/he scored 50 on the test, s/he would be deemed to have a mental age of eight – to have the ability of an average eight-year old. In a similar way the mental ages of five, six, seven, nine and so on would be defined.

From this comparison of mental age and chronological age, the notion of IQ or Intelligence Quotient developed, using a formula for IQ as follows:

$$IQ = \frac{Mental\ Age}{Chronological\ Age} \times 100$$

From this formula, the average IQ for a child would always be 100 because for an average child MA = CA. Children with higher than average intelligence would have scores over 100 and those with less than average intelligence scores less than 100.

IQ tests are designed so that half of all those who take the test will score below 100 and half above. Furthermore, they are designed so that the distribution of scores above and below 100 is predictable and conforms to what is known as the normal curve (see Figure 5.1 below). This means that a high proportion of individuals' scores will lie close to the average of 100 (e.g. 50 per cent will score between 90 and 110). The further up and down from 100 a score is, the less often it will be obtained. At the extremes, scores become very rare. Only one in a million can be expected to score above 160.

IQ scores, therefore, have meaning only in terms of how common or uncommon they are. IQ tests are norm-referenced tests. Scores below 70 are taken to represent mental retardation, or learning disorder, as it now tends to be called in Ireland. Scores above 130 are defined as very superior intelligence. Only a total of about 5 per cent of the population can be expected to have IQ scores above or below that. In practice, the numbers at the lower end are a few percent higher due to a variety of organic disorders, e.g. Down's Syndrome, that interferes with intellectual ability.

While that given above is the generally used definition of IQ, it is only useful for measuring the IQ of children. The problem with adults is that ability does not keep improving with age. There is no reason why a 40-year old should be able to answer more questions on an intelligence test than a 20-year old. It is accepted that mental age stops rising around the age of 16. After that mental ability does not generally improve. Chronological age, of course, continues to rise. Using the above definition, then, IQ would appear to drop as adults get older. This does not happen. Despite this obvious problem, it has been common practice, and still is, to use the concept of IQ to measure adult intelligence. The figures are simply corrected mathematically to avoid the error we have discussed.

In recent years, some intelligence tests for adults have moved away from reporting intelligence scores in terms of IQ. They have adopted the practice of using what is known as standard scores instead. This is a simple idea. It involves translating the score on the test (number of items correct) into a figure (standard deviations) which expresses how far above or below the average that score is. Since the distribution of IQ around the average is known to follow the normal curve (see Figure 5.1 below) it is then a relatively simple matter to identify in which percentile the individual has scored. If the person is found to have performed better than, say, 62 per cent of the population, then the person's score is reported as being at the 62nd percentile. Likewise, if they score better than 88 per cent of the population then that person is said to be at the 88th percentile.

The Normal Distribution of IQ Scores

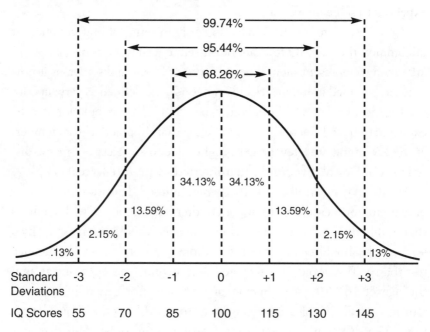

If each person in the population of the world were represented by a grain of sand, each one was marked with that person's IQ score and the sand was piled up with the grains marked average IQ (100) in the middle, those with 99 or 101 on either side of them and so on outwards, the pile would take the shape shown in the diagram. At the edges would be the relatively few grains that differed most from the average. Standard deviation is a scale of measurement reflecting distance from the average (from Locurto, 1991).

The standard scores and the percentile approach are just other ways of reporting intelligence test scores by comparison with the performance of the general population. This is, of course, exactly what IQ scores do as well, except that the problem of a static mental age in adults has to be corrected for. Percentiles have the advantage that they immediately indicate the position of the individual's IQ relative to the population, while with IQ scores you need to be told separately what proportion of the population can be expected to score above or below that score.

It is customary to think of a single IQ score as representing the intelligence of an individual. Despite this, the major IQ tests such as the Stanford-Binet test (the original Binet-Simon test was revised and adapted for a US population at the Stanford University in 1916, was revised several times subsequently, most recently in 1986 and is known as the Stanford-Binet test) and the Wechsler Intelligence scales report a number of IQ scores for each person.

The Stanford-Binet is effectively comprised of four separate tests:

(a) verbal reasoning;
(b) abstract/visual reasoning;
(c) quantitative reasoning; and
(d) short-term memory,

each one reporting an IQ score.

The Wechsler Intelligence Scales (there are different tests for adults and children) divide IQ into a *verbal scale* and a *performance scale*. Separate scores for sub-scales or sub-tests of each of the two scales are also reported.

Why do different IQ tests measure a different number and range of skills? This is because there is no certainty as to how many separate skills make up intelligence. The Stanford-Binet treats verbal reasoning (reasoning with language) and quantitative reasoning (reasoning with numbers) as separate skills. The Wechsler Scale for Adult Intelligence deals with both skills under the verbal scale. This is a slight simplification, but essentially the difference between the two tests concerns the degree of correlation between the various skills that are used to measure intelligence. The makers of the Stanford-Binet may be interpreted as viewing the correlation between verbal and numerical ability to be low enough to warrant them being separated into separate scales. The makers of the Wechsler Scale judge the correlation to be high enough for them to be included in one scale. Of course, the Wechsler Scale also reports separate sub-test scores within each scale so that, for example, there are separate scores given for arithmetic and vocabulary within the verbal scale.

While it is true that an individual who takes an IQ test will score better on some scales or sub-tests than others (one person being better at performance activities like assembling designs with blocks, another being better at verbal or mathematical activities), the overall correlation between the different scales for any individual tends to be reasonably high. This means that, in the main, those who score high on one scale rarely score very low on others, and, similarly, those who score low on one scale rarely score very high on others. Exceptions may be poorly educated individuals who, for example, though intelligent, may have a poor ability to read and will therefore do very poorly on scales that require language skills but may do very well on performance activities. This high correlation among various intelligence skills suggests that they are not entirely separate abilities. Something causes people to do relatively well or relatively poorly across the full range of abilities. This 'something' is often described as *general intelligence* (g), a general ability, which is thought to lie behind all intellectual skills. A person's performance on any scale of an IQ test is then partially a measure of 'g' and partially a measure of the special ability which that scale is concerned with.

Limitations in the measurement of intelligence

As yet there is no direct way of measuring 'g' independently of the various special abilities. It is inferred from the degree of correlation that exists among measures of various aspects of intelligence or intellectual skills. Neither is there any certain way of determining how many special abilities intelligence is made up of. Much of what we measure right now in determining individual's intellectual abilities through IQ tests derives from the activities we focus on in education. This in turn is a product of our own culture – in Europe and North America especially. In Africa many cultures place a very high value on musical and dance abilities. They think of those who are poor at those activities as unintelligent. If IQ tests had developed in Africa, chances are they would have included measures of ability in those areas.

BOX 5. 1

EMOTIONAL INTELLIGENCE

In 1996, psychologist and New York Times journalist Daniel Goleman excited world-wide media interest with his best-selling book entitled *Emotional Intelligence*. Though his insights were not by any means entirely new, he succeeded in raising the profile of the emotions to a plane previously occupied solely by the cognitive domain.

Emotional intelligence, he explained, is made up of characteristics such as self-awareness, ability to manage and control emotions, ability to motivate oneself, empathy with others and the capacity to handle relationships. Without these abilities, the ability to assimilate, recall and apply information (the core of IQ in the ordinary sense) is essentially switched off when it comes to much of life's challenges. He made a convincing case that even those achievements to which IQ is supposed to matter most, such as educational and occupational success, are as much, if not more, impacted upon by emotional intelligence. Other arguably more important aspects of life such as forming relationships and founding stable marriages are almost entirely down to this factor.

The core of emotional intelligence or what Goleman calls the 'master aptitude' is the ability to master and channel one's emotions productively. It is the difference between having one's thoughts and decisions clouded by intrusive negative emotions such as anxiety or anger on the one hand and being able, on the other hand, not only to control one's own emotions, but those of others as well.

Goleman explains that the emotions operate within a neurobiological system in the brain that is partly independent of cognitive awareness and often ahead in terms of response time. Nevertheless, he argues that it is possible to learn to control one's mental and behavioural response to these emotions. That is the skill of emotional intelligence. The future of our modern industrialised societies, in Goleman's estimation, needs less those with IQs of 160 and more those who can understand their own emotions and those of others, who can act with less impulsiveness and who can deal more constructively with interpersonal relations. A proper emphasis on emotional intelligence in child development and education should, he argues, go a long way towards both the success and happiness of future generations.

Some experts in the field of research on intelligence, such as Gardner (1983), Sternberg (1985) and Goleman (1996), point out that other areas of intelligent activity tend to be missing from both our understanding and measurement of intelligence. Gardner draws attention to 'interpersonal' and 'intrapersonal' intelligence. Sternberg refers to 'street smarts' or practical intelligence, the kind of judgment we need for dealing with day-to-day life, especially for dealing with other people. Goleman argues cogently for 'emotional intelligence' (see Box 5.1).

IQ tests, they each point out, fail to measure such abilities. This is probably where *intelligence* and *personality* collide. We all know people who, despite having great academic intelligence, seem to have little or no 'native wit' or 'cop-on' to help them live their lives. We also know those who seem to be ruled by their emotions – by impatience, explosive anger, overriding need to seem right, anxiety or fear of failure – emotions which can spoil the finest intellect. It may well be that both groups are essentially the same. Their deficiencies lie in a failure of personality rather than intellect. The mistake is to imagine that intellect exists in a vacuum. Intellect is better understood as a set of capacities, which require other capacities inherent in personality before they can be drawn upon in any practical or useful sense. After all, no sensible employer will hire a candidate for an important post on the basis of intelligence alone. Personality will be investigated with equal rigour. One is as important as the other for getting things done.

Intelligence tests and work performance

Given that intelligence seems logically to be a significant contributor to performance in a great many jobs, it may come as a surprise that standard IQ tests such as the Stanford-Binet and the Wechsler Scales are rarely or ever used in the selection of employees. The main reason is that such tests have to be individually administered to the test taker by a trained psychologist. They cannot be administered to a group, and considerable practice and expertise is required to administer them correctly. As a result, employers tend to use alternative tests which can be given to groups of candidates at the same time, using a set of standard instructions so that no great expertise is necessary to administer them. Such tests typically measure an individual aspect of intellectual ability such as numeracy or verbal ability and are usually referred to as aptitude tests. They will often show high correlations with IQ tests and, properly used, can act as good predictors of job performance.

Indeed there is evidence that general intelligence or 'g' accounts for a high proportion of job performance across a wide range of jobs. An analysis of job training across the wide range of jobs in the US military indicated that on average 'g' (estimates derived from the battery of cognitive tests used in selecting recruits) accounts for 60 per cent of the observed variance. The more complex the job, the more 'g' matters, with over 77 per cent of the training success differences among nuclear weapons specialists being accounted for by 'g' (Ree and Earles, 1990).

Evidence also exists for the predictive value of 'g' in a wide variety of civilian occupations based on the US Labour Department's cognitive ability selection test: the General Aptitude Test Battery (GATB) (Thorndike, 1986).

Validity and reliability of intelligence tests

IQ tests such as the Stanford-Binet and the Wechsler have high reliability. In other words, they return quite consistent results if expertly administered. Over time, the scores achieved by any individual tend to vary a little but not a great deal. If you achieve an IQ score of 108 at age 20, then you will get a very similar score at age 30 or 40 and so on. This applies, however, much more to adults than children. The variability of individual childrens' and adolescents' scores over time can be consider-able. It should also be noted that, with both children and adults, the impact of factors such as motivation, fatigue and anxiety about doing the test can be great. This is one of the reasons why IQ tests are individually administered, so that a trained tester can detect signs that may indicate the testee is not performing to the best of his or her ability.

It is easy to demonstrate the reliability of IQ tests. Demonstrating their validity is more difficult. The validity of a test, as you will recall, is the degree to which it measures what it is supposed to measure. The problem with intelligence is there is no certainty as to what precisely it means or how, other than through IQ tests, it might be measured with accuracy for comparison purposes. The best that can be done by way of validity checks on IQ tests is to see if they identify individuals whom you would expect to be bright or clever. They do this quite well, showing reasonable correlations with various measures of academic performance and job career success. However, both academic performance and career success are influenced by a variety of other factors such as motivation and opportunity. It follows, then, that the correlations with IQ can not always be expected to be very high – nor indeed are they always very high. IQ test scores also tend to correlate quite well with primary school teachers' judgments of children's brightness. Again, however, other fac-tors influence teachers' judgments of children, such as their sex (boys are underrated) and their personalities (eager, confident, outgoing children are overrated), so that the correlations are not as high as they might. The absence of any pure criterion of intelligence is a fundamental obstacle to demonstrating the true value of intelligence tests, and indeed to demon-strating the accuracy of the concept of intelligence on which they are based. This is why intelligence testing continues to be an area dogged with controversy.

What influences intelligence?

In this context the main issue that has been researched is whether IQ is a result of genetic inheritance or environmental influences. Is it a product of nature or nurture? The evidence suggests that both play a significant role.

Former US President Richard Nixon (on left), son of a county store and gas station owner, featured as a member of the Terman et al (1925) sample of gifted children (IQ above 140) followed up long-term. Though not all made it as far as Richard Nixon, they were more successful educationally, vocationally and health-wise than average (Oden, 1968).

Genetic inheritance

The evidence for the genetic inheritance of intelligence comes from studies of genetically related individuals. Where any characteristic is genetically inherited, closer relatives will on average be more alike on that factor than more distant relatives and of course more alike than individuals who are not related to each other. This is true of scores on IQ tests. The more closely individuals are related, the higher the correlations between their IQ scores.

Based on a summary of over 100 studies world-wide on the correlation between the IQ scores of relatives, the following average correlations (see Box 5.2 below for explanation of how correlation figures work) have been identified by Bouchard and McGee (1981).

Relationship	Correlation
Identical twins (reared together)	.86
Fraternal twins (reared together)	.60
Siblings (reared together)	.47
Parent/child	.40
Cousins	.15

BOX 5.2

NOTE ON CORRELATIONS

A correlation is a mathematical measure of association or similarity between two lists of figures. It can range from -1 to +1. The closer to 0 the correlation is, the less relationship there is between the two lists. The closer to +1 the correlation is, the more accurately larger figures in one list are matched by larger figures in the other. The closer to -1 the correlation is, the more it is the case that smaller figures in one list tend to be matched by larger in the other.

Take the following example:

IQ scores of identical twins

	Twin A	Twin B
Pair 1	100	98
Pair 2	130	126
Pair 3	147	150
Pair 4	88	94
Pair 5	111	120
Pair 6	103	105
Pair 7	107	103

As you can see, when one twin has a high or a low score the other twin tends to have a matching high or low score. This results in a correlation, which is closer to +1 (in this case .968). If, instead, high scores for Twin A were matched with low scores for Twin B in each pair, the result would be a negative correlation indicated by putting a minus sign before the figure.

Now take the following example:

IQ scores of pairs of unrelated adults picked at random

	Person A	Person B
Pair 1	100	136
Pair 2	130	88
Pair 3	147	120
Pair 4	88	94
Pair 5	111	89
Pair 6	103	116
Pair 7	107	90

The relationship between the IQ scores of each pair is random. This results in a correlation, which is quite close to 0, indicating that no real relationship exists between the two lists of figures. The actual computed correlation is, in fact, .045.

Clearly there is a pattern of lower correlations where the genetic relationship is less close. Identical twins share the same genes. Fraternal twins share, on average, 50 per cent of their genes, as do other siblings. Cousins share, on average, even fewer genes. However, the higher correlations in IQ among those who are closely related may be due to something other than genetics. It may be due to their also sharing a more similar environment. There is clear evidence in the figures for this possibility. Fraternal twins share no more genes than do ordinary siblings. Yet they tend to develop much more similar IQs. This must be due to their being treated more similarly and experiencing a more similar environment in general than do siblings. Of course, since identical twins look so alike, it is reasonable to suppose that they experience an even more similar environment (at home, in school and in their neighbourhoods) than fraternal twins and this may account for their higher correlations.

Bouchard and McGee (1981) also identified the following average correlations:

Relationship	Correlation
Identical twins (reared apart)	.72
Siblings (reared apart)	.24
Foster parent/child	.31

An analysis of these figures offers more definite support for the notion that intelligence is influenced by genetic inheritance. It is reasonable to assume that identical twins reared apart by different foster parents or adoptive parents are subjected to environments that differ more than those of fraternal twins reared together. Yet the identical twins still develop more similar IQs. This must be due to their genetic similarity. Similarly siblings, even when reared apart, are still more alike in IQ terms than cousins. It is also notable that children raised by their bio-logical parents develop IQs more similar to them than do children who are fostered compared to their foster parents. It is reasonable to assume that the rearing influences would be broadly the same in both cases, but the children and their biological parents share common genes, which must account for the greater similarity in their IQs

Exactly how much of the variation between individuals in intelli-gence is accounted for by genetic inheritance is still a matter of debate. Different experts have arrived at differing estimates. Based on an anal-ysis of the major studies to date, Bouchard (1998) suggests that the figure lies between 60 per cent and 80 per cent. At the moment great advances are being made in the science of genetics. Before long it may be possible to be more definite about how strong a contribution genetic inheritance makes to intelligence.

Environmental influences

If genetic inheritance accounts for, say, 60 per cent of the variability in intelligence, then the other 40 per cent must be accounted for by various environmental influences. Evidence on the nature of those envi-ronmental influences comes from a variety of research sources, which will be discussed below. First, two striking, though controversial, research studies will be examined.

The Skeels and Dye and the Schmidt Studies

In 1939 Harold Skeels and Harold Dye presented a paper at the annual convention of the American Association on Mental Deficiency in Chicago. They reported on a study they had conducted where 13 children were transferred from an Iowa orphanage to an institution for feeble-minded (retarded) children nearby and cared for there for the subsequent two years. The transfer arose after Skeels and Dye (a psychologist and a doctor) began to suspect that the very low level of personal attention given to the children in the orphanage was retarding their intellectual development. The experience of the children in the orphanage was characterised by a profound lack of mental stimulation. Contact with adults was largely limited to feeding, dressing, bathing and toilet details. In contrast, the 13 children transferred (aged from seven months to three years, mean age, 19.4 months at time of transfer) experienced a very stimulating environment in the institution for feeble-minded children. They were the only babies there. As a result they were given a lot of attention, not only from the adult staff, but also from the more capable 'feeble-minded' patients, who in actual fact were mainly adults ranging in age from 18 to 50, though their mental ages ranged from five to 12.

After two years the average IQ of the 13 children was compared to a comparison group who had remained behind in the orphanage. The report showed dramatic gains for the experimental group. On average their IQ scores had risen by 27.5 points over the two years, while the comparison group showed a drop of 26.2 points. The precise figures must be treated with some scepticism, due to the difficulties of accurately measuring young childrens' IQs. Nevertheless, it is clear that a considerable improvement in intelligence had been achieved by placing children in a more stimulating environment. Skeels and Dye were unsure as to what precisely were the ingredients of the environment that helped stimulate intellectual development. A general description of the characteristics of the environment for the children was given, as follows:

> '... love and affection by one or more interested adults; a wealth of play materials and ample space and opportunity for play with supervision and

*direction; varied experiences such as pre-school or kindergarten atten-
dance and opportunity to be in group gatherings …'*

(Skeels and Dye, 1939)

In 1946 another study was published showing dramatic improvements in IQ, this time of adolescents, being brought about by environmental intervention (Schmidt, 1946). The subjects of this study were 254 adolescents aged 12-14, with an average IQ of 54 – well within the range of mental retardation. The intervention involved a three-year training programme in three special schools. The programme was comprehensive and intensive covering all kinds of skills, from personal behaviour to academic skills to pre-employment experience. By the end of the programme the adolescents' IQ had risen to an average of 72. Five years after the end of the programme their IQ scores were reported to have improved to an average of 89 – very close to normal intelligence. The average gain in IQ exceeded 30 points.

These studies, particularly the Schmidt report, are still regarded as very controversial. They reported truly dramatic increases in IQ, increases of a magnitude not approached in any study since. Furthermore, the outcome of the Schmidt study suggested that IQ remains, even in adolescence, a highly malleable or changeable characteristic of humans. There is no doubt that IQ is affected by the type of environmental influences indicated in the two studies. However, that it can be changed to the extent reported in both studies and at the life stage suggested by Schmidt does not conform to the weight of subsequent research findings.

Further evidence of environmental influence on IQ has since been sought through a variety of means, including adoption studies, comparisons of children reared by their parents with those reared by special child-care workers and examination of the effects of pre-school education.

Pre-school interventions

Particularly in the US and Canada, there have been a variety of pre-school interventions designed to improve the intellectual ability of children from disadvantaged homes. The most famous of these programmes is the *Head Start* Project commenced in the 1960s in a variety of major

US cities. The approach used within *Head Start* varied from area to area. A typical approach, however, was to have special teachers visit the children at home and play with children – building with blocks, naming colours, looking at pictures and teaching them concepts such as 'rough-smooth' and 'big-little'. The teachers also taught the parents how to carry out such activities with their children. The theory behind this was that children from more affluent backgrounds are much more likely to receive such attention from their parents and it was suggested that this might account for the significant intellectual advantage such children have when they arrive in school. In some of these pre-school interventions, samples of children who had been in the programmes were compared with matched samples of children who had not.

The results are a source of considerable disagreement and controversy among psychologists, not least because conclusions reached have considerable implications for government funding for such programmes. Some writers have chosen to interpret the findings as a major success for pre-school intervention (e.g. Atkinson et al, 1993). Others (e.g. Locurto, 1991) have reported the very opposite picture. The more convincing case appears to have been made by the sceptics. It seems that the improvements in IQ have been short-term and that the advantage of those on the programmes over those not on the programmes disappear over time. Pre-school interventions offer only limited evidence, therefore, of environmental influences on intelligence.

Adoption studies

Studies of adopted children have excited much interest as a means of estimating how much can IQ be affected by environment – especially by the home and parenting environment. The key to the value of studying adopted children is that any relationship found with the IQ of their adoptive parents must be down to environment since there is no genetic relationship between them. The most interesting question is whether children from disadvantaged backgrounds who are adopted into affluent middle-class families develop IQs that are like those of their adoptive parents or whether they remain comparable to children who remain in disadvantaged backgrounds. Based on four separate studies (see Box 5.3), which reported clear findings on this issue, Locurto (1991) concludes that an improvement of up to 10 or 12 IQ points results from such adoptions. This, of course, is not to say that only 10 or 12 IQ points are due to environment and the rest is down to heredity. It simply means that the difference in the environment between the disadvantaged backgrounds from which the children come and the nature of the affluent homes in which they are brought up account for a jump in IQ of that much. This is clear evidence that environment plays a part – how big a part is not indicated.

The relationship between IQ and socio-economic status alluded to in the last paragraph would seem itself to suggest that intelligence is affected by environmental conditions. According to Locurto: 'it is one of social science's most reliable findings that differences in social class are associated with differences in IQ' (Locurto, 1991, p. 93).

While individuals with relatively high and low IQ scores are to be found in all social classes, there are a disproportionate number of individuals with low IQ in the poorer social classes and a disproportionate number of individuals with higher IQ scores in the richer social classes. It is tempting to immediately assume that this represents the differences in environment between the social classes. The problem is that it may not be the social class (and its associated environment) that causes the intelligence scores. It may be that it is intelligence that influences social class membership. To the extent that intelligence is genetically inherited, the genes associated with lower IQ are passed down through certain families. This in turn causes the children in each generation to develop low IQs, which goes on to prevent them doing well educationally and in their careers, thereby keeping them in a low social class.

The opposite pattern may apply among the better-off social classes. It is in this context that the adoption studies are of interest (see Box 5.2 below). There is no particular reason to suppose that children from lower social classes put up for adoption are genetically advantaged over those reared by their own parents. The fact that such children, when adopted into higher social class families, go on to develop higher IQs than comparable children not adopted strongly suggests that the change in environment produces the improvement in IQ. If genetics alone were responsible for IQ, then this improvement would not happen.

BOX 5.3

CONTRASTED ENVIRONMENTS ADOPTION STUDIES

Skodak and Skeels (1949) – a study of 180 children, the majority of whom had been placed in foster homes before six months of age. The average IQ of their biological mothers was 86 (based on a study of 63 of them). No IQ data existed on their biological fathers but their educational level was about average and their occupations below average. The average IQ of the adopted children at age 14 was 114, much higher than would be expected had they remained with their biological parents in their social background. The study suggests that the increase in IQ was due to the higher social class (educational/ occupational) backgrounds of the adoptive parents.

Scarr and Weinberg (1976) – a study of 97 black children adopted by upper-middle class white foster parents. At age seven the children had an average IQ of 106, 16 points above the average for the black population in the area of the US from which most of the children came. The interpretation of these findings is rendered more difficult by the fact that some of the children were half white and the group as a whole may have come from more advantaged backgrounds than black children do on average in the US. Nevertheless, some gain in IQ due to a more favourable environment seems to have taken place.

Schiff and Lewontin (1986) – study of 32 French children from very deprived socio-economic backgrounds (poorest 16 per cent) who were adopted by foster-parents in the top 5 per cent as regards socio-economic status. IQ data existed for biological siblings of 20 of the 32 children. The average IQ of the siblings was 95. The average IQ of the adopted children was 107. The suggestion is that the adopted children would have had IQ scores much closer to their siblings had they not been adopted into home environments more conducive to the development of IQ.

Capron and Duyme (1989) – comparison study of 38 children from high and low socio-economic classes who were adopted by foster-parents of either high or low socio-economic status. Children from low status backgrounds developed significantly higher IQs when adopted by high status adoptive parents (average IQ = 104) than if adopted by low status adoptive parents (average IQ = 92). The same pattern was found for children from high status backgrounds (average IQ, 120 vs. 108). The children were tested after an average of 14 years with their adoptive families. This again demonstrates the potential of an advantaged environment to enhance IQ.

The Israeli studies

Another source of evidence for the impact of environment (again rearing experiences) on intelligence comes from Israel. Israel is largely a country of immigrants and their descendants. The Jewish population has its origins either in Europe or in Arabic (Middle Eastern) countries. The average IQ of Jews who are descended from people of European origin is considerably higher than those descended from immigrants from Arabic countries. This difference between the two groups disappears, however, if children are reared in the Kibbutzim – communal settlements unique to Israel where children are not primarily raised by their parents but are entrusted to the care of specially trained child-care workers (Smilansky, 1974). The explanation appears to lie in different child-rearing practices. Jews of Arabic country origin interact much less with their children. Children are expected to be more passive. This reduces the amount of intellectual stimulation they receive, an environmental variable long associated with intelligence. In the Kibbutzim children of all backgrounds receive the same rearing and while there is still considerable variability in IQ among individuals (evidence of genetic influence on IQ), the differences are not associated with country of parental origin.

Why do pre-school interventions not raise IQ in the long term?

If evidence from diverse sources such as adoption studies and Kibbutzim rearing supports the idea that a richer, more stimulating environment improves IQ, why have pre-school intervention studies failed to convincingly demonstrate the same effect? The answer probably lies in the scale and duration of the intervention where the improved IQ has been shown. Adoption, for example, involves a complete life change.

Pre-school interventions studied typically involved a limited number of hours intervention over a few years. Otherwise, the lives of the children remained the same. The scale and duration of environmental change involved in the programmes such as *Head Start* were probably not near enough to offset the effects of a deprived environment in the longer term.

Other environmental factors

While most of the evidence on environmental influences on IQ, as we have just discussed, centres on rearing practices and intellectual stimulation, it is important to recognise that there are a wide variety of other environmental factors that have the potential to inhibit the development of intelligence. Among those associated with lowered IQ are:

1. malnutrition (pre- and post-natal);
2. illness in mother during pregnancy (e.g., rubella);
3. childhood illness;
4. exposure of mother to toxins during pregnancy (radiation, nicotine, alcohol, narcotics, certain medications);
5. exposure to toxins in childhood (e.g., high atmospheric concentrations of lead);
6. anoxia (lack of oxygen flow to brain) during birth.

Toxins, anoxia and both malnutrition and illness of mother during pregnancy all have their impact on IQ through brain damage. Childhood illness and childhood malnutrition, if not directly causing brain damage, may have their effects through reducing the activity of children and their capacity to gain the necessary stimulation to encourage brain development.

BOX 5.4

WHAT IS MEANT BY INFLUENCE ON VARIANCE IN IQ?

If we are to accept that upwards of 60 per cent in the variance in IQ is accountable for by genetic inheritance, what exactly are we accepting? We are concluding that the observed differences in IQ among the members of the population at large have come about more as a consequence of differences in their genetic make-up than differences in their environment such as the way they were reared by their parents, their differing diet, states of health and so on. We should note two things however:

1. The nature of environmental influences and the variation in environmental influences is not fixed.
2. The proportion of population variance in IQ accountable for through genetic and environmental factors does not tell us how much genetic or environmental factors have contributed to any one person's level of IQ.

The importance of the first point can be appreciated if we think of what would happen if it were possible to establish conclusively the best possible environment (rearing practices, food, protection from illness and toxins etc.) for the enhancement of IQ and if this environment were then made available to all children. In this ideal set of circumstances, any remaining variance in IQ would have to be as a result of genetic differences since environment would be at a perfect level for all. Genetic inheritance would now account for 100 per cent of the variance. A perfect environment may be a fanciful notion but all modern advanced societies are making stringent efforts to provide children with an environment that is conducive to their development. To the extent that those efforts are successful, the overall average of IQ should rise in the population and the amount of variance accounted for by genetic inheritance should increase.

The second point above is intimately related to the first. It may be the case that at the moment 40 per cent or less of the observed variance in IQ throughout the population is accounted for by environmental factors but it does not follow that if we take any one individual that this will tell us how he or she came to have his or her IQ score. An individual may well be born with the genes that should lead to a superior level of IQ but if he or she were unfortunate enough to be sufficiently neglected in early childhood – such as was the fate of the children in the Iowa orphanage where Skeels and Dye worked – then s/he would not be expected to rise in IQ terms to 60 per cent of his/her potential. The outcome may well be much worse. Irrespective of genetic inheritance the development of IQ can be altogether undermined by exposure to a bleak enough environment.

The converse is not true, however, to the same extent. Irrespective of how advantageous the environment is, an individual lacking the appropriate genes will not develop an exceptionally high IQ. The best the environment can do is enable each individual to reach his or her potential. The worst the environment can do is eliminate all potential, as in the case of severe brain damage due to injury or anoxia.

Race and intelligence

Very considerable controversy has raged many times over the last hundred years in the pages of psychological journals and in the popular press about the relationship between intelligence and race – specifically over whether certain races genetically inherit a superior IQ to other races. Not surprisingly, the debate has been intimately associated with the whole issue of racism, where one people or race attempt to assert their self-styled 'natural superiority' over some other race or people. Central to assertions of natural superiority are claims to genetic superiority in intelligence – a characteristic that rightly or wrongly is seen as the defining feature of what it is to be human.

A supposed natural inferiority of intellect has been used to justify a great variety of abuses against races or people so defined, not least of which has been the treatment of black people in America, a treatment which has included slavery and legalised segregation.

On the question of race and intelligence, the focus is still largely on African-Americans. This focus is often racist in origin. There is, however, an undisputed feature of African-Americans which requires explanation. On average they have performed on IQ tests roughly 10-15 IQ points lower than white Americans (Atkinson et al, 1993, p. 484; Ogbu, 1986, p. 32; Hernstein and Murray, 1996, pp. 276–7). Furthermore, the difference reduces but does not disappear when social class is the same. Similar findings exist for black West Indians in the UK. This data has been seized upon by those who support the notion that white people are naturally intellectually superior to black people. What evidence exists to support or contradict the genetic explanation suggested by the racists? And if genetic differences do not account for the IQ differences, what does?

Victims of racism: concentration camp survivors at Dachau after World War II. The Nazis claimed that races such as Jews, Slavs and Gypsies were intellectually subnormal, then used this propaganda to justify their subjugation and genocide.

From a biological perspective, the suggestion that white people inherit a superior intellect seems immediately doubtful. Genetically the differences between black and white people are negligible and superficial. They are largely responses to evolution in hotter and colder climates. The within-group genetic differences, insofar as they have been identified, are greater than the differences between the two groups. Quite simply, black and white people are biologically different in only a very superficial way.

What then accounts for the 10-15 IQ point deficit? It is not purely down to social class, since equalising social class does not eliminate the difference. One possibility is that the intelligence tests are biased in favour of white people. This does not appear to be the answer either. There are lots of other minority groups in the US and the UK, such as immigrants from Asia, who would be expected to be similarly disadvantaged by tests developed in the US or the UK. They do not get such low scores. Furthermore, great efforts are made by test developers to avoid items or questions that advantage any group over another.

The most coherent explanation offered to date comes from Ogbu (1986). He quotes data from various countries around the world, such as India and Japan, showing that where a group occupies the status of an 'inferior caste' in any society that group will tend to have on average an IQ score 10-15 points lower than the average in that society. An 'inferior caste' is a group into which one is born, out of which there is no escape (unlike a low social class which can be escaped by education and income) and the members of which are regarded as social inferiors within the dominant society.

This is the status occupied by the Harijans of India (lowest group in the ancient Hindu caste system, known as 'untouchables'). It is the status also occupied by the Buraku of Japan (a group whose ancestors were legislatively restricted to the low status occupation of leather tanning up to 1871 – still regarded as inferiors within Japanese society). What is interesting about these two groups is that they are not racially distinct from the rest of their society but show a 10-15 point deficit in IQ just like the racially distinct African-Americans and the racially distinct UK West Indians. It is a further striking point that among Buraku immigrants to the US, their children perform on intelligence tests and educational activities at least as well as the children of other Japanese immigrants. In the US their separate status is not identified and they receive similar treatment to any other Japanese immigrant. They have effectively escaped from their inferior caste and with this their IQ problems disappear.

Ogbu (1986) suggests that African-Americans and UK West Indians are members of inferior castes within those societies. In a variety of ways they are made to feel inferior purely because of the racial group to which they belong. And because the primary mark of the group is to be black they cannot escape membership by any act of their own. The main effect of this is to produce a way of thinking that emphasises the unfairness of society and the futility of trying to work 'within the system' so as to get on.

Over generations less value is placed on education (seen as a route to success for white but not black people). The importance of developing the skills necessary in high status jobs is not accepted (there is no point in doing so since the system limits black people to menial work). Educational success and the skills, such as communication and problem solving, necessary in high status jobs are the very factors which intelligence tests are designed to predict. It is not surprising then that a group that has for generations seen no relevance to themselves for either the skills or the contexts in which they are used will fail to pass on such skills to its children.

Essentially the very activities, (to measure intelligence one has no choice but to measure specific activities or skills; there is simply no direct route to measuring intelligence) which we use to measure intelligence are the ones that are viewed as irrelevant by African-Americans and UK West Indians. Of course, despite normal genetic intelligence, the failure to develop the skills that underpin IQ tests leaves these groups at an enormous disadvantage in their societies. The abilities that underpin IQ tests are the same ones that enable success in mainstream society. They are the skills one needs to get good qualifications, good jobs and to play an effective part in the social and political system.

There is positive evidence emerging from the US that the drive against racism, commenced in the 1960s with the abolition of racial segregation, is reaping dividends. The degree to which being black consigns individuals to an inferior social caste is reducing. Going together with this there is evidence of improving intellectual and educational performance among the African-American population.

INTELLIGENCE, INTELLIGENCE TESTING AND CULTURE FAIRNESS

Before closing, it is important to emphasise some points made earlier about what intelligence is and about its measurement. Whatever intelligence really is, and that is a matter of some debate, it can never be measured directly. There is no option but to identify tasks and skills that represent intelligent behaviour. Such tasks and skills will, inevitably, differ depending on the type of society you are operating within.

Intelligence tests such as we have been talking about all have their origins in modern, industrialised societies. It is to be expected that tests developed to measure intelligence in other societies, say, hunter-gatherer societies, would be based on different skills and activities. However, if you live in a modern industrial society such as Ireland it is no use to just have the intellectual skills relevant to a hunter gatherer society. One needs to have the intellectual skills that enable one to get on in the society in which one lives.

The key characteristic of a useful IQ test, then, is to predict aspects of success and not to be culture-fair (i.e. not to give an advantage to one culture over another) at the expense of a loss of predictive validity. Doubtless, intelligence exists as a partially inherited universal feature of the human condition. Its measurement, however, can not be universal. To measure intelligence one must measure it through skills that are important and have a practical use in the society concerned. At its roots, then, intelligence may well be universal but its measurement will remain a culturally relative process.

SUMMARY

Intelligence is normally understood and defined in terms of its effects. It is usually described as a characteristic that enables individuals to solve problems, think rationally and deal effectively with their environment.

The characteristic that enables us to do those things is a complex interaction between brain structure or functioning and information processing skills.

Intelligence is always measured in terms of its effects. Tests are used to measure a range of cognitive or mental skills that have been shown to be important. The choice of skills to be measured in intelligence tests is very significantly a product of the culture from which the tests come – that of modern technologically advanced society. The skills demanded by education in this society have had a particular influence. Intelligence tests were originally devised in France to help identify children who were too weak intellectually to cope with normal schooling and needed special help.

Intelligence tests are norm-referenced tests. The scores reported for individuals represent how well they have done relative to the population at large. The first method devised for reporting intelligence test scores was the Intelligence Quotient or IQ. The original definition of IQ was

Mental Age divided by Chronological Age, the result being then multiplied by 100. In adults this definition has to be corrected because of the fact that mental age stops improving in the mid-teens. Another approach now used to report intelligence test scores uses what are known as standard scores, as a measure of how far from the average a person's performance lies. This allows for reporting of scores in terms of which per cent or percentile of the population range the scores falls within.

Intelligence is 'normally' distributed. This means that half the population score above and half below the average. The percentage of the population with scores any particular distance above or below the average is known. In IQ terms the average is 100. Fifty per cent of the population lie within the scores 90-110. The remaining half are split 25 per cent above and below those scores.

Intelligence is measured in accordance with a number of factors or skills, which are to some degree independent of one another. Intelligence tests, therefore, report a number of sub-scores as well as an overall score. Individuals will show some variation of performance across the factors. Because relatively high correlations exist among the various factors, it is assumed that something is preventing individuals' scores on the various skills tested from deviating too widely from each other. This factor is taken to be 'general intelligence' or 'g', a common information processing skill, which underpins all intelligent activity.

The reliability of intelligence tests is good, in that scores for individuals do not normally vary much over time. Their validity is harder to prove. They do show reasonable correlations with educational and vocational success, but since many other factors are known to influence such success it is not possible to say with any certainty how high those correlations should actually be. Ethnic minorities in English-speaking countries and elsewhere in the world have tended to perform relatively poorly on intelligence tests, leading to accusations of culture bias. Efforts to devise tests more sensitive to those minority cultures have resulted in lowered correlations with educational and vocational success. The tests are doubtless a product of the dominant culture of technologically advanced countries but so is everything of importance that they might seek to predict in those countries.

There is very strong evidence indicating that intelligence is partly a function of genetic inheritance. Similarity in test scores increases with closeness of genetic relationship between individuals. More strikingly, identical twins separated shortly after birth and raised without contact by different families due to separate adoptions have been found as adults to have very similar intelligence test scores, more similar on average than non-identical twins reared together by their own natural parents. The greater similarity must be accounted for by the fact that identical twins in all cases share the very same genes while non-identical or fraternal twins share on average just half their genes.

Identical twins, despite sharing the same genes, do not show exactly the same intelligence test scores. Furthermore, when reared separately, the similarity in their scores falls appreciably. The same is true of other siblings. The intelligence test scores of adopted children correlate with their adoptive parents who are not genetically related to them. Environmental aspects clearly have some influence on the development of intelligence. There is convincing evidence that a stimulating environment in early childhood is essential. This evidence comes from a number of sources involving circumstances where it was possible to compare the intelligence test scores of children raised in stimulating environments with matched samples of children raised in less stimulating circumstances. In addition to a lack of stimulation, there are a variety of other environmental factors, such as disease and exposure to toxins, which negatively impact on intellectual development. The precise proportions of variance in intelligence accountable for by environmental and genetic factors are very difficult to compute. The evidence suggests upwards of 60 per cent being accounted for by genetic inheritance.

A controversial issue for a long time has been the question of whether different races, particularly black and white people, inherit different levels of intelligence. Much of the debate has been coloured by racism. The hard evidence used by those proposing a genetic difference is that ethnic minorities such as African-Americans and those of Afro-Caribbean origin in the UK have tended to perform poorly on intelligence tests. The question is why? Socio-economic and test culture bias explanations do not appear to adequately explain their poor test performances.

A more convincing explanation drawing on data from minority groups around the world has been offered by Ogbu (1986). It can be called the 'inferior caste' theory and is based on the finding that any group that is treated within a dominant society as naturally and inescapably inferior tends to internalise its status. People in this group see no point in attempting to pass on to their children the intellectual skills necessary for success in that society, since they are debarred from success by virtue of their group membership. This results in children failing to appreciate the value of and to pick up the skills measured by intelligence tests. African-Americans and those of Afro-Caribbean origin in the UK fit this picture.

A further point from a physiological perspective that casts doubt on any genetic relationship between race and intelligence is that the within-race genetic differences are much greater than the average between race differences, which are small and have mainly to do with superficial characteristics.

REVIEW QUESTIONS

1. Describe the origins of intelligence tests and how those origins may have limited the value of intelligence test scores.
2. (a) It is more accurate to speak of intelligences rather than intelligence. Explain why this is so.
   (b) Explain how intelligence tests operate to take account of this fact.
3. Describe the process of intelligence-testing, including how scores are reported so as to give meaningful information.
4. Intelligence is partly a function of genetic inheritance, partly a function of environmental influences. Discuss.
5. Discuss the evidence against the notion that white people inherit a superior level of intelligence to black people.

REFERENCES

Atkinson, R.L., Atkinson, R.C., Smith, E.E. and Bem, D.J., (1993), *Introduction to Psychology*, 11th Edn, Orlando: Harcourt Brace.
Binet, A. and Simon, T., (1905), 'New Methods for the Diagnosis of the Intellectual Level of Subnormals', *Annals of Psychology*, 11, 191.

Bouchard, T.J. and McGue, M. (1981), Familial Studies of intelligence: A review, *Science*, 212, 1055–1059.

Bouchard, T.J., Jr., (1998), Genetic and environmental influences on adult intelligence and special mental abilities, *Human Biology*, April, 70, 2, 257–279.

Capron, C. and Duyme, M., (1989), 'Assessment of Effects of Socio-Economic Status on IQ in Full Cross-Fostering Study', *Nature*, 340, 552-554.

Gardner, H., (1983), *Frames of Mind: The Theory of Multiple Intelligence*, New York: Basic Books.

Goleman, D., (1996), *Emotional Intelligence*, London: Bloomsbury.

Herrnstein, R.J. and Murray, C., (1996), *The Bell Curve*, New York: Free Press Paperbacks.

Locurto, C., (1991), *Sense and Nonsense about IQ, The Case for Uniqueness*, Praeger: New York.

Nash, J.M., (1997), Fertile Minds, *Time*, 10 February.

Oden, M.H., (1968), 'The Fulfillment of Promise: 40-year Follow Up of the Terman Gifted Group', *Genetic Psychology Monographs*, 77, 3-93.

Ogbu, J.U., (1986), 'The Consequences of the American Caste System', in Neisser, U. (ed.) *The School Achievement of Minority Children*, Hillsdale, NJ: Erlbaum.

Ree, M.J. and Earles, J.A., (1990), *Differential Validity of a Differential Aptitude Test. AFHRL–TR–89–59*. Brooks Air Forces Base, Tex: Manpower and Personnel Division.

Scarr, S. and Weinberg, R.A., (1976), 'IQ Test Performance of Black Children Adopted by White Families', *American Psychologist*, 31, 726-739.

Schiff, M. and Lewontin, (1986), *Education and Class: The Irrelevance of IQ Genetic Studies*, Oxford, England: Claredon Press.

Schmidt, B.G., (1946), Changes in personal, social and intellectual behaviour of children originally classified as feebleminded, *Psychological Monographs*, 160, (5, Serial No. 281).

Skeels, H.M. and Dye, H.B., (1939), 'A Study of the Effects of Differential Stimulation on Mentally Retarded Children', *Proceedings of the American Association for Mental Deficiency*, 44, 114-136.

Skodak, M. and Skeels, H., (1949), 'A Final Follow Up Study of Children in Adoptive Homes', *Journal of Genetic Psychology*, 75, 85-125.

Smilansky, B., (1974), Paper presented at the American Educational Research Association, Chicago.

Sternberg, R.J., (1985), *Beyond IQ: A Triarchic Theory of Human Intelligence*, New York: Cambridge University Press.

Terman, L.M. et al, (1925), 'Genetic Studies of Genius', Vol. II, *Mental and Physical Traits of a Thousand Gifted Children*, Stanford, California: Stanford University Press.

Thorndike, R.L., (1986), The Role of General Ability in Prediction, *Journal of Vocational Behaviour*, 29, 332–339.

Wechsler, D., (1958), *The Measurement and Appraisal of Adult Intelligence*, Baltimore: Williams.

Chapter 6

Personality

LEARNING OBJECTIVES

Having read this chapter you should be able to:

- explain what psychologists mean by the term 'personality';
- describe the *nomothetic* approach to understanding personality
  - distinguishing the trait from the type approach,
  - outlining the main features of the 'Big Five' personality factors;
- explain how personality tests are developed;
- describe the influences on personality, including
  - evidence of genetic origins,
  - evidence for and nature of environmental influences;
- describe the *idiographic* approach to understanding personality, including
  - psychodynamic theories,
  - behaviourist/social learning theories,
  - humanistic theories;
- outline the main applications of personality theory.

INTRODUCTION

The story of Californian, Edmund Emil Kemper is not by any means unique. Around the world there have been many others of his like, both more and less well known. That is a disturbing thought.

He was raised primarily by his mother, a socially ambitious university administrator. She married several different men in the course of Edmund's upbringing and apparently showed him little real affection. His younger sister was later able to recount some of the odd behaviours that had disturbed her about him when he was still a child. He developed a fascination with execution and would have her blindfold him so that he could stage his own imaginary death in a gas chamber. He chopped the head and hands off a doll she had been given as a present. Before he was ten he graduated to killing cats, the first one by burying it alive, another by an attack with a machete. He fantasised about killing people. Eventually he did.

At the age of 14 he was living by his own wishes with his grandparents on a ranch. Without warning one day he picked up a rifle and shot dead his grandmother as she sat at the kitchen table. When his grandfather returned he shot him dead too, then rang his mother and told her what he had just done. He spent four years in a secure mental hospital but was released on parole at age 21. He quickly formulated a grand plan of action. He would become a serial killer. Between May 1972 and February 1973, he murdered and mutilated the bodies of six young women. On one occasion during that time he was interviewed by two psychiatrists associated with the parole board. They concluded that he was no longer a risk to society and recommended that he should now be allowed to get on with his life in the ordinary way despite his previous homicides. As they interviewed him the severed head of his latest victim sat in the boot of his car out in the car park.

All six victims he had picked up in his car as hitch hikers. The first four he took to secluded places before killing them with a knife or by suffocation. The last two he just suddenly shot as he drove along chatting to them.

Edmund Kemper had one last mission to complete. He had decided to kill his mother. He knocked her unconscious with a hammer as she slept in bed and then slashed her throat. He decapitated her as he had some of the others. The next day he decided to kill her close friend, a woman named Sally. On the pretext that his mother had cooked a surprise dinner, he lured her to the house and choked her to death. He got into his car and drove east hour after hour without stopping. He had no clear idea of what he wanted to do. In Eastern Colorado he pulled up at a public phone booth, rang the police back home, several of whom he often drank with, and confessed to what he had done. He had great difficulty being believed but after a long wait local police arrived and arrested him.

Behaviour like Edmund Kemper's seems to defy all possibility of explanation. Immediately one finds oneself retreating to the comforting explanation that he was simply insane. This puts him beyond the realm of responsibility. Yet he was not insane. He knew perfectly well what he was doing when he was doing it. He planned his actions in advance and afterwards methodically concealed his tracks, of which there were a great many bloody ones. Otherwise, in his dealings with people he behaved normally. He was in control.

Any explanations he offered, and he talked a great deal, were striking for one thing. They were explanations that would account for something but just not remotely for something as appalling as what he had done. He grew up feeling angry and unhappy because his mother belittled him. He wanted her love but she just criticised him. He seemed to generalise from her to all women and felt inadequate before them. None of this is particularly unusual. However, it was coupled with a failure to empathise with others. While most of us have a sense of how others feel, Edmund Kemper lived in his own world. He could not identify with others so there was nothing to make him feel bad about killing them. In simple terms, he had an abnormal personality. Where did he get it from? No doubt he was born with part of it and his unhappy upbringing finished the process. It is thought – but difficult to prove – that a lack of ability to empathise with others is not so unusual. Most such people do not kill others. They just tend to treat them rather badly and feel no guilt about it. It is only when the idea of killing emerges, possibly by accident, coupled with the anger to motivate it, that events will take a turn like they did in Kemper's life. Mostly those with abnormal personalities will live out their lives without doing anything terribly extreme. That unbelievable acts like those of Kemper's can be explained away by concepts as mundane as personality and circumstances – not by madness or demonic possession – may seem disturbing. Yet personality is the core of what we are. It is at the heart of our humanity or inhumanity. Personality is as much accountable for the behaviour of Edmund Kemper as for that of Oscar Schindler or Fr. Maximilian Kolbe. Personality and circumstances dictate what we do.

There are few characteristics that define a person to the same extent as personality. Initially, appearance may count for a lot, but in the long run few would disagree that personality is the key to whether we can get on with someone or not, whether we wish to engage with or avoid an individual. Those who suspected Kemper's true personality kept well clear of him. Unfortunately for all of us in our dealings with others, key aspects of personality are often not so easy to detect.

It is not just in the private domain that personality matters. It is also a large component in vocational or professional success. Employers are all acutely aware of this characteristic of employees. Many would argue that in the workplace it matters as much or even more than intelligence or learning. Almost all employers make an effort to judge job candidates' personality before employing them, so as to match them to the tasks they will have to perform. They may not do this very well but few fail to attempt to make predictions about personality, on which job selection decisions hinge. Most employers attempt to judge personality from interviews. Research has shown this method to produce judgments that are, as often as not, mistaken. It is not surprising, then, that more effective ways of measuring personality are in great demand. We will be discussing such measures below.

Quite apart from the area of work, personality has been shown to have profound effects on other dimensions of life. There is much evidence that a variety of physical illnesses, such as heart disease, are experienced more often by individuals with certain particular personality profiles. There is an intimate relationship, too, between personality and mental health. There is no aspect of experience that remains untouched by this central characteristic of the human state.

WHAT IS PERSONALITY?

In the paragraphs above, the concept of personality has been discussed without an attempt to explain what is meant by the term. You probably didn't notice. It was not as if it was something you had rarely heard of. We all use the term to describe others. We assume that others know what we mean. Behavioural scientists, however, cannot afford to make such assumptions. We must be clear as to which aspects of a human we are including under the term. We must define personality.

Once we begin to consider the issue of definition, it proves to be trickier than it initially appeared. Let's ask a number of questions.

Are attitudes part of personality?

Is a person's personality fixed or does it change from time to time?

Does it come from genetic factors or is it a product of the environment?

Can we deliberately change our own personalities?

Is personality to be inferred from how one feels, how one thinks or how one behaves, or from all three?

Do all of our thoughts, feelings and behaviours reflect our personalities or are our personalities responsible only for some of them?

As an exercise you should attempt to answer the above questions using what you have understood personality to mean up to now as the basis of your answers. Then, after you have read the chapter, ask yourself the same questions again. See if your answers have changed.

A careful examination of the writings of psychologists on personality reveals that there are a number of different understandings of what exactly is meant by the term. Hence, different psychologists will offer different definitions. The main issue of disagreement centres on the extent to which personality is a fixed, stable characteristic of humans. To some psychologists it is taken to be a much more fixed characteristic than others take it to be. But first we need to understand what exactly are we saying is either fixed or else open to change.

As a useful start let's take one definition of personality. It is:

'the total pattern of characteristic ways of thinking, feeling and behaving that constitute the person's distinctive method of relating to the environment'

(Kagan and Havemann, 1976, p. 376)

While this definition will not solve all our problems of understanding, it is a useful one to adopt as a starting point. The following key points should be noted about the definition:

Firstly, it describes personality as evident in 'thoughts', 'feelings' and 'behaviours'.

Secondly, not all thoughts, feelings and behaviours are relevant, only those that are characteristic of the person and that are in some way distinctive. By 'characteristic' we mean in effect **stable**; in other words, thoughts, feelings or behaviours that recur again and again across time and across situations. For example, shyness cannot be said to be a significant part of one's personality just because one was shy at the age of 15 or because one is shy on meeting somebody famous. To describe shyness as part of personality, it must be a feeling that keeps on happening. As for the word **distinctive**, a thought, a feeling or a behaviour cannot be said to be a part of one's personality if most people share it. Thinking that it is wrong for someone to criticise you for something that is not your fault does not define your personality. Most people are likely to think that way. Thinking that it is wrong for anyone ever to criticise anything you say or do is distinctive and would be part of someone's personality if they thought that way. It is a distinctive way of thinking. Most people do not think that way.

Thirdly, personality has to do with how the person relates to his/her environment as a whole. It is not something that matters only when dealing with other people, as is sometimes understood by the term. Whether you are inclined to persist or give up in the face of failure is an expression of your personality. Whether you are generally pessimistic or optimistic about the future is a part of your personality. Whether you like to read fact or fiction is an expression of your personality. None of these ways of thinking or behaving have to involve other people. Yet they are part of personality.

The main issue that this definition does not answer is how stable thoughts, feelings and behaviours must be before we call them part of personality.

Some psychologists will incline towards the view that we should only call the personality those aspects of the person that are very stable and can not really be changed. Such psychologists tend to view personality as significantly inherited through the genes. They will accept that there are other aspects of a person that can and do change over time and that most people see those aspects as part of personality as well. They choose, however, to define personality in a narrow way and view those changing aspects as not really personality at all.

Other psychologists, while accepting that there may be some aspects of personality that are genetically inherited and are very fixed and stable, also believe that there are many additional less fixed aspects that can change over time as a result of experience and personal insight. The disagreement is not so much about what is there or not there. It is more about what we should call it.

DEFINING PERSONALITY

Think of the larger circle (enclosing grey and black areas) as the person's total characteristic ways of thinking, feeling and behaving at a given time. Think of the black area as the person's ways that are stable throughout life. Some psychologists see only the black area as personality, while others view the entirety as personality.

DIFFERING WAYS OF LOOKING AT PERSONALITY

Arising out of the definitional debate discussed above, there are two broad views as to how personality should be viewed and understood. One is called the *nomothetic* approach, the other the *idiographic* approach. Without too much simplification it can be said that the nomothetic focuses largely on the black area in the above diagram, while the idiographic attends more to the grey area. Let's look at each in turn.

The nomothetic approach

'Nomothetic' means law-setting or law-giving. This approach to understanding personality starts with a number of assumptions, that in personality we are talking about something that:

1. conforms to a framework that makes it simple to understand –
   specifically that people's personalities differ in a finite number of
   ways and the differences are ones of quantity just like physical
   differences: to understand personality we have simply to identify
   what those differences are;
2. remains stable throughout lifetime, largely because it is a function
   of genetic inheritance;
3. can be measured, or, in other words, turned into, quantities of some
   kind: this in turn enables comparisons to be made between individuals on the basis of the measurements.

Historically, the nomothetic approach has resulted in two differing
attempts to explain personality: *type theories;* and *trait theories.*

Type theories

Down through history there were always those who sought to identify
the laws underpinning human personality. They tried to identify some
kind of structure or framework that would make the seemingly vast array
of differences to be found among humans simple and understandable.
Mostly such attempts resulted in what can be called *type theories* of personality. They tried to divide people up into distinct categories based on
their most obvious characteristics. The most famous of these is the
theory advanced around 400 BC by Hippocrates, a Greek philosopher and
physician. He suggested that all of humanity fell into four personality
types depending on which of the four bodily components was dominant
in that individual. In ancient Greece they did not know what the
material world (including living things) was made up of. We now know
that the known material universe consists of 105 basic elements and that
the human body is comprised of some of these joined together in molecules, which in turn make up the cell structure for the individual tissues
and so on. The ancient Greeks thought the basic elements were earth,
air, fire and water and that the body was made of four substances: blood,
black bile, bile and phlegm. The four personality types into which
Hippocrates thought all of humanity could be divided were as follows:

TABLE 6.1 – HIPPOCRATES' TYPE THEORY OF PERSONALITY

Personality type	Dominant body substance	Characteristics
Sanguine	Blood	Hopeful, confident
Melancholic	Black bile	Depressed, fearful
Choleric	Bile	Active, aggressive, angry
Phelgmatic	Phlegm	Sluggish, slow, apathetic

Despite its lack of a scientific basis, this theory of personality was influential right up into the Middle Ages. There were other type theories of personality also. One suggested that all people could be divided up into personality types based on the exact shape of their heads, particularly the pattern of bumps or unevenness on their skulls. Dividing people into types on this basis was known as phrenology. It had no more scientific basis than Hippocrate's theory. Astrology represents another theory of the same kind – categorising people on the basis of the star sign under which they were born.

Apart from the fact that none of the type theories mentioned have any scientific basis or have ever been shown to work, type theories in general suffer from one major deficiency. They impose much too simple a structure. Describing people as, say, hopeful, in general, only tells you about one aspect of their personalities. In addition to being hopeful, they may be a thousand other things: honest or dishonest, witty or dull, sociable or solitary. The list goes on and on. Dividing individuals into categories or types, even if a lot of categories are used, tells us in each case only one thing about the person. A better approach was obviously necessary. That better approach emerged eventually in trait theories.

Trait theories

This view dominated nomothetic thinking throughout the twentieth century and is now more or less unquestioned as the mechanism through which personality is measured. Psychologists with an idiographic bent of mind will, of course, take a different view. We will come to that presently. First let's see how the trait approach works.

The trait approach takes as its starting point the idea that people differ in their personalities in terms of a great number of traits or characteristics. Traits tend to correspond with words we use in our language every day to describe personality, words like shy, sociable, determined, optimistic, suspicious and so on. Gordon Allport (1897-1967), a US psychologist and important personality theorist, counted more than 4,000 words (adjectives) used in the English language to describe personality. While many of these words may mean essentially the same thing, it is clear that there are a great number of traits on which human personality can differ.

On each trait, people vary along a dimension from very high to very low. Take 'sociable'. Now and again you will come across extremely sociable individuals and now and again you will come across very un-sociable individuals. Most others will distribute in between. It is assumed that the actual distribution of any trait in the population as a whole will be what is known as a normal distribution. You will recall this as the way in which intelligence is distributed (see chapter 5). It means that a high proportion of individuals have scores close to the average and the further from the average you go, the fewer individuals you will find. Hence an extremely sociable person is much rarer than one who is average on that trait. The same is true of an extremely unsociable person.

Clearly, the trait approach to understanding personality allows for far greater complexity than the type approach described above. Now we have literally thousands of ways in which people differ. This seems, however, to leave us with too much complexity to allow for any practical measuring of any one person's overall personality. Fortunately, there is one fact which greatly simplifies the whole picture for us. Traits are generally not independent of one another. They tend to show very significant correl-ations. What this means is that individuals' positions on any one trait will be a very good predictor of their position on a whole range of other traits. Those high on one trait will also be high on many others. Those low on one trait will tend to be low on others. A few examples will suffice to illustrate the point. Those who are high on the trait 'helpful' tend also to be high on the trait 'trusting'. Those who are high on the trait 'imaginative' tend also to be high on the trait 'independent'.

The weight of research in recent years has led to the conclusion that all the traits we can use to describe personality cluster together into five major groups (Costa and McCrae, 1992, 1995; McCrae and John, 1992; Goldberg, 1993; Wiggins, 1996; McCrae and Costa, 1998). Each group represents a super-trait. Psychologists usually describe them as *factors*. The research on this is so consistent that psychologists have begun to call them the Big Five personality factors. They are summarised in Table 6.2 below. For many years psychologists have been examining the relationship between traits but had great difficulty in agreeing how many independent groups of traits or personality factors there actually were. Estimates had varied from two up to around 20. The problem lies in how you measure and estimate the degree of correlation between traits. It is only in the 1990s that a good deal of agreement has been arrived at on this subject. It is, of course, possible that the five-factor model of personality is not the final story.

TABLE 6.2 – THE BIG FIVE FACTOR MODEL OF PERSONALITY

FACTOR	TRAITS OR CHARACTERISTICS
Neuroticism	Worried – calm
	Insecure – secure
	Self-pitying – self-satisfied
Extraversion	Sociable – retiring
	Fun-loving – sober
	Affectionate – reserved
Openness	Imaginative – down-to-earth
	Preference for variety – preference for routine
	Independent – conforming
Agreeableness	Soft-hearted – ruthless
	Trusting – suspicious
	Helpful – uncooperative
Conscientiousness	Well-organised – disorganised
	Careful – careless

(From: Burger, (1997), p. 194)

Each of the factors is made up of many related traits. Like the traits that make them up, the factors show a 'normal' distribution in the population.

204 Introduction to Behavioural Science

This means that for, say, extroversion, a high proportion of people will be close to average with relatively fewer people being very high or very low on the factor. If you think about all the people you know, you will probably agree that while they do vary in how extravert they are, there are very few who are extremely extravert or the opposite, extremely introvert.

Another important characteristic of the five factors is that they are quite independent of one another. It is possible to be extremely high on one factor and yet be high, average or low on any of the others. One's position on one factor does not in any way predict one's position on the others.

Let's briefly consider what the factors mean. Some of the key traits are listed in Table 6.2 above. The easiest way to grasp what a factor means is to consider what someone who is very high on that factor will be like.

If you are high on **Neuroticism,** you will worry a good deal about things and find it difficult to be satisfied or happy. You will experience a lot of guilt feelings. You will tend to be insecure and pessimistic and you will tend to see life as mostly outside your control. You will not have a great sense of well being and instead will often feel 'under the weather' for no particular reason.

If you are very high on **Extraversion** you will have a great need for constant stimulation – for activity and for company. You are likely to know a lot of people and be very sociable. Solitary pursuits and the quiet life will not be for you. You will enjoy parties, having fun and playing practical jokes on others. You will tend to display your feelings easily, though your emotions will not be too deep or long-lasting.

If you are high on **Openness** you will be willing to take on board new ideas and put yourself in the way of them. You will not be fixed in your views. You will be curious and adventurous with a love of change and variety. You will not go along with ideas or fashions just because it is the done thing. Instead you will be independent in your way of thinking.

If you are high on **Agreeableness** you will be easy to get along with and find it easy to accept others. You will tend to trust people and not easily find fault with them. You will be soft-hearted and always willing to help or give the benefit of the doubt to others.

If you are high on **Conscientiousness,** you will be very trustworthy and reliable. You will always strive to do a good job and finish properly what you commit yourself to. You will plan and organise your affairs carefully. You will have a great deal of discipline and willpower.

Looking at the descriptions of the five factors you would be forgiven for thinking that the ideal would be to be very low on neuroticism and high on all of the other four. This is, however, a mistaken perspective. There is no universally good personality profile – it depends significantly on your circumstances.

Firstly it is probably best not to be too extreme on any factor. If you are too low on neuroticism, it means that you will worry about nothing and feel guilty for nothing. That is straying close to the personality profile of a psychopath – someone like Edmund Kemper, who experiences no sense of guilt no matter how awful their actions. Likewise being too high on extraversion would be a considerable obstacle to coping with the educational process. Reading books, sitting quietly in lectures, studying alone would all be very difficult.

Look carefully at the other factors and imagine what problems might arise for someone with extremely high or low scores.

A good way of thinking about personality profiles is to ask what kind of profile would suit various occupations. If you think hard you will probably find some occupation that suits someone who is relatively high or low on any of the factors. It may be difficult to find an occupation that particularly suits someone relatively low on conscientiousness. Employers generally like their workers to be towards the high end on this factor. It is easy to see why.

The overall point, however, is that it is best to view personality profiles as suitable or not to situations, not good or bad in themselves. A sales representative would benefit from being more extravert (because of the need to be more sociable) while an air traffic controller would benefit from being the opposite (because of the need to avoid distractions and spend long periods concentrating on radar screens).

Measuring personality traits

By far the most common approach to measuring personality is through self-report questionnaires or personality tests, as they are usually called.

They normally ask relatively simple questions with a multiple-choice format for answering. An example might be the following:

When travelling unaccompanied on a long bus journey, would you prefer to:

(a) *read a book;*

(b) *converse with a stranger who sits beside you.*

You will probably have already suspected that those who answer (a) are likely to be lower on the trait 'sociability' than those who answer (b). This reflects what is called 'face validity' – the question seems on the face of it to be measuring sociability. It is not necessary that questions in personality tests are face valid. They do, however, have to be valid in a more general sense. In other words there must be evidence from research that they are capable of differentiating between people on the trait that is being measured. Of course no trait would be measured by one question only. Take the above example. If it were our only measure of sociability on a given test (even assuming that it had been shown to be a very valid question for measuring sociability), all it could do would be to divide people into two categories – those less sociable (giving the answer (a)) and those more sociable (giving the answer (b)). To be able to place people on a dimension of sociability from high to low, we need several questions. Those who answer in the sociable direction on more questions will have the higher scores and those who answer in the sociable direction on fewer questions will be given the lower scores. In other words, your sociability score will depend on how many questions you answer in the sociable direction.

How are questions chosen for particular questionnaires? Let's assume initially that we are talking about an attempt to measure one particular personality trait such as sociability. Firstly, lots of face valid questions (or alternatively questions that previous research indicates to be valid for this trait) will be trialled on a sample of individuals. Questions that are given the same answers by most people will be discarded – they are failing to distinguish between people. The correlations between all pairs of questions will then be checked. There are computer programmes and sophisticated statistical procedures for doing this in practice. Questions that show no correlation with others can be assumed not to be measuring the same trait. Take the question example given above. It is supposed to distinguish between more and less sociable individuals. Now let's think of another question that might also measure sociability. Take this one for example:

At a party would you usually:

(a) let strangers take the lead in starting conversations with you;

(b) take the lead in opening conversations with strangers.

If this question were also a measure of sociability, then you would expect a majority of those who answer (a) to the first question to also answer (a) to this one. The same applies to those who answer (b). If this were found not to be the case, then it would seem that the two questions are not both a measure of sociability. In other words, if the answers do not correlate, they are not measuring the same thing. Hence questions that do not correlate with the others will be excluded. This is the **internal reliability** issue addressed in Chapter 2.

Questions used in a personality test must have another characteristic. They must have test-retest reliability. Remember that the nomothetic view of personality assumes it to be stable. If a question is measuring something stable in a stable way, any individual should give the same answer whenever s/he is asked the question. Thus it is essential to trial the questions on the same group on at least two occasions. Any questions that too many people change their minds about from one time to the next have to be excluded. It may be that such questions are open to various interpretations or are overly influenced by mood, attitude or some other unstable characteristic of the test takers.

The final characteristic a test must have is **validity**. It is no good having a set of items that only seem to measure a trait. There must be some more concrete evidence that the test or questionnaire is actually a measure of whatever trait it is supposed to be. The only way of checking the validity of any measure is to compare it with other measures of that variable – even if those measures are just nominal measures.

How might you go about researching the validity of a measure of sociability? One obvious way is to compare scores on your test for a group with their scores on existing tests of that trait. That may be fine if what you are developing is a shorter or simpler measure of a trait for which a well-validated measure already exists. What if no valid test exists for your trait? Then you have to be more ingenious. One way of solving your problem may be to identify samples of individuals who can reasonably be assumed to be high or low on your trait. More sociable individuals can be expected to choose and enjoy certain occupations such as bartender, sales representative or public relations officer. Less sociable individuals may be expected to choose and enjoy other occupations: computer programmer, perhaps, or research scientist, data entry clerk or night security officer, to name a few. If you find that the members of the various occupations score in the predicted direction on your test, then that is evidence for its validity.

Another possible approach to the validity challenge might be to get individuals to nominate their most and least sociable friends, then give those individuals the test. People generally know how sociable their friends are. Again, if the predictions hold true it is evidence of the test's validity.

A third approach might be to categorise individuals as more or less sociable on the basis of observations in, perhaps, an environment created or just being used for the purpose. The situation might be a party where the guests are closely observed. Those who initiate more contacts could reasonably be judged to be more sociable and vice versa – assuming you have controlled for other variables such as how many of those present each guest knows in advance. The judgments are then compared with the individual's personality test scores.

Measuring personality factors

Up to now we have been looking at personality tests designed to measure a single trait. How then are personality tests developed to measure personality factors made up of many traits or to measure overall personality profiles based on all five factors? Essentially, the rules are the same. Only this time one is including questions to measure all known traits. The simplest way to think of it is like this. Imagine that you have a giant questionnaire made up of all the questions that you could conceivably use to measure any and every personality trait. Basically your list of questions about personality is exhaustive. Then imagine you give the question-naire to a large sample of individuals. After that, you follow through the process outlined above for generating a measure of a trait. This time of course you cannot expect all the questions to correlate – because they include questions on every trait, many of which you can reasonably assume are unrelated. You will however find large clusters of questions that do correlate. In fact you will most probably find five such clusters.

Within the clusters not all questions will correlate equally well. On close examination you will find that there are many clusters within each of the five clusters. Each of the smaller clusters is made up of questions that tend to correlate more highly. When you examine those questions you will notice that they seem to correspond with specific traits. While each trait within each of the five big clusters correlates with the other traits in that cluster, traits in one cluster will not correlate with traits in another. In other words distinct patterns as to how questions are answered can be found within the big clusters but no pattern crosses over between those clusters.

It is through this kind of process that the Big Five personality factors have been identified. Tests measuring traits show predictable correla-tions. After looking at a great many correlations between a great many trait measures, psychologists have reached a fair measure of agreement that there are five clusters of unrelated personality traits. They are the Big Five described above.

The word factor comes from a particular statistical technique known as factor analysis that is used to compute the most accurate clustering of personality traits based on the correlations between them. A great deal of skill and knowledge is required in interpreting the results obtained using this technique. Much of the difficulty in deciding how many independent factors or major traits underpin human personality can be traced to dis-agreements over the proper use and interpretation of factor analysis results.

Where do we get our personalities?

Like other human characteristics there are two possibilities. Personality can be a product of genetic inheritance or it can be a product of environmental influences. We have seen that the nomothetic approach tends to view personality as a stable characteristic of humans likely to have a major genetic component. The alternative view – the idiographic approach – though less likely to see personality as something largely inherited, does not deny the possibility that part of it may be inherited. It is just that idiographic personality theorists see personality as something more than core characteristics that have a biological base.

Genetic influence on personality

What then is the evidence supporting the notion that personality is in part genetically inherited? The evidence comes from very similar research to that which indicates that intelligence is partly inherited.

Two major studies in Scandinavia looked at the degree to which the personalities of identical twins correlated as compared with those of non-identical or fraternal twins. Floderus-Myrhed et al (1980) reported a study where 12,898 adult twin pairs were tested for their level of extraversion. The correlations were .50 for identicals but only .20 for non-identicals. The figures are for same sex twins in both cases – identicals will always be the same sex, obviously, but the opposite sex cases among non-identicals might have influenced the figures if they had not been excluded. Girls and boys can be expected to experience different environmental influences on their personalities. The sample accounts for all the traceable twins born in Sweden between 1926 and 1958, making the sample very representative of twins in general, at least in Sweden. A similar picture was obtained for Finnish twins by Rose et al (1988). They tested 7,144 pairs of adult twins, all the traceable living twins born in Finland before 1958. In their study the correlation for identicals was also much higher (.47) than for non-identicals (.15).

There have been many other studies comparing the similarities between the personalities of identical and non-identical twins. Looking at a variety of studies and personality traits, identical twins tend to correlate at on average .50 while non-identicals tend to correlate on average at from .25-.30 (Loehlin and Nichols 1976; Nichols, 1978).

Much of the evidence on the inheritability of traits such as personality and intelligence comes from the study of twins.

These studies suggest strongly that there is a genetic base for personality. The assumption is that the higher correlations for identicals are due to the fact that they have the same genes, which the non-identicals do not have.

While it is very suggestive evidence, it is not altogether proof that personality is inherited genetically. Another possible explanation for why identicals grow up to have more similar personalities is that they are treated more similarly in a variety of ways than same sex non-identicals. Because identical twins look so alike they tend to be treated more similarly by parents, teachers and so on. They are often even mistaken for one another, and so alike that it is difficult to treat them differently. This is not true for non-identicals. As they get older they get less alike. They tend also to drift apart more than identicals, between whom there tends to be a much stronger bond. Even if there were no direct genetic influence on personality, one could reasonably expect identicals to develop more similar personalities.

To test whether the greater similarity between identicals is directly due to genetic inheritance, one would need to separate a sample of identical twins at birth and have them brought up in different homes. Then when they grew up, you could check to see if they were much less alike than identicals reared together or much more alike than non-identicals reared apart. While it is not possible to do this just for an experiment, it has been possible to trace samples of identical twins reared apart (due to separate adoptions) and to check how similar their personalities are as adults. Pedersen et al (1988) reported just such a study. In Sweden, they located a sample of 95 identical twin pairs and 220 non-identical twins, all of whom had been reared separately, and tested them on the extraversion factor. Their findings offer strong support for the genetic explanation. Identicals reared apart (.30) were much more alike than non-identicals reared apart (.04) in terms of their level of extraversion. When they looked at identicals reared together they found a very similar picture to that reported in the Scandinavian studies, that being reared together resulted in a much higher correlation of .54 – suggesting a significant environmental influence as well. When they looked at non-identicals reared apart they found something rather peculiar. This finding will be discussed below under environmental influences on personality.

A major study at the University of Minnesota examining the personality characteristics of identical and non-identical twins reared apart and comparing them to twins reared together has arrived at similar conclusions about the genetic heritability of personality traits (Bouchard et al, 1990; Lykken 1982; Tellegen et al, 1988). They concluded that the average correlation across a wide variety of personality traits was .49 for identical twins reared apart but only .21 for non-identical twins reared apart. Like Pedersen (1988), they report unexpected results for comparisons between non-identical twins reared apart and reared together.

Further evidence for the genetic element in personality comes from studies of brain activity. It has been shown that individuals who are prone to feeling negative emotions such as depression or just feeling upset about events have detectably different brain wave patterns to those who are more resistant to feeling negative (Davidson and Tomarken, 1989). The differences exist not just when the individuals feel unhappy, but all of the time. It seems that we have brains that are more or less resistant to feeling unhappy or upset. This does not necessarily mean that the differences come from genetic inheritance. Differences in brain activity may be a function of diet or lifestyle. However, most physical differences in humans have a genetic component, so it is very likely that brain wave differences do as well.

All in all, the evidence accumulated over the last few decades strongly suggests that genetic inheritance plays an important role in personality.

Environmental influences on personality

Since identical twins reared together do not have identical personalities (correlations of .50 are a long way from 1.0 which would be a perfect match in all cases), we must immediately assume that personality is significantly influenced by the environment. What exactly in the environment is important has proved to be very difficult to identify.

For a long time psychologists have taken it as a fact that child-rearing practices play a major role in the development of personality. Based on this assumption one would expect children reared in the same home by the same parents to develop similar personalities even if they are not genetically related to each other – as in the case of adoptees. This however has not been found to be the case, or at least not to the extent one would expect. Adopted children do not grow up to be very like their adopted siblings.

In the discussion above on genetic inheritance of personality, some unexpected findings in the Pedersen and the Minnesota studies were mentioned. These concerned comparisons between non-identical twins reared together and those reared apart.

The surprising discovery in both cases was that it seemed to matter little or nothing whether such twins were reared together or apart. On average they retained the same degree of similarity in personality test scores. Pedersen et al (1988) found that non-identical twins reared apart had a correlation of .04 on a measure of extraversion. That correlation only rose to .06 when non-identical twins reared together were compared. Evidence from the *Minnesota Study of Twins Reared Apart* (Bouchard et al, 1990; Tellegen at al, 1988; Lykken, 1982) reveals a similar picture. Across a wide variety of personality measures a median or average correlation of .21 was found between non-identical twins reared apart. That only went up to .23 when non-identicals reared together were compared.

Furthermore, the evidence from the Minnesota studies suggests that this pattern is also true of identical twins. Whether reared apart or together, they emerge with a comparable degree of similarity in personality test scores.

It is surely very surprising that being raised in different homes by different parents does not have a major influence on how twins' personalities develop. How can this be explained? We know that the environment in some way has an influence on personality. Otherwise, identical twins would always have identical personalities. This is far from the case. Surely who your parents are is a significant aspect of the environment? How can it be that being raised in a different home by different parents does not cause twins to develop more dissimilar personalities?

Interaction between genes and environment

One possible answer to the questions posed above is that parents in general, whether biological or adoptive, may be very responsive to the innate nature of their child. Thus, the way parents behave towards their children may be more a product of how that child tends to respond and behave than of any attitudes, values or beliefs the parents hold about child rearing. If this were so, a given child may be able to evoke a similar response from most biological or adoptive parents he or she happens to end up with. Basically, insofar as parents are concerned, the child creates his/her own environment. This also means that several children in the one family manage to create differing environments for themselves in so far as parental treatment is concerned. Hence it is not surprising that adopted siblings do not grow up to be very alike. They start off with different inherited tendencies and dispositions. Through these they cause the parents to behave differently to each child.

There is another similar but distinctly different explanation for how it is that twins seem to grow up to have roughly the same degree of similarity in their personalities whether they are raised or not within the same family. This explanation hinges on the importance of perception. Perhaps it matters a great deal less how your parents behave than how you, the child, interpret that behaviour. Following this logic, a pair of non-identical twins being treated in a very similar fashion by the same parents in the same home perceive their treatment as very different. They interpret what their parents say and do in very different ways. Thus, twins growing up in the same home experience very different psychological environments despite similar social environments. The effect is that children growing up together do not turn out as alike as we would have expected. This leads us to the question of where children get their own unique ways of perceiving their worlds from. The answer is almost certainly in part from their genetic inheritance. Since degree of genetic similarity will not be altered by separate adoptions, twins are likely to carry with them some similarity in tendency to perceive the world in a particular way and, as such, to experience similar personal environments in different families. This in turn offers an explanation for why twins reared apart do not drift apart even more in personality terms.

There is a growing appreciation that genetics and environment interact together in a very complex way. Only by understanding that interaction can we hope to understand how personality really develops. It is worth noting that this approach goes a long way to explaining the enormous diversity and unpredictability found in human personality.

As for which of the two theories advanced here (influence on parents or perception) best explains the failure of twins reared together to grow up to have personalities as similar as we would have expected, the answer is probably a mixture of the two. Child development experts generally accept that children do have a major influence on how they are treated by their parents. In addition, all the evidence from the study of human perception (see Chapter 3) suggests that it is not so much the actual world, as the world filtered through our own highly selective and organising perceptual processes, that we end up interacting with. Every child grows up in his or her very own unique world of personal experience.

At this point it should be recalled that the research on genetic and environmental influences on personality described above hinges on the notion that 'personality' is measurable through questionnaires. To the degree that one does not accept the understanding of personality inherent in the nomothetic view, the research loses its relevance. This takes us to the idiographic perspective.

The idiographic approach

Theorists who adopt this view have a number of characteristics in common in the way they view personality. They take it as a feature of humans that is:

1. not reducible to a finite set of traits or factors, since there are an unlimited number of ways that humans differ;
2. not fixed by heredity and therefore stable for life but instead is capable of development and change (an emphasis on how personality develops follows);
3. not measurable or open to being quantified by personality tests or questionnaires – instead the best approach to understanding personality is to explore each individual in depth (this is where the approach gets its name; idiographic means writing about an individual).

The major focus of research among nomothetic theorists concerns the measurement of personality and the identification of the traits and factors of which it consists. Idiographic theorists, on the other hand, are understandably not particularly interested in how personality is structured, since they believe that it allows for an infinite amount of variation and does not conform to some kind of fixed pattern. Anything that has no fixed pattern is not likely to be open to any kind of precise measurement.

Idiographic theorists look mainly at how personality develops. Psychologists who adopt this perspective have drawn up several elaborate theories. These theories fall into a limited number of categories, which will be described in general below.

The main groups of personality theories arising out of the idiographic perspective are:

1. psychodynamic theories;
2. behaviourist/social learning theories; and
3. humanistic theories.

Psychodynamic theories

These include various theories proposed by Freud, Jung, Adler, Anna Freud, Fromm and others. They all have their origins in the work of Sigmund Freud (1856-1939), who was the first to develop a detailed theory of personality development.

Sigmund Freud.

The common characteristics of the psychodynamic approach are an emphasis on innate drives and unconscious processes. To understand this approach, it is best to focus on the original theory from which all the others developed. Freud believed that all humans are naturally driven by powerful drives towards sexual expression and towards aggression. To enable humans to live with one another and survive, it is necessary for some form of control to be exerted over these potentially destructive impulses. In early childhood, he explained, all children are discouraged by their parents from expressing sexual or aggressive impulses. As a result, those impulses become submerged in unconscious memory and normally remain inaccessible. Many experiences and thoughts associated in some way with unacceptable impulses are buried in the unconscious and they continue to exert a powerful influence on our personalities and behaviour unknown to us. Because unconscious memories are not available to be thought about they may cause all kinds of peculiar effects on us but we can not do anything about them unless we can gain access to them. According to Freud, the origins of most mental disorders and emotional disturbances lie in the unconscious.

Freud explained that the structure of human personality could best be explained as three separate mechanisms: the Id, the Ego and Superego.

The *Id* consists of basic selfish drives towards pleasure. Left unchecked it would lead to an extraordinary short-sighted and self-centred approach to life. All children, he explained, are born with a dominant Id and it is through rearing and experience that they develop other parts of the personality.

The opposite of the Id is the *Superego*. This is essentially the internalisation of the rules and demands of society inculcated through socialisation. Those with an overly developed superego are likely to be too constrained and duty-bound, suffering guilt about any personal indulgence. What is needed for a healthy personality is a balance of Id and Superego.

The third part of the personality, the *Ego*, has the job of maintaining this balance through a realistic appraisal of the world. The task of the Ego is not an easy one. On the one hand, it must constantly try to prevent the individual from being overwhelmed by dark and disturbing violent or sexual impulses arising out of the Id. Freud placed considerable emphasis on such impulses as being innate in all humans. On the other hand, it must prevent the individual being crippled by guilt arising from an overly influential Superego. To achieve balance, the Ego is often forced to resort to '*Defence Mechanisms*' or distortions of reality. These are engaged in unconsciously without any deliberate intent on the part of the person.

Freud outlined the following classes of defence mechanism:

Denial – Refusal to even entertain the evidence of whatever is too threatening or unacceptable such as one's anger towards another.

Projection – Attributing one's own emotions to another, as in the case of believing that the person of whom you are jealous is actually jealous of you.

Reaction formation – Reacting to one's unacceptable emotions towards a person or situation by doing the opposite, such as being very considerate and friendly towards someone you actually dislike but feel in duty obliged to think well of – a parent perhaps.

Compensation – Acting so as to make up for an unacceptable emotion; aggression is a common compensation for fearfulness or feelings of inadequacy.

Repression – Pushing what is unacceptable to conscious awareness into the unconscious resulting in complete amnesia about certain past actions or experiences.

Displacement – Shifting the focus of a particular emotion to a safer target; anger, for example, against those we fear to confront may be vented on those over whom we have some degree of power

Sublimation – Turning our unacceptable tendencies into socially acceptable activities; competitive sports may sometimes be a sublimation of aggressive impulses.

Rationalization – Convincing oneself that there are socially acceptable reasons for one's behaviour so as to avoid confronting the real ones; an alcoholic may convince himself that his drinking is just to be sociable or because he is under stress.

Many of these defence mechanisms may be familiar to the reader. Inevitably, we all resort to them at one time or another. The difficulty, as recognised by Freud, is that their benefit is often short-term and in fact may well prevent us from confronting and solving the real source of our problems.

As regards how we each come to have the individual balance of Id, Ego and Superego that we have, Freud outlined a series of developmental stages through which all humans must pass in their early years. The stages differ in terms of the focus of mental energy. Initially, a child begins at the *oral stage*, visibly manifest in the way babies try to suck on everything. This is followed in the second year of life by the *anal stage* when, according to Freud, pleasure is primarily sought through evacuation of the bowels at will. Later between three and five comes the *phallic stage* when the genitals become the source of pleasure. Freud believed that at this stage all children experience strong sexual impulses. During the fifth year this stage gives way to a *latency stage* during which sexual impulses become dormant. These impulses reappear in adolescence when the *genital stage* of development begins. Once more, and for the rest of one's life, mental or psychic energy is focused on the genitals, which are the primary source of pleasure.

The early three stages, according to Freud, are crucial for personality formation in that they involve important conflicts that must be managed. If mismanaged, the person can become fixated at that stage. Too much or too little oral stimulation can result in an orally fixated person, which can manifest itself, for example, in overeating, over-drinking or a tendency to talk too much. Problems at the anal stage may arise due to excessively strict or liberal toilet training. Adult manifestations, symbolic retention or expulsion of faeces, may be stinginess and excessive tidiness, or, conversely, impulsiveness and disorganisation. The phallic stage is famous for the *Oedipus complex* in boys and its female equivalent, the *Electra complex*. Both involve a kind of sexual attachment to the opposite sex parent, which must be resolved by its transfer to the same sex parent so as to avoid the psychological dangers inherent in competing with the mother or father for the opposite sex parent's affections. This stage lays the base for the development of the Superego but, if the conflicts are not negotiated successfully, it can undermine the individual's future ability to relate to authority, the establishment of sexual identity and the ability to form successful relationships as an adult.

Freud and his followers gave much attention to helping clients become aware of their unconscious thoughts and impulses. They developed a variety of techniques for exploring personality by helping to uncover the unconscious – a process or therapy known as *psychoanalysis*. Among those techniques are:

Dream analysis – The assumption is that when conscious control of thoughts is switched off during sleep, the unconscious takes control. Dreams are the result. The individual keeps a careful written account of his/her dreams over a period of time and the therapist analyses them for themes and clues as to the true meaning of the person's unconscious thoughts and impulses. Images are a big issue in dreams, an image representing some other idea. Thus, the recurrent image of a vicious dog may be taken to represent the individual's fear of his/her own aggressive impulses.

Free association – This is where the individual is encouraged to express thoughts in a stream of words or phrases without any structure, through quite literally saying anything that happens to enter the mind. This may also be done by the therapist giving stimulus words, say 'mother', to which the client responds with some word without thinking. It takes practice to do because we are all so used to putting structure on our thoughts. The idea is that when we do not consciously structure our thoughts, then our unconscious takes over, as it may be taken to do in 'slips of the tongue', to which Freud paid much attention.

The Rorschach Inkblot Test – This technique was developed in the 1920s by Herman Rorschach, a Swiss psychiatrist. It consists of a series of ten cards bearing complex designs created by blotting ink on a page and folding it over. The objective was to create meaningless images onto which individuals could project their own thoughts. Clients are asked to report everything each blot resembles. Since the blots do not mean anything in reality, the responses are assumed to arise out of the person's personality in some way.

The Thematic Apperception Test – Devised by Henry Murray at Harvard University in the 1930, it is a similar approach to the Rorschach Test. It consists of a series of pictures of persons and scenes. The client is asked to write a short story of a few paragraphs based on each picture. It is assumed that in the stories individuals will reveal aspects of their personalities. A particularly competitive person may frequently bring issues to do with competition into his/her stories. The therapist searches for themes running through the person's brief sketches in an effort to explore the personality. Unlike most of the other approaches outlined above, this test has been shown to have some scientific validity. It has been possible to show correlations between judgments of such factors as achievement, motivation or aggressive tendencies and actual behaviour bearing this profile out in reality.

The focus on therapy arising out of this theory of personality is based on the view that changes can be brought about in personality. By uncovering unconscious thoughts and drives, an individual can be helped to develop a personality that is more adjusted to the demands of the real world.

Followers of Freud in the psychodynamic tradition introduced modified versions of the overall theory. A major source of disagreement between Freud and those who followed concerned his emphasis on infant sexuality. Alfred Adler, Erik Erikson, Erich Fromm and Harry Stack Sullivan placed social needs as opposed to sexual as central to the development of personality. The enduring aspect of psychodynamic theory is the relevance of unconscious processes.

Behaviourist/social learning theories

Theories in this category suggest that personality is a product of learning, through classical and operant conditioning and through the imitation of role models. Initially the focus on how personality is learned was on the basic behaviourist principles. Behaviourists pointed out how we learn to behave in accordance with what is rewarded (operant conditioning). Children rewarded by their parents for behaving in an extravert fashion will grow up to be extraverts, they reasoned. It was easy to find fairly substantial correlations between what parents approved of and what children learned to do, supporting this view. Genetic influence on personality was not given much attention at the time. Also through the process of classical conditioning there could be significant learned influences on personality. A child, for example, who is being reared by parents who demonstrate a lot of fearfulness or wariness, may well come to associate a lot of stimuli in the environment with fearfulness. Such a child is likely to grow up with a conditioned fear response to many aspects of his/her world and develop a timid personality.

Later learning theory began to focus on learning by example rather than by direct experience. Clearly we learn some things by observing others. It was proposed that aspects of personality might be learned in this way. Theorists such as Albert Bandura (1925-) began in the 1950s and 1960s to focus on cognitive variables such as beliefs, thoughts and expectations in the learning of personality. Humans, it was argued, are not just influenced by stimuli or by events. Their own interpretations and thoughts about those stimuli or events influence them. We saw this point previously in Chapter 4 on Learning when we considered the role of control and prediction in conditioning. According to this view, how one responds to rewards or punishments depends to a great degree on how the situation is interpreted. One person may interpret a setback (a punishment) in achieving a goal as evidence of his or her own incompetence and therefore give up. Another person might interpret the same setback as temporary bad luck and persist. Thus experiences that teach one person to be more persistent may teach another to give up easily. A general tendency either way would clearly be a significant aspect of a person's personality.

However the processes of learning work, this approach to the development of personality clearly presupposes the possibility of change at all times. What we have learned we can unlearn. Therapies based on behaviourist (teaching people new associations) or cognitive (teaching people to think in more positive ways) principles are commonly used in clinical psychology today with much success. They are used to help people with phobias, compulsive personalities, depression and a variety of other conditions. Of course it is possible to disagree about whether or not their success indicates that personality is being changed. Idiographic theorists would say it does. Nomothetic theorists would say that behaviour or attitudes may be changing, that an individual may even learn to behave contrary to his/her basic personality but the basic personality remains the same.

Humanistic personality theory

This perspective is perhaps the most idiographic of all theories of personality in that it focuses more on the potential for change within any person. Humanistic theory emerged as something of a reaction against the determinism of psychoanalytic and learning (particularly behaviourist) theories. 'Determinism' here refers to the notion that personality is dictated or determined by outside forces over which the individual has little or no control. Psychoanalysis had placed great emphasis on the innate sex and aggression drives as dictating the development of personality. Learning theory had suggested that the person's environment (reinforcing stimuli, unconditioned stimuli, role models – cognitive theory, which leaves more control in the hands of the individual, was a later development) ultimately determined what kind of person he or she would become.

Some psychologists in the 1950s and 1960s, notably Carl Rogers (1902-1987) and Abraham Maslow (1908-1970) in the US, were convinced that human personality has more to do with free will than psychoanalysis and learning theory suggested. They proposed a rather optimistic view of personality development, a view that quickly gained a lot of support among psychologists and within society (particularly American) at large. This perspective became known as the humanistic approach.

Like the other approaches discussed above, different individuals proposed different theories, but humanistic theories all have certain characteristics in common. They are based on the idea that it is in the nature of humans to wish to develop and grow as people in all aspects of life. Growth is the goal of human existence. It is society and the world as a whole that prevents this development, not innate negative drives or tendencies in humans. Personality is to be understood in these terms. All people are on a path to developing their full potential. Understanding a person's personality is the same as identifying the point of growth he/she has arrived at. Humanistic theory strongly emphasises the power of the individual to control self-development. Psychotherapy may play a role for some people but it is really all about helping them to help themselves. The logic of this perspective is to see personality change as the norm. Hence it is very much idiographic in the way it views personality. If there are fixed or stable, perhaps inherited, aspects to personality, they are of little interest to humanistic theorists. What matters is constant development towards realising one's full potential.

The nomothetic versus the idiographic perspective

It is natural to wonder whether the idiographic or the nomothetic perspective is more accurate. The answer is neither, because the question is misleading. They are both offering valuable insights into the human state but they are not actually talking about the same thing. They both use the term personality but define it in different ways. From a scientific perspective it is the nomothetic perspective that is likely to achieve more – given its emphasis on precise measurement and its very structured approach. It is the nomothetic approach that the business world and indeed the world of health care rely on to furnish tools that give more reliable measures of aspects of human personality. The question that needs to be asked, however, is whether or not human personality, something that is so much the defining feature of who we all are, can be reduced in total to a set of quantities on a limited number of personality traits or factors. It seems unlikely that this could ever be so. We will need the idiographic perspective to continue to throw light on the rich diversity that is human nature.

PRACTICAL APPLICATIONS OF PERSONALITY THEORY

Throughout the world there are two major areas within which the fruits of research on personality are put to practical use. One is the health care sector and the other is the field of human resources management.

The health care sector draws on both the idiographic and the nomothetic perspectives. Each theory of personality development has given rise to therapeutic approaches designed to help individuals with difficulties in living their lives associated with their personalities. There are behaviourist, social learning, cognitive, humanistic and psychodynamic therapies designed to treat a wide variety of mental and physical disorders. The health care sector also widely uses personality tests that have emerged from research on traits and factors. They are mainly used to help diagnosis, i.e. to give insights into what kind of personality problems may be leading to specific disorders such as stress for example. Traditionally the main application has been within the mental health realm but more recently the relevance of personality to physical health is being increasingly realised.

Human resources management is an activity within all organisations, whatever they do – whether they are manufacturers of goods, government agencies, charities or whatever. Human resources management concerns itself with attempting to ensure that employees can contribute to the maximum extent to the good of the organisation and gain fulfilment and reward in the process. An important aspect of this involves matching the individual to the job or task. Jobs and tasks make demands on personality. The job of sales representative, for example, requires individuals with confident outgoing personalities who like to achieve. Personality tests are used internationally on a widespread basis to help match individuals to jobs and tasks. There is much debate about their use in the selection of staff because of the danger that candidates for jobs can answer questions on personality tests untruthfully and fake results that may seem suited to the job. There is no controversy, however, about the use of personality tests in a closely related area. They are widely used to good effect in careers guidance and counselling. In that context the individual has no motivation to lie and such tests can be of great assistance in helping individuals to understand themselves and to make more suitable career decisions.

SUMMARY

Personality may be defined as:

> *the total pattern of characteristic ways of thinking, feeling and behaving that constitute the person's distinctive method of relating to the environment*

(Kagan and Havemann, 1976).

Personality theorists differ in how stable and enduring those ways of thinking, feeling and behaving must be before they can be said to be part of personality. Nomothetic theorists emphasise high levels of stability and tend to focus on what may be regarded as the core dimensions of personality more likely to have heritable components. Idiographic theorists take a broader view of personality and allow for a considerable degree of change and development due to environmental variables.

The opposing perspectives produce a different approach to understanding personality. The nomothetic perspective focuses on the use of personality inventories or tests to identify the core dimensions or enduring traits that are inherent in personality and how those traits combine to form independent factors. This work has resulted in a high level of agreement that there are five independent factors underpinning personality. They are: extraversion; stability; openness; conscientiousness; and agreeableness. Those factors and the traits of which they consist are measurable through questionnaires resulting in norm-referenced scores.

The idiographic approach to understanding personality rejects the principle that it is a quantifiable characteristic. Idiographic theorists regard such attempts as an over-simplification of individual differences that are too many and complex to reduce to a finite set of measurable traits. Their focus is instead on exploring individual personality in depth and in identifying the mechanisms of development. This approach has evolved a number of different development theories that may be categorised as belonging to either the *psychodynamic, behaviourist, social learning* or *humanistic* schools.

The psychodynamic approach derives originally from the work of Sigmund Freud. It proposes key developmental stages, through which a child must pass. They are the oral, anal, phallic, latency and genital stages. How a variety of conflicts are dealt with during those stages is interpreted as having profound lifelong effects on personality. During those stages, the Id, Ego and Superego tripartite structure of personality is laid down. The concept of unconscious influences on personality is a central idea in this school, resulting in the therapy of psychoanalysis and the development of a variety of techniques such as dream analysis and the Rorschach Inkblot Test designed to gain access to unconscious memories and impulses. There are a number of important defence mechanisms through which the individual can be protected from conscious awareness of threatening aspects of reality. They may, in the long term, prevent the individual from facing up to real problems and may need to be penetrated through psychoanalytic therapy.

The behaviourist approach to personality is based on the notion that personality consists of a complex array of learned or conditioned responses to the environment. Those responses are learned through the processes of classical and operant conditioning. Personality is, in effect, taken to consist of learned habits.

The social learning approach identifies additional learning mechanisms for the development of personality. The focus is largely on the role of vicarious learning – learning from observing the behaviour and experiences of others.

The humanistic approach emerged in response to the determinism of other approaches. It emphasises the power of the individual to self-develop and suggests that this is a natural tendency in humans.

Research evidence on the origins of personality employing twin studies indicates that a significant role is played by both genetic factors and environment. The two operate together in a complex system of interdependency. Inherited tendencies will lead individuals to seek out and create for themselves particular kinds of environments and to interpret their experiences in unique ways. This latter effect causes apparently similar environments such as rearing practices within families to have markedly varying impacts on different individuals.

The main areas of practical application of personality theory and research are within the fields of health care, human resources management and the related field of careers guidance. In health care both the nomothetic and idiographic perspectives are drawn upon for the purposes of diagnosis and treatment. In human resources management, the main application of personality research is the use of personality tests to select employees. This is a controversial application of personality testing due to the capacity of individuals to misrepresent themselves. The value of personality tests in career guidance is much more accepted due to the fact that there is no motivation to lie.

REVIEW QUESTIONS

1. Contrast the nomothetic and idiographic approaches to the understanding of personality.
2. Explain the process of personality test development and the logic underpinning this process.
3. Discuss the origins of personality in terms of genetic and environmental influences.
4. Describe the behaviourist and social learning theories of personality development.
5. Describe briefly the main features of Freud's theory of personality and discuss the implications of defence mechanisms for relationships with others.

REFERENCES

Bouchard, T.J., Jr., Lykken, D.T., McGue, N.L. and Tellegen, A., (1990), Sources of Human Psycological Differences: The Minnesota Study of Twins Reared Apart, *Science*, 250, 223-228.

Bouchard, T.J. and McGue, M., (1990), 'Familial Studies of Intelligence, a Review', *Science*, 212, 1055-1059.

Burger, J.M., (1977), *Personality* (4th ed.), Pacific Grove: Brooks Cole.

Costa, P.T., Jr. and McCrae, R., (1992), *Revised NEO Personality Inventory: NEO Pi and NEO Five-Factor Inventory (NEO FFI: Professional Manual)*, Odessa FL: Psychological Assessment Resources, Inc.

Costa, P.T., Jr. and McCrae, R.R., (1995), 'Primary Traits of Eysenck's P-E-N System: Three- and Five-Factor Solutions', *Journal of Personality and Social Psychology*, 69, 308-317.

Davidson, R.J. and Tomarken, A.J., (1989), 'Laterality and Emotion: An Electrophysiological Approach', in F. Boller and J. Grafman (eds), *Handbook of Neuropsychology* (Vol. 3, pp. 419-441), New York: Elsevier Science.

Floderus-Myrhed, B., Pedersen, N. and Rasmuson, I., (1980), 'Assessment for Heritability for Personality, Based on a Short Form of the Eysenck Personality Inventory: A Study of 12,898 Twin Pairs', *Behaviour Genetics*, 10, 153-162.

Goldberg, L.R., (1993), 'The Structure of Phenotypic Personality Traits,' *American Psychologist*, 48, 26-34.

Kagan, J. and Havemann, E., (1976), *Psychology: An Introduction* (3rd edn.), New York: Harcourt Brace Jovanovich.

Loehlin, J.C. and Nichols, R.C., (1976), *Heredity, Environment and Personality*, Austin: University of Texas Press.

Lykken, D.T., (1982), 'Research With Twins: The Concept of Emergenesis', *The Society for Psychophysiological Research*, 19, 361-373.

McCrae, R. and John, O., (1992), 'An Introduction to the Five-Factor Model and its Applications', *Journal of Personality*, 60, 175-215.

McCrae. R.R. and Costa, P.T., Jr., (1998), 'Personality Trait Structure as a Human Universal', *American Psychologist*, 52, 509-516.

Nichols, R.C., (1978), 'Heredity and Environment: Major Findings from Twin Studies of Ability, Personality and Interests', *Homo*, 29, 158 –173.

Pedersen, N.L., Plomin, R., McClearn, G.E. and Friberg, L., (1988), 'Neuroticism, Extroversion and Related Traits in Adult Twins Reared Apart and Reared Together', *Journal of Personality and Social Psychology*, 55, 950-957.

Rose, R.J., Koskenvuo, M., Kaprio, J., Sarna, S. and Langinvainio, H., (1988), 'Shared Genes, Shared Experiences and Similarity of Personality: Data from 14,288 Adult Finnish Co-Twins', *Journal of Personality and Social Psychology*, 54, 161-171.

Tellegen, A., Lykken, D.T., Bouchard, T.J., Wilcox, K.J., Segal, N.L. and Rich, S., (1988), 'Personality Similarity in Twins Reared Apart and Together', *Journal of Personality and Social Psychology*, 66, 895-910.

Wiggins, J.S. (ed), (1996), 'The Five-Factor Model of Personality: Theoretical Perspectives', New York: Guilford.

Chapter 7

Attitudes

LEARNING OBJECTIVES

On completion of this chapter you should be able to:

- explain what attitudes are, describing the components of which they are made up;
- explain the importance of attitudes to understanding other people and predicting their behaviour;
- discuss the use of open and closed questioning approaches to measuring attitudes;
- describe the four major types of attitude scales:
  - Likert Scale,
  - Osgood's Semantic Differential Scale,
  - Thurstone Scale,
  - Guttman's Scalogram Analysis;
- explain the various origins of attitudes;
- explain the relationship between attitudes and behaviour;
- outline the main factors associated with attitude change under the following headings:
  - the communicator,
  - the message,
  - the medium,
  - the audience.

INTRODUCTION

Think about the pictures shown below. If you had to describe in a word what they represent, what notions they evoke, what would your word be?

Possible words might be: solitude; scenic; old-world; peaceful; quiet. Such images are typical of Ireland's promotion of itself abroad as a tourist destination. Both of the images shown here come from Bord Fáilte promotional literature.

The objective in tourism promotion abroad is to implant in the minds of potential visitors a sense of Ireland that is attractive to them through advertisements in TV, newspapers and magazines.

A quaint old shop with an old-fashioned bicycle outside, golf links beside a scenic inlet overshadowed by a majestic range of mountains. They do exist in Ireland, but it may strike you that an entirely different Ireland could be portrayed, one that is more representative of everyday life. What kind of Ireland do you imagine the IDA portrays when trying to attract manufacturing industry from the US, Germany or Japan? Probably an urban Ireland of high technology, with an educated sophisticated population, possessing advanced infrastructure and telecommunications. That is the sense of Ireland likely to appeal to industrialists.

Even within the confines of tourism promotion, Bord Fáilte is conscious that different markets are attracted by different things. The promotional images of Ireland used in the US are different to those in France, which are again different to those shown in Italy. A shot of a hotel is slipped into the TV commercials in the US, which caters for the American obsession with good accommodation. For the French, there are images of delicious food, responding to their insistence on good cuisine. In Italy, a more youthful, fashion-conscious imagery is employed. Bord Fáilte has invested in a great deal of expensive research since 1994 to try to ensure that Ireland has the right 'brand image'.

All this has to do with the creation of attitudes. A striking thing that Bord Fáilte research revealed is that visitors from abroad arrived with more negative attitudes than they departed with. They arrived with a notion of Ireland as macho, not for the family, unsophisticated and lacking in things to do. They were pleasantly surprised. Somewhere along the line they had picked up false notions that coloured their view of the country. Exposure to the reality had changed those views. Bord Fáilte's task is now to instil a broader range of favourable views in the overseas market. Despite the negative attitudes on some dimensions, many were still coming for the scenery and the expected slow pace of life. Many others were doubtless put off by their attitudes to Ireland.

This chapter explores the whole issue of attitudes so crucial not just to our tourism industry but to virtually every area of life, from who we choose as our friends to the brands we buy in the shops to the political parties we vote for at election time. What exactly are attitudes? Where do we get them? How do they relate to our behaviour? Can they be changed? Can we measure attitudes in any kind of accurate way? These are the questions we will explore.

DEFINING THE TERM 'ATTITUDE'

To kick off, let's try a few standard definitions offered by prominent psychologists. Gordon Allport (1954) defined an attitude as:

> 'a mental and neural state of readiness, organised through experience, exerting a directive or dynamic influence upon the individual's response to all situations and situations with which it is related'.

Kretch, Crutchfield and Ballachey (1962) defined an attitude as:

> 'an enduring system of positive or negative evaluations, emotional feeling and pro or con action states towards a social object'.

You may be immediately struck by the complex language that seems necessary to define such a commonplace concept. The reason is that an attitude is not a single simple concept. It is in fact made up of a number of factors. Any attitude consists of three components:

1. a cognitive component – beliefs about one thing or another being true or not;
2. an affective component – feelings or emotions about the attitude target;
3. a conative or behavioural component – tendencies to behave in some way towards the target.

Take any target about which one might have an attitude, a political party for example. Let's say you have a positive attitude towards that party.

This will most likely mean that you believe the party will do good things, for you or for the country in general, if it gets to power. That is the cognitive component. Also, you are likely to feel more positive emotions when you see a representative of that party speaking, at a rally or on television or wherever, than you feel when you see a member of an opposing party speak. You are likely to even feel more positive emotions in response to the sight of that party's posters than to the sight of posters from the other parties. That is the affective component. Finally, you will most probably have a tendency to behave in a positive way towards the party – being more likely to listen to its party political broadcasts, to vote for it in an election or even to campaign on its behalf, depending on how strong your attitude is. That is the conative component.

The same components exist in all attitudes. If I have a positive attitude towards a particular brand of breakfast cereal, then I am likely to believe that it is good for me (or at least not bad for me). I am likely to enjoy the cereal when I am eating it – the affective component – and I am likely to purchase the product more often and eat more of it than breakfast cereals towards which I have a negative attitude.

Attitudes, then, are a mix of beliefs, feelings and tendencies towards behaviour. In simple terms, they can be defined as our general responses to particular targets. Another simple way of understanding the concept of attitudes is to think of them as our likes or dislikes.

MEASURING ATTITUDES

In principle, people's attitudes can be identified in two ways. You can infer them from their behaviours or you can infer them from answers to relevant questions.

If a person buys a product and does so repeatedly, then you can assume that he/she has a positive attitude towards that product. Inferring attitudes from behaviours is of very limited use in practice. Mostly, those who are interested in people's attitudes wish to use them to predict their behaviours. Producers of products or services wish to know in advance the attitudes of potential customers so that products or services that will sell can be designed. Politicians want to know in advance of publishing their policies what will fit in with the attitudes of the electorate. It would not be clever to suggest that your party will increase significantly the tax on tobacco or petrol if the electorate is known to have negative attitudes to those proposals.

It is highly unlikely that any political party would have risked supporting a change in the constitution to allow for divorce in Ireland if they had any reason to believe in advance that a majority of the electorate had negative attitudes towards divorce. In 1995 all major political parties supported such a constitutional change because they had become convinced from surveys previously carried out that a majority of the electorate favoured such a change and were not opposed to allowing divorce. That the constitutional amendment was eventually carried in the ensuing referendum by only a fraction of one per cent of the vote cast is a salutary warning about the relationship between attitudes expressed and subsequent behaviour, an issue to which we will return below.

If waiting for people to behave to find out their attitudes is of no value, attitudes must be identified from what people say in advance. This involves asking questions and basing the measure of attitude on the answers.

QUESTIONING FOR ATTITUDES

In broad terms there are two ways you can ask questions: in fixed response format or in open-ended format. A fixed response question is one that offers a range of answers from which the respondent (person answering) must choose one. An open-ended question is where you leave the respondent the freedom to answer in any words or at any length he/she chooses.

The clear favourite for 'measuring' attitudes is the fixed response question. This is because of the shortcomings of the open-ended format. When you ask questions to measure attitudes you want to be able to deduce two things from the answers. You want to find out the direction of the person's attitude: whether it is negative or positive towards the target. In addition, you want to know the strength of the person's attitude: whether it is stronger or weaker than that of others who were asked the same questions. It will often not be possible to deduce either direction or strength from an open-ended question. Take this example. Imagine that you go out on the streets of your local town to measure attitudes towards a proposal to ban all car parking on the main street. You stop passers by and ask them an open-ended question: What do you think of the proposal to ban parking on Main Street? The first person you ask gives you this answer:

'Parking on Main Street? Oh, it's a big problem. It's probably for the best that it should be stopped altogether because there's too much abuse of the yellow lines. If you allow people to park at all on the street they will park all over the place at any hour of the day. But all you need really is for the rules to be kept. No double parking and the like. Then again it will be very hard on shops. How are they to get deliveries? And what about people who live over the shops? They won't be able to have their cars nearby. I don't know. Maybe it would stop people shopping in the centre of the town.'

It's not so easy to say whether this person has a negative or a positive attitude to the proposal. At the beginning it seems like a positive attitude is being expressed. Then the attitude appears more negative from further aspects of the answer. This is a big problem with open-ended questions. They are often difficult to interpret. Even if it is clear that the person holds a negative or a positive attitude, it is very difficult to rank order such responses in terms of strength. That takes even more judgment with all the possibilities of being subjective that judgments entail. One response may seem very vehement but that may be due to the way the person uses language to express ideas. Another person holding an even stronger attitude may have a habit of understatement leading to the mistaken appearance of a less vehement attitude.

While fixed response questions are not a guarantee of accurate attitude measurement they are much easier to interpret. Instead of the question asked above about their attitude to parking restrictions you could alternatively read people on the street the statement: *'The proposal to ban parking on Main Street should be implemented'*, then ask them to rate their level of agreement or disagreement by ticking one of the following:

☐ *Strongly agree;*

☐ *Agree;*

☐ *Neither agree nor disagree;*

☐ *Disagree;*

☐ *Strongly disagree.*

This is a fixed response question from which it can readily be gleaned whether a person has a negative or positive attitude. Furthermore, without using any judgment, some indication of the strength of attitude can also be obtained.

In practice, to get a more accurate measure of attitudes to any issue, a number of questions need to be asked, each of them coming at the target from a different angle. The example above illustrates one way in which fixed response questions can be designed. There are several others. In the next section below, we will go on to look at the various ways questions are designed and put together to make up attitude measures or attitude scales, as they are called.

Here we have been emphasising measurement or quantification of attitudes. There are situations where the dimensions of attitudes may not be at all clear and as a result it may not be possible to construct specific questions. This calls for a qualitative approach to understanding attitudes. Market researchers often employ this approach to get a sense of how consumers or potential consumers feel about a product. They assemble a number of focus groups consisting of potential consumers and an experienced researcher leads a discussion in an effort to evoke how the consumers feel. This was an approach taken by Bord Fáilte in finding out what associations people in overseas countries had with Ireland that might influence their decision to visit the country. The approach reaped dividends. It is unlikely, for example, that a quantitative or questionnaire approach would have revealed that when thinking about Ireland potential visitors from abroad did not spontaneously think of Ireland as an island (who would have thought to ask the question?), diminishing the relevance and impact of our wealth of beaches and seascapes.

In the focus group approach, much reliance is placed on the researcher to evoke and then encapsulate the true sense of the groups' attitudes and, of course, quantitative information does not result. However, there is no reason why qualitative information arrived at in this way cannot then be the basis for the development of quantitative measures as described below.

TYPES OF ATTITUDE SCALE

There are four main types of attitude scale:

1. Likert Scale;
2. Osgood's Semantic Differential Scale;
3. Thurstone Scale;
4. Guttman's Scalogram Analysis.

Let's now look at each one in turn.

Likert Scale

This is the simplest, probably the best-known and most commonly used attitude scale, originally devised by Likert (1932). It consists of a series of statements about the attitude target. Respondents are invited to indicate their level of agreement or disagreement to each one.

For example, if you were measuring attitudes towards a political party, Party X, a few of the questions on the scale might look as follows

1. Party X protects the interests of the poor.

Strongly agree	Agree	Neither agree nor disagree	Disagree	Strongly disagree
☐	☐	☐	☐	☐

2. The policies of Party X will lead to unemployment.

Strongly agree	Agree	Neither agree nor disagree	Disagree	Strongly disagree
☐	☐	☐	☐	☐

3. Party X is competent at managing the economy.

Strongly agree	Agree	Neither agree nor disagree	Disagree	Strongly disagree
☐	☐	☐	☐	☐

4. Party X has poor leadership.

Strongly agree	Agree	Neither agree nor disagree	Disagree	Strongly disagree
☐	☐	☐	☐	☐

It is best to express half the questions in a positive direction towards the target (as in questions 1 and 3 above) and half in a negative direction towards the target (as in questions 2 and 4 above). This prevents respondents, who have a generally positive or negative attitude towards the target, from just running down the list and lazily ticking boxes without thinking about the statements, assuming, for example, that since 'agree' or 'strongly agree' is always a positive response, that is all they have to do to fill out the questionnaire. When such people read the items they may not be uniformly positive or negative towards every aspect of the target. To get a more accurate picture of their attitudes it is necessary to get them to read the statements.

For each question the five response options from 'Strongly agree' to 'Strongly disagree' are scored from 1-5. Of course the scoring must be reversed for statements couched in a negative fashion. Otherwise, positive and negative responses to the target would get the same score, which would make summation of the scores meaningless.

To get a person's overall score the scores for all questions are simply added up.

Some experts suggest that there should be one other response option for each question: a 'No opinion' option. This would not be included in the overall score. The logic here is that the middle box 'Neither agree nor disagree' is an undecided response. Psychologically it falls in between agreement and disagreement, in that it reflects the view of a person who feels there are roughly equal arguments both ways. This is different to the position of a person who says that he or she does not know any information on which to arrive at a decision on the issue and therefore has no opinion.

While there is a temptation to use the scale as if it produces an interval level of measurement, Chisnall (1975, pp. 254-5) points out that 'it would not be correct to reach any conclusions about the meaning of the distances between scale points'. It is best to consider respondents as being in a rank order based on their total scores.

Of course, in designing a Likert scale, someone has to decide what statements and how many of them to include. Likert (1932) suggested that before any statement is included, its correlation with the overall measure (the sum of the scores on all the statements) should be checked out in pilot studies. Only items with high correlations should be included. That way you know every statement is a measure of attitude towards the same target. We are back to internal reliability again here (see Chapter 2). Often, in practice, statements are included on the basis of face validity – they look like they are measuring some aspect of attitude towards the target – and no pilot study is done. It is strongly advisable to always carry out a pilot study before using the questionnaire for its intended purpose. This enables statements that should not be included, because people are unsure of their meaning or because they are referring to something other than the target to be identified.

As for how many statements to include, there is no hard and fast rule. Some experts maintain that the more you include the more accurate your measure is likely to be, even if statements are essentially saying the same thing in different ways. In practice you will not want to include too many statements or respondents may be unwilling to take the time to fill out the questionnaire.

Osgood's Semantic Differential Scale.

Osgood, Suci and Tannenbaum (1957) originally proposed this approach. A questionnaire is drawn up where each item or question consists of a pair of bipolar (opposite meaning) adjectives describing the target and the respondents are invited to indicate their level of agreement with the adjectives as descriptions of the target.

For an example, let's pretend you are measuring attitudes towards a new breakfast cereal. Your first item might look like this:

		+2	+1	0	-1	-2	
1.	Healthy	☐	☐	☐	☐	☐	Unhealthy

Respondents would indicate their level of agreement by ticking one box. The nearer the box is to an adjective, the more they agree that the adjective describes the target.

Of course you could use more boxes if you like to allow for more steps of agreement.

Other items would follow using other pairs of bi-polar adjectives, such as 'tasty–tasteless', 'appetising–unappetising', 'refined–unrefined', and so on. An overall measure of the strength of a respondent's attitude, whether negative or positive, can be obtained by summing up their responses over all items.

Osgood et al (1957) originally proposed a seven-point scale as opposed to the five-point example shown above. Morton-Williams (1972) noted that some researchers prefer to use the five-point version and commented that an examination of responses to the seven-point scale indicates that respondents have a tendency to use only four or five points in any event. It may be that in general individuals do not discriminate the strength of their attitudes so finely as to require more than five points.

Again piloting of the questionnaire in advance is advisable. It is important to know whether your respondents are likely to understand the adjectives you use. It is also important to establish if they evaluate them in the same direction as you expect. Take the 'refined–unrefined' example used above. Which is the positive end? Some individuals regard unrefined foods more positively because they are understood to be healthier, while others prefer refined food because they are easier to eat and may be interpreted as tasting better. It is important to establish in advance if the words are interpreted by respondents in the way you expect. Of course checking that each item correlates reasonably well with the overall score is a useful pointer to whether the item is being interpreted as you expected. Imagine, for example, you thought that 'refined' was the positive end of the dimension. Then you discovered that those respondents who had the most positive attitudes overall on the questionnaire towards the cereal had mostly all agreed with 'unrefined' as a description. This should suggest to you that you have been misunderstanding the meaning of refined. Refined is a negative quality in the eyes of respondents.

Thurstone Scale

The scale is called after Louis Thurstone who designed it together with E.J. Chave (Thurstone and Chave, 1929). Similar to the Likert Scale, the Thurstone Scale involves a list of statements. This time, however, the respondents are simply asked to state whether or not they agree with each statement. The important thing about each statement is that it has been rated by a group of individuals as to how positive or negative is the attitude which it expresses towards the target. Thurstone and Chave proposed that each member of this group rate the statement on an 11-point scale, from one (most positive attitude) to 11 (least positive attitude). It does not really matter whether one or 11 represents the most positive attitude, just as long as the process is carried out in a consistent way. After the ratings are carried out, each statement is given a value based on the average rating given the statement by the group. This value represents how positive or negative the statement is towards the target. Statements distributed across the full range of positive to negative will be used in the final questionnaire.

Examples of the kind of statements included in a Thurstone Scale measuring attitude to genetically modified plants (GMPs) might be as follows:

1. GMPs represent a dangerous tampering with nature (8);
2. Increasing world population will require GMPs to ensure adequate food supplies (3);
3. The advantages of GMPs may, in the long run, be outweighed by their disadvantages (7);
4. In an ideal political world, GMPs might be beneficial for all (6);
5. GMPs are the only real hope for resolving world food shortages (1).

Here, higher scores represent statements expressing a more negative attitude. In practice, more statements would be required to construct an effective measure of attitudes.

After the questionnaire is given to respondents and they indicate whether they agree or disagree with each statement, the score for each statement to which they agree is totted up. High overall scores will represent individuals who have agreed with a lot of high scoring statements – ones that, say, have been rated during the questionnaire design stage as indicating a strongly negative attitude.

Guttman's Scalogram Analysis

This method of attitude measurement was proposed by Louis Guttman in 1950, who based it largely on work done by Bogardus in 1925. Like the Thurstone Scale, it consists of a series of statements with which the respondents are simply asked to agree or disagree. The statements are carefully researched and put in a particular order so that agreement with any one statement should logically lead to agreement with all the following statements – since the statements are ordered in accordance with the strength of attitude expressed. The first statement will be the strongest possible expression of the positive attitude and the last the least positive attitude. All statements in between are carefully graded steps or increments between the most and the least positive.

MacGreil (1996) used this kind of scale to measure attitudes in Ireland to various minority, racial, religious and social groups. He used a seven-point scale as follows:

1. 'would marry or welcome as a member of my family';
2. 'would have as close friends';
3. 'would have as next-door neighbours';
4. 'would work in the same workplace';
5. 'would welcome as an Irish citizen';
6. 'would have as visitors only in Ireland';
7. 'would debar or deport from Ireland'.

The logic is that agreeing with earlier statements in the list signifies a more positive attitude to whichever group is being asked about. An individual's score must then be a figure between one and seven inclusive depending on the statement that represents the closest level of association he or she is willing to enter into with a member of the group. Statements 6 and 7 are expressed in negative terms, however, so that those who agree with any of the previous five statements should in logic disagree with those. The most extreme negative attitude is expressed by agreeing with statement 7 resulting in a score of seven. The most positive attitude is expressed by agreeing with statement 1 resulting in a score of one.

The following are the mean or average scores for some of the 59 groups reported by MacGreil (1996) from a national survey using the above scale carried out in 1988-89:

Roman Catholics	1.057
Working-class	1.210
English	1.475
Dutch	1.946
Greeks	2.634
Africans	2.916
Travellers	3.681
Gay people	3.793

Not surprisingly, given that the vast majority of the population in Ireland are baptised Roman Catholics, average attitudes towards this group are close to being as positive as the scale allows. The increasing figures for the remaining groups on the list denotes progressively less positive attitudes towards them.

In drawing up such a scale the statements have to be carefully researched on groups of subjects to ensure that the order is correct. This may prove difficult in many cases. Because of the effort required to identify the statements and research their validity, this is not a very widely used attitude measure.

HOW ACCURATE ARE ATTITUDE MEASURES?

Assuming that the measure is carefully designed and that there are no major flaws such as the use of ambiguous language, how accurate a reflection of attitudes are you likely to achieve?

Even if you are using a well-designed measure there are a few reasons why you should interpret your findings with caution:

1. attitudes are amenable to change;
2. attitudes expressed may be affected by the circumstances of the survey;
3. any measure you take may be true at the time you take it but the individuals surveyed may change their attitudes shortly after – in the light of new information or perhaps in response to deliberate attempts at attitude change.

National surveys capturing attitudes frequently reflect the above. The changes in attitudes towards political parties in the run up to a general election offer a good example. Months or weeks before voting day it may appear from the attitudes expressed in surveys that one political party is going to win. By polling day the electorate has often changed its views and votes in large numbers for a different party.

The British Labour party in the 1980s and early 1990s seemed like it was about to win a number of general elections when the attitudes of voters in the months and weeks ahead of the election were surveyed. Nevertheless, as the elections approached it began to become clear that the Conservatives would win those elections, which they did. It was not that the voters had been lying about their attitudes. They simply changed their minds before voting day. A similar shift of attitudes, mentioned above, was represented in the extremely narrow margin (less than 1 per cent) by which the 1995 constitutional amendment on divorce was passed in Ireland. Opinion polls had previously indicated a much greater margin in its favour among the electorate.

As for sensitivity to the circumstances of the survey, many people have a tendency to answer questions in the direction which they think is socially approved (Edwards, 1964). This is known as the Social

Desirability Response Set. A black person carrying out a survey of racism in Ireland may find considerably less racist attitudes than a white person. A woman may receive answers indicating considerably less chauvinistic attitudes among men than would a man carrying out the same survey. One possible solution to this problem is to carry out the survey in a manner that ensures privacy and confidentiality for the answers given by any respondent. An anonymous postal survey, for example, should do this. Even then there are grounds for concern, as an experiment by Shomer and Centers (1970) indicates.

BOX 7.1

DO ATTITUDES PREDICT BEHAVIOUR?

One particular experiment is regularly quoted to cast doubt on the link between attitudes expressed and behaviour demonstrated. This was carried out in the US by Richard LaPiere (1934). In the early 1930s in the US there was evidence of much anti-Asian prejudice. LaPiere embarked on a journey across the country with a young Chinese couple. They visited a total of 251 establishments such as restaurants and motels. In no establishment were they refused service. Afterwards LaPiere wrote to the managers of those establishments asking if they would serve 'members of the Chinese race'. Over 90 per cent of replies stated that they definitely would not. Only one reply indicated a clearly positive response.

For many years this study cast something of a pall over the worth of attitude surveys as indicators of real behaviour.

More recent research does, however, indicate that attitudes will predict behaviour so long as certain conditions apply. It is those conditions which were lacking in the LaPiere study.

If attitudes are to predict behaviour, clearly the same person must be the subject of both. In many of the establishments LaPiere visited it was not the manager, but another member of staff, who made the decision to serve. Another condition is that the attitude be accessible to the person when they are called on to act (Fazio, 1990, 1995;

Kallgren and Wood, 1986). Decisions on many actions such as serving someone at a bar have to be made in a moment. Only if the attitude comes immediately to mind will it be acted upon. Given time for reflection some of those called on to serve LaPiere's Chinese friends might have declined. A further important condition is that attitudes need to be specific to act as good predictors of behaviour (Davidson and Jaccard, 1979). LaPiere's letter asked about willingness to serve members of the 'Chinese race' in general. The staff of the establishments were not confronted with some negative Chinese stereotype but with a well-dressed couple arriving in a motor car (sign of affluence at the time) in the company of a middle-class white American. Had the couple arrived unaccompanied, shabbily dressed and self-evidently of poor immigrant origins (probably the image in the managers' minds when responding to the letter), their reception might have been generally less welcoming.

Shomer and Centers randomly divided a group of male students into three sub-groups. They asked each group to complete a survey on their attitudes to the role of women in society. The survey was designed to measure how chauvinist or traditional their attitudes were. In this experiment the independent variable was the circumstances under which the subjects completed the survey. Group 1 completed the survey without any women being present in the room. Group 2 were surveyed with an equal number of female students also completing the questionnaire in the same room. Group 3 responded to the survey together with one female student. The dependent variable was the level of chauvinism expressed. The survey was completed anonymously in all cases. Despite that, significant differences in the average amount of chauvinism were found between the three groups. Group 1 expressed the highest level of chauvinism, Group 3 showed the lowest level of chauvinism and Group 2 was intermediate between the other two.

The researchers concluded that the high level of chauvinism in Group 1 resulted from a tendency for men to identify less with women and to think in 'laddish' terms when there are no women about. The low level of chauvinism in Group 3 was interpreted as resulting from identification with the lone isolated female – a kind of protective response or a heightened sensitivity to her circumstances.

Whatever the reasons for the differences found by Shomer and Centers between the three groups, it is the existence of such differences that is a cause for concern. It implies that attitudes or at least those attitudes expressed in a survey are very sensitive to outside circumstances. All kinds of things can raise or lower sensitivity to issues and thus affect attitudes expressed. In the aftermath of the Omagh bombing, where the unionist and nationalist communities suffered together in an unprecedented way, and following the blanket media publicity accorded the tragedy, it is likely that the political attitudes of both communities would have temporarily shown less polarisation. However, as the event faded into memory for those not immediately affected, attitudes probably returned to where they were before. A more accurate measure of real attitudes may then result from a series of surveys over time, rather than from one survey which may be affected by any kind of external event.

WHERE DO ATTITUDES COME FROM?

There is evidence that genetic influences on personality may predispose each of us towards certain types of attitudes (Tesser, 1993). Identical twins reared apart have been found to share remarkably similar attitudes. However, while our innate temperaments may make us more susceptible to certain attitudes, we are not likely to hold them without some kind of learning or experience that leads us in that direction. Such experiences may give rise to attitudes through any of the following routes:

1. beliefs;
2. emotions;
3. behaviours;
4. social influences.

Let's look at each one in turn.

Beliefs

It may strike you when you look at the four origins of attitudes that three of them are the components of which attitudes are made up. The implication is that an attitude may grow out of any one of the components. Because one believes something to be true, it may in turn lead to a particular attitude being developed. Say you read (and believe) that the genetic modification of crops may result in the development of super-weeds, which no pesticide will be able to kill. This may in turn lead you to develop a negative attitude towards genetically modified crops. The attitude, once it has been fully developed, will consist of more than just a belief. It will also include an emotional or affective component. You might feel a sense of foreboding or fear when you hear that such crops are being developed in Ireland. It will also include a conative or behavioural component. You may be willing to sign a petition to ban such crops or you may support a political party like the Green Party that promises to seek legislation against such developments. What began as just a belief may develop into a full-blown attitude.

Emotions

Most people are happy to accept that their attitudes follow from their beliefs. It seems the rational sensible way for them to develop. They are less happy to accept that attitudes may start out as emotions. That seems less rational. Some attitudes doubtless do begin in this way, however.

Why does the population of the US consistently support the death penalty for first-degree murder? There is no evidence that it deters murderers. Indeed, there is some evidence that it in some way encourages them. Perhaps if there is state legitimisation of killing, then it helps to lift the taboo associated with it for individuals. More problematic is the evidence that many on death row have been committed in the wrong and that black and disadvantaged convicts are much more likely to be sentenced to death for the same crimes than those who are white or middle class. The answer to why the US is the only country in the developed world that allows prisoners to be put to death lies in the emotions. The public supports it because of an understandable emotional reaction to the extraordinary high level of gruesomely violent crime in the US. It is an attitude dictated by emotion, not rational thought.

Another area in which there is ample evidence of the power of emotions to dictate attitudes is in the evaluation of other individuals. We are strongly affected by their appearance despite the old maxim that beauty is but skin deep. The effect of appearance is an emotional thing. Research has demonstrated that, for example, on a blind date physical attractiveness is a much more powerful determinant of liking than personality or intelligence (Walster et al 1966). It is easy to see that when we don't like the look of people it is harder to like them in a more general sense, and easier to think negatively about them. This is particularly so if our opportunity to evaluate them is somewhat limited such as in spending a few hours with them at a night-club. The unfortunate reality is that frequently our opportunity to evaluate important others, such as the candidates in a general election, is quite limited too. Looking and sounding good on TV is a major benefit to them.

The power of emotions to dictate attitudes can have very problematic effects for any of us ever attending a job interview. There is evidence that one of the major factors that determines whether you will be successful or not is how attractive the interviewer finds you to be (Kinicki and Lockwood, 1985). While attractiveness is not to be understood here as just physical attractiveness, nonetheless it is a decision based primarily in the emotions. If the interviewer likes you, he or she will come to more positive beliefs (cognitive component of attitude) about you and will then be more inclined to act on this by hiring you (conative component).

Advertisers capitalise on the power of emotions by seeking to classically condition positive responses to products.

Gorn (1982) found that consumers were more likely to opt for a product presented against a background of music they liked than music they disliked. Advertisers use a variety of visual and auditory stimuli, which are designed to evoke positive responses in consumers that will then rub off onto the product. Such stimuli include music, scenery, sex appeal, nostalgia, sophistication, health and many more.

Behaviours

It seems a little unexpected to suggest that attitudes may follow from behaviour. We generally think of the process acting in the other direction. Yet it is quite plausible that some attitudes may indeed have their origins in behaviour. This idea was suggested by Bem (1972).

There are many situations where we may be called on to do something before we have had a chance to form an attitude on the matter. Let's say you are stopped on the street by a friend, who asks you to sign a petition to call on the government to protect the human rights of refugees seeking asylum in Ireland. Pretend for a moment that you have heard little or nothing about the issue of refugees and don't have much knowledge about it. Will you sign the petition? Chances are you will, if only not to offend your friend. Perhaps also you are embarrassed to admit your ignorance on the subject.

At this point, according to Bem, you would be much more likely than before to form an attitude favouring the rights of refugees. This is because you have acted as if you had such an attitude by signing the petition. Bem, and indeed other major writers in the field such as Leon Festinger (1957), suggest that we all seek to have consistency between our attitudes and what we do. We wish to believe that we do what we do because that is what we believe, not because we are forced to do it or embarrassed into doing it. We like to see ourselves as sensible and rational. The only way to achieve consistency when we have already acted in a particular way without having a relevant attitude is to go on to form such an attitude. Thus, in the example used above, information about refugees will now become more noticeable to you and you will tend to interpret it in a way that supports what you have just done. In short you will be more likely to develop beliefs, emotions and further tendencies to behave in a way that is consistent with your existing behaviour. From the behaviour will have sprung an attitude.

Social origins

To a considerable extent, the three origins of attitudes already discussed may themselves come from social influences. We learn many of our beliefs from people that we know. Likewise, we tend to pick up emotional responses from seeing others respond in a particular way. As for behaviour, it is often others who induce us to do one thing or another. To that extent clearly there are social origins in the learning of attitudes. In addition, we frequently pick up our attitudes fully formed from significant people we are involved with. The groups to which we belong in life have profound influences on our attitudes.

The first group to which most people belong is a family. There is no doubt that family has a powerful influence on attitudes. Even in adolescence, when it is generally thought that children drift apart from their parents and come under the influence of peer groups, research evidence suggests that the influence of parents still dominates important attitudes. The peer group tends to dominate in matters of youth culture such as fashion, music, entertainment and use of language (slang etc). Parents are still the dominant influence on moral and social values (Mussen et al, 1990, p. 604).

Inevitably the family is not the only group to which we belong in the course of our lives. As we grow up, particularly after leaving home, there are colleges we attend, groups in the workplace where we earn a living, groups at the clubs we join, friends we live with and so on. They all bring their own influences to bear.

One important general truth seems to be that it is very difficult to hold attitudes in conflict with the groups to which we belong. Attitudes generally need social support for survival. A study by Newcomb (1943) is an interesting illustration of the way attitudes change in response to changes in group membership. The study also illustrates clearly how attitudes require social support to endure. Newcomb studied the political attitudes of students at Bennington College, a university in the US, which in those days catered only for female students. Bennington College was somewhat unusual in that it drew its students mostly from wealthy, conservative, Republican voting backgrounds but was known to have a somewhat radical/liberal ethos. In simple terms you might characterise the families of the students as favouring the status quo – preferring to avoid political change, in that they were doing very well out of how things were. Yet the college (through staff) favoured more political change. Such political attitudes at the time might be given expression in voting for the Democratic party.

Newcomb hypothesised that, in the run up to the 1936 presidential election, first year students – not having been so long away from the influence of their families – would largely prefer the Republican candidate, Alfred M. Landon. Students who had been longer in the college, 2nd and 3rd years, would be less likely to support the Republicans and under the influence of the college would have shifted their preferences towards the Democrats. That is exactly what Newcomb found, as the figures below illustrate.

TABLE 7.1 – BENNINGTON COLLEGE STUDENTS' PREFERENCE FOR 1936 PRESIDENTIAL CANDIDATES IN % (NEWCOMB, 1943)

	1st Years	2nd/3rd Years
Alfred M. Landon (Republican)	62%	15%
F.D. Roosevelt (Democrat)	29%	54%
Socialist/Communist Candidate	9%	30%

The students' political preferences were clearly influenced by their new social contacts in the college.

Given that the students came from wealthy Republican voting backgrounds, it would have been reasonable to expect them to return to such backgrounds when they left college. Did they then go back to voting Republican? A follow up study in 1960 was carried out on a sample of the same Bennington College students (Newcomb, 1967). The follow up surveyed preferences for Richard Nixon (Republican) and John. F. Kennedy (Democrat) in the run up to the 1960 presidential election. It was found that the ex-Bennington women tended to retain their preference for the Democrats. Was this political attitude at odds with that of their friends and associates, whom you would have expected to favour the Republicans? It seems not. Bennington women retained their favourable attitude to the Democrats, but so did their friends and associates. Basically they had stayed within Democrat voting groups, even tending to marry Democrat-voting husbands. It is difficult to hold attitudes at odds with the groups to which we belong but there is nothing stopping us deliberately seeking out groups whose members hold the same attitudes as we do. That is in fact what people do a lot of the time.

THE RELATIONSHIP BETWEEN ATTITUDES AND BEHAVIOUR

In general, we like to maintain a match between our attitudes and our behaviour (see also Box 7.1 above). This, however, can be achieved in at least three ways:

1. developing an attitude first and then behaving in accordance with it;
2. behaving first and then developing an attitude in accordance with the behaviour ;
3. changing our attitudes to bring them back into line with what we do.

The first of these ways seems the most rational and it is how we like to think of ourselves as acting. Doubtless, this is what we do a good proportion of the time. However, as we saw above, sometimes behaviours may logically precede attitudes. Then we are motivated to form an attitude in keeping with our behaviour – otherwise we have to admit that we behaved wrongly, something we avoid doing if we can.

The third mechanism of achieving a match between attitudes and behaviour presents an interesting possibility. It presupposes that we already have an attitude on the issue and that we behave contrary to it for some reason. Why behave contrary to your attitudes? In response to some kind of pressure is the answer. While we all like to think of ourselves as courageous and principled, frequently we fall short of those high ideals. You may have a clear attitude against misleading customers about products. Most of us have such attitudes. However, imagine for a moment that you have taken up a new job and you discover that your bosses expect you to conceal some flaws in the products you are selling. Perhaps you are not exactly told to lie to customers. You are just expected to 'gloss over' the deficiencies in what you are selling. Initially you may have some qualms of conscience about misleading the public. Then you notice that all your colleagues are doing what the company wants.

Chances are you will go along and do what the company wants as well. Evidence on conformity with the demands of authority figures (e.g. Milgram, 1963) and with group pressure (e.g. Asch, 1957) strongly suggests that this is so.

At this point, according to Leon Festinger (1957), you will feel unhappy and uneasy, knowing that your behaviour and your attitudes are at odds (a state of mind he calls *cognitive dissonance*) and you will be motivated to rid yourself of this uncomfortable feeling. The obvious thing to do is to refuse to go on misleading the public but then you fear you will incur the displeasure of your bosses and even your colleagues whom you will effectively be accusing of lying. Perhaps you will lose your job. The other alternative is to change your attitude. You might say to yourself that one cannot be too pure about the truth in a tough world or that you are not really lying, only failing to tell people the truth, or that the lie is not that important, or maybe that you are just carrying out instructions and that the company or your bosses hold the moral responsibility for your lies. One way or another, it involves a change of attitudes. What previously you would have defined as unacceptable, you now declare to be OK. The benefit is that it brings your attitudes and behaviours back into line. If you observe people closely you will inevitably come to the conclusion that there is a strong tendency for individuals to hold attitudes that suit their circumstances. The concept of cognitive dissonance does much to explain this.

Festinger and Carlsmith (1959) carried out an interesting experiment demonstrating the existence of cognitive dissonance. They had a group of students carry out a particularly boring set of tasks as part of a research experiment. They then asked them to tell their colleagues how interesting the experiment had been. Half the group were offered a one-dollar bribe to tell the lie, the other half a 20-dollar bribe. The researchers hypothesised that many of the students in both groups would comply with the request, because people tend to comply with what figures in authority demand. They also hypothesised that most of the students would hold attitudes against telling such lies. They would then have to explain their behaviour to themselves. Their prediction was that those who were paid the 20-dollar bribe would conclude that to tell a white lie for 20 dollars was something anyone would do but those paid only one dollar would have greater difficulty justifying their actions to themselves, since these actions were contrary to their attitudes to lying. The researchers therefore predicted that the one-dollar group would develop a more favourable attitude to the experiment so as to justify telling others that it was interesting. This is, in fact, what was found. Presumably the only other explanation (the true one) that they had lied because an authority figure asked them to was too much of a blow to their egos.

IS IT EASY TO PRESSURE SOMEONE INTO VIOLATING HIS/HER ATTITUDES?

While individuals may find it unacceptable to their egos to admit that they will contravene their own attitudes if an authority figure demands, that is just what research has shown and shown very dramatically in one famous instance.

Milgram (1963) recruited a group of volunteers to participate in a research experiment, which they were told concerned learning. They were told that they were each being assigned to the role of 'learner' or the role of 'teacher'. In fact they were all assigned to the role of 'teacher' and unknown to the participants the 'learner' was always the same person, a confederate of Milgram's. Each participant was dealt with separately and each of them was treated exactly the same. In each case they were put in charge of a machine which they were told would deliver electric shocks to the 'learner' who was tied into a connected apparatus in an adjoining room. They were introduced to the learner before the experiment began. During the experiment they were instructed to ask questions of the learner who answered through a communication system. When the learner gave a wrong answer the 'teacher' was told to give him an electric shock using one of a row of 30 switches on the control panel of the machine. The switches were marked from 15 to 450 volts and had descriptive labels ranging from 'Slight shock' up to 'Danger, severe shock'. To the right of the 450-volt switch were two switches just labelled ominously as **XXX**. Each time the learner gave another wrong answer they were to raise the level of the shock delivered.

Milgram was interested to discover the extent to which volunteers would comply with the bizarre instruction to deliver electric shocks to someone whom the participants believed was just a volunteer like themselves. To make it more difficult for them, the 'learner' was instructed to begin to bang on the wall and to shout and scream to be released after the shocks reached a certain level, then to go silent completely and to stop responding after the shocks reached a higher level. A scientist dressed in a white lab coat accompanied the 'teacher' in each case. He gave the instructions. Typically the subjects turned to the scientist for guidance, especially when the 'learner' began to bang on the wall. The scientist was instructed to say the same thing in all cases:

'Please continue';
'The experiment requires that you continue';
'You have no other choice; you must go on'.

No other pressure was put on the participants to go on. Milgram reported that 65 per cent of them were obedient to the very end – even pressing the XXX switches, despite the banging, the shouting and the ominous silence that followed. According to Milgram, the participants showed great signs of anxiety and unhappiness at what they were doing, yet, in the majority of cases, somehow seemed unable to take the obvious stance of refusing to go on. Needless to say, no actual electric shocks were delivered, but the participants had been entirely fooled that there were. This is what Milgram (1965) wrote afterwards:

> 'If in this study an anonymous experimenter could successfully command adults to subdue a 50-year old man and force on him painful electric shocks against his protests, one can only wonder what government with its vastly greater authority and prestige can command of its subjects.'
>
> (Milgram, 1965, p. 262)

The lesson appears to be that humans are remarkably inclined to do what people in authority tell them to, even if that means violating very basic attitudes they hold.

Naturally one might be inclined to wonder if there was something unusual about Milgram's sample. Perhaps they held peculiar attitudes towards authority or towards torturing others. Would the same results be found elsewhere with other samples? Are both men and women equally compliant? As for the latter question, Milgram studied both female and male subjects and found the same level of compliance. A subsequent study in Australia (Kilham and Mann, 1974) found women markedly less willing than men to continue administering electric shocks under the Milgram experimental circumstances but that may have been due to the fact that their 'victim', unlike the one in Milgram's study, was also female. As for the former question concerning how representative Milgram's subjects were, there are at least eight studies around the world that have replicated his experimental design with broadly similar results. Sixty-five per cent of Milgram's subjects persisted delivering shocks to the end. The comparable figures from studies elsewhere in the US and in other countries are:

Spain (Miranda et al, 1981)	90%+
US (Rosenhan; in Milgram, 1974)	85%
Italy (Ancona and Pareyson, 1968)	85%
Germany (Mantell, 1971)	85%
Austria (Schurz, 1985)	80%
Jordan (Schanab and Yahya, 1978)	62%
UK (Burley and McGuiness, 1977)	50%
Australia (Kilham and Mann, 1974)	40% (males)
	16% (females)

It is indeed a disturbing finding that in so many modern civilised countries it seems so easy for authority figures to get individuals to carry out instructions to harm others when surely such behaviour is contrary to their basic attitudes and values.

ATTITUDE CHANGE

Attitude change is attempted all the time by all kinds of people. Advertisers try to win customers around to more favourable attitudes towards products or services. Politicians try to win the electorate around towards more favourable attitudes to their policies. Government agencies try to change public attitudes to drink driving, to smoking, to diet and to a variety of other health- and safety-related issues.

An attempt at attitude change can take on a variety of forms. Among other things, it can be a face-to-face conversation, an article in a newspaper, a TV advertisement or even a billboard poster.

Every attempt at attitude change or persuasion involves four components:

1. a communicator;
2. a message;
3. a medium;
4. an audience.

Under each of those four headings, we will now look at what research tells us about changing attitudes.

The communicator

The communicator is the person or organisation who is putting out the message in an attempt to change attitudes. In a party political broadcast or a speech it is the person or persons doing the talking. In a newspaper advertisement it is the originator of what is said. This will often be the organisation paying for the advertisement but it may also be someone else being quoted in the advertisement as in a celebrity endorsing a product.

Communicators are more influential if they are:

1. credible or believable (Hovland and Weiss, 1951, Kelman, 1961, Petty et al, 1997);
2. attractive (Kelman, 1961; Eagly and Chaiken, 1975; Joseph, 1982; Petty et al, 1997).

Credibility comes from perceived expertise and perceived sincerity. Is the communicator seen as an expert in the topic at issue and is he or she telling the truth? Advertisers try to get 'experts' to endorse products. This explains the use of models or film make up artists to endorse cosmetics. Watch out for this practice on TV. Where health care products are concerned, doctors or nurses may often be used. In the case of baby care products, washing powders and so on, a 'typical' mother may be employed as the relevant expert.

It is one thing to accept that experts know what they are talking about. It is quite another to be confident that they are telling the truth. The problem advertisers have is that the viewing or listening public know that those who endorse products are paid, often a great deal, to do so. This undermines their credibility. A solution is to quote communicators who have said good things about the product without being paid or rewarded to do so. If the new make of Ford or Toyota has won a 'European Car of the Year' award as judged by an independent panel of motoring journalists, then you can be quite sure that this will be widely quoted in the advertisements for the car. The communicator then becomes the independent panel of motoring journalists rather than someone paid for by the company. Their sincerity can be assumed. Why would they lie? The endorsements of novels by reviewers often printed on the back cover fall into the same category.

Where there is a visible or audible communicator as in the case of a TV advertisement or a party political broadcast or a member of the Mormon community on your doorstep trying to win converts, the look and sound of the communicator matters. How should a communicator look and sound? The issue of looks is already taken care of if the communicator is familiar to the audience, such as a well-known politician or a celebrity endorsing a product. The impact then derives from what the audience associates with this individual. Note in this context how quickly advertisers run away from celebrities when they become associated in the media with something negative. Take the case of Michelle De Bruin, the most successful Olympic competitor Ireland has ever had after winning three gold medals and a bronze in 1996. At first, she was regularly on TV endorsing hair care products and the Irish language. After she became embroiled in controversy about performance-enhancing drugs and sample contamination she disappeared entirely from view. The same fate befell world record-holding Canadian sprinter, Ben Johnson, for the same reason. Even singer Michael Jackson, with his world-wide following, was dropped by Pepsi when he was accused, though never convicted, of child abuse.

But what of a communicator who is unknown to the audience? How should he or she look? The answer would appear simple. He or she should look as the audience expects. Otherwise perception of expertise and sincerity will be undermined. A doctor doing an advertisement, for example, should look like people expect doctors to look – probably not too young or old, neat, clean, fairly conservative in dress, no odd hairstyle or jewellery and so on. The same applies to members of other professions or groups. Basically one tries to appeal to the popular stereotype. What do you imagine a pop star should look like? How do you think you should look to convince an interview board to give you a job in the business world? Don't forget that in an interview you are the communicator trying to win round the attitudes of the interviewers. The key to credibility in so far as looks are concerned is to 'look the part'.

A glance back at Chapter 3, particularly the sections describing how our perceptual systems lead us into errors when appraising other people, should be helpful at this point.

Another factor about looks that has been found to be influential is attractiveness. Communicators found attractive by the audience – partially but not entirely a feature of looks – have been found to be more persuasive. Other things being equal, the better-looking politician is likely to get more people to believe his or her arguments. As for advertising, on balance it is better to have your product fronted by someone who is pleasing on the eye.

As for the sound – voice and accent – of the communicator, again, to be convincing and credible it is probably best to sound as the audience expect you to sound. As with looks, it is a matter of appealing to the popular stereotype. It has been the subject of recent debate in Britain whether individuals with strong regional accents are considered to be less credible than those with a more standard unaccented way of talking – the way one associates with newsreaders on TV, for example. Many feel that there is a general bias against those with strong regional accents and they are assumed to be less educated and less informed. Ask yourself honestly if you have a bias one way or the other.

Research from the US suggests that slow talkers are taken to be less knowledgeable and less objective than faster talkers. Presumably in the US talking slowly is taken to mean that you are making it up as you go along. This might not be true in Ireland, where there is a tendency to associate fast talking with dishonesty – with the type of person who might sell dodgy goods from the back of a truck.

The message

Three issues to do with the message will be considered here:

1. When does the message matter more than the communicator?
2. Is it better to give a balanced or a one-sided argument in your message?
3. How effective are attitude change messages based on fear arousal?

Research evidence suggests that the communicator matters less and the content of the message more when the audience members are able and willing to attend closely to the message (Petty and Cacioppo, 1986, Chaiken, 1987). A number of factors can influence attention to any message such as an advertisement or a party political broadcast. The audience may be distracted by other calls on attention, as is often the case when watching TV. The message may be of greater or lesser personal relevance to any individual, thus engaging or failing to engage attention as the case may be. The content of the message may be more or less understandable to the audience depending on factors to do with current state of knowledge. The less understandable, the less likely attention is to be maintained. When, for one reason or another, attention is not maintained, the communicator matters more. This can be a short cut to evaluation, eliminating the more onerous task of considering the merits of the arguments advanced. All one has to do is decide if a communicator is to be trusted and follow the advice given.

An important finding about how attitudes are arrived at is that attitude change based on analysis of the content of the message is more durable and tends to last longer than attitude change arrived at by reliance on more superficial factors such as who the communicator was (Chaiken, 1980). This has obvious practical implications. Those influenced to favour a product by 'expert' endorsements are just as likely to change preference to another product endorsed by another 'expert'. If, on the other hand, the first product has real advantages of which the consumer has been convinced, then loyalty is likely to be maintained.

As for the one-sided/two-sided issue, this can be a tricky decision to make. You wish to get the audience to adopt a certain attitude. You have some good arguments that favour your position. You are aware, however, that there are counter-arguments. Should you mention them or not? The answer is that it all depends on knowing your audience. Two-sided arguments are best when dealing with an audience that may be:

1. sceptical about your position (Sawyer, 1973, Szybillo and Heslin, 1973);
2. well-educated and aware of the opposing arguments (Belch et al, 1987).

Based on the first point, the advice is not to shy away from addressing arguments against your position if your audience may be biased against you. Imagine you are a politician on the campaign trail. You arrive to give a speech in a town and are advised that many of the waiting crowd have previously voted for another party. You can assume that they may be sceptical about your party and its policies. They will not be receptive to a simple litany of self-praise. You would be wise to address some of the criticisms that have been mounted against your policies and dispose of them as best you can. Otherwise, the audience may feel you are afraid to address the problem areas and you may lose credibility with them.

On the other hand, you should not introduce discordant notes among favourable audiences by mentioning opposing arguments. Just concentrate on the positive points. If instead of a negatively biased audience you are addressing a meeting of the party faithfully, your job now is to firm up conviction that they support the right party. You can see that it would be counterproductive to make reference to criticisms of your policies that have been voiced elsewhere. To do so would simply be sowing seeds of doubt where doubt did not exist.

On the matter of educated, well-informed audiences, the advice is similar – face up to criticisms and opposing arguments, but only if the audience is already aware of them. You should not introduce negative suggestions where they are not likely to exist already. Imagine you are designing an advertising campaign to promote favourable attitudes among the local community towards a new chemical plant being set up in the locale. In the past, your company and others like it have come in for major criticisms in relation to pollution of the environment. The company has taken significant steps to eliminate the dangers of pollution. In designing your campaign, do you raise the issue of pollution and address it or do you just concentrate on all the economic and social benefits the company will bring to the area? It all depends on whether the local population is likely to know about the pollution concerns. If they do not – as is often the case among less well-educated populations found in third world countries – then mentioning such issues in the advertising campaign may have the effect of creating fears that would otherwise not exist. If, however, you suspect that pollution and general environmental threat may be well understood in the local population, as is often the case nowadays in the developed world, then it is best to address those issues, and, if possible, lay the concerns to rest.

Regrettably, many commercial, and indeed government, organisations have been only too aware of this advice and behaved with shocking cynicism in capitalising on the ignorance of local communities around the world and particularly in the poorer third world.

As regards the issue of fear arousal, the question here is how effective is it to attempt to frighten the audience into a change of attitude. The question is most pertinent to government health and safety campaigns. Take the need to encourage more negative attitudes towards smoking. Should TV advertisements be designed which graphically illustrate what it is like to be in the advanced stages of lung cancer or other serious smoking related respiratory disorders? Surely seeing and listening to a long-time smoker literally drowning in his own phlegm at the age of 45 would convince other smokers to change their attitudes towards cigarettes. Likewise, surely a shocking illustration in a TV ad of what a body looks like after being cut from the wreckage of a 70 mile per hour crash would convince motorists to change their attitudes to speed? Logically you would think so. But research since the 1950s suggests that you should approach fear appeals with caution. If the message is too upsetting it seems that the audience switches off. That may literally mean switching channels or simply avoiding looking at or thinking about the message.

The evidence is that where the message is too upsetting viewers can screen it out and any potential effect on behaviour is inevitably lost.

Janis and Feshback (1953) illustrated the dangers of fear arousal in an experiment attempting to improve the attitude of students towards oral hygiene. They used different messages with three randomly chosen groups. The messages were deliberately varied in terms of fear appeal. The high fear group was given a frightening lecture on all the terrible infections that can result from poor oral hygiene, accompanied with slides of decayed teeth and gory mouth infections. Those students were subsequently found to brush their teeth less often than the other groups who were given medium and low fear appeal presentations. Similar findings have since been made about the effects of fear appeals in relation to condom use to avoid AIDS and in relation to efforts to discourage drinking and drug use among teenagers (Hill, 1988; Rothenberg, 1990).

Some fear may be useful to grab attention and make the message more memorable, but if it is over-done the whole attitude change attempt may backfire and achieve nothing. Another important factor is whether or not the message offers a clear way to reduce or eliminate the fear (Leventhal et al, 1967). Consider this scenario. As part of a campaign to encourage more responsible attitudes to child-care among young parents, they are warned about the vulnerability of infants and told about 'cot death', a frightening condition where seemingly perfectly healthy babies die in their sleep without any known cause. This is not likely to have much effect on their attitudes or behaviour unless they are told how to minimise the risk of cot death. Parents are likely to try to forget such a worrying prospect. However, if they are also advised that simple precautions (such as putting the baby to sleep on its side or back, not allowing it to get over-heated and not allowing anyone to smoke in the same room as the infant) significantly reduce the risk, then the message is likely to have a real impact. In fact, campaigns in recent years bringing this message to parents have been successful in significantly reducing the rate of cot deaths or Sudden Infant Death Syndrome, as it is now called.

The medium or channel

The medium or channel is the vehicle for carrying the message to the audience. It may be face-to-face conversation, TV, radio, the written word, billboard posters or the internet.

A distinction should be drawn between personal and impersonal media. Face-to-face communication is personal, whereas newspapers and TV are examples of impersonal media, in that they do not involve one-to-one communication. It is generally held that the personal approach has the greatest power to persuade, because the message can be tailored to the circumstances of the target. Personal or direct selling has a variety of such advantages over advertising (Cash and Crissy, 1965). Of course, the mass media has the advantage of getting to a very large audience at once, while there is an obvious limit to how many doors even the most committed Mormon or door-to-door salesperson can knock upon.

Impersonal media can be divided into permanent and transient media. A permanent medium is where the message is presented in such a way that the audience can go back over what is said again and again without much difficulty. Clearly the written word falls into this category, as does the internet. Public speeches, TV and radio fall into the transient category. This is where the audience gets one take. They cannot easily get a repeat. Technically, the TV can be videotaped, making it a permanent medium. Advertisers and politicians, however, can hardly rely on people taping their messages. Billboard posters, though they have the appearance of permanence, are actually a transient medium. They are largely designed for passers by. While the message stays up there permanently, the audience is transient, going past in a car or on foot.

Whether one should use a transient or a permanent medium is dependent on the nature of the message. If the message relies on appeals to the intellect, containing, say, a lot of fact and figures, then a permanent medium is necessary. It is a mistake to over-estimate the capacity of the human brain to process information quickly. If the message is complex, people will need to go through it at their own pace. Only a permanent medium allows this. The transient media, particularly TV with its power to appeal to both the eyes and ears, are more suited to messages based on emotional appeal. Torin Douglas in his *Complete Guide to*

Advertising puts it like this:

> '*Nothing can create a brand image more dramatically or sell more persuasively than film, with its use of such elements as music, emotion, humour, animation and personalities.*'

(Douglas, 1984)

If a politician in a party political broadcast wishes to convince the electorate of the benefits of recent tax changes, he or she could attempt to get at the viewers through their intellects or through their emotions. The intellectual approach might consist of a careful presentation of detailed figures such as an economist or an accountant might require to assess the real impact of the tax changes. In a TV broadcast there would be a real danger that much of the detail would go over the heads of the viewers. Very soon many of them would be lost and stop watching.

The alternative emotional appeal might consist of a single case presentation. It could follow the pattern of '*Here are John and Mary, a married couple with two children, earning the average industrial wage. They will now explain what the tax changes have meant for them*'. The objective is to get the audience to emotionally identify with the couple. What might have been a dry accounting lesson has now become a human-interest story – you see real people who have been able to take their first holiday in years. That is an emotional appeal. Transient media are best used for that purpose. That is not to say that appeals to the intellect cannot be made on TV and radio. One must, simply, be careful not to overestimate the attention and retention span of the audience.

Billboards also have limited value for intellectual appeal messages. Billboards are best used for pictures or graphics that evoke an emotional response. Where text is used, it must necessarily be limited in quantity. Otherwise your audience will have passed by and only seen a portion of the message. Striking visual images or slogans with an emotional appeal such as '*Speed kills*' are commonly used in this medium.

The audience

Inevitably, in dealing with the other elements of attitude change, we have already discussed several characteristics of the audience: whether or not they pay close attention, whether they are well informed and whether they are favourably disposed in the direction of the attitude sought.

There are a number of other factors about the audience that influence how likely its members are to be persuaded by an attitude change attempt:

1. intelligence;
2. self-esteem;
3. age;
4. perceived expertise;
5. involvement with the message.

More intelligent people are more resistant to persuasion (Rhodes and Wood, 1992), presumably because they are better equipped to attend to the content of messages and tend to require better arguments to be convinced.

People with high self-esteem are less persuadable. Those who do not think so highly of themselves are easier to influence. Religious cults are infamous for being aware of this. They often seek to target individuals who feel low in self-worth, who feel that they are unloved and perhaps not worthy of being loved. Armed forces are conscious of this also. They like to get recruits who are young and whose sense of self-esteem is still very much dependent on external validation. That way they can mould their attitudes as required. As people mature their sense of self worth becomes less dependent on being popular with others. They become somewhat (though not always a great deal) better able to stand alone and are, therefore, less amenable to having their attitudes moulded. By and large people are most open to persuasion between the ages of 18 and 25 (Krosnick and Alwyn, 1989, Sears, 1981). Before then, attitudes tend to be tied to those of parents, and afterwards a great many attitudes have been arrived at personally and are harder to change. It may also be that group affiliation tends to have been fixed by the age of 25 so points of reference do not change as much thereafter.

Apart from one's general sense of self-esteem, there is a kind of localised or subject specific sense of self-esteem as well. This is a person's

sense of self-perceived expertise in a given area. The more a person perceives himself or herself as expert on a topic, the more resistant s/he is to
persuasion. Parents who are rearing their third child can be expected to be
less open to the advertising pressures from baby product manufacturers.
The latest fad in 'unisex' disposable nappies will seem less impressive to
them. That is because they have had an opportunity to build up a sense
of expertise in that area – parenting – and to form more fixed and in their
own eyes at least, more informed, attitudes. Likewise a mechanic will be
less influenced by any kind of slick motor car advertisement than the
average customer will.

Another relevant factor about the audience is the degree to which its
members become actively involved in the attitude change attempt. The
more actively involved they become, the more likely they are to be persuaded. Janis and Mann (1965) manipulated audience involvement in a
series of experimental attempts to change attitudes to smoking. They
found the most successful approach to be a very high involvement technique where the subjects agreed to play the role of a person being told by
a doctor that he or she had lung cancer.

Good orators often seek to create audience involvement when given a
speech by asking questions which the audience can be expected to answer
mentally, even if they do not answer them out loud. Imagine an opposition
politician berating the government of the day during an economic reces-
sion. *'Are you now poorer than you were two years ago? Who is responsible
for that?'* Inevitably, members of the audience will find themselves
answering these questions in their own minds. This means they have
been drawn in and become actively involved in the speech. This gives the
speech more impact.

SUMMARY

Attitudes are not simple uni-dimensional concepts. This makes them more
difficult to define. Every attitude is made up of cognitive, emotional and
behavioural components.

Attitudes are valuable for helping to predict behaviour, though the
relationship between attitudes and behaviour is not always simple.

Attitudes can be inferred from behaviour or from replies to questions.

Frequently the objective is to predict behaviour so the latter option is favoured for measuring attitudes.

Closed format questions are preferable for measuring attitudes because they are easier to interpret. In practice, attitudes are normally measured through the use of several questions, each coming at the target from a different direction. Qualitative approaches such as focus groups are also used to explore attitudes, particularly where the dimensions of an attitude may not be well understood.

There are four main types of attitude questionnaire or attitude scale. They are: the Likert Scale; Osgood's Semantic Differential Scale; the Thurstone Scale; and Guttman's Scalogram Analysis. They differ in how questions are chosen, designed and interpreted.

Attitude measures must be interpreted with caution. Some people tend to answer questions in the way they believe is socially desirable – the Social Desirability Response Set. Even anonymous surveys are not necessarily immune to the effects of circumstances on the answers given. Another reason for caution is that attitude surveys may be a true snap-shot of attitudes at the time but attitudes can change within a short time frame.

Generally, it is expected that attitudes will lead to behaviours that are consistent with them. This is not always true. Sometimes, due to external pressure, individuals may behave contrary to their attitudes, even in quite extreme ways. Research has shown that they may then change their attitudes to fit their behaviour due to cognitive dissonance. Occasionally behaviour may precede attitudes, when one is called on to act on a matter about which one has not yet formed an attitude. In such circumstances individuals are likely to form attitudes that fit with their behaviour.

Attitudes can grow out of beliefs, emotions or behaviours, each of which in turn tend to have social origins. Attitudes may be received ready-made from groups to which an individual belongs, such as his or her family. It is difficult to hold attitudes that are contrary to those of a group to which one belongs.

Every attitude change attempt involves four components: a communicator; a message; a medium; and an audience. Research has focused on aspects of the four components that tend to determine whether an attempt at persuasion will be successful.

The important factors concerning the communicator are whether he or she is credible and attractive. More credible and attractive communicators tend to have more success. Credibility derives from perceived expertise and perceived sincerity. Attractiveness derives partly, but not entirely, from looks.

As regards the message, it tends to be more important than the communicator when the audience is able and willing to give it closer attention. Attentiveness derives from personal relevance, absence of distractions and such personal factors as intelligence and education. More balanced messages that mention contrary arguments are more effective when dealing with a less favourably disposed audience and an audience that is likely to be aware of such counter arguments to the position being proposed. Messages that rely on encouraging attitude change through fear run the risk of back-firing. If too much fear is provoked or if no obvious course of action to reduce the fear is available, then people tend to put the whole message out of their minds and little or no attitude change is achieved.

Media may be divided into personal and impersonal depending on whether a one-to-one interaction is involved. Personal approaches are generally held to be superior in that the message can be tailored to fit the audience. Mass media approaches – much more cost-effective for reaching large audiences – are impersonal. Impersonal approaches can be divided into transient or permanent depending on whether or not the audience can go back over the message. Permanent media are required for messages containing lots of facts or figures. Transient media such as TV are more suited to emotional appeals.

Audiences are more open to attitude change when they consist of individuals who are less intelligent, do not have very high self-esteem, do not perceive themselves as experts on the issue, are aged between 18 and 25 and become actively involved in the attitude change attempt.

REVIEW QUESTIONS

1. Explain the challenges inherent in both defining and measuring attitudes.
2. Describe the four main scales used to measure attitudes.

3. Discuss the relationship between attitudes and behaviour.
4. Describe the main characteristics of the communicator, message, medium and audience that facilitate attitude change.
5. Discuss the various origins of attitudes.

REFERENCES

Allport, G.W., (1954), *The Nature of Prejudice*, Reading, Massachusetts: Addison-Wesley.

Ancona, L. and Pareyson, R., (1968), 'Contributo Allo Studio Della Aggressione: La Dinamica Della Obbedienzia', *Archivio di Pssicologia Neurologia e Psichiatria*, 29, 340-72.

Asch, S.E., (1957), 'An Experimental Investigation of Group Influence', in *Symposium on Preventive and Social Psychiatry*, pp. 15-17, Walter Reed Army Institute of Research, Washington DC: US Government Printing Office.

Belch, G.E., Belch, M.A. and Villereal, A., (1987), 'Effects of Advertising Communications: Review of Research', in *Research in Marketing*, Greenwich, Conn: JAI Press, 9, 59-117.

Bem, D.J., (1972), 'Self-Perception Theory', in L. Berkowitz, (ed.), *Advances in Experimental Social Psychology*, Vol. 6, New York: Academic Press.

Bogardus, E.S., (1925), 'Measuring Social Distance', *Journal of Applied Sociology*, 9, 299-308.

Burley, P.M. and McGuiness, J., (1977), 'Effects of Social Intelligence on the Milgram Paradigm', *Psychological Reports*, 40, 767-70.

Cash, H.C. and Crissy, W.J.E., (1965), 'Comparison of Advertising and Selling', *The Salesman's Role In Marketing, the Psychology of Selling*, 12, 56-75.

Chaiken, S., (1980), 'Heuristic versus Systematic Information Processing and the Use of Source versus Message Cues in Persuasion', *Journal of Personality and Social Psychology*, 39, 752-766.

Chaiken, S., (1987), 'The Heuristic Model of Persuasion', in M.P. Zanna, J.M. Olson and C.P. Herman, (eds), *Social Influence, The Ontario Symposium*, Vol. 5, 3-39, Hillsdale NJ: Erlbaum.

Chisnall, P.M., (1975), *Marketing: A Behavioural Analysis*, UK: McGraw-Hill.

Davidson, A.R. and Jaccard, J.J., (1979), 'Variables that Moderate the Attitude Behaviour Relation: Results of a Longitudinal Survey', *Journal of Personality and Social Psychology*, 37, 1364-1376.

Douglas, T., (1984), *The Complete Guide to Advertising*, London: Macmillan.

Eagly, A.H. and Chaiken, S., (1975), 'An Attribution Analysis of Communicator Characteristics on Opinion Change: The Case of Communicator Attractiveness', *Journal of Personality and Social Psychology*, 32, 136-244.

Edwards, A.J., (1964), 'Social Desirability and Performance on the MMPI', *Psychometrica*, 29, 295-308.

Fazio, R.H., (1990), 'Multiple Processes by Which Attitudes Guide Behaviour: The MODE Model as an Integrative Framework', in M.P. Zanna (ed.), *Advances in Experimental Social Psychology*, Vol 23, pp. 75-109, San Diego: Academic Press.

Fazio, R.H., (1995), 'Attitudes as Object-Evaluation Associations: Determinants, Consequences and Correlates of Attitude Accessibility', in R. Petty and J. Krosnick (eds), *Attitude Change: Antecedants and Consequences*, pp. 247-282, NJ: Erlbaum.

Festinger, L., (1957), *A Theory of Cognitive Dissonance*, New York: Harper and Row.

Festinger, L. and Carlsmith, J.M., (1959), 'Cognitive Consequences of Forced Compliance', *Journal of Abnormal and Social Psychology*, 58, 203-210.

Gorn, G.J., (1982), 'The Effects of Music in Advertising on Choice: A Classical Conditioning Approach', *Journal of Marketing*, 46 (Winter), 94-101.

Guttman, L., (1950), 'The Basis for Scalogram Analysis', in S.A. Stouffer (ed.), *Measurement and Prediction*, Princeton, NJ: Princeton University Press.

Hill, R.P., (1988), 'An Exploration of the Relationship between AIDS Related Anxiety and the Evaluation of Condom Advertisements', *Journal of Advertising*, 17, 35-42.

Hovland, C.I. and Weiss, W., (1951), 'The Influence of Source Credibility on Communication Effectiveness', *Public Opinion Quarterly*, 15, 635-650.

Janis, I.L. and Feshback, S., (1953), 'Effects of Fear-Arousing Communications', *Journal of Abnormal and Social Psychology*, 48, 78-92.

Janis, I.L. and Mann, L., (1965), 'Effectiveness of Role Playing in Modifying Smoking Habits and Attitudes', *Journal of Experimental Research in Personality*, 1965, 1, 84-90.

Joseph, W.B., (1982), 'The Credibility of Physically Attractive Communicators', *Journal of Advertising*, 11, 3, 13-23.

Kallagren, C.A. and Wood, W., (1986), 'Access to Attitude-Relevant Information in Memory as a Determinant of Attitude Behaviour Consistency', *Journal of Experimental Social Psychology*, 22, 328-338.

Kelman, H.C., (1961), 'Processes of Opinion Change', *Public Opinion Quarterly*, 25 (Spring) 57-78.

Kilham, W. and Mann, L., (1974), 'Level of Destructive Obedience as a Function of Transmitter and Executant Roles in the Milgram Obedience Paradigm', *Journal of Personality and Social Psychology*, 29, 696-702.

Kinicki, A.J. and Lockwood, C.A., (1985), 'The interview process: an examination of factors recruiters use in evaluating job applicants', *Journal of Vocational Behavior*, 26, 117-25.

Kretch, D., Crutchfield, R.S. and Ballachey, E.L., (1962), *The Individual in Society*, New York: McGraw Hill.

Krosnick, J.A. and Alwyn, D.F., (1989), 'Aging and Susceptibility to Attitude Change', *Journal of Personality and Social Psychology*, 57, 416-425.

LaPiere, R.T., (1934), 'Attitudes vs. Actions', *Social Forces*, 13, 230-237.

Leventhal, H., Watts, J.C. and Pagano, F., (1967), 'Effects of Fear and Instructions on How to Cope with Danger', *Journal of Personality and Social Psychology*, 6, 313-321.

Likert, R., (1932), 'A Technique for the Measurement of Attitudes', *Archives of Psychology*, 28, No. 194.

MacGreil, M., (1996), *Prejudice in Ireland Revisited*, Maynooth: St Patrick's College.

Mantell, D.M., (1971), 'The Potential for Violence in Germany', *Journal of Social Issues*, 27, 101-12.

Milgram, S., (1963), 'Behavioural Study of Obedience', *Journal of Abnormal and Social Psychology*, 67, 371-378.

Milgram, S., (1965), 'Some Conditions of Obedience and Disobedience to Authority', *Human Relations*, 1965, 18, 57-75.

Milgram, S. (1974). *Obedience to Authority: An Experimental View*, New York: Harper and Row.

Miranda, F.S.B., Caballero, R.B., Gomez, M.N.G. and Zamorano, M.A.M., (1981), 'Obediencia a la Autoridad', *Psiquis*, 2, 212-21.

Morton-Williams, J., (1972), Questionnaire design, in Worcester, R., (ed.), *Consumer Market Research Handbook*, Maidenhead: McGraw-Hill.

Mussen, P.H., Conger, J.J., Kagan, J. and Huston, A.C., (1990), *Child Development and Personality*, (7th Edn), New York: Harper Collins.

Newcomb, T.M., (1943), *Personality and Social Change*, New York: Dryden Press.

Newcomb, T.M., (1967), *Persistence and Change: Bennington College and its Students After Twenty-Five Years*, New York: Wiley.

Osgood, C.E., Suci, G.J. and Tannenbaum, P.H., (1957), *The Measurement of Meaning*, Urbana, Illinois: University of Illinois Press.

Petty, R.E. and Cacioppo, J.T., (1986), *Communication and Persuasion: Central and Peripheral Routes to Attitude Change*, New York: Springer-Verlag.

Petty, R.E., Wegener, D.T. and Fabrigar, L.R., (1997), 'Attitudes and Attitude Change', *Annual Review of Psychology*, 48, 609-647.

Rhodes, N. and Wood, W., (1992), 'Self-esteem and Intelligence Affect Influenceability: The Mediating Role of Message Reception', *Psychological Bulletin*, 111, 156-171.

Rothenberg, R., (1990), 'Talking too tough on life's risks', *New York Times*, 16 February.

Sawyer, A.G., (1973), 'The Effects of Refutational and Supportive Advertising Appeals', *Journal of Marketing Research*, 10, 23-37.

Schurz, G., (1985), 'Experimentelle Uberprufung des Zusammenhangs zwischen Personlichkeitsmerkmalen und der Bereitschaft zum destruktiven Gehorsham gegenuber Autoritaten', *Zeitschrift fur Experimentelle und Angewandte Psychologie*, 32, 160-77.

Sears, D.O., (1981), 'Life Stage Effects on Attitude Change, Especially Among the Elderly', in S.B. Kiesler, J.N. Morgan and V.K. Oppenheimer (eds), *Aging: Social Change*, New York: Academic Press.

Shanab, M.E. and Yahya, K.A., (1978), 'A Cross Cultural Study of Obedience', *Bulletin of the Psychonomic Society*, 11, 267-9.

Shomer, R.W. and Centers, R., (1970), 'Differences in Attitudinal Responses Under Conditions of Implicitly Manipulated Group Salience', *Journal of Personality and Social Psychology*, 15, 125-132.

Szybillo, G.J. and Heslin, R.H., (1973), 'Resistance to Persuasion: Inoculation Theory in a Marketing Context', *Journal of Marketing Research*, 10, 396-403.

Tesser, A., (1993), 'The Importance of Heritability in Psychological Research: The Case of Attitudes', *Psychological Review*, 100, 129-142.

Thurstone, L. and Chave, E.J., (1929), *The Measurement of Attitudes*, Chicago: University of Chicago Press.

Walster, E, Aronson, V., Abrahams, D. and Rottman, L., (1966), 'Importance of Physical Attractiveness in Dating Behaviour', *Journal of Personality and Social Psychology*, 5, 508-516.

Chapter 8

Motivation

LEARNING OBJECTIVES

When you have read this chapter you should be able to:

- explain what is meant by the term 'motivation';
- describe the difference between innate drives and learned motives;
- describe the following theories and explain their relevance to the management of staff in the workplace:

  universal needs theories
    (i) Maslow's Hierarchy of Needs theory;
    (ii) Alderfer's ERG theory.

  work related needs theories
    (i) McClelland's Acquired Needs theory;
    (ii) McGregor's Theory X and Theory Y;
    (iii) Herzberg's Dual Factor theory.

  decisional process theories
    (i) Vroom's Expectancy theory;
    (ii) Adam's Equity theory;
    (iii) Reinforcement theory.

INTRODUCTION

Motivation is the difference between doing and not doing, between continuing or giving up. For John and Selina Hanrahan, it took an awful lot of motivation not to give up in despair.

John Hanrahan operated a 265-acre dairy farm at Ballkurkeen in the rich pasture lands of the Suir valley near Carrick-on-Suir. In 1977 a kind of mysterious plague descended upon the holding. He first began to notice that his cows were at times suffering from a discharge from their eyes and coughing peculiarly. At those times he would notice that his own eyes and even exposed skin were stinging as well. A kind of brownish fog would be visible swirling in the air. The natural assumption was that the only source of the strange gas that seemed to descend on his farm was the large Merck, Sharp and Dohme industrial plant, which manufactured pharmaceuticals nearby. Complaints to the plant managers resulted in promises that the matter would be investigated but the problems continued. The Hanrahans were not the only people affected. Lots of others were bothered by the inter-mittent smells. Investigations by Merck failed to produce an explanation. A County Council investigation prompted by local complaints identified the smell in October 1980 as resulting from a chemical called thioanisole, a foul-smelling but harmless compound, which came from the Merck plant.

By now most of the members of the Hanrahan family were suffering health problems – chest pains, coughing, headache, irritation of the eyes, nose and throat. A Dublin chest specialist concluded that there was strong circumstantial evidence that John's condition had to do with the fumes from the plant. Calves were dying or born dead on his farm at an alarming rate, and at the end of December 1980 the first adult cow died. Many more died later. In 1981, 46 animals in total died on the Hanrahan farm, and in 1982 40 more, an enormous increase in normal mortality rates. Cows were refusing to eat grass in certain fields, vomiting when they did. Silage mysteriously decayed. Garden plants began to grow abnormally.

A plethora of official investigations by the County Council and the Department of Agriculture failed to come up with anything conclusive. John Hanrahan was convinced that nobody in authority wanted to find Merck at fault in case it caused them to relocate their operations or undermined the chances of attracting similar firms to the vicinity. He commenced a legal action in February 1982 against the plant to restrain it from discharging fumes over his farm. Merck at all times denied that they were discharging anything harmful. Later that year John and his family moved to a rented house ten miles away, and he travelled back and forth to the farm each day. Immediately their health began to improve.

By 1983 the issue was on the Government's agenda. Further investi-gations were ordered. The Hanrahans were now caught up in a complex web of scientific claim and counter-claim. Day in and day out they pursued the issue through all available channels. Official investigations proved unable to access relevant information and with the information available could explain nothing. No cause could be established for the terrible state of animal and human health on the farm, which continued unabated. Scientific investigations commissioned by the family found evidence of abnormal pollution. State agencies produced contrary scientific findings. Meanwhile, animals ailed and died.

At the centre of the mystery lay Merck's incinerator and what exactly came from its smoke-stack. Was chemical waste being burned at high enough temperatures to ensure safe destruction? One candidate for all the problems was known to be an almost unbelievably toxic compound called tetrachlorodibenzodioxin, the most deadly substance ever created. Low incinerator temperatures might result in such a compound. In June 1984, the County Council engineer for Tipperary South publicly declared in favour of Merck – that they had been operating their incinerator in accordance with planning permission.

A civil suit for damages was now the Hanrahans' only option. In 1985, the High Court eventually heard the Hanrahan case against Merck, Sharpe and Dohme. After all kinds of conflicting scientific evidence it ruled against John Hanrahan. Were seven years of ill-health, cattle deaths, ceaseless battling with officialdom and endless inconclusive investigation now to be followed by his total ruin? It seemed so. Including legal costs, he now owed three times the total worth of his farm, stock and contents. Most would have given up in despair. John Hanrahan did not. He lodged an appeal to the Supreme Court. It was the last hope. The farm was put up for auction but did not sell. Two-thirds of the stock were auctioned off to pay some of the debts.

On 5 July 1988, the Supreme Court ruled in favour of the Hanrahans. The judges concluded that the only credible cause for all the human and animal health problems was emission from the Merck, Sharp and Dohme plant. They ruled that damages must be set by the High Court. The company offered £500,000. If the Hanrahans refused and the High Court ruled for that or a lower sum, the huge costs of the hearing would fall back on the Hanrahans. The sum offered was scarcely able to cover their outstanding debts, let alone recompense them for the misery they had suffered. It was a terrible dilemma. Again, John Hanrahan and his family somehow found the motivation to go on. They lodged a claim for £1.8 million. Eventually, in November 1990, the company settled privately out of court for a figure rumoured to exceed £1 million.

After 12 years of endless battle against a huge multi-national corporation, with enormous resources and with every official hindrance possible put in their way, they had prevailed. Their health restored, the factory emissions having ceased in the middle of the battle, John Hanrahan and his family returned home and built up the farm again to its former high level of success.

What drove the Hanrahans on? What motivated them? It may have been the need to right the injustice they perceived. It may have been a determination to retain their way of life, come what may. Even they themselves would probably find it hard to identify the total nature of their motivation. The Hanrahan case is an extreme and dramatic one involving exceptional motivation to continue. The same basic concept, however, underpins all of our actions – even the most trivial and mundane.

Motivation is about the 'why' of human behaviour. Why do people behave as they do? Why do different individuals behave so differently under similar circumstances? What drives them to act as they do? These are questions that behavioural scientists have long been concerned with. They are questions also of great practical interest to anyone who seeks to lead others – to managers in workplaces, for example, or to trainers of sportsmen and women. If you wish to lead others, you need to know what will motivate them. What will get the best out of workers on the job or out of players on the field?

Mitchell (1982) offers the following simple definition of motivation:

'Motivation is the degree to which an individual wants and chooses to engage in certain specified behaviours.'

Unfortunately, there does not appear to be any simple easy answer to why individuals choose and want to engage in the great variety of behaviours that they do engage in. No universal key to motivation exists. What will motivate one person will demotivate another. At different times and under different circumstances we are all motivated by a variety of factors.

Inevitably, motivation is a complex mix of several human characteristics that we have explored in previous chapters. Perception, learning, intelligence, personality and attitudes all play a role in what drives any individual in any particular direction. For example, one may be born with a genetic predisposition towards being sensitive to the opinions of others and towards a higher level of intelligence. Then, if one is brought up in a family that places a high premium on scholastic achievement, one learns early on that the good opinion of adults is won through doing well in educational activities. In an intelligent child, for whom scholastic success comes with relative ease, it is not difficult to imagine very positive attitudes to education being developed with a strong motivation to succeed in this area of life. Change any one of the inputs and a different outcome in motivational terms may ensue. Place the same child in a family that has no regard for educational success or alter the genetic predisposition to below average intelligence and an individual with no motivation towards academic success is easily produced.

Because motivation is a complex multi-dimensional concept, it is no surprise that a variety of theories of have been developed, each attempting in its own way to explain what has been observed about the subject. Research has been able to provide evidence that some of these theories are at least partly true. On others, research outcomes are less clear. In this chapter we will discuss eight theories.

DRIVES AND MOTIVES

Writers on the subject often draw a distinction between two classes of motivators – drives and motives. Therefore, we need to be clear at the outset what the distinction is. Drives are unlearned or natural sources of motivation. Hunger and thirst are said to be drives. Humans do not have to learn to feel them as urges to action. Even a new-born baby will cry when s/he feels hungry or thirsty. Other drives are to avoid pain and to preserve normal body temperature.

Motives are things we learn to want. Hence they are also referred to as 'wants'. Most material goods fall into this category. Nobody is born with a need for a Porsche or a villa in the South of France. Nobody is born with a need for designer label clothes. A great deal of what is seen to motivate much of human behaviour is in fact learned. It is possible, however, that learned wants only have the power to motivate because they satisfy deeper natural needs. A review of Chapter 4 on Learning may be worthwhile at this point for a reminder of how associations between wants and innate needs can be formed. The real satisfaction to be obtained through a sports car may be that it gives the owner a feeling that others respect him or her as a result of having it. Whether or not they are actually respected is of little importance – it is the belief that counts. Need for the respect of others may be a natural human drive, which lies within us all. Universal human need theories discussed below follow this kind of logic.

THEORIES OF MOTIVATION

Some theories of motivation focus on innate or natural drives. Some focus on learned wants or motives. Some theories pay less attention to what motivates and more to the process of how behaviour follows from whatever needs (drives or motives) a person has.

We will examine theories under three headings: *universal needs theories*; *work related needs theories*; and *decisional process theories*.

Universal needs theories

Theories in this category propose that there are a limited number of needs that naturally arise in all humans. They are, therefore, drives. Everything we do in our lives is in an effort to satisfy one or other of these needs. When we feel and act on the need to buy those designer label clothes, we are really trying to satisfy some basic, natural human need – perhaps the need to be held in high esteem (to be respected) by others. The same is true of all other human actions. We will look at two closely related theories of this kind: Maslow's Hierarchy of Needs theory and Alderfer's ERG theory.

Maslow's Hierarchy of Needs theory

For the sake of ease of understanding this theory will be described here in a slightly simplified form, leaving out some of the complexities that Maslow dealt with. Abraham Maslow (1943, 1954, 1971) described five human needs, which together account for the bulk of human behaviour. The five needs occur in a loose hierarchy as illustrated above.

The hierarchy is meant to illustrate the way humans are normally affected by the various needs. The lower down the hierarchy, the more immediate the need is – each lower need must be satisfied before the individual comes to feel the need above that as a source of motivation. Let's see what the classes of need mean so that we can understand how this works.

Physiological needs – These are basic survival needs, for food, water, to avoid pain and to avoid excesses of heat or cold. While one is experiencing such needs, one is not very conscious of any other need. Starving people are willing to risk great danger to get food.

Safety/security needs – We are talking here about freedom from fear or threat. The idea is that if your survival is not under immediate threat from say hunger or thirst, you are likely to feel a motivation to avoid other environmental dangers to your well-being in a more long-term sense. The starving person may risk his life attempting to kill a dangerous animal to eat but the better fed one will have more concern about his safety.

Affiliation needs – These are the needs to relate to other people, to love and be loved, to have friendly relationships with others. Maslow suggests that when threat to security is lifted from individuals' lives, they are usually motivated then to satisfy affiliation needs. Most of us are fortunate enough to know no serious lack in relation to the first two needs, but we have all felt strongly motivated by this need.

Esteem needs – This is the need to be respected by others and to respect ourselves for what we are or what we achieve. The theory proposes that this need will only be a significant influence on the behaviour of those who are reasonably satisfied in terms of the three needs previously discussed. The idea is that those longing for love or affection are less likely to feel much of a need to be respected for their achievements.

Self-actualisation needs – Only those who know satisfaction of the other needs will feel this. It is the longing to develop oneself to the greatest degree possible – to fulfil one's own potential. It is the need for growth and self-development in all areas of life. This, according to Maslow, is the ideal situation for a person to be in – seeking to satisfy this need. It is an open-ended need, however. It can never be fully satisfied. Those who are fortunate enough to achieve satisfaction of the lower needs and move on to this level will continue to feel this need as a constant motivator. In Maslow's view, we are only in a truly mentally healthy set of circumstances when we are attempting to self-actualise. It is in effect the goal of human existence.

According to this theory, all human actions can be explained as an attempt to satisfy one or other basic human need. There is, however, no simple way to identify which need is behind a given action. A person may seek work promotion so as to gain more money with which to feel more secure from want in the future, or to gain more respect or esteem from others, or indeed to gain the opportunity to do work which will assist self-development or self-actualisation. This is a defect of the theory in that it explains everything and nothing at the same time.

Since its original publication, writers on work motivation have given a lot of attention to Maslow's theory. This is mainly because it brought about a focus on the higher level needs, particularly the idea that we are all really striving towards self-actualisation. Such needs were traditionally paid scant attention in considering the motivation of workers. It was broadly assumed that work – a necessary evil – was there to satisfy lower survival and security needs. The message to be obtained from Maslow is that work which does not allow for higher level needs to be satisfied is not likely to be motivating for very long. Money alone will not satisfy workers if their jobs are repetitive and boring. Only if they are caught in a permanent survival struggle will they be motivated by such work.

The lesson for employers is that, if possible, work should provide for the chance to self-develop and, lacking that, at least for the chance to gain esteem or respect for achievement.

Alderfer's ERG theory

This is a very similar theory to that of Maslow.

It suggests, however, that all needs can be classified into three groups: *existence needs*, *relatedness needs* and *growth needs*.

Existence needs are made up of Maslow's physiological and safety needs.

Relatedness needs consist of all the social benefits which we derive from other people – love, positive regard, friendship, respect and so on.

Growth needs are similar to Maslow's self-actualisation needs and concern the desire humans have to develop their skills, abilities and personalities.

In effect, Alderfer is saying that Maslow's five needs can be repackaged into a simpler set of three.

Maslow stressed the hierarchical nature of the needs more than Alderfer. Maslow held that a higher level need could not be a source of motivation until those below it in the hierarchy are satisfied and that once satisfied needs tend not to recur later as sources of motivation. Only the top-level need – self-actualisation – can act as a constant, continuing motive. Alderfer, on the other hand, though suggesting a loose hierarchy of needs with existence at the bottom and growth at the top, believed that individuals can return to lower level needs, particularly if frustrated in their attempts to satisfy higher level ones. His theory suggests that an individual whose job fails to offer opportunities for growth or self-development may seek to compensate for this by placing a greater emphasis on relationships or indeed on the money which the workplace may provide.

Maslow's theory strongly suggests that workers will only be satisfied in their jobs if the higher level needs – particularly self-actualisation, towards which all people are driven – can be satisfied through those jobs. Alderfer, in contrast, suggests that individuals may derive motivation in their jobs from the two lower level needs even if growth opportunities are absent. This seems to fit somewhat better with the reality in many workplaces, where workers often seem satisfied without much in the way of self-development opportunities.

Comments on universal needs theories

It is unlikely that any simple theory of motivation can effectively explain human behaviour for all people in all places. The best such theories can do is draw attention to what may be general trends. There is also the danger that such theories are overly influenced by the culture within which they were developed – the modern industrialised society in the United States. It may be the case that such theories with their emphasis on 'higher level' needs are applicable among relatively well fed, well-off individuals who are influenced by a society that places a high emphasis on individual achievement. They may not be so applicable in say, third world societies where the struggle to survive is more acute and where there is often much less emphasis on the individual and more on the group.

A further deficiency of universal needs theories is that they fail to offer any insights as to how an individual comes to choose specific wants as the vehicles for satisfying any particular need. Why does one person seek material goods as the route to 'esteem' while another chooses service to the community as a means to being held in high opinion?

Universal needs in Irish society

It is interesting to examine the application of the universal needs theory to developments in Irish society throughout the 20th century (see Chapter 11 for a detailed discussion of such developments). Particular relevance for the theory can be found in attitudes towards work and marriage. Early in the century, when a very large proportion of the population lived on the land in the shadow of material want, marriage was largely viewed in material/contractual terms. Parents either chose or had a major influence over the choice of marriage partners for their sons and daughters. The criteria used in choosing were largely economic. Parents sought husbands for their daughters who would have the means to support them and their children. For their sons, they sought wives who would bring material wealth in the form of dowries, who would be hard-working and thrifty and who would come from a family that might be of help in times of shortage or difficulty. Little attention was paid to relatedness needs such as love or friendship. The emphasis was largely on existence needs. Only with relatively greater affluence and a somewhat greater confidence in the satisfaction of existence needs did relatedness issues begin to predominate in the marriage context.

Likewise with work. There are many older people who remain somewhat mystified by the younger generations' emphasis on work satisfaction, on the need to enjoy one's job. For the majority of the working population of Ireland, before the economic growth commencing in the 1960s, work was viewed solely as a means to survive. People were glad to get any kind of job and thought little if ever about enjoyment of the tasks involved. Permanence and security were valued above all other job characteristics – even above immediate financial rewards. The relevance of job satisfaction with its emphasis on the intrinsic nature of the work and on opportunities to satisfy esteem, growth and self-development needs was not widely recognised until greater job opportunities allowed many to rise above the threat to basic survival.

It is important, therefore, to recognise that, while there may be universal needs that can potentially motivate, their actual impact on any person in any time or place will inevitably be mediated by the nature of society and its general economic state. Upward progress on the hierarchy of needs can easily be impeded by lack of opportunity to satisfy lower level needs.

The impact of society on work related issues will be further explored in Chapter 11.

Motivation is not just relevant to adults. Teachers are only too aware of how different motivation is among children. Think about why that may be.

Work related needs theories

Included here are the theories of McClelland, McGregor and Herzberg. What they have in common is they deal only with needs that are suggested to be important in the context of motivation at work. Unlike the previous category of theory, they make no pretence to be universal or to explain all of human motivation. Each one will be described in turn.

McClelland (1961) – Acquired Needs Theory

According to McClelland, there are three important needs that are central to why individuals are motivated to work. They are the needs for achievement, affiliation or power, abbreviated by McClelland to nAch., nAff. and nPow.

We are not born with those needs. They are acquired or learned in childhood and perhaps later. There is evidence that, at least in so far as achievement (nAch.) is concerned, we can learn as workers to experience it to a greater extent if given the correct kind of training. Again, we must fall back on learning and also personality theory to understand the development of such needs in the individual.

The need for achievement (nAch.), is the need to know that what we are doing is making a difference, to know that our efforts are being productive and that we are not just time-serving. People with a high level of this need seek feedback. They need to see the outcome of their efforts. Working as a small cog in a big wheel is not for them. They are not happy to just put in a hard day's work. They want to feel sure that it has been worthwhile. People with a high need for achievement make good sales personnel, work hard and constantly seek to improve. Good managers must have a healthy need for achievement. It drives them on to get things done. Indeed, in any job where striving to improve is likely to result in demonstrable improvements in productivity or quality, those with a high need for achievement will tend to excel.

The need for affiliation (nAff.) is the need to maintain good, cordial relations with others. It is the need to be liked. If one's job involves dealing a lot with others it is generally good to have a fairly high need for affiliation. Managers who lack this need are likely to be remote from those they manage – to manage from behind closed doors. Too much of the need can, however, be a disadvantage, particularly if unpopular decisions have to be made in the interests of the common good. If managers have too great a need to be liked, they may become indecisive, trying to please everyone all the time and end up pleasing no one. They may also shy away from unpleasant duties – like making staff redundant – that are sometimes necessary for the long-term good of the organisation. Managers may be better to have only a moderate need for affiliation.

The need for power (nPow.) concerns the need to have control over others, to make decisions that affect others. It is often the driving force behind political aspirations. It is also often the driving force behind the quest for promotion in the workplace. McClelland and Boyatzis (1982) in a long-term follow up study of 235 male managers at the AT&T company found that those with higher needs for power were more likely to get promoted in the workplace. There is a risk, however, that while the need for power may result in individuals seeking and winning promotion, they may do so at the expense of the organisation. They may use power for their own advantage rather than the common good. The same applies to politicians.

Depending on which of the three needs we feel more strongly, we will each be motivated to do different kinds of work. According to this theory, we will only be satisfied in jobs where our particular needs, the ones we feel more strongly, are likely to be satisfied. For example, those with a high need for power will not be happy carrying out research in a laboratory. Those with a high need for achievement may be very happy carrying out research in a laboratory, so long as they are getting something important done. Those with a high need for affiliation will not be happy working in isolation from others or where they are required to do unpopular things.

The general lesson for managing and motivating workers is to match workers to jobs that suit their profile across the three needs. Motivation is largely a recruitment and selection challenge. Get the right person in the job and s/he will be motivated. Insofar as achievement is concerned, training can also be employed to get workers to focus more on this need, which in turn causes it to be felt more keenly. This causes workers to effectively do more or work harder so as to satisfy their enhanced need to achieve.

The relationship between nAch. and a variety of measures of achievement has been well-established through research. Ambrose and Kulick (1999) in a review of studies on employee motivation published between 1990 and 1997 reported relationships between nAch. and 'sales performance', 'job satisfaction' and 'entrepreneurial success'. They also reported an interesting finding from a study by McClelland and Franz (1992) that parenting achievement pressure in the first two years of life was associated with adult need for achievement and earned income. While, of course, association or correlation does not prove causation, this finding points in the direction of potential influences on the development of nAch.

McGregor (1961) – Theory X, Theory Y

From his observations on the manner in which different employers treat their workers, McGregor concluded that employers act as if human motivation conforms to one of two theories, Theory X or Theory Y. His own view was that Theory Y is a much more accurate reflection of workers in general. The theories differ in what they suggest about the needs humans seek to satisfy in the workplace.

According to Theory X, workers are largely driven by the needs for:

1.   money – with which to buy material goods; and
2.   job security – so as to know that the money will always be available.

Workers are not interested in achievement or in taking responsibility. They will only work if it is necessary to earn the money and to maintain job security. If they can arrange to achieve those two objectives without working they will gladly do so. It follows, therefore, that they must be constantly pressurised or coerced into working by threats that they may lose their jobs if they do not. Only constant supervision will maintain effort and there is inevitably an ongoing tension between workers who wish to do as little as possible and their employers who wish them to do as much as possible.

BOX 8.1

HIGHER LEVEL NEEDS – CAN THEY MAKE US WORK HARDER?

Yes! but not all of us in the same way, according to Robert McHenry, Chairman of Oxford Psychologist's Press, writing in *People Management*, the Journal of the Institute of Personnel Development.

Both the universal and the work related needs theories discussed in this chapter emphasise the importance of higher level needs in motivating human behaviour. Those theories have had a real impact on management thinking. It is now fashionable to assume that a sense of achievement, respect for one's contribution, a feeling that one's work is important and opportunities to develop oneself are required for high levels of work motivation.

Of course, the important question for managers is whether or not providing such need satisfaction causes employees to work harder and, if so, how.

McHenry (1997) draws his conclusions from 3,000 returns obtained through a survey of Human Resources Management personnel distributed through People Management and from work carried out by Leigh and Brown (1996) on senior salespeople in the US. He reported that among both personnel and sales people those who have a greater sense of job involvement work harder, devoting more time to their jobs and applying themselves more intensely. Job involvement is the degree to which one's job constitutes a major source of satisfaction in one's life. This is not at all surprising. Where the picture gets more interesting is when the pathways to job involvement are explored for the two groups. Here there is a striking divergence.

Salespeople derive their sense of job involvement from two factors, *Psychological Safety* and *Job Meaningfulness*. The former refers to feelings of being given authority, being supported by their bosses, knowing what is expected of them and being praised for their achievements. The latter refers to encouragement to express their personalities at work, seeing that their efforts make a difference and being challenged by the job demands. Both factors are a necessary prerequisite to motivation.

Personnel workers on the other hand seem to require only *Job Meaningfulness* to become deeply involved in their work and to work harder and more intensely. Interestingly, though they do not need *Psychological Safety* to drive them on, they acquire it in some way as a bi-product of the efforts they make.

McHenry concludes that the conditions for motivation will differ from job to job. Different types of individuals with different needs may be attracted to sales and personnel. He also suggests that to encourage more committed workers, employers might do better to focus on organisational climate issues fostering a sense of *Job Meaningfulness* rather than on the more traditional carrot and stick approaches such as Performance Related Pay systems.

The moral of the story is that the satisfaction of higher level needs can indeed produce harder workers but not always in the same way.

Source: *People Management*, 24 July 1997.

According to Theory Y, workers are driven by the needs for:

1. achievement;
2. growth;
3. recognition;
4. the knowledge that they are doing a good and important job.

It follows that workers need little supervision since they wish to do a good job for its own satisfaction. Money is not seen as the key motivator. Only having the opportunity to know that they are doing something important is likely to maintain motivation.

Theories X and Y are diametrically opposed views of employees. To refer back to Chapter 3 on Perception, different employers possess radically differing schemata for the category 'worker'. McGregor observed that much of industry this century has behaved as if Theory X is true. This has led to the assembly line – a system of doing work that breaks down the whole process into the simplest tasks. Obviously it is wise to do this if employees can be expected to have no interest in working except to gain reward. By giving each person a simple task, they are relieved of any need to apply themselves except in the most mechanical way. Also, it makes the work easy to supervise. It becomes possible to count and quantify output to which reward can then be pegged. Clocking in and fixed duration work breaks are other inevitable outcomes of an emphasis on this theory.

McGregor held that Theory Y is much truer of employees at large. He held that if given responsible challenging work, workers would rise to the challenge and begin to enjoy the work for its own sake. All humans, he believed, are essentially creative and wish to achieve. If they are given no opportunities in this regard and treated as if Theory X is true, they will begin to behave as if it were. If they are treated as if Theory Y is true, they will behave as if it is true with all the benefits for employers that flow from that. It is in the nature of a schema, particularly one governing a human category, to not only direct attention towards confirming evidence but to act as a self-fulfilling prophesy. If you believe sufficiently that members of a group have certain attributes and behave accordingly, chances are they will behave in a way that matches your belief.

Herzberg's Dual Factor theory

Herzberg (1966, 1968, 1987) derived his theory from surveys of largely professional employees – accountants and engineers. He asked them to list the factors that lead to satisfaction in their jobs and the factors that lead to dissatisfaction. One would expect the same factors to appear in both lists. For example, you might expect some individuals to say that their jobs are satisfying because they pay well and others to say their jobs are dissatisfying because of poor payment. He found, however, that by and large different factors were listed in each case.

Herzberg concluded that only the factors that are capable of bringing about satisfaction are actually motivators in any positive way. The factors which may cause job dissatisfaction but are rarely listed as bringing about satisfaction he called 'hygiene' factors.

The motivators he identified were:

1. responsibility;
2. personal advancement;
3. recognition;
4. nature of work;
5. sense of achievement.

The hygiene factors or dissatisfiers were:

1. salary;
2. work conditions;
3. company policies;
4. interpersonal relationships;
5. security.

Hygiene factors can at best only prevent workers from being actively unhappy with their jobs. If there are problems with them, this will certainly undermine motivation. On the other hand they will never get workers to feel a positive sense of satisfaction and motivation in their jobs. In other words, one can pay people lots of money – more money than the employee expects – but unless the motivators are present, he/she will not be motivated in a positive way by the job.

Comments on work related needs theories

Clearly the views of McClelland, McGregor and Herzberg have much in common. They all emphasise achievement as a central need which individuals seek to satisfy through work. McGregor and Herzberg have a similar conviction that money and security are not central to work motivation. They both emphasise intrinsic motives – the satisfaction that is obtained through knowing that one is doing a good job.

The main criticism of these theories is that they may well be true of better paid, more educated and more skilled workers but less true of other employees. Such workers have, in any event, a greater sense of security in their lives and they tend to be more removed from the risk of poverty. In Maslow's terms they have satisfied their physiological and security needs and can therefore afford to have an emphasis on achievement, recognition and growth.

Workers who are closer to the poverty line, and who have greater reason to fear an insecure future, may well derive much more satisfaction from money and job security. The same criticism as that made against the universal needs theories may also apply here. They may well be applicable in the developed industrialised world but not so relevant in the poverty stricken third world. Some research from different countries in the 1990s supports this view. A study of directors of child-care centres in Australia (higher level jobs in a highly developed country) reported a greater emphasis on interesting and challenging work and on a sense of achievement than on salary as a source of motivation (Savery and Wingham, 1991). In contrast, hotel workers in the Caribbean (lower level jobs in an under-developed region) cited higher wages and better working conditions as more important motivating factors (Charles and Marshall, 1992).

Decisional process theories

Theories in this category do not seek to identify the specific needs that lead to motivation. Instead they seek to explain *how* motivation follows from any need that an individual may have. They assume that needs will lead to motivation only where the individuals involved make certain decisions and arrive at certain conclusions. It is the nature of those decisional processes with which the theories are concerned. Under this heading we will examine Expectancy Theory and Equity Theory.

Expectancy theory

This theory has its origins in the work of Edward Tolman, an American cognitive psychologist, in the 1930s. Vroom (1964) is credited with developing the first systematic formulation of expectancy theory for explaining work motivation.

Essentially, the theory explains motivation in terms of the expectations or beliefs that the worker has concerning the outcomes of his/her applying effort to work. The individual will only be motivated to work hard if he/she concludes that certain outcomes will result or certain conditions apply. There are three conditions which must apply: expectancy; instrumentality; and valence.

Expectancy is the conviction that one's effort will result in the work getting done. It amounts to the belief that one is able to do the work. Without this belief, effort will not be applied. A number of factors could undermine this belief: the employer's expectations being unrealistic; the worker not being adequately trained; insufficient resources in terms of material and machinery to do the job; or inadequate back up from colleagues or managers. Any of these might lead an individual to conclude that there is no point in trying since failure will inevitably be the outcome. This means that expectancy is lacking.

Instrumentality is really another kind of expectancy, a second order expectancy. It is the conviction that if the job is done satisfactorily then it is likely to lead to outcomes that may potentially be of benefit or value to workers. Such outcomes might include more money, greater job security, the esteem of the employer, fame or promotion – in short, anything that might potentially be valued by workers. Without instrumentality, the theory suggests that there will be no motivation to work well. The sense of instrumentality will be absent if in general it is perceived by workers that there is no certain relationship between doing a good job and obtaining whatever benefits the workplace has to offer. If, for example, promotion is seen to flow from saying the right things and not from doing a good job or if good workers and bad workers are paid the same, then instrumentality will be obstructed.

Valence is a measure of the value a given worker places on the instrumental benefits that may flow from doing a good job. Some workers may place a high valence or value on money, others on promotion and others on praise and so on. Unless the instrumental benefits have a high valence for a given worker s/he will not be motivated to work hard even if both expectancy and instrumentality are present.

The lesson for employers and managers flowing from this theory is that they should attempt to identify what instrumental benefits are valued by their workers, ensure that those benefits follow only from good work and ensure that employees are always confident that their efforts, if applied, will result in the appropriate standard of work to gain those benefits. It includes a focus on setting reasonable, understandable goals, training and supporting workers adequately and managing the workplace to ensure that good work is rewarded with promotion, bonuses, job security, praise or whatever it is that workers value.

It should be kept in mind that certain instrumental outcomes of value to workers may actually flow from applying less effort in the workplace. Colleagues often put pressure on each other not to work too hard. They fear that one very hard worker may raise the employer's expectations for all of them (see description of Hawthorne Studies in Chapter 9). Thus, keeping in with one's colleagues (an important instrumental benefit to many workers) may require that you do not work as hard as you would be otherwise happy to do. Likewise, not working too hard may save you from tiredness or stress or may leave you more free time (by avoiding overtime, for example) to do things you prefer to do. These are clearly instrumental outcomes that may have high valence for many workers.

Employers have to seek to make the positive outcomes of working harder even more attractive than the negative outcomes as workers are assumed to sum up the negative and the positive instrumental outcomes and only if positive valence remains are they willing to apply more effort. It clearly explains why the chance to make more money is not always a way to get more effort from employees. They may value their free time more than extra money. Extra holidays may sometimes be a better way of getting workers to apply more effort than extra money. It is up to the employer to identify what has valence for employees and make that available.

BOX 8.2

EXPECTANCY THEORY IN THE BANKING WORLD

In October 1998, the Royal Bank of Scotland launched a radical new approach to rewarding over 18,000 staff members in 700 locations. It is the biggest 'Menu Reward' scheme in the UK.

The objective is to make staff feel better rewarded and give them more real value for the rewards they receive. It is all built on the expectancy theory principle of valence – giving individuals rewards they value more highly. Previously, a limited range of perks in addition to salary did not satisfy the needs of many. Company cars were not so highly valued by those who lived in cities. Private medical insurance had little value for someone whose partner already had such insurance covering the family.

Under the new scheme, called RBSelect, everyone is offered the total value of their reward package to 'draw down' in the way that suits them most. The total menu of options includes life assurance, holidays, contributions to pension schemes, company car, childcare vouchers, retail vouchers, a Christmas bonus and a legal rights helpline. All benefits on the menu have a costed value and are interchangeable. An employee can choose any combination up to the value of his/her total reward package. There is even the facility to buy or sell up to three days leave.

The idea is clear. What has a given level of valence for one individual has a very different level for another. Giving such an elaborate set of options maximises the worth of the reward package for each member of staff. Of course, anyone can choose to have their total reward as salary. Better value for money may be obtained, however, through taking some or all of the non-salary options. After all, large companies by purchasing in bulk can obtain products at a lower cost than the average employee can.

Source: *People Management*, 6 May 1999.

The logic of this approach leads to menu reward schemes – a system where work is rewarded from a menu of available benefits as the employee chooses (see Box 8.2). Such a menu may include extra holidays, a shorter working week, more money, a company car, life insurance, enhanced pension rights and so on.

Ultimately, expectancy theory rests on individual decisions, for which the theory does not offer any explanations. What leads a given worker to conclude that he or she is unable to perform the task or that such performance does not lead to personal gain? How do workers evaluate the valence of outcomes? This leads Ambrose and Kulik (1999) to suggest that there is a need for an integration of research into decision theory and expectancy theory, an integration for which they detect little evidence to date after having reviewed the relevant literature. We are back to the issue of perception addressed in Chapter 3 and how people make sense of and come to conclusions about the circumstances around them.

Equity theory

Equity theory derives from the work of Adams (Adams, 1963, 1965). Like expectancy theory, it allows that any worker may be motivated by a variety of different needs, the satisfaction of which they may perceive as rewarding. In this theory, the focus is not on the relationship between work effort and rewards but on the relationship between the rewards a given worker gets and those obtained by comparable workers. According to Adams, workers are motivated to achieve equity of reward with those obtained by individuals they compare themselves with. Each worker first estimates what his/her inputs to the job are. This will include a variety of factors such as:

1. level of responsibility carried;
2. work hours invested;
3. skills and education;
4. unpleasant aspects of work endured – danger, disruption to family life, etc.

Workers also estimate the outcomes or benefits they gain from the job, which may include:

1. pay;
2. fringe benefits – car, health insurance, etc.;
3. status;
4. personal autonomy;
5. job satisfaction;
6. growth opportunities.

They then compare their inputs to their outcomes and estimate the ratio between them. This, of course, is a mental calculation, not expressed in a figure but in a sense of how good a deal they have. This deal is then compared with their perception of the deal obtained by comparable workers of whom they are aware. This comparison may result in three outcomes:

1. a perception of equity – in which case the worker will continue to be as motivated as he/she already is;
2. a perception of negative inequity – others are getting a better deal – in which case motivation will drop, resulting in a drop in inputs (effort) until equity is restored;
3. a perception of positive inequity – others are doing less well – in which case motivation will increase and effort will increase until equity is restored.

This theory does indeed seem to explain the behaviour of workers. It is at the core of the Irish government's fears of awarding exceptional pay increases beyond the guidelines of national pay agreements, even where such workers are able to make a plausible and popular case for exceptional treatment. The first national nursing strike in Irish history in 1999 offers a good example. The government was clearly anxious to satisfy nurses' demands for greater pay and recognition for the undoubted contribution they make to society. However, they were convinced that if they conceded an award to nurses beyond the terms of the national agreement it would encourage other employees to agitate for better pay as a result.

Clearly, giving nurses better pay would not have made other workers less well off. It would simply have upset their notions of equity. Teachers, for example, had always been paid more than nurses. If nurses were seen to catch up, it was anticipated that teachers would feel that for what they themselves put in (four years of earnings foregone while at college, high stress levels, high academic demands) they would now be doing badly compared with nurses. Nurses, of course, perceive the equity ratio in the opposite direction.

Equity theory also explains the extraordinary financial rewards demanded by some categories of workers. Top professional sports stars expect to earn millions of pounds or dollars per year. No top ranking professional footballer in the UK today will be happy to work unless he is paid many thousands of pounds per week and unless he earns very large sums from advertising on top of that. Not many years ago professional footballers earned only a fraction of this. They would continue to be happy with much less except that they see other sports stars, such as US professional basketball players, earning vast sums. It is not the absolute earnings that matter but the comparison.

If supermodel Linda Evangelista can say 'we don't get out of bed for less than $10,000', one can hardly expect Naomi Campbell, Elle McPherson, Helena Christensen or Claudia Schiffer to put themselves outside that 'we', unless they are willing to concede their inferiority. Tom Hanks might be happy to act in a film for a few hundred thousand dollars but not if Leonardo De Caprio or any other actor is able to command millions. Reward becomes a measure of relative worth and status.

At the other end of the scale many extremely gifted scientists, who have devoted at least eight years of poverty to gaining qualifications, work for little more than the average industrial wage. This is because they view their rewards more in terms of the intrinsic interest value of the work than in terms of financial outcomes. They could use their talents to earn much more money in some other field but choose to stay in lowly paid research jobs because they value so highly the work itself. In computing the outcomes from the job, they place a high value on how interesting the work is to them. They may also place a high value on the chance that they may some day be famous for a great discovery. Thus, pay becomes less important. They presumably feel in a reasonable state of equity despite the fact that they may have friends with inferior intellects and abilities who earn far more than them.

A flaw in equity theory as an explanation for behavioural change is that positive inequity can be rectified without applying more effort to the job. Instead of actually putting more effort into one's work so as to raise one's inputs to a level that justifies the outcomes, one can mentally raise the inputs. You can say to yourself that you are getting a better deal than those people you have been comparing yourself with because you have been underestimating your inputs. It is easy to convince yourself that you are doing a better job, are more skilled, carry more responsibility or whatever. On the other hand, in the case of negative inequity, the option of mentally revising inputs in a downward direction is rarely taken. Real de-motivation seems to generally result followed by a drop in effort if outcomes or rewards can not be raised.

Central to equity theory is the whole question of how individuals arrive at their evaluations of inputs and outcomes both for themselves and reference groups or individuals. As with the decisions inherent in expectancy theory, one must fall back on research into perception and decision theory for answers. We have seen in Chapter 3 that one's perceptions about the world are highly selective and are furthermore based on a very personal organisation of the information detected by the senses. Biases and errors are inevitable. The whole process of equity evaluations must be prey to those same problems. It is not surprising therefore that Ambrose and Kulik (1999) conclude from their review of the literature that equity theory's predictions regarding the effects of undercompensation have proven to be very robust but there continues to be ambiguity about the effects of overpayment inequity.

The implications of this theory for managers and employers mainly concern the management of rewards. Generally it is agreed that the effective management of pay or rewards in organisations must take account of both internal and external equity. Internal equity demands that within an organisation, jobs be paid in accordance with their value to the organisation and in accordance with the demands on the worker. External equity demands that jobs in an organisation be paid as well as similar jobs in other organisations within that labour market i.e. within the area over which individuals may move to take up that job. The area may be the globe for some jobs. For others it may be only daily travelling distance. Even today not many jobs have a truly global labour market. Individuals usually look for a job in their own country of origin. That is why there are great disparities of pay for many jobs between one country and another.

Finally it is important to note that it is the perception of inequity even more than the reality that matters. This offers human resource managers the often considerable challenge of not only rewarding workers equitably but convincing them that such is the case.

Reinforcement theory

This theory is more commonly discussed in contexts others than motivation such as learning and personality development. In Chapters 4 and 6 we have already explored the fundamentals of this theory and its other applications. It is, however, a theory that has much to offer in helping to explain the process through which outcomes are likely to motivate specific work behaviours. It is a source of additional insight particularly when placed alongside expectancy theory.

Reinforcement theory has its origins in the work of psychologists Watson (1930) and Skinner (1938). Skinner, in particular, is credited with outlining the process known as operant conditioning, which is at the core of this theory. In simple terms operant conditioning occurs when an individual comes to associate a behaviour with a particular outcome or consequence. If the outcome is desirable or reinforcing, it encourages repetition of that behaviour. If the outcome is undesirable, it discourages repetition of that behaviour. The individual is said to be conditioned by the outcomes to behave in a particular way. According to the theory, behaviour can be easily shaped or moulded simply by the use of reinforcement. If, for example, you wish your employees to be more careful in terms of safety, identify safe behaviours and ensure they are rewarded through praise, or, perhaps, financial bonuses.

Up to this point the theory seems too obvious to offer any new insight into work motivation. After all, everyone knows that one is likely to do whatever wins reward. The real value of the theory comes from the detailed understanding of how behaviour-reinforcement associations are built up, retained and lost. Much of the experimental work involved has been carried out on animals, but the principles established apply equally well to humans, with some modifications.

It has been demonstrated that the behaviour-reinforcement association will be effective only if the individual perceives the reinforcement to result from his or her actions (Maier and Seligman, 1976). In other words, to motivate a particular behaviour, it is not sufficient for that behaviour to be followed by reinforcement. The individual must be convinced that the two are inextricably tied together, that his or her behaviour is capable of winning the reward. This condition is frequently lacking in workplaces. Workers often have a very uncertain conviction about their power to affect the level or nature of reward. Likewise with promotion. If employees are unclear as to what the performance criteria are to win promotion, they are not in a position to have their performance influenced by this potential outcome.

Another insight arising out of reinforcement theory is that it is not only simple discrete actions that can be motivated in this way. Even animals such as rats can learn that a lengthy or complex series of actions will be followed by reinforcement and can be motivated to act accordingly. In fact the evidence suggests that allowing reinforcement to be too easily obtained simply results in immediate de-motivation where there is any failure of the system to deliver. Having learned that reward may require considerable effort encourages persistence.

Reinforcement may, however, have unforeseen effects. There is a strong tendency towards generalising from one reinforced behaviour to other related behaviours. In the workplace it may be expected, for example, that if workers are rewarded for bending the rules in one context they will soon begin to do likewise elsewhere. This is how a culture of behaviour is created. Workplaces need to be consistent. Entertaining good or bad habits in one area will lead to their eventual spread to other parts of the organisation and soon a general culture or set of norms of behaviour is established. Allowing minor breaches of safety regulations to go unchecked today can, if an organisation is not careful, result in major breaches tomorrow. Social learning theorists like Bandura (1977) emphasise another kind of generalisation, from one person to another. While reinforcement or operant conditioning theory focuses on the effects on the individual being rewarded, social learning theory points to the effects on observers. Observing another person being reinforced for a particular behaviour is sufficient to motivate the observer to behave in a similar way expecting to be rewarded in turn.

Reinforcement theory suggests a very careful identification of the behaviours one wishes to motivate in any context and an equally careful emphasis on ensuring that those, and only those, behaviours result in reinforcement. It also suggests the need to ensure that persons to be motivated must clearly perceive the relationship between their actions and the rewards obtained. A further important insight it offers is into the contagion-like spread of reinforced behaviour from one person or one context to another throughout an organisation. The overall lesson is that reinforcement is a powerful tool but one that needs to be handled with care and precision.

There is considerable research evidence concerning the effectiveness of reinforcements for improving employee performance. Stajkovic and Luthans (1997) analysed those organisational behaviour studies published between 1975 and 1995 where reinforcements were introduced for specific behaviours and before and after measures of performance were compared. They concluded that, on average over all the studies, a 17 per cent improvement in performance was obtained.

COMMENTS ON MOTIVATION THEORIES

While, as stated above, many theories of motivation may be culture bound – true only of the industrialised world – they have nevertheless had considerable influence within that zone. The main influence has been to focus attention on higher level needs (as per Maslow) and to depend less on pay and job security to encourage staff to work better. A variety of initiatives aimed at making work more interesting and stimulating have become common. These include job enlargement (giving a greater variety of tasks to each employee) and job enrichment (giving more control and responsibility to workers in the doing of their work). Other initiatives have focused on giving workers a bigger say in the running of organisations. These include consultation committees where all workers are included at some level in the decision-making process within the organisation. The European Commission has been pressing for more worker consultation mechanisms to be made obligatory by law throughout the EU. The Irish Congress of Trade Unions has also been campaigning in favour of such mechanisms in Irish workplaces. Another approach to giving workers a say is the mechanism known as Quality Circles. These are voluntary committees of workers that convene regularly to examine and propose solutions to work related problems. Traditionally, that activity was the sole preserve of managers.

All staff involvement initiatives assume that workers are motivated by the opportunity to achieve, to develop their skills and to be creative in solving problems. If Theory X were really true, there would be no point in these activities.

Other developments arising out of motivation theory concern the management of rewards. Giving workers a share in the profits, or bonuses for special achievement or rewarding them from a menu of options are all approaches designed to meet the requirements of expectancy and reinforcement theory.

The decisional process theories are important for their insights into the conditions under which rewards or the satisfaction of needs may lead to work motivation. They need, however, to be augmented by psychological research into the mental processes involved in making what are usually very individual decisions.

No single theory explains the totality of human or even worker motivation, but the theories described above, taken together, provide a framework within which motivation can be understood and decisions made on how it can be encouraged in any set of circumstances.

SUMMARY

'Motivation is the degree to which an individual wants and chooses to engage in certain specified behaviours.'

(Mitchell, 1982)

Because no universal key exists for explaining motivation, a variety of theories have been advanced, each offering its own insights into the subject.

Certain theories seek to explain motivation in terms of the needs or wants being satisfied by the behaviour observed. Needs may be distinguished from wants on the basis that needs are naturally occurring, whereas wants are learned. Wants may derive their motivating force from their capacity to satisfy underlying needs.

Theories of motivation fall into three general categories: universal needs theories, work related needs theories and decisional process theories.

Universal needs theories suggest that all behaviour is designed to satisfy a limited number of naturally occurring human needs. Maslow's Hierarchy of Needs theory identifies five major classes of need: physiological needs, security needs, social needs, need for esteem and need for self-actualisation. The needs arise throughout humanity in a hierarchy following the order listed here with physiological needs at the bottom and need for self-actualisation at the top. The implication of the hierarchy is that it is necessary to be reasonably confident that needs lower down will be satisfied before one experiences needs further up the hierarchy. In all humans there is an upward drive towards the ultimate goal of self-actualisation. Alderfer's Existence-Relatedness-Growth theory is a somewhat simplified version of Maslow's theory. The main relevance of universal needs theories to the workplace is their emphasis on an inevitable drive towards progress up the hierarchy. This suggests that any class of needs except the needs for self-actualisation has a limited power to motivate.

The major work related needs theories are those of McClelland, McGregor and Herzberg. They specify needs or wants that have particular relevance to motivation in the workplace.

McClelland's Acquired Needs theory identifies the learned needs or wants for achievement, power and affiliation as particular driving forces in relation to work related behaviour. These needs are acquired by different individuals to different degrees and one is likely to be satisfied only in jobs where the work allows for satisfaction of one's particular needs profile. The need for achievement is the need to see results for effort employed. The need for power concerns the desire to have influence over the lives of others while the need for affiliation involves the maintenance of good relations with others.

McGregor's Theory X and Theory Y are contrasting visions of work related needs. Theory X suggests that the prime motives to work are material reward and security. Theory Y, which McGregor holds to be true, suggests that individuals are primarily motivated by factors intrinsic to work activities such as the interest value of the work, the challenge to achieve and be creative and the challenges to give a good service and accept responsibility. Rigid bureaucracies and systems such as the assembly line are based on an acceptance of Theory X. Theory Y leads towards less supervision, greater delegation of responsibility and an emphasis on making work interesting and challenging.

Herzberg's Dual Factor theory identifies work motivation as synonymous with work satisfaction. It identifies a set of factors that will produce positive satisfaction or motivation in the job. These include personal advancement recognition, the nature of the work, and sense of achievement. These factors are contrasted with those that can only prevent an active sense of dissatisfaction in the workplace, which Herzberg refers to as hygiene factors. They include salary, work conditions, company policies and interpersonal relationships.

Decisional process theories are less concerned with identifying precisely which needs or wants lie behind behaviour and concentrate on the process by which they actually result in behaviour changes. Such theories include Vroom's Expectancy theory, Adam's Equity theory and Reinforcement theory.

Expectancy theory suggests that needs or wants can only result in motivation in the workplace if three conditions apply for the workers concerned: expectancy, instrumentality and valence. Expectancy is the confidence they possess that the objectives which they are set can be achieved through their own efforts. Instrumentality refers to the conviction they have that personal benefits in the workplace follow from achieving those objectives. Valence is the measure of importance or worth placed by the worker on the instrumental outcomes or benefits that ensue.

Equity theory describes the process by which outcomes or rewards for any action, e.g. work performance, are evaluated as being motivating or not. The suggestion is that it is not the absolute value of the outcomes or rewards that count but how they compare with the outcomes achieved by other comparable individuals who are perceived as investing a similar level of input in terms of skill, effort, responsibility and so on. If the comparison is unfavourable it results in a desire to increase outcomes and failing that a tendency to decrease inputs. A favourable comparison is said to result in an increase in inputs. The desire is for equity in the input-outcome ratio comparison.

Reinforcement theory explains the process by which behaviours and reinforcing stimuli become associated resulting in motivation. It suggests that it is insufficient for reinforcement to follow a given behaviour for the association to be formed. The individual must in addition be convinced that it is his or her actions that control the reinforcement. Even in animals, reinforcement need not follow each discrete behaviour to motivate. The evidence, on the contrary, is that if reinforcement is too easily obtainable, it simply results in rapid de-motivation if the system ever fails to deliver. The effects of reinforcement are not always predictable. There is a natural tendency to generalise from one behaviour to related behaviours. Therefore, the reinforcement of one behaviour can unintentionally result in motivation to perform other related but possibly unexpected behaviours.

Certain theories of motivation, particularly those that emphasise the importance of specific needs may well be culture bound and reflect the society from which they arise. However, since their common home is the US, with which we share a good deal of cultural values, they should have a reasonable application in the Irish context. No theory of motivation is sufficient to explain such a complex phenomenon. A consideration of the variety of theories discussed in this chapter should provide a framework for a more informed view on the topic.

REVIEW QUESTIONS

1. Discuss, with examples, the relevance of universal need theory to motivation in the workplace.
2. Describe the work related needs theories of McGregor and Herzberg, explaining their common message.
3. Explain Vroom's Expectancy theory and identify its implications for the effective management of employees.
4. Explain how Maslow's Hierarchy of Needs theory may be drawn on to help resolve the conflict between McGregor's Theory X and Theory Y.

5. Describe the insights offered by Reinforcement theory into how to achieve improvement in performance through reward.

REFERENCES

Adams, J.S., (1963), 'Towards an Understanding of Inequity', *Journal of Abnormal and Social Psychology*, November, 422-36.

Adams J.S., (1965), 'Injustice in Social Exchange', in L. Berkowitz (ed.) (1975), *Advances in Experimental Social Psychology*, New York: Academic Press.

Alderfer, C.P., (1969), 'An Empirical Test of a New Theory of Human Needs', *Organisation Behaviour and Human Performance*, May, pp. 142-75.

Ambrose, M.L. and Kulik, C.T., (1999), 'Old Friends, New Faces: Motivation Research in the 1990s', *Journal of Management*, 25, 3, 231-301.

Bandura, A., (1977), Social Learning Theory, N.J.: Prentice Hall.

Charles, K.R. and Marshall, L.H., (1992), 'Motivational Preferences of Caribbean Hotel Workers: An Exploratory Study', *International Journal of Contemporary Hospitality*, 4, 25-29.

Herzberg, F., (1966), *Work and the Nature of Man*, Staples Press: New York.

Herzberg, F., (1968), 'One More Time: How Do You Motivate Employees?' *Harvard Business Review*, Vol. 46, No. 1, pp. 53-62.

Herzberg, F., (1987), 'Workers' Needs the Same Around the World,' *Industry Week*, 21 September, pp. 29-30, 32.

Leigh, T.W. and Brown, S.P., (1996), 'A New Look at Psychological Climate and its Relationship to Job Involvement, Effort and Performance', *Journal of Applied Psychology*, August, 81, 4, 358-368.

Maier, S.F. and Seligman, M.E.P., (1976), 'Learned Helplessness: Theory and Evidence', Journal of Experimental Psychology: General, 105, 3-46.

Maslow, A., (1943), 'A Theory of Human Motivation', *Psychological Review*, Vol. 50, No. 4, pp. 370-96.

Maslow, A., (1954), *Motivation and Personality*, Harper & Row: New York.

Maslow, A., (1971), *The Farther Reaches of Human Nature*, Penguin Books: Harmondsworth.

McClelland, D. C., (1961), *The Achieving Society*, Van Nostrand: Princeton NJ.

McClelland, David C. and Boyatzis, Richard E., (1982), 'Leadership Motive Pattern and Long-Term Success in Management', *Journal of Applied Psychology*, Vol. 67, No. 6.

McClelland, D.C. and Franz, C.E., (1992), 'Motivational and Other Sources of Work Accomplishment in Mid-Life: A Longitudinal Study', *Journal of Personality*, 60, 697-707.

McGregor, D., (1961), *The Human Side of Enterprise*, McGraw-Hill: New York.

McHenry, R., (1997), 'Spurring Stuff', *People Management*, 24 July.

Mitchell, T.R., (1982), 'Motivation: New Directions for Theory, Research and Practice', *Academy of Management Review*, 7, 1, Jan.

Savery, L. K. and Wingham, D.L., (1991), 'Coping With the Career Plateau: Motivators for Directors of Child-Care Centres, *Leadership and Organisation Development Journal*, 12, 20-23.

Skinner, B.F., (1938), *The Behaviour of Organisms*, New York: Appleton-Century-Crofts.

Stajkovik, A.D. and Luthans, F., (1997), 'A Meta-Analysis of the Effects of Organizational Behaviour Modification on Task Performance 1975-95', *Academy of Management Journal*, 40: 1122-1149.

Vroom, Victor H., (1964), *Work and Motivation*, John Wiley: New York.

Watson, J.B., (1930), *Behaviourism*, New York: Norton.

Chapter 9

Groups and Leadership

LEARNING OBJECTIVES

On completion of this chapter you should be able to:

- explain the characteristics of a group;
- distinguish between formal and informal groups ;
- distinguish, within the category of formal groups, 'command' from 'task' groups;
- distinguish, within the category of informal groups, 'friendship' from 'clique' groups;
- describe the five-stage process of group development according to Turkman and Jensen (1977);
- draw on research evidence to discuss the influence of groups on members;
- describe, with examples, the eight team roles identified by Belbin (1981), showing the relevance of each role to group effectiveness;
- explain the concept of leadership in terms of what it achieves;
- discuss what is required for effective leadership.

INTRODUCTION

On 21 November 1915, Irish-born Captain Ernest Shackleton, with his crew of 27 and 74 sledging dogs, abandoned their ship, the *Endurance*, as it was crushed by the enormous power of the Antarctic pack ice in the Weddell Sea, one of the coldest, wildest and most forbidding places on earth. Their dream to be the first explorers to traverse the ice-capped continent on foot was abandoned and a feat of leadership and human endurance without parallel began.

They had already spent over nine months on board ship trapped in the ice. Now, men and animals stood exposed in the middle of a giant ice field. The nearest land was 350 miles away. They had salvaged a number of lifeboats, but with hundreds of miles of ice in all directions they might as well have had boats on the American prairies. There was no choice but to survive on the ice as best they could and hope to drift northwards. For nearly five months they lived in tents so thin that the moon shone through, sleeping on ground sheets that were not waterproof in temperatures so cold that sleeping bags froze solid around the sleeping men. Attempts at dragging the boats over the ice to get to open water proved impossibly exhausting and were abandoned. Food supplies ran dangerously low. Much to the regret of the crew, the dogs had to be shot so that their food could supplement the men's diet. The younger dogs were eaten. They lived in constant fear of the ice cracking beneath their feet and dumping them into the freezing water or, worse still, crushing them as the crack suddenly closed. Some began to doubt if there was any chance at all of survival.

At last, on 9 April 1916, the ice had sufficiently broken up to launch the three open boats: the *James Caird*, the *Dudley Docker* and the *Stancomb Wills*. They set out to row to Elephant Island, a bleak uninhabited rock. What followed were seven nightmarish days and nights. With scarcely any sleep, men whose strength was sapped by a lack of carbohydrate in their diets, their bodies erupting in boils from being constantly wet through with salt water, fought against the most terrible seas to row and navigate. Some suffered from frostbite in temperatures as low as -7F. For the last two days and nights they had no water. When, against all the odds, the three boats landed on an inhospitable beach at Elephant Island many of the men had partially lost their senses.

While the island offered temporary refuge of sorts, a more hostile spot could scarcely be found on the planet. It was without any form of shelter or vegetation, lashed constantly by howling blizzards and so far from any shipping lane that there was no chance at all of their ever being found. By this time the crew had been a total of 497 days at sea, in the *Endurance*, on the pack ice or in the boats. Any form of solid land was welcome.

Food, mainly in the form of seal meat, was abundant, but the weather and conditions were atrocious. Quickly, many of the party began to fall into hopeless despondency and lay helpless in their sodden bags. Shackleton announced a daring plan. He and five others would set out in the largest of the boats, the *James Caird*, and attempt to sail to the whaling stations of South Georgia, 800 miles away. The desperate challenge they would face defies adequate description. The open boat was twenty-two and a half feet long. It was a voyage of ten times the distance they had just completed. It would be through the worst piece of ocean on earth, with winds at 80 miles per hour and waves of 60 feet in height. With the most basic of navigation equipment they would have to use the sun to strike a tiny land-fall in the middle of the vast Atlantic. In winter in those parts there was no guarantee of ever seeing the sun.

On 24 April 1916, the epic voyage of the *James Caird* began. On board with Shackleton was Tom Crean, from Annascaul near Dingle in Co Kerry. Shackleton chose him for his enormous strength, endurance and loyalty. He had previously accompanied the ill-fated Captain Scott on his two polar adventures. Also on board was another Irishman, McCarthy, whose perform-ance on the previous boat journey singled him out. The other members of the crew were Worsley, a gifted navigator, McNish and Vincent. McNish was a skilled carpenter and both he and Vincent had also proved their mettle on the boat journey to Elephant Island. Shackleton had another motivation for including the latter two. Both had proved troublesome and he feared that if left behind they might undermine the morale of the party remaining on the island. They were left under the command of the one man, Frank Wilde, whom Shackleton trusted more than any other.

Food supplies were estimated as enough to last four weeks, the out-side that Shackleton reckoned they could survive at sea. It was three days before the first sighting of the sun on which they depended for navigation. Worsley was to manage only four more sightings of the sun to guide them to South Georgia. The seas were mountainous, requiring constant baling of water to save them from going under. The cold was so intense that spray formed ice, which built up on the boat and had to be exhaustively chipped away lest its weight take it down. The men were constantly wet through and frostbitten, afflicted with salt-water boils and their legs were white and swollen. Sleep was nigh impossible. Vincent and McNish fared the worst. In Worsley's view they were close to death. Again they ran out of water. Yet, against all the odds and after 17 days at sea, on 10 May they landed on South Georgia.

Even then, they still faced seemingly insurmountable obstacles in getting help. They had been forced to land on the uninhabited side of the island. Between them and the whaling stations lay a great frozen and entirely uncharted mountain range. With the currents and winds, sailing round South Georgia in the *James Caird* was impossible. The island would have to be crossed on foot. Shackleton, Crean and Worsley set out on 16 May, leaving the others behind. For four days they tramped up and down across glaciers and through deep snow, often climbing peaks from which they had to return as they had arrived, being faced with impossible precipices beyond. For the last 36 hours they marched without stop and finally staggered into a Norwegian whaling station. At long last, they had regained contact with civilization. A ship was immediately dispatched to collect McCarthy, McNish and Vincent, and eventually a rescue ship reached Elephant Island to save the remaining party of 22. Not one man was lost. All hands were saved.

There is no doubt from the diaries and subsequent publications of the crew that their survival against all the odds was largely down to the exceptional leadership qualities of Shackleton and to his extraordinary grasp of human group dynamics.

His achievement lay partly in an heroic capacity to maintain a spirit of optimism in the face of overwhelming odds and to command respect from those around him, but no less in his attention to a myriad of human details. The choice to take the more problematic McNish and Vincent on the *James Caird* displayed his grasp of how group spirit can be undermined. A collapse in morale among the Elephant Island party could have spelled doom for them. During the long tedious months when the *Endurance* was trapped in the ice, one of the scientists on board, Thomas Orde-Lees, injured his back and was confined to bed and became lonely and depressed. Lees was no favourite of Shackleton's on account of his neurotic pessimism. Despite this he took him into his own cabin and checked regularly on him, bringing him cups of tea, in a very successful effort to raise his spirits. He knew that the spirits of one affected the spirits of all and, besides, every man was his responsibility.

On the iceflows, after abandoning the *Endurance*, lots were cast for the better quality, hide sleeping bags. It seems Shackleton rigged the draw to ensure that the more junior ranks got the best bags. He calculated that their morale was more vulnerable and a little creature comfort would help. He had behaved similarly when distributing winter wear on board the *Endurance*. On the *James Caird*, Shackleton insisted on organising hot food or milk every four hours. He carefully gauged the physical condition of each of the men, and if he noticed a man seeming extra cold or shivering he ordered hot milk immediately for all so that the man would not know it was on his account.

Shackleton regarded his crew of 27 as if it were a single living entity. What happened to one he perceived as profoundly affecting all. The loss of one would be as painful as losing the lot. It was his capacity to turn 28 disparate men (himself included) into a unified group that ensured their survival against enormous odds.

This chapter deals with the twin concepts of *groups* and *leadership*. Previous chapters have to some degree focused on individuals as if their behaviour is independent of others. We have, for example, examined perception, intelligence, personality and attitudes and found them to be characteristics on which people vary. Each person carries around his or her particular way of being. Thus, understanding any person's personality, attitudes and so on will help us to predict how he or she is likely to behave in any given set of circumstances. That is only part of the picture, however. There is another significant source of complexity. Each person is influenced by every other person with whom he or she deals. In other words, we all behave somewhat differently depending on whom we interact with. Thus, a better idea about how anyone will behave in a given situation can be gleaned by looking, not only at his or her personal characteristics, but by also taking into account the kind of individuals he or she will have to interact with and how they behave. It was this reality that Ernest Shackleton faced so starkly when he and his crew of 27 were alone in a most hostile world.

That anyone's behaviour is partly a function of their own characteristics and also of the characteristics of the people they interact with has very significant practical implications in circumstances less dramatic than a polar expedition. Take employers, for example. They wish to recruit employees with the characteristics – personality, intelligence and attitudes – which suit the job on offer. They also, however, need to take into account the fact that most work is done in co-operation with other workers. The prospective employee will function well in the workplace not only by being able to do the tasks that are required but by also being able to get on with the other workers, the group with whom it will be necessary to co-operate. It is a matter of fitting in. A new employee needs to fit in with the existing team. Unlike the crew of the *Endurance*, a failure to fit in is not likely to be fatal, but it will have knock-on effects beyond the individual. If you think about it, the very same thing is true in sport – perhaps more so. An excellent player with great technical skill may be unable to get on with the other members of the team and may, as a result, not only play badly but cause others to play badly as well.

Let's now see what exactly a group is, how it comes about and how it functions and affects the behaviour of individuals within it.

WHAT IS A GROUP?

Just because a number of people happen to be together does not mean that they are a group. A collection of individuals is a group only if certain conditions apply. The following conditions for the existence of a group were outlined by Buchanan and Huczynski (1997):

1. At least two individuals – obviously you cannot have a group of one, but you can have a group of just two.
2. A shared communication network – it must be possible for all the members to communicate with each other without much difficulty. Communication can be through conversation but it can also be through writing or the internet (the members of a group do not have to be in the same place) or through some system of signs. Members of sports teams rely a lot on interpreting each other's movements or behaviour to communicate. They may not speak much to each other during a game. Yet nobody would doubt that the members of a successful team communicate effectively with each other on the pitch or court. Obviously as the numbers in a group grow larger the difficulties of communication increase. Larger

groups often break down into a number of smaller groups. Have you ever observed conversation among a group of a dozen or so friends or associates who are out for an evening together, say in a bar? They may sit in one large group initially but as the evening goes on the large group tends to break down into several smaller groups having separate conversations. The members of a group must also be willing to communicate with each other. If some members will not communicate then they may not effectively be a part of the group at all.

3. A shared sense of identity – members of a group must have a conscious sense of belonging to the group, a sense that they in some way are united by their membership of the group and that there is a difference between those outside and those inside the group. If you belong to a set group of friends, you will be conscious of that feeling when an outsider happens to be present. You are more comfortable with just the group members and you may have a distinct feeling that this other person is an outsider. Members of groups do not see themselves as acting independently. They very much see themselves as acting together as a unit.

4. Shared goals – for a group to exist, there must be a purpose that unites them. The members must have a reason for being together. The shared goal may be nothing more than to have a good time as in the case of a friendship group. It may be to get a job done as in a work group or it may be to win a match or a competition as in the case of a sports group, which we normally call a team. The goal must be something that is sought by all and achievable only through co-operation.

5. Group structure – all groups will have a structure, which consists of rules of behaviour and roles for members. Both the rules and the roles may be formal or informal. A group of friends may have – without them being consciously aware of them – a set of conventions or unwritten rules that govern their behaviour. Such rules may involve loyalty towards each other, or it may not be the done thing in the group to act in bad humour. Individuals may be expected to keep up a good face when together and not burden each other with personal problems – a common convention among male friendship groups particularly. *Consider any friendship groups to*

which you belong or have belonged. Are there or were there unwritten rules governing behaviour? In other groups such as work groups or sports teams the rules may be formally agreed – even written down. The rules of play for a team are understood by all and exist somewhere in a written form. As regards roles, this refers to the unique position each member of any group occupies. In a work group each individual has his or her own job. In a sports team each player has a position. In a friendship group there are no formally agreed roles but individuals typically take on their own unique roles nevertheless. For example, one person may take on the mantle of leader and will be looked to by the others to make decisions. Another may be the funny person who is expected always to be a source of amusement. In the context of work, as we will see in more detail later, these informally assumed roles are of great importance too.

In summary then, a collection of individuals will constitute a group if they are in communication with each other in some kind of co-operative venture to achieve an objective and if they possess a sense of group identity or loyalty.

DIFFERENT KINDS OF GROUPS

While they work in many ways along similar lines, clearly there are differences between groups, say between a work group and a friendship group. The difference is one of formality. This is the first major division along which groups can be distinguished. There are *formal groups* and there are *informal groups*. While both types of groups exist in all kinds of contexts let's explore them as they exist within organisations such as workplaces. We will examine formal groups first.

Formal groups

Formal groups have the following characteristics:

1. Consciously set up – someone always deliberately sets up a formal group for a particular purpose. They do not evolve accidentally in the way that, as we will see later, informal groups do.

2. Overt rules and roles – the rules of behaviour and the roles of the members are set down openly by some authority and real sanctions can be brought by that authority against members who fail to fulfil their responsibilities as implied in those rules and roles. In a work group the organisation allocates jobs (roles) to each of the members and requires that they abide by certain rules such as hours of work and the type and quality of work to be done.

3. Organisationally purposeful – formal groups are set up to contribute to the organisation's overall purpose. In a commercial organisation, the overall purpose is to make a profit for the owners or shareholders. Even groups such as social committees (which arrange sports and social events for employees) fostered by the organisation are set up with a view to profit. The logic is that their activities will promote better relations among employees, which in turn will lead to better co-operation and more productive work. Members of formal groups are expected to be clear about the task or tasks they are there to carry out. They are assigned the tasks by the organisation and they devote their efforts to accomplishing those tasks.

4. Controlled life span – a formal group remains in existence until its job is done. Just as it comes about through deliberate intention, it remains in existence until a formal decision is made to wind it up. In the case of a task group described below, once its specific purpose has been accomplished it is normally disbanded. In the case of command groups (also described below), they remain in existence until such time as it is decided to reorganise the doing of work in a different way. Such groups tend to take on a permanent nature. Even if individual members leave the group due to retirement or job change, the group carries on with new members. While this may interfere with the effectiveness or satisfaction of its members, the group must carry on regardless.

Types of formal groups in organisations

If you were to undertake an analysis of all the formal groups within any organisation, you would have to trace two different kinds of groups: *command groups* and *task groups* (Sayles, 1957). The major difference between them is that employees work on a permanent basis within command groups, while they may or may not belong to task groups at any given time. A task group does not stay in existence on an ongoing basis. It is set up to perform a task and terminated when the task has been completed.

Command groups

Generally, command groups and their membership are identifiable from an organisation's staff chart. Let's take a typical commercial organisation's structure. You will find that it will be divided up into departments and within each department will be different sections with groups of staff co-operating to carry out specific functions of that department. An example might look like this

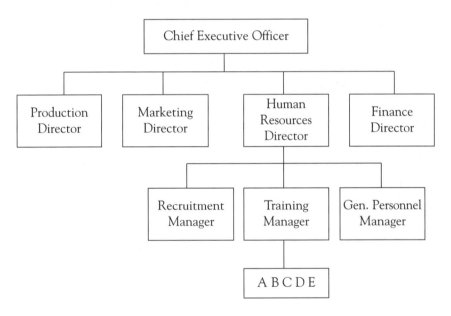

In this example a command group is made up of the Training Manager and the five staff (represented by letters A-E) who work at that activity. Similarly, if one traces the chart down through any of the four departments headed up by directors you will find lots of other command groups. At the top end of the organisation the Chief Executive Officer, together with the four directors, makes up a command group. This is the group that co-operates to make the major decisions on behalf of the organisation.

A command group is so called because it is the mechanism through which commands or instructions are passed down to staff and acted upon. All staff will be in one command group or another. Command groups are in fact the main vehicles through which work is done. If you examine how any of these groups operate you will find that they do indeed function as a group and satisfy the conditions for the existence of a group as described above. Ask members of staff where they work in an organisation and you will be told which command group they belong to. 'I work in the Recruitment section', might be an answer. There will be a clear sense of co-operating to do the job and each individual will have his or her own role. Even if a role seems to be a minor one, it will be essential so as to enable others to do their work. Thus, the members of a command group will need to communicate and co-operate with each other to get the job done.

The last time you went into the library in your college to borrow a book, you inevitably interacted with a member of a command group. The library staff consists of one or more command groups. The person who checked out your book works in co-operation with others to provide a library service to students. He or she could not have checked out your book if someone had not ordered and shelved the book, if someone else had not set up a record system to keep track of books and if someone did not manage the budgets to ensure there was money there to buy them. The library staff who do all this operate as a command group, each one with his or her own role. Instructions are passed down through their manager as to how things are to be done. The group will remain in existence so long as the work is organised in this way.

Task groups

The other type of formal group is a task group. This is set up when a task is identified which does not comfortably fit within an existing command group and when it is not worthwhile to set up a new command group to undertake it. Let's imagine for a moment that a commercial organisation, say manufacturing electrical goods, is finding that there is a diminishing demand for its products. As a solution, the Chief Executive Officer decides that they must diversify into a new product range – the question is which products can be produced efficiently, for which there will be a demand and through which profits can be made.

Video conference: a seven-person task group.

Identifying the products is a task that is partially a production, partially a marketing, partially a human resources and partially a finance problem. The task does not fit comfortably within any particular command group. The solution will probably be to create a task group – set up a working party or a committee with members drawn for their expertise from the various areas of the organisation. This group will continue to meet on a regular basis until it has done its work. Then, when it has identified a suitable new range of products, it may be disbanded again.

At any one time, organisations typically have a number of such task groups in operation for various purposes. The members will of course at the same time retain their positions within their command groups, where they will perform most of their tasks. Only a proportion of their time – often a relatively small one – will be devoted to the task group.

Formal groups outside the workplace

Formal groups can be found in all kinds of circumstances independent of the workplace. If you play a team sport you are a member of a formal group. A football team, for example, is deliberately set up by someone for a purpose – to win a competition, to provide healthy enjoyment to the members or, perhaps, to foster a team spirit or a co-operative ethic among young people. The team members are assigned roles or positions in the team. They must operate according to strict rules that are formally laid down and enforced by a referee. Communication among all the members, often by interpreting each other's movements, is essential during play and clearly there is a common goal (to win) that can only be achieved through co-operation. A sports team is, in fact, one of the clearest examples of a formal group.

Other examples of formal groups outside the workplace are residents committees, Alcoholics Anonymous meeting groups and youth club organising committees.

Informal groups

Side by side with the formal group structure of any organisation lies another reality. This is the informal group structure of the organisation. Identifying this structure is a bit like looking at the world through infra-red glasses. Suddenly a whole new reality becomes visible. It is not a reality that the organisation has in any way sought to create, but it will always have profound effects on how work is done and on how individuals experience the organisation.

An informal group is a collection of individuals who evolve into a group over time as a result of the fact that they are in communication with each other and due to their developing interdependencies for the satisfaction of personal needs. Nobody deliberately sets out to form an informal group. It just develops. It will only emerge if individuals have an opportunity to communicate and if they can use this opportunity to communicate about personal issues or matters not strictly required for the doing of their work.

Think of any collection of individuals in a command group. Imagine them occupying an office space together. Inevitably they will communicate about issues outside of work demands. They will gossip, swap stories and tell each other about their private lives. They will talk about their views on current affairs and so on. Often they will grow to enjoy each other's company. Most people have needs – particularly social needs – which their jobs do not satisfy. They use informal relations with work colleagues to satisfy those needs. You will recall that it was suggested in the discussion of Alderfer's ERG theory of motivation in Chapter 8 that, where the nature of work will not satisfy the higher level growth needs, work motivation may be sustained through the satisfaction of social needs. If you could quantify all the communication that goes on in any organisation that is not strictly necessary for the doing of work, you would in most cases discover that it is a large part of the total. It is in this way that informal groups develop. The members discover that they can satisfy their personal needs for communication and friendship through them.

Informal groups will not mirror the existing formal groups, though there may be a fair degree of overlap. A command group may be made up of, say, seven employees who co-operate together to carry out some part of the organisation's operations. Within that group there may emerge two informal groups of two and three friends, with two individuals remaining aloof and not being particularly friendly with anyone or being a member of either informal group. That individuals are members of informal groups will be evident from their behaviour. They will chat more together, share confidences, trust each other with information and do things together, like going for coffee breaks. They may also socialise with each other outside of the workplace. There will be a distinct sense of group identity, carrying with it the notion of an in-group, out-group divide. Others who work with them will be conscious of the group as being such.

Think about the existence of informal groups in your own life. Are you a member of one or more such informal groups? Think about your class at school. Can you recall how many informal groups it broke down into? Have you ever felt excluded by a group? Have you ever felt like excluding someone from a group to which you belonged?

Types of informal groups in organisations

Some writers who have examined the notion of groups in organisations distinguish between what they call *friendship groups* and what they refer to as *cliques or interest groups* (Sayles, 1957). In simple terms, the distinction concerns the motivations of the members, though any group is likely to be a mixture of both. A friendship group may be said to be based on nothing more than the common goal of enjoying each other's company. A clique involves a more material gain or benefit where a group evolves for mutual professional advantage. An 'old boys network' constitutes an example of this. Here we have a group that holds together to help each other gain advantage such as promotion or perhaps to pass on useful information to each other and even to keep information away from others. Women in organisations often complain that they find themselves disadvantaged by the existence of such informal cliques among their male colleagues from which they are subtly excluded because of their sex (Kanter, 1977).

Sometimes cliques exist to help individuals get over some of the information flow barriers that exist in organisations. Generally the departmental structure of organisations constitute one kind of information flow barrier. Knowledge does not make its way as efficiently from department to department as it does within departments. This is often due to the fact that informal groups do not cross over departments and as information often flows most quickly through the 'grapevine' or system of informal contacts, employees may find it hard to discover what is happening in another department. Likewise there is another information flow barrier created by occupational status or position in the management hierarchy. Those at the same level in the hierarchy tend to communicate much more with each other than do individuals at different levels, particularly in an informal way. Thus more senior managers may have no informal contacts with junior staff to find out what they really feel about matters.

In response to these information flow problems individuals sometimes cultivate cliques with members drawn from diverse parts and levels of the organisation. Initially the group may come from friendships fostered throughout individuals' work histories in various roles, perhaps as they progressed up the hierarchy. Those friendships may later be maintained and used as a mechanism for gaining access to informal channels of information. A manager who has been promoted up through the ranks may find it expedient to retain contact with former colleagues he or she was friendly with along the way as a mechanism of overcoming the communication barriers described above.

While it may be useful to distinguish between cliques and friendship groups, it is important to recognise that no informal group will be a pure instance of one or the other. All friendship groups will act to the material advantage of the members. Members are likely to be more loyal to each other and to give each other advantageous information and so on. Likewise, any clique will survive only if the members like each other and retain some degree of friendship. You are not likely to retain a mutually beneficial relationship with someone you dislike. Inevitably, cliques involve some degree of friendship as well. It is the weighting towards one set of objectives or the other that makes a group tend towards being a clique or a friendship group.

THE DEVELOPMENT OF GROUPS

Putting a collection of individuals together and assigning them a set of common objectives does not in itself guarantee that they will become a group. Just because a number of employees have been selected to make up a committee or to staff a section in an organisation, it is not inevitable that those individuals will take on the characteristics of a group we discussed above. In all cases, whether we are talking about formal or informal groups, the individuals involved will have to go through a process of development to arrive at the status of a true group. They may well fail along the way. One particularly insightful view of the development of groups has been offered by Tuckman and Jensen (1977). They suggest a five-stage cycle in the life of any group, i.e. forming, storming, norming, performing and adjourning, the first three stages of which are developmental. Let's look at each of the stages in turn:

Forming – This stage commences as soon as the members are thrown together and have the opportunity to communicate with each other. A number of employees who find themselves sharing an office is a good example. Initially, according to Tuckman and Jensen, they will all be rather wary of each other, anxious to make a positive impression and not to reveal anything about themselves that may not be acceptable to the others. As an employee in such a set of circumstances you may, for example, be wary to reveal that you are a member of a Communist party and regard all work as the exploitation of the masses by organised capitalism. Likewise, you might be slow to reveal that you used to be a big fan of *Abba* or that you support, say, the Wimbledon football team. You may also be unwilling to admit that you hate your job and would rather chat all day long if you could get away with it, or, alternatively, that you see your job as very important and wish that the others would take their jobs more seriously. In short, it is a stage of impression management.

Nobody tends to be too open or honest until by degrees they each get some sense of what the others are like. The forming stage involves a lot of subtle information gathering with members trying to establish the attitudes, motivations and personalities of the others without having to give too much away themselves. Gradually, by revealing a little and gaining acceptance, confidence grows among the group and they begin to open up and communicate more honestly with each other. Also, at this stage, some tentative steps toward the evolution of group rules are taken. Simple things like how informally or formally to address each other may be sorted out, whether it is OK to use some colourful language in each other's presence and so on.

In some cases this stage may fail to progress. Simply, the small overtures that individuals make may not be reciprocated or else do not result in positive responses. In such circumstances the group may get stuck at the forming stage and never move beyond. Each individual remains aloof from the others and communicates only as much as is absolutely necessary. This can be a considerable impediment to getting work done, as a spirit of real co-operation and trust will never emerge.

If, on the other hand, a group makes it beyond the forming stage, gradually a new stage emerges.

Storming – The storming stage is characterised by members being more honest about their own needs and wishes. Individuals feel confident

enough to reveal their hands, so to speak. Inevitably there will be conflicts of interests and motives, hence the term storming. It is a relatively
stormy period in group development. The earlier placid veneer may be
stripped away. In a potential friendship group it may, for example, emerge
that there are two dominant individuals who vie for attention and to
have their ways. Even the existence of a number of very talkative parties
who compete for a hearing can be the cause of conflict. In work groups,
whether command or task, differences of objectives or approaches to
work may emerge. All of this has the potential to cause a group to get
bogged down in disagreements and even acrimony or hostility. It is worth
remembering that two individuals in a relationship can be considered to
be a group. If you have had the experience of dating somebody, you may
recall that initially everything appeared rosy. Then at some point
disagreements may have surfaced and either those disagreements were
handled or the relationship suffered and possibly ended.

If a group is to develop, the storming must gradually give way to a
stage where methods of resolving differences are arrived at. This is the
next stage of group development.

Norming – As the title suggests, norming involves arriving at norms of
behaviour, ways of acting that are acceptable to all. In this stage the
group arrives at some kind of consensus on how things should be done
and who should do what. Basically the rules and roles of the group are
arrived at. In a formal task group, say a committee, the rules may be
openly discussed and agreed. One person may be appointed a chairper-
son. He or she will be given the authority to say who can speak and who
cannot at any given moment when the group is together. This is to prevent everyone talking and nobody listening. Times of meetings and ways
of deciding what will be done may be agreed.

In an informal friendship, group roles may also become fairly fixed
and accepted. The members may accept that one person is rarely serious
and makes a joke out of everything. Initially that may have caused confusion and even resentment. Now it is accepted that the person is just
'like that'. Informal rules are also agreed without them having ever to be
spoken about openly. A rather pushy individual who originally had a
habit of trying to get his own way may come to accept that decisions are

made logically after discussion. That's the way it works and he accepts it. Because some individuals object to politically incorrect – say racist – humour, it may become the norm that nobody makes comments or tells jokes that could cause offence. Norms of behaviour evolve in this way, which the group then observes.

Not all groups will achieve norming successfully. Some will find it difficult to resolve conflicts. Groups that are held up at the norming stage will be noticeable for the amount of time and effort they spend trying to decide how to do things. They will have difficulties making decisions, arguing about how it should be done. You may be aware of couples who are stuck at this stage. They are forever arguing about how to decide things. One says: 'I did the washing up yesterday, you should do it today'. The other responds: 'But there is much more washing up today than yesterday, I'm always getting caught to do it when it is a big job'. Where norming has been achieved there is little argument or discussion over how to decide things.

Acceptance of roles may also be a problem for groups. If one person has a tendency to lead and the others accept that, then there will be no difficulty. The norm is that X is the leader. If that norm is not acceptable to others then there will inevitably be conflict. The same is true for any other role that an individual adopts. Until members of the group are happy with the roles that each person is given or adopts, norming will not have been achieved successfully.

Performing – If norming is complete, then the group will devote most of its energies to getting on with its purpose and rarely have to revert back to sorting out rules or roles. This is the next stage of the group life cycle. A performing work group will get work done efficiently without obstructive or time wasting disagreements. This is not to say that disagreements will be avoided. Indeed, the members of a well-developed group should feel free to disagree because they will have developed norms as to how disagreement is to be handled. In an efficient group disagreements are constructive and result in analysis and discussion. This allows the group to make the best decisions in light of the available information. Imagine you are with a group of friends with whom you get on very well. One of them suggests that you should all go to see a band that is playing in a pub across town. You have been there previously and found the place exceptionally overcrowded and uncomfortable. Chances are you would have no hesitation in saying this to your colleagues. This would result in a discussion as to whether that is likely to be the case on the evening in question and whether if it is, that is a sufficient reason to adopt some alternative plan. Other possibilities might be considered and eventually a consensus is arrived at. The point is that if you thought you had good reason to disagree with a suggestion among good friends you should have no reason to conceal your disagreement. Indeed they might not thank you if you failed to disagree and allowed the group to make a bad decision.

Disagreements, then, are not a sign of a malfunctioning group. It is a failure to handle disagreements and benefit from them that indicates that a group has not arrived at the performing stage and is still stuck at the norming stage.

Adjourning – This refers to the closing down or termination of a group. It may happen because the group has accomplished its purpose, as in a task group, or because some of the members are leaving, as in the case of an informal group. Even command groups effectively become new groups when members leave and new ones arrive. The loss of even one member can so radically alter the dynamic of the group for those remaining that it may amount to an adjourning.

When groups have functioned or performed well, adjourning is usually a source of regret for the members. Membership of an effective group, whether formal or informal, is rewarding.

FAILURE IN GROUP DEVELOPMENT

From the above section on the stages of group development it should be clear that groups can develop more or less effectively. This applies both to formal and informal groups. Failure in an informal group typically results in the exit of one or more members. If you fail to find common purposes or ways of achieving them with a group of friends you will eventually give up on the effort and decide to look for friends elsewhere. Of course you may spend a long time trying to make things work before you give up. During this period there will be a badly functioning group.

Anyone who followed the enormously popular Channel 4 *Big Brother* series in the summer of 2000 will recall how conflict diminished as time went on and as the less co-operative characters were eliminated. With the exit of Nick, Caroline, and Nicola, relative calm descended on the household. Little signs of friction were evident in the closing days when only the final three contestants, Darren, Anna and Craig remained. They had endured to the end because they were simply better group players, more capable of dealing with the variety of others they had been thrown in with. If the group did not have the safety valve of eliminating its problems through successive evictions, an entirely different and almost certainly explosive dynamic may have built up as the weeks went by. On the other hand, though it seems unlikely from the mix of characters involved, they might have evolved a set of norms to enable harmonious co-existence.

Where formal groups are concerned, development failure is more problematic because the group members do not typically have the option to give up. You cannot just ignore the other members of your command group in the workplace because you do not get on with them. Members of a task group cannot decide to give up on the project because they have difficulties co-operating. In these contexts, failures to arrive at common objectives or ways of achieving them will inevitably mean poor communication, poor co-operation and as a result work will not be done as well as it could. Employers have a powerful motivation to encourage the development of effective formal groups.

THE INFLUENCE OF GROUPS ON MEMBERS

The broad effect of groups on their members is to cause them to perceive, think and act in a similar way. It is as if a group has a mind of its own and is capable of getting its members to go along with its views. Down the years, a variety of sources of research has amply demonstrated this. Let's look at a few examples.

The Hawthorne Study

Back in the 1920s a major research project was mounted within the General Electrics Company in the US to identify the effects of environmental variables, such as heating and lighting, on productivity among factory workers (Roethlisberger and Dickson, 1939). The project, known as the Hawthorne Study after the plant near Chicago where it was based, quickly concluded that psychological factors, not physical or environmental variables, were the key to understanding productivity. Something within the dynamics of groups seemed to be the key to the problem. A special study was set up at the Hawthorne plant to look into this. It became known as the Bank Wiring Room Observation Study because it involved workers who worked in a particular room in the plant putting electric wires into components known as 'banks'.

The principal finding of the study, which observed two formal groups of workers for several months, was that over time the workers in the room evolved two informal groups. One group emerged at the front of the room and the other at the back and they even came to know each other as the 'group in front' and the 'group in back'. A few workers remained aloof from both groups. More importantly, these groups developed their own informal work rules that dictated the pace at which individuals operated. Workers were prevented from working too quickly or too slowly. If anyone deviated from the accepted pace, he would be tipped off by a colleague or the group would begin to make jokes about him suggesting that he was a 'speed king' or a 'a slave'. Individuals quickly came back into line. It was an informal rule also that no worker would say anything to a supervisor or manager that might in any way reflect poorly on a colleague or get him into trouble. Loyalty was the order of the day.

The Bank Wiring Room Study was an early demonstration of a now well accepted phenomenon. Informal groups in workplaces have a major impact on how workers behave. Essentially, humans like to belong and to be accepted. Informal groups are a vehicle through which that need is satisfied. The price that must inevitably be paid is a giving over of some individual freedom or decision making rights to the group. A group must act as one for the good of all. In the Bank Wiring Room Study the faster workers would have created the effect of putting pressure on their slower colleagues by demonstrating to managers that the job could be done faster. If managers were faced with workers who did not vary much in their level of productivity they would be less inclined to put pressure on anyone. In effect there would be no evidence that the work could be done more quickly. In this way by setting and policing a common pace of work, the informal groups were acting to protect all their members. The price to be paid was everyone having to behave in a similar way. Individualism is stifled in groups.

The Sherif Study

The first well-known experimental demonstration of the power of the group to define the judgment of individuals was carried out by Muzafer Sherif (Sherif, 1936). He had individuals estimate the degree of movement of a pinpoint of light in a dark room. The light was in fact stationary but due to an optical illusion known as the auto-kinetic effect such a light takes on the appearance of movement if it is not illuminating other objects in the room against which its position can be checked. Sherif's key finding was that when individuals were alone in the room making the judgments of movement, they varied quite a lot in how much movement they perceived. Yet when individuals were together they arrived at very similar perceptions of the degree of movement. Furthermore, they were not consciously aware of the way they were influencing each other, each one still believing that he was independently making his own judgments. A further interesting finding was that, having arrived at a group consensus or norm in this way, individuals tended to continue to stick with it even when they were subsequently alone making further estimates of the degree of movement of the light.

Sherif interpreted the finding to mean that where individuals are faced with an ambiguous situation, they will depend on one another for clues as to how to respond or interpret the situation. A high proportion of decisions we make in work and in other aspects of life requires us to make judgments about information that is not entirely clear. Simple examples are how to interpret other people's behaviour or predict how others may react to our behaviour. The implication is that the groups to which we belong – work colleagues and friends – will have a major influence on our decisions and on what we do.

The Asch Study

Another demonstration of the effect of groups on individuals comes from a famous study by Solomon Asch (Asch, 1956). The experiment involved decisions about much more objective, less ambiguous information – the kind of information that you could expect people not to need the help of others to make judgments about. Asch set up an experiment where subjects were asked to judge which one of three lines shown on large cards hung on an easel at the front of the room most closely matched in length a fourth line presented alongside. The lines were drawn so that the answer would be obvious. The subjects viewed the cards in the company of several others and then each person was asked to call out his judgment.

Unknown to the subjects each group judging the line lengths together included only one subject. The rest were confederates of the experimenter who had been instructed to call out the wrong line. The objective was to see what the subject would say. Would he say what he saw or would he somehow be influenced into conforming to the judgments of everyone else? In each group the subject was left towards the last to be asked for his response so he had heard all the others agree on the wrong line before him. To aid the credibility of those reporting the wrong judgment, each subject had sat through previous trials involving other lines where correct judgments had been made by all members of the group. In fact a high proportion of subjects went along with the consensus. Only 26 per cent of subjects were able to consistently resist the pressure to conform to the error over the 18 separate trials which the experiment involved.

Why then did subjects give the wrong answer? In the main they were convinced that the evidence of their own eyes was correct but lacking any explanation for how the consensus was to the contrary, they simply lacked the courage to stand alone and be the odd one out. They felt it was better to conform. In trials where there was one other dissenter from the consensus – even where the dissenter seemed so visually impaired as not to be able to see the lines – conformity dropped very significantly (Allen and Levine, 1971).

This was a striking illustration of the power of groups to dictate how individuals behave, not least because the group here was not a true group at all. It was just a gathering of individuals who had been given no time or reason to develop a group spirit. Yet individuals were driven to conform. Presumably they had generalised from other real groups that it is best not to be the odd one out. It is safer to stick with the crowd in judgment and behaviour. It seems to be in the nature of people to fall in with the crowd. A review of a large number of replications of the Asch experimental design in 17 countries revealed that the conformist effect is more striking in countries with a collectivist or group orientated culture (see Chapter 11 for a discussion of this cultural dimension) and that the level of conformity has shown a decline in the US since the original Asch study (Smith and Bond, 1993). This latter finding may represent a drift over time towards individualism in the US.

Attitude expression and group decision making

Similar conformity effects have been experimentally illustrated on self-reports of attitudes (Crutchfield, 1955). In his study subjects were led to believe that there was a consensus among others on agreement with statements such as 'Free speech being a privilege rather than a right, it is proper for a society to suspend free speech whenever it feels itself threatened'. This produced 58 per cent agreement among subjects tested. Yet in a control group, where they were not led to believe that such a consensus existed among others, only 19 per cent endorsed the statement. In this experiment the subjects could not even see the individuals among whom the consensus was supposed to exist but were aware that those individuals would be informed of their response. It would be even harder to express contrary views to a consensus among a group to which you feel a sense of loyalty and where you are directly faced with the other members.

The difficulty of expressing views contrary to the perceived group consensus can, under certain circumstances, cause groups to make decisions or carry out actions against the better judgment of all the individual members. Janis (1982) has described a phenomenon called 'Groupthink' which can affect high morale, highly cohesive groups. In simple terms the phenomenon amounts to individuals being so loyal and placing such trust in the group that they will not voice dissenting opinions even when they suspect the group may be making a great error. They lull themselves into a false sense of security that if there is the consensus then it must be right. The problem is that everyone is feeling the same and no one says anything. The result is highly ill-advised decisions.

An exacerbating factor is the tendency for groups to make more extreme decisions than individuals. This was originally thought to be a tendency towards the extreme in one direction – towards more risk decisions (Kogan and Wallach, 1967). This became known as the Risky Shift phenomenon. Other researchers, however, identified that the group tended to carry individuals' initial stances further in the direction towards which they were already leaning (Teger and Pruitt, 1967; Myers and Arenson, 1972). Thus, individuals who are inclined towards safe decision-making are likely to play it even safer having discussed the matter as a group. Those who are predisposed towards being 'gung ho' are likely to be even less cautious in a group.

Some of the worst political decisions of the US government over the last four decades (such as the Bay of Pigs invasion of Cuba in 1961) have been attributed to 'Groupthink' among policy advisers (Janis, 1982). Doubtless, a careful investigation would reveal similar influences of 'Groupthink' on high level decision making in this country. The now much maligned dramatic government 'spend, spend, spend' budget of 1977 designed to bolster consumer demand and provoke economic growth may well be a case in point. It marked a radical departure from the hitherto generally conservative financial management of the state's finances and has since been widely identified as a serious mistake and as sowing the seeds of our economic slump in the 1980s. It is doubtful if any one member of government would have felt safe indulging in such enormous borrowing as was entailed. One wonders if any cabinet member counselled against such a risky strategy or if, consumed by 'Groupthink' they felt convinced they could do no wrong. It should be recalled that the party in power at the time, Fianna Fáil, had won the previous general election by an unprecedented margin – a sure source of high morale.

Other group effects

Producing conformity in perception, judgment and behaviour is a major effect of groups. It is not the only effect, however.

One of the major reasons for the widespread use of groups to carry out work is that different members can bring different strengths, knowledge, skill and personality to bear on the task. The effect may be that in combination a group can achieve something more than the sum of individual efforts. Even the simple presence of the other members of a group can have an enhancing effect on performance. Armies the world over make use of this phenomenon where a group dynamic can produce feats of courage and endurance in individuals which on their own they would be quite incapable of achieving. Sports teams produce the same effect.

Not all work is best done in groups, however. There is evidence, for example, to suggest that if a task involves unfamiliar activities, individuals perform better without the presence of others.

In a similar vein, it is commonly assumed that a group brainstorming session will produce a richer variety of ideas as to how to solve a problem due to the fact that in the group one person's ideas will spark off new trains of thought in others. However, research evidence suggests that the opposite is the case. Instead of helping each individual, the group acts to inhibit the flow of ideas. Studies have identified a number of reasons why this is so, including pressure for individuals to conform (e.g. Hoffman, 1979) and too great an impact of high status members (e.g. Hare, 1976). Napier and Gershenfeld (1999) report that eight separate studies involving 228 groups consistently demonstrated that greater success resulted where the group members first worked separately to generate the ideas and later came together to evaluate the overall list.

GROUP EFFECTIVENESS

Since groups are so commonly used to perform tasks or make decisions in the workplace, what makes a group more or less effective is of considerable practical interest. This question has been addressed in a variety of ways by different researchers.

One focus of research in this context has been on the characteristics that individuals display in a group. Belbin (1981) suggests that the key to group (or team, as he calls them) effectiveness is a mix of individuals who will take on complementary roles. Having observed management groups on training courses over several decades, Belbin concluded that there are eight individual roles that any person may adopt in a group. Any one person is likely to consistently display one or two of these roles when working with others. The roles individuals adopt are due to their own personality dispositions. All the roles are informal, in that nobody allocates such a role to each individual. They simply act that way.

To understand the nature of each role and the kind of contribution it involves, let's imagine that we are talking about a group of individuals sitting down together to plan an operation. Let's pretend that they are a group of students who have been formed into a committee to plan the events for next year's rag week. The following, then, is a description of each role with the titles given them by Belbin (1981):

Chairman – The title indicates that those who adopt this role are inclined to act as if they had been appointed as chairpersons. They seek to co-ordinate and control the contributions of the others, to act as a kind of referee, if you like. They stop people from talking over one another or failing to listen. Imagine a group of students, several of whom have their own ideas about the events that should be run, all talking together. The chairman will be the one that says: 'Let's each take our turn here or nobody will get a hearing'. The chairman will also seek to allow the quieter members to make a contribution and help to stop the more dominant ones from taking over. When there is a disagreement, the chair will suggest how it is to be resolved – perhaps by drawing up the advantages and disadvantages of each opposing view on a whiteboard. The great value of the chair is in enabling the group to function and to allow individuals to contribute. The chair is valuable not so much for the content of suggestions or ideas but for giving method and structure to the group. In short they keep order and allow the group to function.

Shaper – The shaper imposes a pattern on the discussion or on the task. Shapers hate confusion. They hate when group discussions are going round in circles. They naturally strive to see a way in which things can be simplified and given a kind of order that will guide the discussion and allow progress to be made.

In our imaginary group of students a great variety of suggestions may have been made as to events that would be nice to run – far more suggestions than there will be time, resources and opportunities to implement. The shaper is the person who is likely to find the means by which the list of suggestions can be limited to something manageable – perhaps by suggesting that the group focus on only those activities which do not demand resources that are not readily available. They may propose that only events with a track record of being successful should be focused on. One way or another, shapers limit discussion to more manageable confines. They set priorities and direct attention to the setting of clear objectives. Their contribution is to bring focus and so enable the group to make progress. Without a shaper a group may go round in circles forever.

Shapers inevitably set boundaries to thought. This is always necessary if progress is to be made but they must be stopped from doing it too quickly. Sometimes when priorities are set too quickly without adequate general discussion, important points are missed out and the group funnels its thoughts in such a way that they forget important points. For example, too hasty an acceptance by the group that only events which have been tried and tested should be looked at will stifle innovation. Likewise, a shaper who causes the group to overly focus on innovation may lead them to eliminate perfectly good events, which have worked well before and might work well again.

Plant – Plants are ideas persons. They are very creative and can come up with a great variety of suggestion or solutions to problems. They tend to think laterally and, therefore, will tend to spot less obvious ideas or strategies that others may never think of. They are likely to be innovative. In our student group, when some novel events are sought the plant will come up trumps. Plants may not be the most practical of people and their ideas may not always be sensible, though they are likely to be enthusiastic about them (at least until the next idea strikes them). A group heavily dominated by plants is unlikely to make much progress but together with more practical people their creativity can be invaluable.

Monitor-evaluator – This is a good role to complement that of plant. Monitor-evaluators are critical thinkers. They are likely to identify quickly what is good and bad about suggestions. They will be able to see why something will not work or what advantages it may have. They will be able to break a problem down into its components and make sense of it. You can see that a Shaper and a Monitor-evaluator may well be the same person, just as you can see that a Shaper and a Plant are hardly likely to be one and the same. Monitor-evaluators may not be very creative in their own thinking, and therefore may not come up with many suggestions, but they are very useful for separating the wheat from the chaff in others' proposals. They stop the group from wasting time following up on proposals that ultimately will not work.

Company-worker – They are so called because employers love them. They are hard working, systematic, practical individuals. They focus on action rather than ideas. They love to turn proposals into working procedures and will then carry out plans systematically. If they have a weakness it is that they may not think enough. Left to their own devices they may well set about the implementation of bad ideas with considerable enthusiasm. It is up to individuals such as the Monitor-evaluator to ensure that the right ideas are being implemented. 'Tell me what to do and I'll see that it's done', is the motto of the Company-worker.

Team-worker – The team worker's concern is neither about ideas nor actions but about people. This person focuses on how others in the group are feeling, on human relations. The team-worker will seek to help others with their weaknesses and to encourage them in their strengths. They will be anxious to help more timid members of the group make a contribution and to ensure them a sensitive hearing if they attempt to involve themselves. They will back up someone who feels put down (perhaps because his/her idea was rubbished rather insensitively by a Monitor-evaluator) and they will rush to improve a bad atmosphere (when, perhaps, a disagreement is getting personal), often through humour. Their big contribution to a group is to help maintain morale. They may not contribute much in the way of ideas or analysis but, nevertheless, can be invaluable in helping the others get along together.

Completer-finisher – The main contribution of this role player is to maintain a sense of urgency in the group, to keep it focused on the clock or the calendar so that deadlines are met and decisions are made in good time.

They will also look to the detail and stop the group forgetting things that need to be done. In our hypothetical student group planning the rag week events, the Completer-finisher is likely to introduce a note of realism when discussion is going on too long and point out that the plans have to be ready by a certain date. It is easy to imagine an individual being both a Shaper and a Completer-finisher. The difference between the roles is that the Shaper will be wedded to a certain vision of how things should be which may hold up progress. The Completer-finisher is likely to be more pragmatic and will be flexible so as to ensure that the job is done on time.

Resources investigator – The focus of the Resources investigator is outwards towards the larger organisation or the larger context within which the group operates. They tend to be individuals with a lot of contacts and are always willing to seek information or resources from elsewhere. When the group needs someone to negotiate on its behalf, this role player volunteers. He/she acts as a valuable link between the group and the wider world. One can easily imagine a Resources investigator being an extravert who is not very happy sitting down discussing things but has lots of contacts and friends, which he/she is only too happy to use on behalf of the group

Belbin (1996) added another team role called the **Specialist.** These are individuals who bring some specific unique skill or source of expertise into the group. They tend to apply themselves within the limited realm of their particular speciality and may not show much interest in the overall project. Nevertheless their special skill or knowledge may be invaluable for group success.

According to Belbin, a group works well if it has a good mix of individuals who will bring the various roles into play. Groups made up of individuals who are too alike may fail in a variety of ways. Too many Shapers are likely to result in disagreements and acrimony about how things should be done. An over-reliance on Company-workers may lead to plenty of action but a lack of imagination and good ideas, while too many Plants will result in a wealth of ideas but little practical progress. Too many Monitor-evaluators may produce lots of clever analysis but little creativity or lateral thinking, a mix that is likely to result in conservatism and little innovation. One could go on and on, but you can see the point. The various role-players are needed to complement each other. They each bring unique strengths to bear, making a group a more potent force than individuals on their own are ever likely to be. Very few individuals will be capable of all those roles.

Finally, it is important to recognise that groups may differ in the degree to which they take on the characteristics of a group as outlined early in this chapter. This will significantly dictate the effect they will have on individuals within them. If the members have a very strong sense of group identity and agreement on common goals they are more likely to be influenced by a group spirit. What the nature of that influence is depends on the norms, values and expectations of the group. In a workplace those factors may influence the members in the direction of higher or lower performance. Clearly the groups studied in the Bank Wiring Room Observation study at the Hawthorne Plant had evolved norms of work that served to restrain output and productivity, at least for the faster workers.

The overall message for employers is that groups can have powerful influences on individuals but by no means always in the direction that employers would like. The challenge for employers is to find ways of harnessing group forces to beneficial effect. The concept of leadership immediately presents as the answer.

LEADERSHIP

The concept of leadership is not easy to define. Napier and Gershenfeld (1999) suggest that it has attracted over 100 separate definitions. The difficulty of pinning down a common definition is largely concerned with the 'how' rather than the 'what' of leadership. In other words, the problem is in agreeing how a leader achieves what he or she achieves. What a leader achieves is much easier to establish. For definitional purposes, therefore, let's avoid the 'how' and concentrate on the 'what'.

Leadership, then, means influencing the behaviour of others towards the achievement of common goals.

The leader directs and motivates. Without the leader, the individuals or groups concerned would not adopt the same objectives and/or would not work together as effectively to achieve them.

Leadership is a role that may be formally given to an individual or may be assumed informally. In a formal group, whether it is a command or a task group, a leader is typically appointed. It is formally understood that this person is responsible for directing the activities of the group so that its goal is achieved. In an informal group there may well be a very obvious leader also but, typically, in this situation leadership is evident not from some formal designation but from the fact that someone comes to be accepted and relied on to fulfil this role.

It is important to understand that in both formal and informal groups leadership may rotate among members. Even if there is a designated formal leader, the actual influence on the group in relation to a particular matter may come from another group member as a result of such factors as personality or expertise.

The concept of leadership can, and frequently does, extend way beyond the group. Leaders may influence the behaviour of a great many groups or individuals even to the point of influencing whole nations and societies. Consider the extent of influence wielded by leaders such as Adolf Hitler or Nelson Mandela, to put together two historical characters from opposite poles of the moral spectrum. The modern mass media, particularly television, makes it easy for leaders to project their appeal to a widespread audience. Nevertheless, if leaders were unable to exert influence on those around them in an immediate personal sense their appeal to a mass audience would be of little consequence. Even Hitler, despite the captivating hold he could exert on crowds when he made speeches at the monster rallies organised by the Nazi party, could not have led Germany in the way he did were he not able to get those around him to do his bidding without question or doubt. His real power lay in the hold he could exert over those in his immediate circle. Albert Speer, one of the Nazi elite who was closest to Hitler, described the nature of Hitler's personal influence:

'One thing is certain: everyone who worked closely with him for a long time was exceptionally dependent on him. However powerful they were in their own domain, close to him they became small and timid.'

(Sereny, 1996, pp. 136-7)

Speer, like others who had been close to Hitler, never seemed able to explain what exactly it was about him that exerted such influence. When pressed he fell back on a word used repeatedly by the others as well: hypnotism (Sereny, 1996, pp. 137, 250).

Unfortunately, as we will see below, it has not proven easy to identify what exactly the personal qualities involved in influential leadership are.

THE 'HOW' OF LEADERSHIP

How do leaders lead? Is it something in the way they behave that enables them to influence others? If so, what is it about their behaviour that matters and how do they come to behave in that way? Are leaders born or made? Is there a common formula for leadership or does the nature of effective leadership depend on a variety of circumstances? These are the questions that lie behind the 'how' of leadership.

Is leadership about behaviour or position? This is the first question we need to examine. There is no doubt that position confers influence over others. Irrespective of how you behave, if you end up in a position of power you will inevitably influence the behaviour of others. A singularly unintelligent, weak-willed, feckless individual who happens to inherit a multi-million pound company will have immediate influence. Employees will do as he or she instructs, at least within certain limits. Whether this influence will take the form of anything that can be called leadership is open to question. Leadership requires the ability to set goals and the stamina to pursue them, while maintaining influence over others to do likewise.

While there is no doubt that having a position of power considerably increases the chances of someone actually leading, it does not at all guarantee that he or she will. The unintelligent, weak-willed and feckless company inheritor is more likely to end up being sidelined in leadership terms and the real running of the company assumed by some senior employee. Now if the same inheritor was unintelligent and feckless but strong-willed, a different outcome might result. The company might very well be led to its destruction.

Leadership then seems to involve personal characteristics. This has led to a hunt for those characteristics that great leaders have had in common. What characteristics did Ernest Shackleton, discussed in the introduction to this chapter, have and are the same traits to be found in other successful leaders? The quest has not proved to be as fruitful as one might expect. While some modest relationships between personal characteristics and leadership have been identified, such as intelligence, desire for power, charisma, social skill and flexibility, no strong relationships are in evidence from research (Aronson, Wilson and Akert, 1999, p. 343). The source of leadership effectiveness must then be sought using a more complex analysis, involving both the leader and the circumstances within which the leader is operating. This is the basis of Fred Fiedler's contingency theory of leadership (Fiedler, 1967, 1978).

FIEDLER'S CONTINGENCY THEORY

Fiedler's theory suggests that there are two important approaches to leadership or styles of leader. One is the *task-oriented leader* who focuses mainly on the objectives to be achieved. The other is the *relationship-oriented leader* who focuses on the feelings of the group being led and on maintaining good relationships among them. Whether one approach or the other is more successful depends on the circumstances, particularly on the amount of control the leader has over the group. Control depends on a variety of factors, such as how clear the goals are, how easy it is for the leader to see whether they are being achieved, how much perceived choice the group members have not to comply with the leader's demands and how committed they are from the outset towards the same goals. If control is very high or very low, according to Fiedler, task-oriented leaders are likely to be more successful. In moderate control situations, relationship-oriented leaders work better.

In high control situations there is no need to spend time on maintaining relationships. The group members will do as directed either because they see no choice or because they are very much committed to the leader's objectives and it is easy to establish whether they are doing so or not. In low control circumstances, particularly where there is a difficulty in establishing what the objectives are, task orientation is called for to avoid confusion and to point the group members in the same direction. The idea is that group members, need to know what to do predominates over their relationship needs. This may well be an application of Maslow's Hierarchy of Needs theory of motivation discussed in Chapter 8. Confusion and uncertainty induces insecurity, which is a need that must be satisfied before individuals come to focus on social or relationship needs. In the moderate control situations the group members perceive that doing as instructed is a matter of some choice and they are not driven by insecurity to cling inevitably to leadership when it is offered. In such circumstances the capacity of poor relationships to interfere with the achievement of objectives is magnified. The leader therefore needs to be able to maintain good relations and morale within the group.

Fiedler's theory has been supported in research across a variety of leadership roles including business managers, college administrators, postmasters and military commanders (Aronson, Wilson and Akert, 1999, p. 346). There is evidence, however, that the theory is only applicable in cultures that emphasise individualism such as found in the US and Western Europe. Collectivist cultures that emphasise the importance of group membership and belonging over individual needs, such as those prevailing in Japan, India and Brazil, require leaders to be high on both task and relationship orientation (Misumi, 1985; Bond and Hwang, 1986; Sinha, 1981).

A reflection on Ernest Shackleton's inspired leadership, discussed at the beginning of the chapter, reveals that he was certainly high on relationship orientation, going to great ends to maintain a positive spirit and morale among his crew. He was also high on task orientation, taking full responsibility for setting the objectives and deciding how to achieve them. Indeed it was his unremitting emphasis on one clear objective – that every member of his crew should escape alive – that enabled its ultimate realisation. Had he suffered any ambivalence in this respect by, for example, crewing the *James Caird* with all the best and most reliable men, he would have deprived the group left on Elephant Island of leadership. They might not have survived so well the four bleak months of the Antarctic winter.

Shackleton, in 1916, should probably be understood to be leading men from cultures that were then more collectivist or group orientated than they would be today. Most members of his crew were British. In those days people in Britain, as in most European countries, came from small tight knit communities, whether urban or rural. His emphasis on both relationships and tasks in leading his men was essential to success, as it would be today, in leading those who come from such collectivist cultures. It is striking that other famous sea captains of the past noted for their leadership, such as Nelson and Cook, had similar reputations for not only being decisive and leading with authority, but also being particularly concerned about the wellbeing of the men under their command.

TRAITS AGAIN

It may strike the more perceptive reader that Fiedler's contingency theory does not really manage to side-step the knotty issue of what personality characteristics contribute to effective leadership. In fact it leads right back in that direction. While effectiveness depends on more than just leadership style, it must also take account of the circumstances of control prevailing in the situation. Does it not follow, however, that the person most suited to be a leader will be the one who can detect the leadership style required in any given situation and then effectively apply that style? This would appear to eliminate anyone who lacks the capacity to judge the situation, is too rigid to adjust accordingly or simply does not have the personal attributes such as decisiveness or empathy necessary for employing the two leadership styles. The converse then should also be the case that those who have the right characteristics ought to be more successful as leaders across a range of situations.

Hogan et al (1994) suggests five traits that appear to fit the bill. They are:

surgent (outgoing and charismatic);
agreeable (co-operative and diplomatic);
emotionally stable (consistent in mood and response, self-controlled);
conscientious (achievement-oriented, motivated to do the right thing); and
having a good *intellect* (clever, penetrating and open to new ideas).

Perhaps in time it will be possible to obtain sufficient research evidence to support this or an alternative formulation of the characteristics of a generally effective leader. It must be kept in mind that those who lack that broad description may be quite effective as leaders in certain circumstances. Agreeableness, for example, matters a lot less if a leader has considerable control over a group.

CAN LEADERSHIP BE LEARNED?

As with so many questions in the field of behavioural science, the answer is: partly.

Management and leadership training is certainly not a waste of time. It is possible to teach people to become better at analysing a situation so as to identify the leadership style required and to enable a more proficient application of those styles. It is always much easier, however, to row with the tide. Those whose innate dispositions make them more agreeable and who are more stable in temperament will always find it easier to build up good relationships with others. Those who have better intellects will always find it easier to analyse a situation and identify the most effective response to carry others with them. Being found to be correct in your judgments is a great basis from which to build the trust necessary to get others to follow you. The cleverer and more temperamentally balanced you are, the more often you will 'get it right'. The personality characteristics identified by Hogan et al (1994) conform very closely to the five-factor model of personality outlined in Chapter 7, for which there is evidence of heritability. In addition, as we saw in Chapter 5, intellect is also inherited to a significant extent. This would suggest a major innate component in leadership ability.

However, just as it is with passing exams in school or college where you do not have to be born with all the ideal characteristics to succeed, leaders can be effective too without coming into the world equipped in the perfect way. But, it helps a lot if they are. Hard work can make up somewhat for a lack of intellect in passing exams, but one is likely to do even better with both hard work and intellect. Leaders can learn to improve their styles but it will be much easier for them if they are naturally disposed in the right direction.

Conversely, being born with all the right personal characteristics such as being clever and conscientious is not enough if you do not apply those characteristics appropriately. Correct application must be learned either through experience or by benefiting from the experience and research of others. To that extent, then, learning is an indispensable prerequisite for effective leadership.

The overall culture and structure of both the workplace and the wider society within which the groups operate have immediate relevance here. It is to those topics that the remaining chapters will be devoted.

SUMMARY

A collection of individuals does not necessarily make up a group. Individuals will only form a group if they are co-operating towards a common purpose, have a sense of group identity, some kind of group structure and are able and willing to communicate with each other.

Groups may be either formal or informal. Formal groups are set up deliberately to achieve a particular purpose. Roles are assigned to individuals and rules are enforced by authority. Formal groups remain in existence as long as the authority that sets them up sees the need for them.

Formal groups can be divided into 'command' and 'task' groups. Within any organisation the command groups are typically identifiable from the organisational staff chart. They are the groups to which employees are assigned and within which they are managed so as to run the day to day operations of the organisation. Task groups are set up on an *ad hoc* basis to carry out some activity that does not fit well within the command group structure.

Informal groups are groups that emerge because individuals are in communication with each other and develop interdependencies for need satisfaction. They are not deliberately established and unlike formal groups they will disband if the members do not find them satisfying.

Informal groups can be divided into 'friendship groups' and 'cliques'. They differ in their objectives. The former emerges purely to satisfy the members needs for friendship and social contact. The latter emerges to provide more instrumental benefits, such as access to information or promotional opportunities, for the members.

Groups of any kind take time to develop. Tuckman and Jensen (1977) have outlined the stages of group development as: forming; storming;

norming; performing; and adjourning. Groups may fail for a variety of reasons to evolve properly. The effect of this is that either they perform poorly or go out of existence.

Groups have powerful influences on the behaviour of individuals. The most notable effect is to cause individuals to conform to group norms in their perceptions, judgments, attitudes and behaviours.

Groups can enable individuals to achieve objectives that would be impossible without the co-operation involved. This is most self evidently true when different skills are combined to produce an overall effect. Groups can also facilitate feats of individual courage or endurance that would not be possible for a person in isolation.

There are situations where groups can have a detrimental effect on performance. 'Groupthink' is a phenomenon where the critical faculties and sound judgment of members can be undermined in a group context with the effect that, collectively, foolish decisions are made, which would be unthinkable for each individual acting alone. Groups can also inhibit performance where a skill is novel or unfamiliar to a person. Another example where individual effort proves better than group effort is in the generation of ideas or solutions to problems. Groups can have inhibiting effects on ideas and suggestions voiced.

A significant factor in the performance of groups concerns the mix of individuals of whom the group consists. Belbin (1981, 1996) identified nine separate team or group roles which individuals may take on when contributing to a group. Each person tends to have one or two preferred roles that are characteristic of him or her regardless of the group involved. The key to group effectiveness is to have a mix of individuals who will be able to take on a range of complementary roles. Individuals who are too alike in their approach to group-work limit the effectiveness of the group.

Leadership may be defined as influencing the behaviour of others towards the achievement of common goals. In groups there may be a designated formal leader or leadership may be assumed on the basis of such factors as personality or expertise. Leadership may rotate within a group with different individuals leading under differing circumstances. Leaders may exert influence long beyond the groups to which they belong though their main impact will be achieved by getting those around them to do their bidding.

It has proved difficult to pin down the personal characteristics necessary for effective leadership. This is because different approaches are effective under differing circumstances. Fiedler (1967, 1978) has proposed a contingency theory of leadership. It suggests that in situations of high or low 'control' task-oriented leadership is more effective. In situations of medium control, relationship-oriented leadership is better. This theory has been supported by research in a variety of situations in individualist cultures. In collectivist cultures where group belonging is seen as more important than individual satisfaction, research evidence indicates that both forms of leadership are important in all circumstances. Hogan et al (1994) suggest that individuals who are strong on the personal characteristics of 'surgency', 'conscientiousness', 'openness', 'stability' and 'intellect' are equipped to make better leaders.

Leadership involves a set of skills that must be learned but those who have suitable personal characteristics are at a considerable advantage in learning and effectively applying those skills.

REVIEW QUESTIONS

1. Describe:
   (a) the essential characteristics for the existence of a group;
   (b) the types of formal groups found in work organisations.
2. Explain, with the aid of examples as appropriate, the stages of group development according to Tuckman and Jensen (1977).
3. With an emphasis on their contribution to group effectiveness, describe the team roles identified by Belbin (1981, 1996).
4. Discuss the effect of group membership on individual behaviour.
5. Discuss the contribution of Fiedler's contingency theory to an understanding of what effective leadership involves.

REFERENCES

Allen, V.L. and Levine, J.M., (1971), 'Social Support and Conformity: The Role of Independent Assessment of Reality', *Journal of Experimental Social Psychology*, 5, 389-399.

Aronson, E., Wilson, T.D.and Akert, R.M., (1999), *Social Psychology*, (3rd Edn), p. 90, New York: Longman.

Asch, S.E., (1956), 'Studies of Independence and Conformity: A Minority of One Against a Unanimous Majority', *Psychological Monographs*, 70, 1–70.

Belbin, M., (1981), *Management Teams: Why They Succeed or Fail*, London: Heinemann.

Belbin, M., (1996), *The Coming Shape of Organisation*, London: Butterworth Heinemann.

Bond, M.H. and Hwang, K.K., (1986), 'The Social Psychology of Chinese People', in M.H. Bond (ed.), *The Psychology of the Chinese People*, Hong Kong: Oxford University Press.

Bond, R. and Smith, P.B., (1996), 'Culture and Conformity: A Meta-Analysis of Studies Using Asch's (1952b, 1956) Line Judgment Task', *Psychological Bulletin*, 119, 11-137.

Buchanan, D. and Huczynski, A., (1997), *Organizational Behaviour: An Introductory Text*, (3rd Edn), London: Prentice Hall.

Crutchfield, R.S., (1955), 'Conformity and Character', *American Psychologist*, 10, 191-198.

Fiedler, F., (1967), *A Theory of Leadership Effectiveness*, New York: McGraw Hill.

Fiedler, F., (1978), 'The Contingency Model and the Dynamics of the Leadership Process', in L. Berkowitz (ed.), *Advances in Experimental Social Psychology* (Vol. II, pp. 59-112), Orlando, FL: Academic Press.

Hare, A.P., (1976), *Handbook of Small Group Research*, New York: Free Press.

Hoffman, L.R., (1979), 'Applying Experimental Research on Group Problem Solving to Organisations', *Journal of Applied Behavioural Science*, 1593, 375-391.

Hogan, R.C., Curphy, G.J. and Hogan, J., (1994), 'What We Know About Leadership Effectiveness and Personality', *American Psychologist*, 49, 6, 493-504.

Janis, I.L., (1982), *Victims of Group Think: A Psychological Study of Foreign Policy Decisions and Fiascos* (2nd Edn), Houghton Mifflin: Boston, MA.

Kanter, R.M., (1977), *Men and Women of the Corporation*, Basic Books.

Kogan, N. and Wallach, M.A., (1967), 'Risk-taking as a Function of the Situation, the Person and the Group', in Newcomb, T.M. (ed.), *New Directions in Psychology III*, Holt, Rinehart and Winston.

Misumi, J., (1985), *The Behavioural Science of Leadership: An Interdisciplinary Japanese Research Program*, Ann Arbor, MI: University of Michigan Press.

Myers, D.G. and Arenson, S.J., (1972), 'Enhancement of Dominant Risk Tendencies in Group Discussion', *Psychological Reports*, 30, 615-623.

Napier, R.W. and Gershenfeld, M.K., (1999), *Groups: Theory and Experience*, New York: Houghton Mifflin Company.

Roethlisberger, E.J. and Dickson, W.J., (1939), *Management and the Worker: Technical vs. Social Organisation in an Industrial Plant*, Cambridge, Mass: Harvard University Press.

Sayles, L.R., (1957), 'Work Group Behaviour and the Larger Organisation', in C. Arensberg et al (eds.), *Research in Industrial Relations*, New York: Harper and Row.

Sereny, G., (1996), *Albert Speer: His Battle with Truth*, London: Picador.

Sherif, M., (1936), *The Psychology of Social Norms*, New York: Harper.

Sinha, J.B.P., (1981), *The Nurturant Task Manager: A Model of the Effective Executive*, Atlantic Highlands, NJ: Humanities Press.

Smith, P.B. and Bond, M.H., (1993), *Social Psychology Across Cultures*, Hemel Hempstead, England: Harvester Wheatsheaf.

Teger, A.L. and Pruitt, D.G., (1967), 'Components of Group Risk Taking', *Journal of Experimental Social Psychology*, 3, 189-205.

Tuckman, B.W. and Jensen, M.C., (1977), 'Stages of Small Group Development Revisited', *Group and Organisational Studies*, pp. 419-27.

Chapter 10

Organisational Design and Culture

LEARNING OBJECTIVES

When you have read this chapter you should be able to:

- explain what is meant by an 'organisation';
- distinguish between an organisation and a group;
- explain what is meant by 'organisational design';
- describe the features of the organisational design known as a 'bureaucracy';
- outline the objectives of the bureaucratic design in terms of its effects on employees;
- explain the 'External Control–Internal Control' dimension of organisational design;
- describe the mechanisms through which an Internal Control approach is realised;
- describe the main influences on organisational design;
- explain the concept of organisational culture, its origins and its impact on behaviour.

INTRODUCTION

Imagine leaving college and taking up a job in an organisation with the following characteristics:

1. no job titles or assigned job roles;
2. no bosses or managers;

3. no chains of command;
4. no pre-determined channels of communication;
5. no rules except to:
   - treat everyone else fairly,
   - encourage help and allow other workers to grow in knowledge skill and scope of responsibility,
   - make one's own commitments and keep them,
   - consult with other workers before undertaking actions that might impact on the reputation of the company.

This is not a fantasy organisation dreamed up by some idealistic organisational theorist. It is the lattice system of W.L. Gore and Associates founded in Delaware in 1958 by Wilbert L. and Genevieve Gore. The organisation was in the top 200 of the Forbes top 500 privately-held companies in 1999 with world-wide sales of $1.23 billion. It is best known for Gore-Tex, the rain-wear fabric but produces a range of products for electronic signals transmission, medical implants and a variety of other uses.

Bill Gore was much influenced by Douglas McGregor's views on management published in his 1960 book *The Human Side of Enterprise*. McGregor proposed in his Theory Y, discussed in Chapter 8 of this textbook, that humans are inherently self-motivated to work and require little management or control. Gore set out to design an organisation that would give maximum freedom to this motivation and release workers from the constraints of bureaucracy and hierarchy.

At W.L. Gore every employee is an 'associate'. It is up to each associate to decide what contribution he or she is most suited to making. Each associate is assigned a 'sponsor' (a more experienced associate) to act as a personal guide and mentor. 'Leaders' emerge naturally due to their contribution and their attraction of followers. Leadership is not an assigned role. Different leaders will guide associates in different activities depending on expertise. Work is largely carried out by small groups or teams. There is no hierarchy of communication. Each associate interacts directly with whichever other associates are relevant at the time and for the purpose in hand.

Reward is based on contribution to the enterprise, as defined by peer rankings twice yearly with the objective of internal equity. Rewards are benchmarked against other companies to maintain external equity.

' The simplicity and order of an authoritarian organisation makes it an almost irresistible temptation. Yet it is counter to the principles of individual freedom and smothers the creative growth of man. Freedom requires orderly restraint. The restraints imposed by the need for co-operation are minimised with a lattice organisation.' – Bill Gore.

Depending on your view of human nature or perhaps on your own attitude to work, you will no doubt have come to your own conclusions about what it would be like to work in an organisation like W.L. Gore. Whatever your views, you will doubtless conclude that the effects of an organisation set up in this way will be profoundly different to that of the way, for example, that an army is designed. In Gore there are no ranks, grades or titles. In an army, rank is everything. In Gore you decide what to do in consultation with your colleagues. In an army you are given orders. In Gore there is no hierarchy of management or line of communication. In an army there is a crystal clear rigid hierarchy of management and communication comes straight down, rarely any other way. The differences go on and on. The two types of organisation are opposite ends of a spectrum of organisational design. This chapter is concerned with the nature of that spectrum and the way in which organisations impact upon the behaviour of those who belong to them.

While, of course, organisations are not human entities and not directly the subject matter of behavioural science, their very considerable effects on people are of great interest to the study of human behaviour. Most individuals, particularly in advanced industrial societies such as ours, spend a great proportion of their time operating within organisations. How they influence our behaviour is, therefore, an important question to explore. Furthermore, organisations, as we will see below when we explore what exactly they are, can best be understood as collections of individuals. Of course organisations also consist of non-human elements such as buildings, equipment and legal frameworks but what they are really like, how they are designed and how they impact on individuals is mainly a function of human decision-making, preferences, motivations, values, attitudes and personalities. To that extent organisations are in many ways 'human' and to be understood through an exploration of human behaviour.

Before the concept of organisational design can be explored, however, it is necessary to be clear about what exactly is meant by an *organisation*.

WHAT IS AN ORGANISATION?

An organisation may be defined as '*a social arrangement for the controlled performance of collective goals*' (Huczynski and Buchanan, 1991).

In simple terms, we are talking here about an arrangement or a set-up involving people that somehow controls or guides the activities of those people so as to get them to achieve a set of common goals. The goals must be formally agreed in some way. If you think about it, this definition would apply to the college in which you are studying. It is an organisation in the sense described here. There are people – the staff and students of the college – and there are arrangements to ensure that they work towards a common purpose or set of objectives. The objectives are to provide teaching and qualifications to students at third level and to do other things such as research and consultancy. There are arrangements to ensure that the staff work together to achieve the objectives. Those arrangements involve such things as:

1. a set of jobs to which staff are assigned – lecturer, registrar, librarian and so on;
2. buildings and equipment to enable the work to be done, such as rooms laid out for classes and laboratories equipped for practical activities;
3. rules governing what staff must do – lecturers must attend to give lectures as per the timetable, for example.
4. a system for paying staff – different salaries for different jobs, payment by credit transfer on set dates.

These are set arrangements that also apply to students. A quick glance through the student rules and regulations, which you were probably given when you entered the college, will give you a summary of those arrangements. The rules are designed to ensure that students co-operate with the systems for education within the college (concerning such issues as lectures, practicals, library and computer facilities) and do nothing to disrupt the process for others.

WHERE DOES ONE FIND ORGANISATIONS?

Employers are normally organisations whether they are big or small.

Consider this question: *Is the shop in which you most commonly buy groceries an organisation?*

Whether it is a branch of a large supermarket chain or a local corner shop, it is still an organisation. There are people who staff it – owners or employees. There are systems for controlling their performance towards a common objective – to make profits by the provision of a retail service to customers. The systems include hours of opening, mechanisms for ordering and recording stock, cash registers for recording the flow of stock and cash, roles and jobs to which employees are assigned and so on.

Sometimes the people involved in an organisation are not employees at all. A sports club may have no employees. The people who help it achieve its objectives are volunteers. Yet they are organisations because they are a mechanism for controlling the performance of people to achieve some common or collective purpose or purposes.

Take some time to give thought to the following: *What do you think are the objectives of your local golf or football club? Think about how such clubs control the behaviour of club members so as to achieve those objectives. Consider what kind of behaviour would result in a member being excluded from the club. It would have to be something that seriously interferes with the realisation of the club's objectives.*

WHAT IS NOT AN ORGANISATION?

It is actually easier to find what are examples of organisations (Iarnród Eireann, the United Nations, The Samaritans, the Department of Social Welfare, your local corner shop and so on), than what are not. There are situations in which people do things together but are not organisations. What they lack is either common agreed purposes/objectives or a system for controlling behaviour and performance. The members of a crowd attending a football match are doing something together, but there is nothing controlling the behaviour or performance of each person. Within the limits of what others will put up with or what the law allows, each person can behave as he or she pleases. In an organisation, each person is under the control of the organisation. The employees cannot behave as they please.

The best way to think about what is and what is not an organisation is to consider activities or tasks that individuals are engaged in and identify whether those activities are under a structure of control leading towards certain objectives. Activities that are engaged in solitarily or together with a few friends or volunteers do not typically involve an organisation. A collection of individuals who meet every Sunday to go for a walk together in the hills does not constitute an organisation. These individuals may, however, evolve into an organisation, if they set up a club with rules, perhaps governing safety, with a mechanism for raising finances, with equipment and with defined roles such as treasurer and walk leaders. The day-to-day activities of the residents of a housing estate or a block of apartments are not under the control of an organisation, in that each person or family operates independently. If they establish a residents' association, it may take on the form of an organisation, however, dictating the behaviour of those who belong to it.

A family: is it an organisation?

Is one's family an organisation? Families are not commonly thought of as organisations. Yet they can have most, if not all, of the necessary characteristics. They have common objectives: the survival, comfort and well-being of the members. They have arrangements for controlling the behaviour of the members so that those objectives are attained by all. Arrangements include agreed mechanisms of obtaining, controlling and spending finances, norms and rules of behaviour such as meal times, bed-times and modes of communication. Property is obtained and used for the common good. Arrangements are policed by authority. Parents usually decide what children may or may not do. If one parent acts contrary to the interests of the family, such as drinking or gambling money needed for housekeeping, the other normally applies pressure to restrain such behaviour. In extreme cases, just as an employee may be fired from a work-place, a family member may be excluded from the family for seriously undermining the common objectives. Examples occur where disruptive delinquent adult sons or daughters are told to move out or where a woman gets a 'barring order' through the courts to exclude a violent partner.

There is one way in which a family might be considered different to other organisations. Other organisations normally have an impersonal dimension. They have an existence above and beyond the individuals that belong to them. Take an organisation like the Samaritans. Even if all the volunteers who currently staff its centres were to leave and be replaced by others the organisation would still be essentially the same. The same is true of a shop (or pub) when sold by one owner to another. If the new owner takes on an entirely new set of staff, it can still retain its organisational identity. This is often reflected in the fact that the name of the shop (or pub) is not changed by the new owners. A given family does not have this impersonal dimension. It has no reality outside of the members. Should they all be killed in a tragic accident, the organ-isation would cease to exist. One should not, however, overemphasise the impersonal dimension in organisations. If there is a radical change in the membership of any organisation its true reality may change so much that it remains in name only. For members it may be entirely a new organisation.

If we are to categorise a family as an organisation, it presents us with the challenge of how to distinguish an organisation from a group. This distinction is easier when an organisation is clearly made up of a collection of groups as in a large workplace. In such an instance a great many individuals may have no contact or communication with each other at all and yet are controlled by the systems of the organisation so as to achieve its objectives. What is the situation when all the members of an organisation are in regular contact with each other, when the organisation consists of a single group? In this instance is the group and the organisation one and the same thing? Let's examine any distinction there may be.

WHAT IS THE DIFFERENCE BETWEEN AN ORGANISATION AND A GROUP?

Think back to what you read in Chapter 9 about the characteristics of a group.

Groups must have a common purpose and always exert control over the behaviour of individuals. Sometimes a formal group may make up all the people in an organisation. Clearly, it would not be a very big organisation, because if the group became too big the members would have difficulty communicating with each other and they would typically break up into several smaller groups. The challenge then facing the organisation is to co-ordinate the activities of all the groups.

Where one group makes up the full membership of an organisation, such as in the case of a family or a small corner shop, the distinction between group and organisation becomes blurred. In communication terms organisational and group communication becomes the same. Likewise, sense of identity or belonging to the organisation is merged with identity with the group. The distinction that remains is that a group is a psychological phenomenon. It is understood in terms of human perception, communication and behaviour. An organisation is, in addition, a material and legal entity. It owns property such as buildings or equipment. It typically has a certain legal dimension or status associated with property held and with responsibilities undertaken. The break up of a family, for example, usually involves legal arrangements about how property is to be divided and how finances are to be organised. An organisation such as a school may possess a culture or ways of doing things and objectives that are retained by tradition even if all the members change. In that sense it is more than just the group or groups that belong to it. It has a reality, both material and cultural, beyond its membership.

Typically, organisations include collections of groups. Think of all the groups that exist in the organisation where you are studying! The achievement of an organisation is to control the performance of all the groups – involving possibly thousands of people, many of whom will not even know each other. Imagine all the individuals involved in a large organisation like the Ford motor car corporation with factories all over the world.

WHAT DO WE MEAN BY ORGANISATIONAL DESIGN?

Just as, say, a car has a design – a plan as to how it is put together and how all the parts relate to each other – organisations always have a design. The design involves the arrangements it has decided on for controlling the behaviour and performance of its members. The design will include all the rules governing behaviour, and the way the organisation assigns different roles to each person. It will also include the mechanisms the organisation uses to allow for communication between the people who belong to it. Think again about how W.L. Gore is designed in terms of rules, roles and communication.

A careful examination of organisations in detail reveals that in design terms they fall along a dimension between two extremes. One extreme is represented best by military organisations – armies, air-forces, navies – the other by organisations such as W.L. Gore. How do they contrast from one another? While the practical differences experienced by employees are myriad, they have one common denominator. This concerns the degree to which the organisation relies on external restrictions on behaviour. All organisations seek to control the behaviour of their members so that they work to achieve its objectives – that is by definition what an organisation is about. The difference lies in the nature of the control.

On the one extreme there is the 'External Control Design', involving a great many rules, tightly defined jobs and close supervision such as one finds in an army. This approach derives to a significant extent from

McGregor's Motivation Theory X (see Chapter 8) in that there is an assumption that unless employee behaviour is externally restricted, organisational objectives will not be met. In contrast is the approach that relies heavily on 'Internal Control Design', the notion that employees internalise the objectives of the organisation and will work towards them all the more effectively and creatively if they are not restricted by tight job definitions and rules about how things should be done. There is no need for close supervision and the associated hierarchy of management because workers can be relied upon to do what is best for the organisation. W.L. Gore exemplifies the Internal Control Design, which derives from Theory Y assumptions about employees.

It is important to understand that what is being described is a dimension of organisational design along which organisations may lie at any point. There is rarely or ever a pure case of Internal or External Control Design. Usually in practice there is some degree of both. For the sake of understanding, however, we will begin exploring the dimension by examining what are the characteristics of 'External Control Design'. It is best to view the dimension from this end because, in practice, every organisation encompasses features of external control and most organisations rely a great deal on this approach to ensure their objectives are met. External Control Design is the norm, not the exception.

The sociologist Max Weber offered a comprehensive account of the design characteristics of an External Control Design organisation which he called a *bureaucracy* (Weber, 1947).

BUREAUCRACY

According to Weber (1947) a bureaucracy is an organisation designed so that it has the following characteristics:

Specialisation – Each job in the organisation is clearly defined in terms of what its holder should do or not do. There are clear tasks and responsibilities which are part of the job and others which are clearly not. The lines between jobs are very clear. This means that job-holders have little freedom about what they can choose to do or get involved in. All that is clearly laid down by the organisation. This has the advantage of clarity.

Everyone knows what he/she should be doing. It has the disadvantage of preventing workers from responding flexibly to situations as they arise. For example, if workers are faced with customer queries, which they can answer, if it is not part of their job in a bureaucracy they are discouraged from providing the answer and must pass it on to the correct person. Specialists work together with similar specialists and with those in closely related areas. Out of this emerges a system of departments where those who do similar work are managed together. Thus an organisation will then tend to consists of departments for such functions as production, purchasing, marketing, human resource management and finance.

Rules – How employees are to conduct themselves and how work is to be done is laid out in detailed rules. Procedures – how a job is to be done – are as important and often seen as more important than getting the job done. Rules may be so detailed as to lay down the way a particular kind of letter is to be phrased, the words that are to be used and not used. This cuts a lot of uncertainty out of work and may ensure that relatively inexperienced workers do things properly by just following the rules and procedures. On the other hand it inhibits flexibility and creativity. A worker may know of a better way to perform a given task, but must still do it 'by the rules'.

Hierarchy of management and responsibility – There is a clear hierarchy of management, often involving many layers. Every employee has a manager to which he/she reports and is responsible. An army is a good example. Every rank is under the supervision of the one above it. Privates answer to NCOs, NCOs to Lieutenants, Lieutenants to Captains and so on up. Normally there are clear 'badges' of authority such as different uniforms or bigger offices. Each rank is expected to show respect and accept the authority of the one above it. Authority tends to derive from rank or grade rather than knowledge or expertise. 'The boss may not always be right, but he's always the boss!'

Impersonality – Employees are expected to carry out their duties without fear or favour. In other words, the rules are to be implemented for everyone, without exception. Civil servants, for example, are expected to treat their relatives and friends no more favourably than anyone else. If your brother or sister is a senior official in the Department of Social Welfare, it should give you no more chance of gaining social welfare entitlements than if you knew nobody there. The clearly defined jobs or roles, the precise rules and the hierarchy of management help to ensure impersonality.

Appointed officials – Employees are selected on the basis of merit and competence. In a bureaucracy, nepotism (giving jobs to one's relatives) is never practised. Neither are employees elected. The Civil Service is a bureaucracy – the Dáil is not. This practice further ensures impersonality and the absence of corruption. It also ensures efficiency. Before the 1840s, the British Civil Service widely practised nepotism. Whole families were regularly employed. It led to appalling inefficiency. Charles Dickens in his novel *Little Dorrit* gave us a fascinating and humorous portrayal of what the British Civil Service was like before it was reformed to make it into a bureaucracy – well worth a read. In the tradition established at that time in Britain, the Civil Service and public sector organisations in Ireland and Britain still adhere closely to the bureaucratic model.

Full-time/career officials – The jobs in a bureaucracy are normally the employees' main or only work activity from which they earn an income. They are, therefore, fully committed to the organisation and its objectives without any competing loyalties. The jobs offer the potential for a career through promotion. Good workers have the opportunity of rising up the hierarchy and taking on more responsibilities for which they are paid higher salaries. All this encourages long-term commitment to the organisation and ensures that employees over time develop the knowledge and skills necessary for doing the work.

Private/official split – In a bureaucracy there is no confusion as to what is the property of the organisation and what is the property of the individual. An employee may handle millions of pounds each day but can make no private use of it. It is like the contrast that exists between modern states ruled democratically and states ruled by Kings and Queens in former times. In the old days the King levied taxes on his subjects, some of which might go to public uses like road building or financing the army. Much of it, however, might also go to building private palaces for the King or funding his lavish lifestyle and those of his family and friends. Modern states levy taxes also but Taoiseachs, Prime Ministers or Presidents do not (or at least should not) get to spend any of it on their own personal needs. The system of government now works much more like a bureaucracy. Similarly, the President or Chief Executive of a large company may have a plush office, a large company car and even an executive jet at his/her disposal. But if he/she is replaced in the job, the property remains part of the company and the new President or Chief Executive gets to use all of it. There is no confusion between the official property of the organisation and the private property of the individual employed by the organisation.

Those characteristics of a bureaucracy, described above, are designed to ensure the following effects:

1. To ensure that the organisation can do its job effectively when old staff members go and new come. The procedures and rules should be capable of being implemented in roughly the same way by any employee. Close supervision guarantees that they are. Furthermore, the existence of permanent/career officials provides a continuous supply of capable staff at all levels in the organisation. When staff members leave, new ones can be obtained through promotion or outside appointment. Effectively, nobody is irreplaceable.

2. To capitalise on the benefits of specialisation. By defining jobs narrowly and restricting individuals to a limited number of tasks, it is possible to promote a higher level of skill through constant practice and to utilise more efficiently individuals' strengths. The logic follows the old proverb that 'a Jack of all trades is a master of none'.

3. To ensure that there is no corruption or favouritism. The organisation should implement the rules without fear or favour. This is especially true of state organisations. Knowing somebody in an organisation should not be a way of gaining advantages. This applies also to private sector commercial companies – it does a company no good at all if contracts are awarded to subcontractors because they have friends in the organisation. Such decisions

should be made on purely commercial grounds for the good of the company. The bureaucratic approach is designed to achieve this. The bureaucracy is also designed to prevent employees benefiting themselves at the expense of the organisation. The emphasis on private/official split and the clear hierarchy of responsibility, where everyone is answerable for his/her actions to a superior, helps to achieve this objective.

Ultimately, the bureaucracy is a system designed to maximise external control over employees. While it is based on a relatively dim view of human nature, one can hardly doubt its achievements throughout the 20th century when the norm in organisational design tended strongly in this direction. Through the assembly line approach in manufacturing industry it facilitated production on a scale entirely unknown in previous times. With this came huge advances in wealth and the kind of lifestyles we enjoy today in the developed world. The bureaucratic approach also enabled the development of state services in the 20th century on a wholly unprecedented scale. It is difficult to see how any other organisational design approach could have achieved the feat of human effort co-ordination that brings us our educational, health and social welfare services.

The External Control Design is not, however, without its downside. It encourages great rigidity and can be very dehumanising and demoralising. Everyone is expected to continue doing things in the traditional way and to stick rigidly to their own jobs. Jobs are reduced to sets of rules, which the employee implements like a machine. While all this may ensure a common standard of performance by all employees in all situations it can be a big problem in times of change. The huge developments brought about by computers in recent decades were a major problem for bureaucracies. Suddenly there were new, more efficient ways of doing everything from typing letters to designing machine components. The old traditional ways had to go. That is very difficult when an organisation has long emphasised doing things as they were always done. Workers find it hard to change. There are no mechanisms in place to help retrain them in new skills. In recent years there have been rapid changes in the kinds of goods and services the public demand. This means that organisations have to design and produce new goods and services. Major change like that is difficult for bureaucracies.

Not a lot of room for individuality and initiative in this organisation.

Even when there was less change and the bureaucratic method was more suited to the demands of the world, this approach to organisational design tended to create very boring jobs. If you are allowed to take no initiative but must stick to doing a narrow limited number of tasks 'by the book', tedium and a sense that you are just a small irrelevant cog in a big wheel are often the outcomes. Say you work for the Department of Social Welfare. Your job simply involves sending out Forms P14 and Forms K18 to the right people and then checking that they are properly completed when returned. You are hardly likely to feel satisfied with your day's work as you go home each evening. Likewise, if you work in a car assembly plant and your sole task is to bolt on the wheels to each new car as it passes along the assembly line, a high level of job satisfaction is not going to follow. This can in turn lead to low motivation, high labour turnover, poor quality work output and high levels of absenteeism.

Recognising the deficiencies of the External Control Design and possessing a conviction that employees more closely conform to Theory Y, many employers have sought to move towards Internal Control. How this is put into practice will now be discussed.

INTERNAL CONTROL DESIGN

Generally, moves in the direction of Internal Control have involved a variety of specific alterations to the basic bureaucratic blueprint without the overall External Control Design being erased. Occasionally the changes are so radical as to leave few External Control features intact, as is the case at W.L. Gore. Typical changes include the following:

1. flattening the management hierarchy;
2. decentralisation and devolution;
3. informalisation;
4. team working;
5. matrix reporting arrangements;
6. blurring organisational boundaries.

Let's now examine each in turn.

Flattening the management hierarchy

If it is decided that close supervision of employees is unnecessary and even damaging through inhibition on individual creativity, then the number of layers of management in an organisation can be reduced. Close super-vision requires a narrow *span of control*. In other words each supervisor can only watch closely a relatively small number of individuals. With an organisation employing 1000 individuals at the lowest level, where a narrow span of control, say six, is adopted, there is need for 167 first line supervisors, 28 managers at the next level, five at the next and one overall general manager. This is a five-layer hierarchy. If the span of control is extended to 20, the number of first line supervisors can be reduced to 50, the next layer of management to three and the fourth layer consists of just the general manager. A whole layer of management can be eliminated with an overall saving of the costs associated with 147 management jobs, which have been culled. This is the process of de-layering, in which many major organisations around the world have indulged during the 1990s, partly to achieve the savings involved, but also to empower staff and eliminate the communication and decision delays associated with information going up and down through many layers.

Decentralisation and devolution

The desire to externally control others naturally tends towards central-isation of power and decision-making. If the owner of a business places little trust in anyone, then permission to take courses of action, even on relatively minor matters, will have to be obtained from the boss. Once an organisation reaches a certain size, the act of seeking permission and awaiting a response becomes a serious source of delays. The mentality that underpins de-layering also favours decentralisation with the power to make decisions being devolved as close as possible to those who identify the need for action and must implement it. If employees can be trusted then they can safely be allowed to make decisions within their field of competence and costly delays can be eliminated.

Informalisation

This term has been coined here to reflect a deliberate avoidance of formal rules and distinctions. The external control mentality naturally favours rules and prescriptions about how work is to be done. Following the logic that individuals can be trusted to behave intelligently with the interests of the organisation at heart, it becomes possible and even desir-able to dispense with many of the rules. Without the constraints involved, individuals are empowered to act as the situation demands and not fall back on rules that may not apply to the situation. Use of initiative is encouraged. Likewise, the distinctions between jobs and between the layers in the organisation's hierarchy are often arbitrary and inappropriate. Individuals should be encouraged to perform whatever duties or activi-ties are required, given their capacities and what the situation demands, and not adopt an 'it's not my job' approach. This is the logic behind the absence of job titles and descriptions at W.L. Gore. Badges of status, such as different dress codes and enclosed offices, also act as artificial behaviour barriers. They tend to cut managers off from the very people they are supposed to be managing and vice versa. Organisations that take Internal Control to heart are often striking for the fact that there are no overt status barriers. Everyone may be informally dressed and more senior staff may occupy work stations in open plan offices together with everyone else. Everyone eats together in the same canteen and addresses each other on a first name basis. In this way communication and ideas flow much more freely throughout the whole organisation and the waste associated with artificial barriers is minimised.

Team working

In many instances the creation of work teams involves a further instance of informalisation in that they break down another kind of formal barrier that tends to exist in organisations, the barrier between departments. While it seems logical to organise workers into groups based on the functions they carry out, whether that be an aspect of production or of marketing or whatever, the effect is often to lose sight of the overall organisational objectives. Locked away in their separate departments, workers' focus tends to become limited to localised objectives. Often, other departments are viewed with some suspicion, as when the marketing staff are exasperated by what they see as unwarranted production delays while the production staff view the marketing department as having unrealistic expectations. Frequently also there are battles about resources. Within a third-level college, staff of the business department may look with resentment at the amount of money that is devoted to the purchase of equipment for the science department, whereas the science staff may view their budget as sadly deficient in terms of the work they need to do.

Organising work not around functions but around products or customers is seen by some organisations as the key to better co-operation among employees. Teams are created drawn from across departments and in some cases the notion of departments is dispensed with entirely.

Multi-skilling is a process commonly associated with the team work approach. It is the reverse of specialisation. Those who previously concentrated on a specific task or activity are trained in a variety of skills. The advantage is that they are easily re-deployed if the need arises and individuals can replace each other without difficulty. In this way a more self-sufficient and flexible workforce is created.

Matrix reporting arrangements

A matrix structure involves a dual line management and reporting structure. The traditional bureaucracy adheres tightly to the principle that each employee should have one and only one line manager to whom he or she reports and who supervises his or her work. The argument is that any other arrangement will inevitably involve conflicts of priorities and interests, with the attendant stress and confusion for the employee. The dictum is that 'one can not serve two masters'. From an External Control Design standpoint this view makes sense. If, however, employees are to a large extent autonomous, require little or no direct supervision, are able to identify and make decisions on priorities and require managers just for co-ordination and advice purposes, a dual reporting structure does not seem so problematic. Of course there has to be a good reason for such an approach. The requirement arises from the reality in some organisations that work cannot be organised within departments or set groups and therefore single reporting lines are insufficient.

Take the Institute or University where you are studying: the academic staff will belong to one or other of several faculties, schools or departments and report to whoever is the head of the entity to which they belong. However, frequently each member of staff may be called on to perform activities such as course development, consultancy, teaching or research that cuts across several departments. The solution is to have a second set of managers who are responsible for leading activities that cut across departments. At the same time then, a given member of the academic staff may be reporting to one manager in relation to consultancy activities, another in relation to research being undertaken and to his/her own departmental head in relation to a variety of other duties. This is the matrix approach. It is of course up to the individual to negotiate work-load and priorities with the various managers and is suitable only where the assumption of internal control is warranted.

Blurring organisational boundaries

To a large extent we have been discussing the organisation as if it were an enclosed entity. In fact organisations that tend towards the External Control Design seek to act as if this were true. Because they can exert maximum control over what goes on within their own boundaries they seek to ensure that influence from outside is minimised. The most extreme example is the enclosed religious order. Enclosed orders of nuns and brothers seek to eliminate all outside influences by requiring their members to have little or no contact with the outside world. Members remain at all times within the physical confines of the convent or monastery and visits from even close relatives are strictly curtailed. All behaviour and activities within the institution must follow a rigidly enforced regime.

Ordinarily, organisations cannot eliminate outside influences to anything approaching this level but they can make quite an effort. Rigidly enforced work hours during which employees' locations and activities are clearly prescribed eliminates any interference from outside, as do restrictions on the use of telephones, internet and general computing facilities. The aim is to ensure that when employees are at work, they are working and not doing anything else associated with their life outside the organisation.

Another approach to ensuring maximum internal control is to extend the organisation's sphere of activities up and down the input-output chain. A food processing organisation may find that it has greater control of supplies if it owns its own farms on which the appropriate crops are grown and greater control over distribution if it owns its own fleet of trucks. It may then decide to exert control over sales of its products by setting up or otherwise acquiring its own retail outlets. In this way an organisation can take within its boundaries the full chain of activities from earth to table, so to speak. The influence of the outside world is minimised by sucking as much of it as possible within the boundaries of the organisation.

Over the last decade or so there has been a marked trend towards blurring or breaking down the boundaries between organisations and the external world. The trend has manifested itself in a number of forms.

Subcontracting is the opposite to that described in the food processor example. Instead of extending their remit of direct control, some organisations limit their activities to a core in which they specialise. Everything else is bought in or sub-contracted out to other organisations. Dell Computer Corporation, which has a large plant in Limerick, is a major supplier of personal computers. The corporation does not, however, manufacture any of the component parts. Everything is bought in and simply assembled on site. Direct control over a lot of the process is lost and the boundary between one organisation and another loses much of its clarity. A great deal of liaison and co-operation between contractor and sub-contractors is necessary with employees of one spending much time with employees of the other. The advantages to the contracting organisation are that much less capital and resources are necessary to produce the product and flexibility is enhanced. If it should be necessary to change the size, shape, colour or indeed any aspect of the personal computer, Dell does not have to worry about modifying the assembly lines associated with the production of the relevant parts. That headache will have to be endured by someone else.

The forming of strategic alliances between organisations is also a breaking down of traditional organisational boundaries. Instead of taking over or buying out other companies, with all the attendant risks and responsibilities, it has been possible for organisations to remain separate yet benefit from each other by forming alliances. Mutually beneficial arrangements can be reached on access to markets, facilities, research know-how and so on. Increasingly this is a characteristic of the air transport industry where it is generally agreed that no future exists outside of a limited number of strategic alliances.

A further form of boundary blurring involves new patterns of working. With recent improvements in telecommunications such as the internet and video conferencing, it has become possible for employees to work from home. Certain types of work involving information processing are particularly suitable for this approach since data can easily be sent to any part of the world via e-mail and the processed outcome e-mailed back with virtually no communication delays. The advantage for employers is that they do not have to carry staff accommodation costs in the form of offices and that employees who would not travel to take up such

occupations may be availed of. The advantage to employees is the elimination of travel time, costs and associated stress each day, coupled with
the opportunity to reshape the working day around other aspects of life
such as family commitments.

The boundary being crossed in this case is that between private and
work life. Telecommuters, as they are known, are at the opposite end of
the spectrum from the members of an enclosed order. Whereas the
organisation in the latter case incorporates the complete private life of
the individual, in the former case it is the individual's private life that
encompasses the work activities. While the organisation retains some
degree of control by fixing deadlines and such like, a great deal of trust is
required that the employee is not misrepresenting how long it will take
to complete tasks and in fact devoting much less time or energy to the
organisation than is pretended. The assumption is that employees are
internally controlled and are motivated by the organisation's objectives.

INFLUENCES ON ORGANISATIONAL DESIGN

What are the factors that drive an organisation towards the Internal or
the External Control Designs? Robbins (2001) identifies four primary
influences on organisational design:

1. strategy;
2. size;
3. technology;
4. environment.

Strategy – Organisations differ on whether they depend on a risk-taking
innovative approach or whether they rely on a cost and risk minimisation strategy. The former are likely to tend towards the Internal Control
Design whereas the latter are likely to tend in the direction of External
Control. Innovation, by definition, relies on new things being done or
old things being done in new ways. This requires the harnessing of
creativity. Progress of this nature cannot be made without a culture of
risk-taking. Software developers, fashion design houses and new players
seeking to invade old markets by offering something new or different all

require the freedom and creativity that too much external control will stifle. On the other hand, those who are seeking to maintain market share for well known products and seek to do so through cost minimisation are likely to rely on the predictability afforded by the External Control Design.

Size – The loose framework associated with the Internal Control Design is difficult to maintain as the number of employees grows. The challenges of co-ordination presented by growth encourage the development of more and more external constraints such as the formation of separate departments, specific job definitions and reporting hierarchies. Of course, within large organisations there may well be some areas that tend towards one end of the design spectrum while others tend towards the opposite. The research and development arm of an automotive corporation may well rely on internal control while the manufacturing arm demonstrates all the rigidity of a bureaucracy.

Technology – This concerns how an organisation turns its inputs into outputs. The general trend is that where the technology involves activities that cannot be routinised or standardised, the tendency is towards Internal Control Design. Where the technology is predictable and involves relatively repetitive procedures, External Control tends to dominate. Clearly there is a skill level factor inherent in this dichotomy. Jobs that can be reduced to simple repetitive routines are mainly of the low skill, low pay variety such as assembly line work. Those that are too unpredictable or complex to be prescribed in any simple way are largely of the high skill, high pay type such as research and design activities. It may be that employers find or assume that a different kind of organisational structure suits the two varieties of employees.

Environment – Included here are all those external factors that impact on the organisation: the public, nature of markets, competitors, suppliers, legislation, government agencies, the economy and so on. The more an organisation is open to impact from the environment the more uncertain a world it occupies. This requires flexibility to enable rapidity of response and will cause an organisation to avoid the rigidities associated with the

External Control Design as much as possible. If, however, an organisation, by virtue perhaps of its size, dominance in the market place or lack of competition, feels insulated from environmental shocks, then it is likely to express its sense of security in the External Control Design. Public sector utilities in Ireland, such as Telecom Eireann (now Eircom) and the ESB, emerging from the environmentally insulated world of state owned monopoly can be expected to have a structure that is ill-suited to post-privatisation global competition. The collapse in the price of Eircom shares shortly after its privatisation in the summer of 2000 is indicative of this situation.

Large private corporations can also find themselves insulated from the environment and grow rigid and complacent. The Digital Equipment Corporation, a US multinational and once Galway city's largest employer was, for decades, a global giant in the manufacture of mainframe computers. It failed, however, to respond to technological changes that brought about the dominance of the small personal computer or PC. In the crisis that ensued it was forced to close its giant hardware plant in Galway and later in 1998 the whole corporation was taken over by Compaq, an organisation that had thrived on the international demand for personal computers. Technological, market and even political changes can very quickly turn environmental insulation into extreme vulnerability. Only those that can adapt survive. External Control Design impedes the flexibility required for adaptation. Thus, de-layering, multi-skilling and decentral-isation are common organisational responses to environmental exposure.

ORGANISATIONAL CULTURE

Even those organisations such as W.L. Gore that rely heavily on Internal Control Design features retain a very powerful External Control mechanism. This is organisational culture. The sociologist Anthony Giddens offers the following definition of the concept 'culture':

> *'Culture consists of the values the members of a given group hold, the norms they follow and the material goods they create.'*

> (Giddens, 1993, p. 31)

If one takes the employees or members of any organisation, one typically discovers that they share a culture to a greater or lesser extent. Certain values are held throughout the organisation such as a high premium on creativity or on risk-taking. Alternatively, creativity and risk-taking may be frowned upon, and conventionality, together with the avoidance of mistakes, valued highly. Values naturally encourage matching norms of behaviour. Where a high value is put on mistake avoidance it becomes the norm to check with superiors before making decisions and to delay action until there is a great deal of support for that course. Where risk-taking is valued, decisions will be made more rapidly and without so much recourse to upward referral. All of this has a knock-on effect on the type of material goods created in an organisation. One, for example, can expect a greater flow of novel products where the associated risks are supported by the culture.

Quite apart from their specific values and norms, organisations differ in the strength or power of their cultures. In some it is all-pervasive impacting upon virtually very action of every member. The Disney Corporation is famed for the strength of its culture, which to many observers seems to have produced a workforce of young, good looking, and by Irish standards at least, peculiarly up-beat, enthusiastic clones. In other organisations the culture may not be so influential but will always exist to some extent.

WHERE DOES AN ORGANISATION GET ITS CULTURE?

It is common for the founder or founders of an organisation to establish its culture. This may be deliberate on their part or may simply be an expression of their personalities and attitudes. A very autocratic-minded individual may insist on making all the decisions, select only employees who will do as they are told and promote into senior positions those who will not insist on a share in the decisional process. In this way a culture is created and sustained over time.

Cultures can also evolve from circumstances. A high degree of informality may understandably characterise a small organisation where the employees all communicate with each other on a daily basis. Written procedures and rules may be unnecessary because it is easy to standardise action among a small group. As the organisation grows the existing members, particularly the more senior ones, being used to the informal approach wittingly or unwittingly encourage its continuation. Their disregard for formal procedures will naturally be passed on to new recruits. A culture that suited when the organisation was small is thus retained, though no longer appropriate. With expansion in size comes the need for more formal systems of control, systems the organisation now fails to develop. This can result in a dangerously erratic approach and divergence of action away from organisational objectives.

It is important to recognise that a strong organisational culture can, if it reinforces the right kind of behaviour, replace to a significant degree formal rules and systems. Take for example, the culture associated with customer service expressed in the maxim that 'the customer may not always be right but is always the customer'. An organisation can give thorough and reliable expression to this philosophy by a careful enforcement of rules defining the obligations of all staff members towards customers. Better expression can probably be achieved by a strong customer service culture through which all staff are inculcated with personal commitment to this ethic.

However an organisation evolves its culture, it is passed on both through selection and socialisation. The selection effect involves the natural tendency of those who recruit new members to the organisation to favour those who are judged to fit in with the established norms and values. In addition, those who conform better to the culture are more likely to remain with and thrive within the organisation. All new members joining the organisation quickly become aware that certain behaviours are rewarded and other ones discouraged. The learning process is both formal and informal. Through Human Resource Management activities such as training and performance appraisal, employees are instructed in what the organisation expects of them. Side by side with the formal learning arrangements there are the daily lessons to be picked up from observing the behaviour of other employees, listening to advice and hearing stories of past failures and successes that circulate among the workforce. Gradually the individual becomes imbued with the culture of the organisation.

The socialisation process in the workplace is similar to that experienced by children in all societies through which, with the help of parents, teachers, other adults and peers they learn the values and norms of their own culture. In organisations, socialisation is assisted by the fact that more suitable individuals can be selected and less suitable ones avoided or rejected, often through their own choice. If one predicts that the norms and values of an organisation are not going to be to one's liking, one is hardly likely to seek a job with it. Furthermore, those who make the mistake of joining an unsuitable organisation typically make the choice to get out as soon as they can. In contrast those who fit more comfortably within the culture are more likely to get promoted and assume positions of greater influence. Overall, the net effect is to reinforce and perpetuate the existing culture within organisations.

THE EFFECTS OF ORGANISATIONAL CULTURE

Diana Baumrind, a psychologist in the field of child development, has described the distinction between authoritarian and authoritative parenting styles. The former relies heavily on the enforcement of rules through punishment for breaches. The latter relies on continuous communication with the child explaining the reasons why certain norms of behaviour are required (Baumrind, 1968, 1991). It is generally accepted among experts on child development that the authoritative approach results in a much greater internalisation of values and norms by children. The effects of organisation culture can be likened to authoritative parenting. While the enforcement of rules and standards of behaviour can produce the same effect as culture, formal rules on their own require constant supervision to ensure implementation. Culture on the other hand tends to be internalised so that employees come to believe in the organisation's approach and are happy to do things 'the company way' without any external pressure. In that sense, culture is a kind of paradox. While it initially involves a very powerful external controlling influence on behaviour, as it becomes internalised it is no longer noticed and simply becomes the individual's preferred way of behaving. A strong culture can replace a great deal of external control.

It is culture that gives organisations their 'personality' and sense of continuity. It can give a large and geographically scattered workforce a strong sense of unity and commitment to common objectives. A father and daughter joining a company 20 or 30 years apart may be aware of essentially the same 'feel' in the organisation, though the overlap of employees is minimal. While this can have great benefits, it is also a potential disadvantage of organisational culture. It tends to have great resilience over time and is typically resistant to change. 'The way we do things here' is often doggedly maintained long after external circumstances demand change. It proves very difficult to 'teach the old dog new tricks'. Many organisations have been dragged down by their cultures having outlived their usefulness.

STRUCTURE AND CULTURE

Organisational structure and culture are not independent realities. They are intertwined and mutually supportive in a variety of ways. Indeed, structural changes, particularly isolated initiatives, tend not to survive in the face of a contrary culture. Employee involvement exercises such as Quality Circles or Joint Consultancy Councils (see Chapter 8) will prove difficult to establish or sustain in the context of a culture that strongly favours centralised decision-making and top-down management.

Together, organisational structure and culture exert very powerful moulding influences on the behaviour of employees. Whatever one's motives, personality and attitudes, it is difficult to resist this influence. Those who do not personally fit the mould generally succumb or decide to leave. Even those introduced at a high level to organisations with, perhaps, the explicit mission to bring about change can find the challenge daunting. If the culture is particularly strong, the task sometimes proves impossible even when the consequences involve the demise of the whole organisation. The reality is that organisations are something more than the sum of the people of which they consist.

SUMMARY

An organisation is a social arrangement for the controlled performance of collective goals. It involves a collection of individuals who may or may not be in direct communication with each other and whose efforts are guided towards common objectives. Control is achieved through rules and roles, physical arrangements and systems of supervision. Workplaces are ordinarily organisations, as are clubs and voluntary bodies. Though not commonly thought of as such, families can be defined as organisations, the objectives of which are the survival, comfort and wellbeing of the members.

Organisations differ from groups in that typically organisations are made up of several groups, the efforts of which need to be co-ordinated. In a small organisation the members may constitute a single group, in which case the distinction is that the group is a psychological reality based on communication whereas the organisation has additional material and legal dimensions.

Organisational design refers to the way the organisation is structured so as to maintain control over the behaviour of the individuals belonging to it. Design includes features such as role definitions, systems of management and supervision, physical layout of work-space, rules and norms of behaviour and systems of communication. Organisational design tends to vary along a dimension ranging from Internal to External Control. The latter approach features a variety of rigid systems for governing the behaviour of individuals, such as precise job definitions, detailed rules and close supervisory arrangements. The former is based on the notion that employees internalise the objectives of the organisation and will operate better without external restrictions. Decision-making tends to be devolved, supervision is minimised and individuals are given a great deal of autonomy in relation to their work.

Most organisations possess, to a lesser or greater extent, features of the External Control Design. Weber (1947) in describing the characteristics of a bureaucracy outlined the features of External Control Design: specialisation of roles, rule-based approach to performance, a hierarchy of management and responsibility, impersonality of treatment for clients or customers, officials appointed on merit, full-time career employees and a clear distinction between private property and that of the organisation.

The purpose of the bureaucratic design is to ensure that the objectives of the organisation are met irrespective of who is doing the work, to capitalise on the benefits of specialisation and to prevent corruption or favouritism. That these objectives, essentially shared by all organisations, can be achieved only through External Control is in keeping with McGregor's Theory X.

The problem with too great a reliance on external control is that it leads to excessive rigidity, limited individual autonomy, unrewarding roles and failure to adjust to novelty or the unexpected.

Wishing to avoid the problems associated with the External Control Design of bureaucracies, many organisations have introduced a variety of design and management initiatives. They are aimed largely at achieving greater flexibility and rely on internal control in keeping with McGregor's Theory Y. Such initiatives include flattening the management hierarchy, decentralisation/devolution, informalisation, team working, matrix reporting arrangements and the blurring of organisation boundaries.

Whether an organisation tends towards Internal or External Control Design depends on the overall strategy it relies on, the size of the organisation, the nature of its technology and its openness to environmental impact. Being larger, having a cost/error minimisation strategy, using simpler more repetitive technology and being insulated from environmental effects leads organisations in the direction of External Control Design. Being smaller, concentrating on a strategy of innovation, employing more complex technology and being exposed to environmental impact tends to encourage a greater reliance on Internal Control Design.

All organisations possess a culture which may be stronger or weaker. Organisational culture consists of the values and norms of behaviour held in common by the members of the organisation. Cultures tend to have their origins with the preferences and personalities of the organisation's founders and with the circumstances in which the organisation evolved.

Once established, organisational culture is self-perpetuating, through staff selection, socialisation and promotion. Those who do not fit the culture tend to leave, those who fit more comfortably are likely to get promoted and become more influential. While culture initially exerts a powerful external controlling influence on individual behaviour, as the values and norms are internalised it allows for the substitution of external with internal control. Those imbued with the organisation's culture perceive 'the company way' as their own preferred way.

An organisation's culture offers a strong sense of unity and continuity to the members of an organisation. It welds them into a like minded workforce with common objectives and a common approach. This is very beneficial so long as the values and norms involved suit the overall circumstances of the organisation. If, however, major change is necessary, culture can act as a powerful obstacle. Organisations' cultures have been known to resist all efforts at reform even to the point of the demise of those organisations themselves.

REVIEW QUESTIONS

1. Explain what is meant by an organisation and discuss the function of organisational design.
2. Describe the characteristics of the bureaucratic approach to organisational design according to Weber (1947).
3. Explain the Internal-External Control dimension of organisational design and describe the factors that influence organisations in either direction.
4. Describe the concept of Organisational Culture and explain how it influences employee behaviour.
5. Describe the organisational design mechanisms that can be employed to enable an organisation to avoid the rigidities associated with the External Control approach.

REFERENCES

Baumrind, D., (1968), 'Authoritarian vs. Authoritative Control', *Adolescence*, 3, 255-272.

Baumrind, D., (1991), 'Effective Parenting During the Early Adolescent Transition', in P.A. Cowan and E.M. Hetherington (eds), *Family Transitions: Advances in Family Research Transition*, pp. 11-163, Hillsdale, NJ: LEA.

Giddens, A., (1993), *Sociology*, (2nd Edn), Cambridge: Polity Press.

Huczynski and Buchanan, (1991), *Organizational Behaviour*, (2nd Edn), London: Prentice Hall.

McGregor, D., (1960), *The Human Side of Enterprise*, New York: McGraw-Hill.

Robbins, S.P., (2001), *Organizational Behaviour*, 9th ed., Upper Saddle River, NJ: Prentice Hall.

Weber, M., (1947), *The Theory of Social and Economic Organisation*, translated by A.M. Henderson and T. Parsons, Oxford: Oxford University Press.

Chapter 11

Society, Culture and Work

LEARNING OBJECTIVES

On completion of this chapter students should be able to:

- explain the concepts of 'culture', 'society' and 'socialisation' and their impact on behaviour;
- explain the origins of the society and culture that characterised Ireland between independence and the 1960s;
- draw on supporting data and statistics to contrast the nature of society and culture in Ireland today with that prevailing prior to the 1960s;
- describe the main causes of change in Irish culture and society over the last 40 years;
- explain how culture, society and work behaviour are interrelated, with particular emphasis on contemporary Ireland.

INTRODUCTION

Imagine the Taoiseach today making a broadcast to the nation in the following terms:

'That Ireland which we dreamed of would be the home of a people who valued material wealth only as a basis for right living, of a people who were satisfied with frugal comfort and devoted their leisure to the things of the spirit; a land where countryside would be bright with cosy homesteads, whose fields and villages would be joyous with sounds of industry, the romping of sturdy children, the contests of athletic youths, the laughter of comely maidens; whose fireside would be the forums of the wisdom of serene old age.'

The passage is drawn from a Radio Éireann broadcast by An Taoiseach, Eamon De Valera, on St Patrick's Day, 1943.

Leave aside the poetic style, which would be the cause of some raised eyebrows today, and examine the passage for its essential message. Note the key phrases and sentiments:

'material wealth' valued only as 'a basis for right living';
'people who were satisfied with frugal comfort';
'leisure' devoted to 'the things of the spirit'.

One can not fail to be struck by the enormous gap between this vision of Ireland and that which has been sought and to a large extent achieved by the present generation of Irish politicians. De Valera espoused an anti-materialistic message of frugal self-sufficiency, based largely on small-scale agricultural enterprises and cottage industry. If the current leader of the government or indeed any politician were to speak in such terms today he would be judged to have taken leave of his senses. What has changed since 1943?

In a word one could reasonably answer: everything. 'Everything' can, however, best be summarised in terms of two concepts: 'society' and 'culture'. Irish society and culture have, in the meantime, gone through an enormous transformation, one which has had a tremendous impact on how people in this country view their world and behave within it.

In previous chapters we explored the effects of individual differences, group interactions and organisational membership on the behaviour of the individual. In this chapter we will examine another far-reaching moulder of behaviour, the society within which one lives. De Valera was able to think and speak as he did because of the society he lived in. His was then a widely-shared vision. It would not be possible to think and speak in this way today. In the famous words of L.P. Hartley: 'The past is a foreign country. They do things differently there'.

SOCIETY

What is 'society' in the context of a country like Ireland? It is a word used more with assumed meaning than in accordance with a strict definition. We tend to speak of Irish society as growing more affluent or less religious or more educated. 'Society' is, in effect, often used as an alternative term for population. When we speak about society, we are frequently speaking about 'the people'.

Properly understood, the word society means much more.

The sociologist Anthony Giddens defines society as:

> 'the system of interrelationships which connects together the individuals who share a common culture.'

> (Giddens, 1989, p. 32)

Population and society bear much the same relationship to each other as do the raw materials to a completed building. Without society the members of a population are like a random assortment of bricks, timber-work and slates scattered about without any order or unity.

'Society' implies some kind of order being brought to bear on the population, some kind of system of inter-relationships and bonds that tie people together into an organised whole. Of what do those 'inter-relationships' and 'bonds' consist?

The connections are achieved by a series of institutions or organisations with which the members of society interact. Tom Bottomore identifies the key institutions or processes involved:

> 'The minimum requirements seem to be:
>
> (1) a system of communication;
>
> (2) an economic system dealing with the production and allocation of goods;
>
> (3) arrangements (including the family and education) for the social-ization of new generations;
>
> (4) a system of authority and of distribution of power; and perhaps

(5) *a system of ritual, serving to maintain or increase social cohesion,*
and to give social recognition to significant personal events such as
birth, puberty, courtship, marriage and death.'

(Bottomore, 1987, p. 111)

The systems, then, through which people in society are connected are:
family; the educational system; economic arrangements such as production and trading institutions; government; and religious institutions. As
regards the system of communication, the mass media play an important
role in modern large scale societies.

A degree of independence is necessary to declare the existence of a
separate society. If a population is not at all autonomous but is simply a
subset of a larger group on which the members depend and with which
they share a variety of important institutions, then it can not be said to
have a separate society. Thus counties or provinces in Ireland, sharing as
they do the economic, political and educational systems with the rest of
the country, can not be said to be separate societies. On the other hand,
despite the fact that Ireland is growing ever more dependent upon and
increasingly sharing institutions with the other members of the European
Union, we have sufficient autonomy to be clearly a separate society from,
say, Britain or France, our nearest neighbours.

Another important element of Giddens' definition of society given
above is that it applies to individuals who share a common culture. The
concept of 'culture' must now be explored.

CULTURE

Culture is both a product of a given society and at the same time a
shaping influence on that society. Mícheál MacGréil defines culture in
the following terms:

'*Culture is the inter-related set (configuration) of learned, created and*
borrowed beliefs, ideas, values, norms, and symbolic meaningful systems
which characterise and influence the human behaviour of a people.'

(MacGréil, 1977, p. 181)

In adopting this definition, MacGréil leaves out the material products of a people such as works of art, architecture and functional artefacts. Presumably he views such material items as the outcome or consequence of culture, while culture itself, though to some degree inferable from them, lies within the collective consciousness of the population.

Gert Hofstede adopts an essentially similar approach to culture, which he describes as:

> 'the collective programming of the mind which distinguishes the members of one group or category of people from another'.
>
> (Hofstede, 1991, p. 5)

Other sociologists, such as Anthony Giddens, include the products of culture within the definition of culture itself:

> 'Culture consists of the values the members of a given group hold, the norms they follow and the material goods they create.'
>
> (Giddens, 1993, p. 31)

Values refer to those objectives that are deemed important and desirable among the members of the group or society concerned. Norms are ways of behaving that are generally regarded as acceptable or normal.

For practical purposes the distinction between the definitions of MacGréil and those of Giddens or Hofstede is of no great importance. To MacGréil and Hofstede, culture lies within the minds of a people in that it refers to their shared values, norms, understanding and ways of think-ing – their collective programming. To Giddens, culture also refers to the things people do and create in response to their shared ways of thinking – to the products of their shared understanding. Whether one refers to these as culture or products of culture is of no great consequence. For the sake of avoiding confusion the MacGréil/Hofstede approach will be adopted here. Culture will therefore be taken to refer to the *shared values, norms, beliefs and ways of thinking that characterise the members of a society.*

IRISH CULTURE

If we take Ireland to be a society – and if we limit ourselves to the bound-aries of the State, in other words to the Republic of Ireland – its people must have a common culture. What then are the shared beliefs and ways of thinking that characterise the members of this society? At the start of the third millennium the answer to this may well, for the most part, be identical to that for the rest of the industrialised world. Tom Inglis expressed this idea in the following passage:

> 'Irish people behave in much the same way as people from other Western societies. They work at the same kind of jobs. They are taught the same things at school. They live in similar kinds of houses. They worship in the same kind of churches. They have similar manners and habits. They watch the same television programmes. They read the same articles and stories in newspapers, magazines and books.'

> (Inglis, 1987, p. 215)

To what extent Irish culture is indeed virtually identical to those of the other Western societies is a matter of debate at the present time. What there is much less debate about is that Ireland did have a distinctive culture in the past, a culture which was significantly different to our neighbours in Europe and to those countries further afield with which we shared a common language and heritage. This culture defined Irish society in the age of De Valera, and understanding it makes his St Patrick's Day broadcast to the nation in 1943 understandable. For ease of communication this culture will be referred to as 'traditional Irish culture'. Later we will contrast it with 'emergent Irish culture', the culture prevail-ing today. The use of the adjective 'emergent' is intended to indicate that it is still very much in the process of creation and the ultimate form it may take on is a matter of speculation.

Traditional Irish culture

To a large extent the existence of Ireland as a separate State and a separate society is owed to traditional Irish culture, which remained largely intact and unchanged into the 1960s. Without a widely shared sense amongst the 'Irish' of their being alike and having a common view of the world and being different to other people, most particularly the English, Ireland would not be an independent State or society. If Ireland and England had a shared culture we would not now be separate States. The most potent element of this sense of unity and separateness for the last few centuries has been religion. Other elements were history, traditions, language, the land and a collective approach to life in general. These elements will now be analysed.

Catholicism in traditional Irish culture

The Irish remained Roman Catholics and very much identified themselves as such; the English became Protestants after the Reformation. A great deal of the sense of unity among the Irish and their resistance to incorporation into the British nation resulted from the shared beliefs and attitudes derived from Catholicism.

This concept is thoroughly described in a passage from Terence Brown's *A Social and Cultural History of Ireland*:

> 'Crucial to the institutional and popular achievements of the Church in the period following the famine until very recent times was the role played by Catholicism in confirming a sense of national identity. The Church with her recently regularised rites and practices offered to most Irishmen and women in the period a way to be Irish which set them apart from the rest of the inhabitants of the British Isles, meeting the needs thereby of a nascent Irish nationalism at a time when the Irish language and the Gaelic culture of the past were enduring a protracted decline.'

(Brown, 1985, p. 28)

History, tradition and language

Religion was by no means the only component in Irish culture that enabled the unity required for independent nationhood. A sense of shared history and tradition, the possession of a distinct language, literature, music and styles of dance – those factors which Brown described as enduring a protracted decline in the period after the famine – were also essential components of Irish culture. It is striking how these components are emphasised and to some degree exaggerated by those who seek to foster a sense of national unity and separateness.

This phenomenon was most evident in the foundation and subsequent activities of the Gaelic League in 1893 by Eoin MacNeill and Douglas Hyde. The objectives of the organisation were evident in the title of a lecture given by Hyde in November 1892: *On the Necessity for De-Anglicising the Irish People*. The founders of the Gaelic League were ultra-conscious of Brown's 'protracted decline' and its destructive effects on the consciousness of the Irish of themselves as a separate people. The League sought to achieve its de-Anglicising objective specifically by revival of the Irish language but its members had a wider agenda. A somewhat acerbic description by the historian R.F. Foster reveals their vision of Irish culture:

> '... an idealisation of the lifestyle of the west became the theme of Gaelic League zealots: where Balfour's administrators saw an economic disaster area, the League saw the remnants of a Celtic "civilisation" that implied a spiritual empire far greater than England's tawdry industrialized hegemony'.

> (Foster, 1989, p. 448)

Here we see the same anti-materialist theme evident later in De Valera's vision of an Ireland whose people are satisfied with 'frugal comfort' and devote their leisure to 'the things of the spirit'.

The anti-English theme of separateness, which, according to Foster, characterised the Gaelic League, was present also in the origins of the Gaelic Athletic Association, which was founded in the previous decade.

The noted historian F.S.L. Lyons quotes Archbishop Croke, the first patron of the GAA:

> '... if we continue travelling for the next score years in the same direction that we have been going in for some time past, condemning the sports that were practised by our forefathers, effacing our national features as

*though we were ashamed of them, and putting on, with England's stuffs
and broadcloths, her masher habits, and such other effeminate follies as
she may recommend, we had better at once, and publicly, abjure our
nationality.'*

(Lyons, 1986, p. 226)

Lyons credits the GAA as not only reviving 'the Irishman's local pride in
his county, but his national pride in his country' (p. 227). This enormous
cultural contribution to Irish society has proved to be a most enduring
phenomenon, far outliving its determinedly separatist origins.

The Irish language theme has endured also, with much less success.
The establishment of Irish as the first official language of the State, and
its mandatory learning in all schools in a country where the vast majority spoke and continued to speak only English is an example of the exaggerated emphasis placed upon specific aspects of culture so as to generate
unity within and separateness from those without.

This exaggeration also existed in the GAA through its long-standing
ban on members or players having any association with foreign sports.
Even attendance at a soccer or a rugby match could result in suspension
or expulsion from the GAA. After the ban was lifted in 1971, contrary to
the fears of its remaining supporters, there was no signs of haemorrhage
of either players or spectators from the GAA. Indeed, in the interim it
has gone from strength to strength, despite periods of enormous national
interest in the feared 'foreign' sports. The unproductive coercive
approach to the fostering of the Irish language may have eased somewhat
but the courage to lift it in its entirety has not yet been achieved.
Alongside it, a more optimistic constructive approach has taken root,
evident in the founding of Radio na Gaeltachta and in TG4, the Irish
language television station.

History, too, suffered from exaggeration and simplification. Myth and
legend were woven into a heroic Celtic history which had been inter-
rupted by English invasion. All that was required was for the invaders to
be expelled and the heroic Celtic tradition would continue from where
it left off seven centuries earlier.

The land in Irish culture

Most people in Ireland are only a few generations removed from the land. Up until a few decades ago, the country was predominantly rural. The first census taken after independence was in 1926. It found that 61 per cent of the population lived outside towns or villages, with 53 per cent of those gainfully employed working in agriculture. Of those, just under 20 per cent were employees, the rest were owners or their relatives who worked the land with them. Farms were, in the main, small- or medium-sized, around half of them being under 30 acres. Large farms were very much the exception. Ireland was essentially a nation of small farmers and those such as shopkeepers and publicans and tradesmen on whom farming families relied to give them essential services. Manufacturing industry was too small to have any major impact on the nature of society except by its absence.

Threshing oats on a small farm in County Galway (circa. 1931).

This economic structure, centred so predominantly on the land, was a product of Ireland's colonial history, though the precise mechanisms by which Ireland failed to industrialise are a matter of some dispute. F.S.L. Lyons, referring to the 19th century, points to the fact that *'over most of Ireland the conditions for speedy, extensive and successful industrialisation simply did not exist'* (Lyons, 1986, p. 55). He goes on to list various obstacles to industrialisation, including the post-famine decline in population, the land system and its prevention of the accumulation of savings, the poverty of the people, transport problems, lack of coal and raw materials and the free trade system which favoured far more highly-developed competitors.

Whatever the reasons for a lack of industrial development, after the famine most of the population that remained were dependent on land tenancies. Following the experience of the famine, when the major burden of starvation fell upon the landless underclass of cottiers, the population knew that survival meant having land and especially land from which one could not be easily evicted. This consciousness, together with a natural desire to improve security against destitution, led to the Land War of the 1880s and the consequent land reforms brought about through a series of land acts. Land was purchased from the landlords and granted to tenants on a lease purchase scheme. A Congested Districts Board was established to resettle farmers from smaller to larger holdings under the new system. Smaller and larger are very much relative terms here, the former referring often to less than one acre, the latter to rarely much more than 30 acres. The Ireland of small farmers had been established. With it came a very important cultural element of particular relevance to the economic domain.

Not only did the bulk of the population have a powerful emotional attachment to the land, but the land became an end in itself rather than a means to a living. The mindset of the farmer was towards maintaining or enlarging his holding rather than maximising his income from it. This was, no doubt, at least in part, an inheritance from the tenancy days when to invest in one's holding was to invite rent increases or to risk losing the investment due to the insecurity of tenure. It was a mentality also fostered by a religion which condemned the material and the pleasures of consumption and preached that reward was attainable only in the hereafter. Another cultural element stemming from those circumstances was a drive towards homogeneity, perhaps not surprising when people lived generation after generation in the same close rural communities. To be the same as (or as good as) everyone else was the objective, while to be different to (or better than) everyone else was to invite popular criticism and rejection. This did not encourage consumerism. To be seen to use one's wealth to acquire anything new or different risked accusations of getting above one's station. De Valera's 'frugal comfort' was indeed satisfactory to such people.

Collectivism in traditional Irish culture

Scholars such as Ferdinand Tonnies (Tonnies, 1887), Louis Wirth (Wirth, 1938) and Gert Hofstede (Hofstede, 1980) each distinguish a similar dimension of culture and society which is helpful in understanding the nature of traditional Irish society and how it later evolved. They draw attention to the degree of personal contact and interdependence that exists among people. Tonnies distinguishes between societies that are characterised by what he calls a *Gemeinschaft* (community) and those characterised by a *Gesellschaft* (association) way of life. Wirth distinguishes between *integrated societies* and *urban existences*. Hofstede contrasts *collectivist* with *individualist* cultures.

While there are some differences in detail between the various formulations of this dimension, in summary they are contrasting ways of life that differ in the following manners. The Gemeinschaft, integrated, collectivist societies involve individuals maintaining long-term associations with each other within a community, tending to know each other well and to have a general sense of obligation towards each other. In such circumstances an individual is defined and self-defines as a member of a group and has a powerful motivation to belong and be accepted. The Gesellschaft, urban, individualist way of life involves relationships that are more fleeting, compartmentalised and instrumental. One relates to others for particular purposes such as to receive services, to enable work to get done or to engage in social activities. Different individuals fit each role so contact with each is limited. Individual needs, not community membership, define contact with others and each person's self-concept is individualist and not based so much on group membership. Accordingly, the need to belong and fit in is diminished.

Traditional Irish society very much matched the *collectivist* model. Those who did not emigrate and leave Irish society largely remained within the community of their birth. They lived among a network of relatives and neighbours whom they knew intimately and whose families had known each other for generations. Being an individual in the sense of being self-made was impossible since one was always known as a member of such and such a family from this or that townland or street. An individual disgrace was a family disgrace for generations. One's behaviour in all aspects was conducted under the eyes of the whole community.

Smith and Bond (1993) suggest a number of features that characterise collectivist in contrast to individualist cultures. They describe the manner in which homes and territories are less clearly demarcated in collectivist societies. It is striking how the typical thatched cottage home in traditional Irish society was designed in this respect. The external door entered directly into the living area or kitchen. Doors were left open or else 'off-the latch' and neighbours felt no obligation to knock but walked straight in when they came to call. To this degree, the home was included in the community space. Contrast this with the current norms on door usage and home entering in Ireland.

Smith and Bond also draw attention to differing perspectives on time. Following Hall (1983), they distinguish between 'Monochronic' and 'Polychronic' time. The former refers to an emphasis on time as somewhat of a strict task master, involving schedules and appointments and an effort to hurry and meet deadlines. The latter involves much less emphasis on time or punctuality. Time is seen to be subservient to other more important demands derived from obligations to others. It is more important to converse and maintain good relations with those to whom you are giving a service than to hurry so as to do your business quickly. The general expectation of punctuality is low and time is understood in very approximate terms. Levine and Bartlett (1984) showed striking correlations across a number of countries between such time related factors as the accuracy of clocks in public places, the speed at which people walked down the street and the speed at which a post office clerk completed the sale of a small denomination postage-stamp (Smith and Bond, 1993). While survey data on time-keeping in traditional Irish society is difficult to come by, anyone with experience of rural Ireland, in particular, cannot but be struck by the casual attitude to punctuality among the population even to the present day.

Smith and Bond (1993) show convincing evidence that another behavioural characteristic associated with collectivist cultures is conformity – a tendency to go along with the views of others. Having examined experimental studies across a variety of countries and societies that used the Asch (1951) design, described in Chapter 9 of this book, they found a consistently higher rate of judgment conformity in collectivist societies. You will recall that the measure of conformity in the Asch (1951) study was the number of subjects who followed confederates' deliberate errors in reporting judgments on the relative length of lines.

The widely-held view of traditional Ireland as being highly conformist fits neatly with this evidence. In simple terms it is more difficult to hold or voice contrary opinions or views among those with whom you are bound up with in everyday life in a highly interdependent way. The apparent unwillingness of the population to disagree with authority, particularly in the form of the Catholic Church, may well have had as much to do with fear of falling out of step with the community than a fear of authority figures per se. That republican revolutionaries during the war of independence and afterwards during the civil war were able to resist highly personalised condemnation from the altar in many parishes throughout Ireland suggests that where there was an assurance of community support for such a stance, resistance to authority was possible. Revolutionary activists were even known to walk out of mass on a Sunday in protest at priestly condemnation of their guerrilla war. Nevertheless, it must be accepted that authority figures will inevitably wield greater influence over others than those without power by their control in various ways of rewards and punishments. Those who have been brought up to fit in, as in a collectivist culture, are ill-suited to resisting authority figures.

There is one incongruent piece of evidence as regards this picture of Irish culture in the past being collectivist as opposed to individualist. It comes from the work of Geert Hofstede who rank ordered the cultures in 50 countries and three regions based on responses given in 1968-1969 and 1971-1973 to survey instruments in those locations (Hofstede, 1983). He identified Ireland as occupying rank 39 of the 53 locations in terms of individualism, the lower ranks being the least individualist. This placed Ireland above Switzerland and Norway and just below France.

The most individualist countries were the US, followed by Australia. While Ireland had changed considerably in the 1960s, it is difficult to believe that we could rank so high on individualism at that time.

The sample used in Hofstede's survey may, however, explain our unexpected positioning. The sample in every country and region consisted of employees of the giant US computer manufacturer, IBM. The numbers in each national sample varied depending in part on how many employees IBM had in that country, from a low of 37 in Pakistan to a high of 7907 in Germany. Overall, the sample used to compare the 53 countries and regions involved some 70,000 questionnaires. While the size of the Irish sample was not given, it can be assumed to be on the smaller rather than the larger side. More importantly, it is highly unlikely that IBM employees at that time in Ireland were typical of the nation at large. Their atypicality would have been further increased by the fact that only marketing and service personnel were included in the survey, i.e. employees who would generally have been more educated and trained than average.

Further evidence on the peculiarity of the Irish results on individualism comes from the finding that average individualism scores for nationalities correlated strongly (.84) with national wealth (per capita GNP in 1970). Irish GNP lay close to that for Greece (22), Spain (31), Argentina (28-29), Singapore (13-14), Hong Kong (16) and Venezuela (4), all countries that ranked, as indicated by the figures in brackets, well below Ireland in individualism. Ireland ranked alongside countries that had 2-3 times its level of GNP.

Hofstede's findings may have been a sign of things to come in Irish culture, but hardly representative at the time.

Traditional Irish society

In discussing traditional Irish culture, the nature of the society which fostered and was fostered by this culture has inevitably been described in part. This was a society that showed little change between the foundation of the State in 1922 and 1960. Thereafter rapid transformation began to occur. Let's now explore further what traditional Irish society was like.

There are a few key elements to its understanding. Traditional Irish society was predominantly rural, Catholic, conservative and insular. Returning to our earlier analysis of society as being made up of the various interrelated institutions within which the people relate with each other, what were they like in traditional Irish society and what were their effects on the area of work?

Family and marriage

Firstly, extended family units were the norm. Grandparents, parents, frequently uncles or aunts and children lived together as units in the family home. Farms were inherited by a son, typically the eldest son, and usually on the death of his parents. The social order was strongly patriarchal. One striking effect of this described by Arensberg and Kimball (1940) was that a man with a wife and family living and working on a farm which he would eventually inherit, would ordinarily have little or no economic or decision-making independence until his father died. Power was therefore invested largely in the relatively elderly. In 1946, a third of all farmers were over the age of 65, according to Lyons, a situation he describes as an 'infallible recipe for rural conservatism' (Lyons, 1986, p. 606).

The dominance of the elderly in society was assured by the peculiar population structure generated by the land system and the lack of industrialisation. While families tended to be large, only one could inherit a farm or business. For the others the economic prospects were bleak. The effect was that they either emigrated or remained unmarried. From early in the 20th century, up to the 1980s, Ireland's marriage rate fell below European norms. Indeed, for most of that time it was about the lowest in Europe. This trend was most evident in the economic sphere of agriculture. The 1951 census, for example, revealed that of males aged 45-54, 39.9 per cent of those defined as farmers, farmer's relatives or farm managers were unmarried. Of those defined as involved in 'other agricultural occupations' 44.9 per cent of the same age cohort were unmarried. These figures contrast markedly with 9.7 per cent for 'higher professionals' and 11.4 per cent for 'salaried employees'. An examination of the subsequent censuses up to 1981 reveals little change in the pattern. Agriculture, which was the dominant economic pursuit, did not facilitate marriage.

What the above figures do not reveal is another strong trend. Those who inherited farms did tend to marry. The bulk of those unmarried men involved in agriculture were relatives assisting on the farm or agricultural labourers. Farmers, when they did marry, married late. This again produced a trend in Ireland markedly in contrast to European norms. Inglis (1987) contrasts the proportion of men and women aged 25-34 in 1936 who were unmarried in Ireland with the numbers unmarried in France. In Ireland the figure for males was 74 per cent and for females 55 per cent, compared with 17 per cent and 15 per cent respectively for France.

Low overall marriage rates, late marriages and high emigration among young adults guaranteed an ageing population, a dearth of young people and a wide age gap between children and parents – a sure recipe for conservatism, to reflect Lyon's sentiments.

The family and the workplace were essentially one and the same insofar as the dominant economic activity, agriculture, was concerned. The same order applied to all the other small businesses such as shops and pubs that existed in rural Ireland. Insofar, then, as organisations influence behaviour, the workplace in traditional Irish society was simply an extension of the family and added little of novelty. This was equally true of men and women. The effect was that there were no opportunities for young people in rural Ireland to experience influences or develop attitudes in the workplace that differed in any way from that of the family. Again this perpetuated conservatism – an adherence to the same values and attitudes from generation to generation.

The Catholic Church

Moving beyond the family and the associated sphere of work, the monolithic organisation of the Catholic Church loomed large over all. The vast majority – around 95 per cent – of the population were Roman Catholics. The influence of the Church on this population was extremely far-reaching. According to Inglis 'being Catholic and being Irish have become synonymous' (Inglis, 1987, p. 11). This was discussed above in terms of Catholicism being an essential ingredient for the Irish in maintaining a sense of unity and separateness from the English, characteristics which were essential to the establishment of independent nationhood. The Catholic Church was to the Irish very much their own, a church which in no way did they perceive as being imposed but which they were proud to belong to. The fact that rule was from Rome was entirely irrelevant. The hierarchy and clergy were their own. It was to them they related with special loyalty. The net effect was an unquestioning acceptance that what the Church preached was right in all spheres of life. To be disloyal to the Catholic Church was to be anti-Irish.

Education

Education was, in the main, an extension of the Catholic Church. Primary schools were either owned and run by religious orders or managed by the local parish priest. Secondary schools were in the main owned and run by either religious orders or the local dioceses. Primary school teacher training was invested entirely in the hands of priests, brothers and nuns. The university system, though more independent of the Church, was still very much under its influence. The clergy were most careful to ensure that more sensitive posts insofar as thoughts on social issues were concerned, such as professorships of philosophy, sociology and later psychology, were held by priests. To study at the one university not under the influence of the Catholic Church, which was Trinity College in Dublin, Catholic students were obliged first to receive permission from the Archbishop of Dublin. This position prevailed up to 1970. Overall the educational ethos was universally and unquestioningly Catholic. What was preached from the pulpit was reinforced in the classroom. The Church's teachings were passed down unfailingly in the schools. Alternative perspectives on attitudes or values were never to be heard.

Other State institutions

The other important State institutions, legislature, executive, civil service, policing and judiciary were nominally secular. The Catholic Church had no direct formal powers within them but in reality had enormous influence. The 1937 Constitution began (and still does) with the following words:

'In the name of the Most Holy Trinity, from Whom is all authority and to Whom, as our final end, all actions both of men and States must be referred,
We the people of Ireland
Humbly acknowledging all our obligations to our Divine Lord, Jesus Christ …
Do hereby adopt, enact and give to ourselves this Constitution.'

(Bunreacht na hÉireann, p. 2)

This indicates the religious character of the State as widely accepted at the time. The precise nature of this religious character was defined in a subsequent article of the Constitution, which recognised '*the special position of the Holy Catholic and Apostolic Roman Church as the guardian of the faith professed by the great majority of its citizens*'. This article was removed in 1972 after a referendum. The hierarchy at the time favoured its removal.

Just as the Church reflected the mindset of the people and the people that of the Church, the State institutions faithfully reflected the same monolithic culture. Given the degree to which basic values were shared, it would be next to impossible for State institutions to do otherwise in a functioning democracy. Nothing emanating from the State, therefore, was ever likely to upset the existing social order. If it is the function of government in a democracy to balance the needs and demands of the various groups within society, then the government in Ireland had little of a balancing act to perform. Except for small minorities that could conveniently be ignored, the population had a common view of how things should be.

Work in traditional Irish society

Work was largely seen through the eyes of the capital owner – typically the farmer. Property was the means to survival, not the sale of labour. Security, a dominant need in a poor society, was to be obtained through the accumulation and safeguarding of property rather than the generation of income. Investment meant risk, which was to be avoided. It was not a society designed to produce an entrepreneurial class.

The wage earner perspective was minimised through primarily a massive outflow of those who were surplus to the requirements of the agricultural system. Those who did not inherit or marry an inheritor were forced to emigrate in enormous numbers. By the early 1920s when the State was founded, 43 per cent of Irish *born* men and women were resident abroad (Brown, 1985, p. 20). In the 1950s alone, around 400,000 Irish people left the country. Those who would have profited from an alternative perspective on work were in the main absent.

Work was largely an extension of family life, which operated on a patriarchal and hierarchical model. Authority was derived from position (inherited and traditional) and those without power were discouraged from thinking about questioning that situation by the all-encompassing educational and religious system and the essentially collectivist nature of the culture. In practice, authority was wielded by men and, more particularly, by older men. Women and younger men largely occupied subservient positions. It was a system guaranteed to produce a marked authoritarianism. The worst excesses allowed by this mentality have come to light in recent years in the form of physical and sexual abuse meted out by those in authority to those under their influence or care. The authoritarian mentality permeating society which defined position and right as synonymous is most evident in the inability of victims to gain any response to their cries for help.

Women occupied a peculiar position in relation to work. In the typical farm family, women were expected to care for the children (the absence of birth control ensured a plentiful supply), to wash, clean and cook within the home and to contribute directly to the farm enterprise within the farmyard area – feeding pigs, poultry, calves and milking cows. In addition, when the occasion required, they would also be expected to work in the fields, saving hay, corn and so on. In practice then, women probably contributed more in an economic sense to the family unit than did men, yet their contributions were viewed as somehow subsidiary. The peculiarity about women's roles in relation to work arises out of the strongly-held view in society that married women should not work outside the home, a view enshrined in Article 41.2 of the 1937 Constitution which states that:

'The State shall, therefore, endeavour to ensure that mothers shall not be obliged by economic necessity to engage in labour to the neglect of their duties in the home.'

(Bunreacht na hÉireann, Article 41.2)

The implication was that women, particularly mothers, should not be in paid employment because it was the role of a father to provide for his family. Apart from the prevailing norms of behaviour, women were obliged to resign from employment in most public sector occupations on their marriage. This sits oddly with the reality that married women in the predominating family circumstances – on farms – were expected to contribute very considerably in economic as well as domestic terms.

The seemingly contradictory logic involved in requiring married women to make a major economic contribution outside the home on farms but preventing them from doing so elsewhere may be amenable to an economic explanation. Paid employment was in chronically short supply. If married women had been allowed to compete with men for this scarce resource, the effect would have been that many more families would have been without any financial support while others would have had two incomes. The obstacles to married women taking up paid employment can be viewed as a system of income rationing, one per family.

On farms the opposite problem prevailed. The difficulty was to find enough hands to do the labour intensive work involved and yet make the small-holdings economically viable. The solution was to draw to the maximum extent on labour that did not have to be paid for. This included not only married women but children from a relatively young age. Into the 1960s it was still common practice for primary school age farming children to be absent from school for a considerable amount of the time while assisting on the family holding. One of the consequences for such children was an inhibition on their chances of educational success and on their preparation for anything other than manual or unskilled work.

Conservatism and insularity

The overall effect of the land structure, the Church and the paranoia about the dangers of foreign ('British') influences was to produce a profoundly conservative unchanging society looking in on itself and determined to ignore the rest of the world to a large extent. It was a society that sought but could not attain the idyll expressed in De Valera's 1943 St Patrick's Day broadcast. It wished to be rural, self-sufficient, Catholic and unchanging. Why and how it failed to sustain itself will be addressed below, when we examine how Ireland came to change in the 1960s, but first we must examine how a society, particularly its associated culture, is transmitted from generation to generation.

SOCIALISATION – THE ENGINE OF CULTURE

Society consists of the institutions or organisations within which people behave and interact with each other. Those institutions will change from generation to generation if there is not some way to ensure that young people come to adopt the same ways of thinking as their elders.

Take education, for example. An authoritarian (or indeed any other) approach will continue to characterise institutions if each successive generation of teachers and managers believes in rigidly enforced discipline and an unquestioning consumption and regurgitation of 'facts' by students. While this remains the shared ways of thinking or the culture of teachers, educational institutions will remain the same. Should a generation of teachers or educators begin to question this approach, the institutions will inevitably change. The same applies to any other institution in society such as the family. The nature of the family will go unchanged so long as each generation of parents take on the culture (attitudes, values, beliefs, ways of thinking) of their own parents. Conversely, changes in ways of thinking will produce changes in institutions and in society at large.

The system for replication of a society and its culture in each new generation is 'socialisation'.

'Socialisation is the process through which children acquire the behaviour, skills, motives, values, beliefs and standards that are characteristic, appropriate and desirable in their culture.'

(Newcombe, 1996, p. 346)

While a very large proportion of socialisation is, as the above definition suggests, achieved in childhood, it continues to some extent through life insofar as an individual arrives in new situations where appropriate behaviour has to be learned. The young adult leaving college and going into the workplace will inevitably be socialised into appropriate behaviours peculiar to that particular organisation. We saw in Chapter 10 how different organisational designs and cultures encourage different types of behaviour.

The process of socialisation is to be understood in terms of the learning principles described in Chapter 4. Early in life every child is conditioned to behave in accordance with their parents' expectations. They are rewarded for certain behaviours, punished for others. In addition they observe adult role models displaying the behaviours that are appropriate in that society. This process is continued outside the home in contacts with other adults in school and elsewhere. In addition, children are formally taught and encouraged to remember the rules of society and the consequences for breaching them, particularly those that are part of the law of the land or of the rules of institutions such as schools to which they are attached.

The agents of socialisation include family, peers, education and the media (TV, radio, cinema, newspapers, magazines, books and recently the internet). Anything that offers role models and directly or indirectly encourages particular modes of behaviour has the potential to socialise. This encouragement can be quite subtle, as in the example of selected media images of youth, beauty or maturity. The association of smoking with sophistication and veritable emaciation with beauty are two unhappy cases in point.

In circumstances where the various agents of socialisation are at one with each other, the outcome is in the main fairly predictable. The culture will be replicated in each successive generation. Where there are contradictions among the various agents, the outcome is much less predictable. The result will be the product of the relative strength of influence of the different agents. In any event the potential for change will now exist. This is essentially what began to happen in Ireland from the 1960s. Before the 1960s, the agents of socialisation were teaching a largely homogenous message. Parents at home, teachers at school, newspapers, periodicals and books available in the shops, radio and cinema preached a common set of values. Elders and those in authority should be respected. They knew what was right. There was a God from whom all authority derived. His teachings could only be accessed through the one true Catholic Church. The teaching of its hierarchy was therefore the word of God. Sexuality, being dangerous and dirty, should be repressed, as should implications of its existence in dress, word or deed. Ireland was an island of spiritual purity in a sea of materialistic sinfulness. It was essential to foster the virtues of true Irish culture and insulate it from the sources of decay seeping in from abroad.

Of course there were always holes in the seamless fabric of socialisation. Women's hemlines went up and down roughly in step with the rest of the industrialised world. Even in the 1920s priests found it necessary to preach against the shorter skirts and the more expressive dance styles that penetrated from America. At this superficial level Ireland was not insulated from the rest of the world and some contemporary writers interpreted this as a thoroughgoing 'modernisation' or 'anglicisation', particularly in the towns. Writing in 1943 about the contrast between the representation of Ireland in the literature of the day and his own experiences of Ireland in towns such as his native Templemore in County Tipperary, Neil Kevin wrote:

> ' The fact that the overwhelming majority of the people in Ireland are in step with the rest of the English speaking world is not deductible from the literature that is written about Ireland ...
>
> The country town with a wireless-set in the houses of rich and poor, with a talkie-cinema, with inhabitants who wear the evening clothes of London or New York and dance the same dances to the same music – this town has not yet appeared in Irish literature, but it is the most typical Irish country town.'

(Kevin, 1944, pp. viii-ix)

Certainly, the inhabitants of towns may have taken on the superficial appearance of being from the same culture as the rest of the English speaking world. But what they were allowed to hear on the wireless or see in the cinema, though enough to encourage them to adopt foreign styles of dress, music and dance, was certainly not enough to contradict any of the essential messages of traditional Irish culture.

How the unity of socialisation finally began to fragment is the topic of the next section.

CHANGE IN IRISH SOCIETY FROM THE 1960S

The glaring failure of the self-sufficient, insular, hermetically sealed, pure, traditional Irish society was that it could only be sustained by an enormous outflow valve. The majority of its children were forced to emigrate to other countries – particularly Britain and the United States, the very societies whose influences Ireland sought to insulate itself against. Despite a tendency towards large families, high levels of emigration (e.g. over half a million between 1946 and 1961) coupled with late age of marriage and low marriage rates meant that Ireland's population never increased between independence in 1922 and 1961. In fact population declined over that period. In 1922 the population of the 26-county Free State stood at 2.9 million. By 1961 it had dropped to 2.8 million.

To those that Ireland did support, it afforded a relatively poor living. Income per head in the first decade of independence was at about 60 per cent of the UK level and declined thereafter (Breen et al, 1990, p. 30). By 1965 it stood at 58 per cent (Breen et al, 1990, p. 83).

A simple conclusion was evident. Ireland could only sustain its brand of society by ensuring that a large proportion of its population lived outside it. If the safety valve of emigration did not exist then the pressure of such a large unemployed underclass would very quickly result in radical change of one kind or another. The status quo was only possible to maintain by literally exporting a large proportion of the population. Even then, Irish society which existed prior to the 1960s could only support an ever-declining number of citizens at a declining level of income. In the 1950s the future of Ireland was in question by anyone with the wit to question it. Change was essential to survival.

In the late 1950s economic planners and politicians performed a major about-turn in the way our economy was to operate. It was to have enormous implications beyond the sphere of economics. It was decided that Ireland should open itself to the developed economies of the world and abandon its objective of self-sufficiency. Protective tariffs (heavy taxes on imports making home products more competitive) for native industry were gradually dropped. Foreign capital was invited to invest in industry in Ireland and financial incentives offered for it to do so. Agriculture was encouraged to focus on being competitive in the rich European markets with a view to enriching the country through exports. The overall objective was to industrialise the economy and thereby create enough employment to stem the tide of emigration and raise national income to European levels. This required Ireland to open itself up to influences from the outside world, influences it had sought with such determination to avoid.

From the point of view of employment two major down-sides had to be faced. To make the price of agricultural produce competitive in the European food markets, farms would have to grow larger and more mechanised. Competition would spell the death knell of the small marginal farmer. The land would support fewer families. The second down-side was that Irish industry, long protected by tariff walls, would inevitably lose out to cheaper foreign imports. The gamble was that the loss of employment in agriculture and native industry would be far outweighed by an increase in employment by the industries set up through incoming foreign capital.

In both the short and the long run, this radical policy paid handsome dividends, with, admittedly, a major hiccup in the 1980s that was not as a result of the policy itself but of serious economic mismanagement involving excessive public borrowing. In the meantime, the process was given a major fillip when Ireland joined the European Economic Community or EEC as it was then known in 1973, now entitled the European Community or EU. This greatly hastened and to a large extent eased the pain of Ireland's integration with the rest of the industrialised world. Through the Common Agricultural Policy and the Social and Structural funds of the EU, Ireland has been the net beneficiary of many billions of pounds in aid to help with infrastructural and educational development and to support agriculture.

How did this great economic change impact on Irish society?

EMERGENT IRISH SOCIETY AND CULTURE

The nature of Irish society today contrasts vividly with that prevailing up to the 1960s. Of course, the change occurred over time, and is not evenly distributed geographically or in terms of the various components of society. It is to be expected that elements of traditional Irish society will continue to live on in a recognisable form. The issue of interest here is change rather than continuity. Those changes can be summarised in a number of striking statistics, which will be discussed below.

Population

Taking the most basic issue concerning society first – the number of people it encompasses – the 1961 census revealed a population low of 2,818,000. Thereafter it increased (albeit with a slight decline between 1986-1991) reaching 3,626,987 in the most recent census of 1996. The increase in population is due to the fact that in the intervening years Ireland evolved an economic system capable of supporting its own people. In the 1950s, as described above, there was a mass outflow of mainly younger members of the population through emigration. Today the situation has been reversed, with a net surplus of inward migration from abroad consisting of returning emigrants, job seekers from other EU nations and individuals seeking refugee status from troubled parts of the world. The main problem facing the labour market in Ireland now is not a shortage of jobs but a shortage of individuals available to fill them. Employers have been forced to go as far afield as Latvia and Newfoundland in an effort to attract employees to Ireland.

The economy

The economic progress made in Ireland, which enables it to support its population, is self-evident in key statistics. Output per head of population was 5.3 times greater in 1998 than 1949 (Redmond, 2000). A more revealing analysis of wealth in Ireland comes from a comparison with UK figures. Based on current exchange rates and expressed in dollars, the Gross Domestic Product (a measure of wealth produced in a country) per person was 97 per cent of the UK level in 1998 (OECD1).

When differences in purchasing power were taken into account, GDP per person exceeded the UK levels. As stated above, income per head in 1965 was only 58 per cent of the UK figure. Admittedly, around 11 per cent of the wealth created in Ireland in recent years has gone abroad annually (largely due to the scale of foreign ownership of business in Ireland which repatriates profits made in Ireland). Taking account of this, income in Ireland has not quite caught up with the UK, but it is not far behind, a dramatic change since 1965. Compared with the 15 members of the European Union as a whole, Ireland is just over the average in terms of wealth production per person and exceeds that average by nearly 9 per cent if account is taken of the variance of purchasing power of income across the various EU states. Again, the outflow of profits must be factored in, however.

The economic transformation has been achieved by a huge increase in the size of the manufacturing and service sectors and a relative decrease in the agricultural sector.

In 1949 agriculture accounted for about 31 per cent of the overall output of the economy. By 1998, this proportion had shrunk to just 5 per cent (Redmond, 2000). The decline in the proportion of the workforce in agriculture is even more striking. In 1950 48.7 per cent of the working population were engaged in agricultural occupations. This fell to 27.5 per cent by 1970, to 17.1 per cent by 1986 and to 11.2 per cent by 1996, is now below 10 per cent and projected to be at 5 per cent by 2010 (EUROSTAT, DG VI Agricultural Statistics).

An economy in which the principal exports in 1949 were cattle, horses, eggs and alcoholic beverages has been replaced by one that today has four main categories of exports: computer equipment; organic chemicals; electrical machinery; and medical/pharmaceutical products (Redmond, 2000, pp. 92-93). Employment, so dominated before the 1960s by agriculture, has now been replaced by service and industrial occupations. In 1997 Ireland's occupational pattern mirrored reasonably closely that of the EU as a whole. The services sector (including education, health, retail, financial services, hotel and catering) and industry (manufacturing and production) accounted for 61.7 per cent and 28.4 per cent respectively of civilian employment. The averages for the 15 EU countries are 65.2 per cent and 29.8 per cent (OECD2).

The actual impact on Irish society of the transformed economy just described have been much more extensive than simply more people in employment working at a different range of activities. The economic reality has only been made possible by three other very major changes in the nature of Irish society. The first one concerns where and how people live, the second their level of education and the third the position of women in society. A fourth major change, a reduction in the influence of the Catholic Church and its teachings, though not as directly associated with economic development, is probably an inevitable consequence of features attendant on such development.

Urbanisation

As Ireland moved from being a predominantly agricultural society to a technologically advanced industrial one, there was a matching drift of the population from the countryside into urban areas. In 1946 over 60 per cent of the population lived in the countryside or in small towns or villages with populations below 1,500 persons. The 1996 census found that 58 per cent of the population lived in urban areas. The most dramatic change has been the growth in population of Dublin City and its heavily urbanised county surrounds, which together had a population of 1,058,300 in 1996, an increase of 66 per cent since 1946. This area now accounts for over 29 per cent of the overall population of the State.

The nuclear family

Family structure has also changed radically. Even in rural areas and among those involved in agriculture, the nuclear family (mother, father and children) has replaced the extended family which included grandparents and possibly uncles or aunts. When couples marry or otherwise form permanent partnerships (recent years have seen a considerable increase in unmarried couples cohabiting at least temporarily) they acquire their own accommodation. The typical family no longer includes grandparents or other relatives. This of course is only made possible by the young family having sufficient independent economic means to set up on their own. Growing affluence, from the 1960s onwards, allowed for this development. Attendant on it is inevitably a diminished level of power and influence among the elderly. Indeed, the elderly have tended to become marginalised, often now ending their days in nursing homes, isolated from their families.

Birth rate and family size

Another major change concerns the number of children being born. The birth rate per 1,000 of the population remained quite stable up to the early 1980s, after which it fell dramatically from a previous norm of around 21.5 to 14.5 in 1998. This is largely due to women delaying the age at which they have children and having far fewer of them. In 1971 25 per cent of women in the 25-29 age cohort gave birth. That was down to 10 per cent in 1998. The fertility rate (estimate of how many children on average women are likely to have) has dropped from 4 in 1971 to 1.9 in 1998 (Redmond, 2000). The estimated rate necessary to maintain population size is 2.1. In the absence of inward migration Ireland's population is set to age and decline.

Marital stability

There is an increase in marital instability in Ireland. Between the 1991 and 1996 censuses there was a 60 per cent increase in the number of individuals declaring themselves to be separated or divorced (Redmond, 2000). The absolute numbers are, however, still very small in comparison with other EU countries and with the US.

International comparisons

While all this represents a considerable change in the circumstances in which the majority of the people live in Ireland, it contrasts sharply in one respect with the pattern in other industrially developed countries. Figures for 1995 quoted by the United Nations show that, for example, the percentage of urban residents in the UK is 89 per cent, Germany 87 per cent, Denmark 85 per cent, France 75 per cent, Italy 67 per cent and the US 76 per cent (Population Division of the UN Secreteriat, 1998). Within the EU, Ireland is comparable to Portugal and Greece on the level of urbanisation, two countries which Ireland has outstripped by a factor of over 100 per cent in terms of economic output or GDP. The relatively low level of urbanisation coupled with the high level of economic development is an unusual situation and may be a function of late industrialisation.

Education

An important element in the foundation supporting Irish economic development is education. The change here since 1950 has been dramatic. At the upper end of the educational spectrum, only 116 postgraduate degrees were awarded in Ireland in 1950. Today about 7,600 such degrees are awarded annually. As regards undergraduate degrees about 14 times more are now awarded each year than in 1950 (Redmond, 2000). A great number of others also receive national diploma and certificate qualifications each year .

The huge increase in third level educational awards mainly through the University and Institute of Technology sector has been facilitated by a dramatic expansion in the proportion of young people entering and completing third level education. Much of this increase is down to the introduction in 1967 of a comprehensive system of free secondary education and free transport to school from rural areas. In the school year 1963-1964, 66.4 per cent of 14 and 51.5 per cent of 15 year olds were in full-time education. By 1984 those figures had climbed to 99.4 per cent and 94.4 per cent respectively (Redmond, 2000). The vast bulk of children were by then progressing to second level. The numbers completing second level education and obtaining the Leaving Certificate qualification has increased over five-fold from just over 12,000 in 1965 to around 64,000 a year at the end of the 1990s (Commission on the Points System, 1999). This represents a current completion rate of about 81 per cent of the relevant age cohort.

Expenditure in Ireland on education, 92 per cent of which is derived from public funds, was in 1995 close to the average of OECD (main developed economies of the world). Ireland spent 5.3 per cent of GDP on education in comparison with a mean of 5.6 per cent. In 1997, public expenditure on education in Ireland amounted to 4.6 per cent of GDP, which at £2,399m represented a considerable real increase since 1991 when it stood at £1,434m or 4.8 per cent of the then prevailing GDP.

Ireland has become an educated nation with an emphasis on formal education similar to the rest of the industrially developed world. This emphasis has been widely credited as the most significant single factor contributing to the level of economic success achieved.

The situation of women

The third major change in Irish society associated with economic change has occurred in the situation of women. The economic and social circumstances of women in traditional Irish society were discussed above. The most significant development has been their increased participation in the labour force, coupled with a widespread acceptance that women are equal to men and have a right to play an equal role to them in decision making and in fashioning society. Based on the European Values survey carried out in 1990 across nine EU countries, Turley (1995) reported that Irish sex role attitudes were in keeping with the European norms of equality. This contrasts with the situation prior to the 1970s when married women were debarred from almost all public sector employment and the primary role of women in society was viewed narrowly in terms of the, albeit very important, functions of child rearing and home making.

The 1970s brought about a considerable reappraisal of the role of women in society driven in part by the active women's liberation movement and by the increasing need to fit in, especially after accession to the EEC in 1973, with the norms prevailing in other European countries. Legislation was introduced in 1974 to outlaw differential pay for women and men doing similar work and in 1977 to prevent discrimination on the basis of gender in the hiring of employees or their treatment in the workplace. Technically, equality of access between the sexes was to be guaranteed, though equality of success in the workplace was not to be achieved.

Labour force participation by women

The immediate trend, which followed on the changes in how women viewed themselves and how they were viewed in society, was a growing participation in the employed labour force. In the first quarter of the year 2000 46.8 per cent of women in the 15-64 age cohort were in the workforce. This includes a much higher proportion of younger than older women. The overall participation rate is similar to the average for the EU where in 1997 45.6 per cent of women in this cohort were in the labour force (Ruane and Sutherland, 1999). A major change also has been the proportion of married women in the workforce up from 14 per cent of the total female workforce in 1971 to 52 per cent in 1997 (Ruane and Sutherland, 1999).

The delayed age at which women have children and the fact that they now have much smaller families is a major factor in enabling participation in the workforce. This of course ties up with attitudes to contraception and the divergence in behaviour on social issues with Catholic Church teaching discussed below.

Participation and performance in education by women

The increased participation rates in the workforce is mirrored by increased educational participation rates for women. The number of females outstrips that for males at all three levels of education (Redmond, 2000). At primary school level this reflects a slightly higher level of female over male births. At second and third level, however, it reflects greater participation rates by females. Achievement at second level measured by Leaving Certificate CAO points (criterion for entry to third level courses) is higher for females. However, despite arriving in third level education with better Leaving Certificate results, females do not perform as well as males do in this sector. A study carried out by the Department of Education Commission set up in 1997 to investigate the system of entry to third level courses found that in the University/Colleges of Education sector, 39 per cent of males obtained upper second or first class honours degrees as opposed to 29 per cent of females. A similar situation was found in the Institute of Technology sector with the sole exception of business qualifications where females performed better (Lynch et al, 1999). This trend of sex differences in educational performance is by no means unique to Ireland.

There have been several explanations put forward for the reversal of female fortunes in third level education. They range from under-performance by males at second level due to the later onset of puberty, to sex differences in competitiveness favouring males at third level, to inherent sex bias in the definition of higher level performance. It is likely that all three factors contribute to some degree.

Earnings of women

Whatever the causes of the apparent under-performance by females in higher education, their level of subsequent under-performance grows more stark in the workforce. In terms of average income in the manufacturing sector, the only area for which separate data on male and female income earnings is available, the March 1999 figures from the Central Statistics Office showed that the average industrial wage for women was only 64 per cent of that for men. A 1994 ESRI analysis of the employed Irish work force as a whole revealed that women's earnings were 82.4 per cent of men's (Barrett et al (2000)). This is due to their considerably lower representation in the ranks of high status, high paid jobs such as senior management, the upper echelons of the civil service, academic posts, the judiciary and management posts in education. It is also due to the greater preference of women for part-time work. A recent UN report commented on a number of reasons for this sex difference in vocational success in Ireland. They highlight in particular the 'persistence of the emphasis on the role of women as mothers and caregivers' as an obstacle to equality in vocational success (UN Committee on the Elimination of Discrimination against Women, 1999).

It should be noted that the average earnings of women do not equal that of men in *any* country. Average hourly earnings of women in Sweden, a country noted for its egalitarian practices, are still 13 per cent below men. In the UK they are 25 per cent below men (O'Connor, 2000). While on the face of it, this disparity seems undesirable and in some way discriminatory, it is possible that the situation can be viewed otherwise. There are certain opportunity costs associated with high earnings, which women may quite rationally and voluntarily be more inclined to avoid than men. Higher paid work often involves greater responsibilities, more stress, less leisure time and longer hours away from family. At a human level, as opposed to an economic one, the foregoing of higher earnings may be a sensible choice. The much greater life expectancy of women in industrialised societies (currently 77.9 and 72.3 years in Ireland according to CSO figures, Redmond, 2000) may at least in part be a testimony to this possibility.

A further important factor is that the direct labour of nurturing/ rearing children does not feature in statistics on earnings unless sub-contracted by parents to others. This inevitably distorts downwards the economic evaluation of the work carried out by women, since a much greater proportion of child rearing activity is carried out by them. While child rearing is one of the most fundamental functions in society, it has never been allocated an official economic value, however. To the extent that women more than men continue to engage in child rearing in pref-erence to other 'paid' activities in society, they will inevitably be found to have lower average earnings as a result.

The Catholic Church in emergent Irish society

Even in the late 1980s it was possible for an Irish sociologist to write the following in respect of the Ireland he witnessed at the time:

> 'One of the first impressions of the country that marks it out as differ-ent from other Western societies is that the Catholic Church is a strong and active force in everyday life.'

> (Inglis, 1987, p. 1)

Survey data from around that time bears out the picture Inglis paints. In the census of 1991, 92 per cent gave their religion as Roman Catholic. Weekly attendance at mass was very high by the standards of other 'Catholic' countries. MacGréil (1996) reported a national average of 82 per cent weekly attendance from a 1988-89 survey, though this dropped to 69 per cent attendance for residents of Dublin City and County.

Other indices measured by MacGréil indicated a high level of reli-giosity among Roman Catholics (94.2 per cent of his national sample). These included reception of Holy Communion (63 per cent, once a month at least) and attendance at confession (only 11 per cent said 'never'). Of the overall sample 82.7 per cent agreed that it was either 'fairly' or 'very' important that children be brought up in the same religious views as parents and 83.3 per cent agreed that their religion had been a help in some way in their personal development.

Religious observation

The intervening decade since MacGréil's survey has been one of considerable change, however. Two relatively recent national surveys of Catholics show that attendance at mass weekly or more often is down to somewhere between 60 per cent and 66 per cent (Council for Research and Development, St Patrick's College/Irish Marketing surveys, 1997 (Hanley, 1998a); RTE *Prime Time/MRBI* survey, 1998 (Hanley, 1998b). An even more recent national survey in November 1999 conducted by IMS/Gallup (Hanley, 2000) found that 57 per cent of the population attend a religious service once a week or more often. The survey did not differentiate attendance by religious denomination but since 94 per cent of the sample claimed to be Roman Catholics, attendance for Catholics can only be a few percentage points either way.

The CRD/IMS survey found that among urban males aged 25-34 weekly mass attendance was down to 31 per cent and the RTE *Prime Time/MRBI* survey found that only 38 per cent of the overall 18-24 age group attended mass on a weekly basis.

Religious vocations

An even more striking change, with very major immediate repercussions for the Catholic Church in Ireland, has been the collapse in vocations. Data supplied to the author by the Council for Research and Development, St Patrick's College, Maynooth shows the following picture of decline. It should be noted that as the Catholic Church operates on an all-Ireland basis, the figures refer to the whole island.

In 1965, 282 men were ordained as diocesan priests and 377 ordained into the religious orders. In 1999, the numbers had dropped to 34 and nine respectively. In 1999 there were 46 vocations to the Diocesan Clergy and 23 to the Clerical Religious Orders. In 1970, the comparable numbers were 164 and 261.

The ranks of the clergy have also been hit by a high number of departures from the priesthood, an action that was virtually unthinkable a generation ago. The remaining priests, numbering 7,605 in 1999 in contrast to 11,890 in 1970, are heavily weighted towards the older end of the spectrum. Half of all priests in the Republic were aged 55 or over, according to the 1996 census.

Among nuns and brothers the fall-off in vocations has been particularly extreme. In 1999, only 21 women joined a convent as opposed to 52 in 1990. In 1970, by way of comparison, 227 women had entered convents in Ireland. Orders of Brothers have been hit even more severely. They received only one vocation in 1999, down from eight in 1990 and 98 in 1970. There were 18,662 nuns and 2,540 brothers on the island of Ireland in 1970. The comparable figures for 1999 were 10,987 and 925 respectively.

The effect has been wholesale reorganisation, involving closures of convents and monasteries and widespread disengagement from the former dominant role in education. In 1970, there were 3,700 second level teachers in religious orders in the Republic. By 1998 this had dropped to 740, despite an increase in the overall number of teachers in the meantime. At primary school level 3 per cent of teachers were in religious orders in 1998, down from just under 20 per cent in 1970 (Redmond, 2000).

While most schools remain, nominally at least, under religious control, the day-to-day role of the Church is growing ever more distant from the classroom, with increasingly lay principals being appointed even in some of the diocesan colleges. Religious orders, former bastions of the educational system such as the Christian Brothers and the Mercy and Presentation orders of nuns, have been closing boarding schools and abandoning the running of schools altogether due to the lack of members.

Changes in social and religious values

The Catholic Church has survived the 1990s with much of its old authority and status eroded. In 1995 a referendum accepted an amendment to the Constitution, albeit by the slimmest majority imaginable, to allow for divorce legislation to be passed, legislation which has subsequently been enacted. In 1992 the electorate, while supporting the constitutional ban on abortion, rejected proposed constitutional amendments designed to prevent pregnant women from obtaining advice on abortion and from travelling abroad for the purposes of obtaining an abortion. Both the latter decisions on abortion and that on divorce represent a divergence of the people and the law from the position of the Church. Further divergence has occurred on the issue of the sale of contraceptives, long prohibited in Ireland. Over the 1980s and 1990s the legal restrictions were relaxed, eventually bringing Ireland into line with the rest of the developed world. Despite the Vatican's prohibition on any form of artificial contraceptive, their use is as widespread in Ireland as anywhere else.

The scale of divergence on social and moral values between Catholics and the Church is evident from the 1998 *Prime Time/MRBI* poll, where only 19 per cent agreed with Church teaching on contraception and 30 per cent with its stance on divorce. The decision to remove the constitutional ban on divorce, the growing rates of marital separation and divorce (though still comparatively low by European and US standards) and the fall in family size due to contraceptive use represents the behavioural as well as the attitudinal parting of the ways between the population and the teachings of the Catholic Church.

A further much more public divergence between accepted norms of behaviour and Church teaching prevails in the area of pre-marital sexual relations and extra-marital cohabitation. This is reflected in the high level of non-marital births. Between 1949 and 1979 the proportion of births outside marriage ranged between 1 per cent and 5 per cent. Thereafter there was a steady climb to 28 per cent in 1998 – higher than the EU average (Redmond, 2000).

What was formerly a very much taboo practice – the bearing of an 'illegitimate' child – has now become an accepted part of Irish cultural reality. In a survey of 780 unmarried women around the country who had just given birth, 40 per cent of them had a positive attitude to the fact that they had a child outside of marriage, a figure that went up to 55 per cent of those describing themselves as cohabiting (Mahon, Conlon and Dillon, 1998). The vast majority of those single women, who were not particularly happy to have given birth, nevertheless intended to raise the child themselves with or without the help of the father. As against that, the number of single women giving Irish addresses at British abortion clinics (circa. 4,500 per year) indicates that around 25 per cent of Irish non-marital pregnancies end in abortion. This again represents a major private deviation from Catholic Church teaching. The Church is unequivocal in teaching that the unborn are living human beings and that abortion is in direct contravention of the fifth commandment.

Religiosity in Ireland today

While religious practice and acceptance of the moral teaching authority of the Church may be in sharp decline in Ireland, religiosity or the importance of religion in people's lives is not showing the same decline. Only 1 per cent in the 1999 IMS/Gallup survey described themselves as having no religion and 86 per cent said that God was important or very important in their lives. The nature of this religiosity is showing clear signs of very considerable deviation from organised religion. While 94 per cent of the national sample in the IMS/Gallup survey described themselves as Catholics, only 58 per cent said they believed in a personal God. Based on answers to other questions in the survey it is also possible to deduce that among those who describe themselves as Catholics, 10-15 per cent are either atheists or agnostics. Clearly, for some at least, the definition 'Roman Catholic' is taken to mean baptised as such as opposed to any expression of religious belief.

Factors influencing the decline of religion in Irish life

There is little doubt that economic changes have given young people a range of options that are more attractive than religious life and this has steered them away from vocations. Additionally more open attitudes to sexuality has led to a greater unwillingness to accept a life of celibacy. Another factor hastening the decline of religious vocations must be the scandals that have rocked the Church in Ireland throughout the 1990s. The 1998 *Prime Time/MRBI* poll found that 73 per cent of Catholics interviewed felt that scandals had damaged the Church authority to a substantial degree.

Chief among those scandals has been the raft of trials and convictions of priests and brothers for paedophile offences. By March 1989, 27 priests, brothers and ex-clergy had been convicted in the courts of the Republic. Twelve further cases were pending either in the Republic or

Northern Ireland. The Church was also traumatised in 1992 by the revelation that Dr. Eamonn Casey, the then Bishop of Galway, had fathered a child back in 1974 while serving as Bishop of Kerry. Dr. Casey resigned his bishopric. Small in the moral scale of the paedophile revelations that were to come, the Casey affair, nevertheless, revealed the hierarchy to be all too human. His conservative moral stance on social issues was retrospectively cast in a hypocritical light and considerable harm was done to the status of the church as a source of moral teaching.

From the point of view of socialisation and culture, not only has the authority of the Church been undermined from within itself, but it must now compete with a variety of contrary influences from outside, especially from the mass media. This is in marked contrast to the situation that prevailed up to the 1960s when there was literally no socialising influence which the Church did not control to a significant degree. Nowhere is this transformation in society more striking than in the realm of sexuality. The Church preaches that sex is acceptable only within the confines of marriage and strongly associates it with procreation through its ban on artificial contraception. The media, through television, advertising, cinema, magazines, and newspapers, portray sexuality as a desirable pleasure to be indulged in by all, whether married or single. Clearly the media are winning the battle or at least reflecting more accurately the values of Irish society.

A further powerful influence pressing the behaviour and attitudes of the population of Ireland in the direction it has been taking derives from economic circumstances. As indicated above, the rejection in practice of Catholic Church teaching may have been essential to allow for the development of the economy we have. Early onset of child bearing and large families, in the absence of the use of contraceptives, would keep the majority of young women out of the labour force and starve the economy of essential labour and talent.

The development of the nuclear family as the norm is necessary to allow for the mobility required in a technologically advanced economy. Families must follow work. The extended family imbedded in the wider local society is simply not mobile. The level of psychological demands placed on each other by men and women in the nuclear family situation removed from the supports and restraints of extended family and wider community leads inevitably to higher marital breakdown and the eventual acceptance of divorce as a common reality.

It is not accidental that those countries that have for a long time been richer and more economically advanced, such as the UK, have also long had low levels of religious observation, coupled with high levels of contraceptive use, sexual permissiveness and divorce. The economic and social systems come as a package, a theme that will be further explored below in the context of culture.

There can be little doubt also that the growth in female consciousness from the 1960s onwards, prompted by a vocal feminist movement, militated against the position of religion in Irish society. In a great many ways it was realised that Catholic teaching was discriminatory and entirely patriarchal. It was a Church within which power was vested almost entirely in the hands of men. The strong emphasis on a particular brand of sexual morality acted in a far more restrictive way on women. The absence of artificial contraceptives, condemned as sinful by the Church, resulted in large families. This had the effect of restricting women to the home for a long period of their lives and preventing them from assuming a more general and influential role in the affairs of society.

Men, on the other hand, were left free to take full charge of the organs of power. By being the income earners they also controlled the purse strings, which further disempowered women in general. A Church wedded to a system of values which rendered women second-class citizens, was bound to lose support once education enabled them to grasp the nature of their circumstances and to realise that change could be achieved. Reform was not forthcoming within the Catholic Church. Since the accession of the present Pontiff, Pope John Paul II, in 1979, all reforms that might have served to equalise the position of men and women within the Church have been forestalled. Women have been left with two options. Diverge from Catholic teachings or accept their discriminatory nature. Many have clearly opted for the former.

AN EMERGENT CULTURE

While the engine driving change in Ireland has been primarily the economy, inevitably such wholesale economic change is accompanied and to some extent, perhaps, preceded, by a variety of developments of a social and cultural nature.

Culture, as we saw earlier, involves shared views on values – what is desirable and accepted in society. Clearly, the disregard for material success inherent in De Valera's 1941 broadcast to the nation could not have acted as a cultural platform from which to launch the kind of economy we now have. It was no accident that it awaited a younger generation of politicians and officials, led by De Valera's successor Sean Lemass, to adopt the radical about-turn in economic policies which led us to where we now are.

Having seemingly embraced wholeheartedly the notion that material wealth is essential to the good of society, how have we been affected in other respects? How different now is our culture to that prevailing in, say, the 1940s?

INDIVIDUALISM IN IRISH CULTURE

Traditional Irish culture was characterised above as firmly at the collectivist end of the cultural dimension identified by Hofstede, Tonnies and Wirth. Conforming, fitting in and not upsetting the group was a dominant value. Individuals perceived themselves as belonging to a social group associated with their local community. Associations were long-term and personal in character, involving a sense of obligation. Work was, for many, an extension of the home, and education an extension of a Church to which there was unswerving and unquestioning loyalty. Irishness and Catholicism were synonymous. The socialisation process was homogenous, lessons taught in the home being reinforced in church and school and vice versa. Access to conflicting notions about values was strictly curtailed.

All this has very significantly changed, though in varying degrees depending on one's situation in society. The separation of work from home and local community following on industrialisation and the decline of occupations in agricultural has shifted relationships from the personal to the instrumental. Associated urbanisation has hastened this process. The norm now is to deal with individuals in a particular instrumental context: as work colleagues, friends, service providers, neighbours or family members. One deals with others in particular roles, not in their totality. Contact with each is limited. This has inevitably led Irish culture towards the individualist perspective.

The fact that behaviour is carried out and life lived in a variety of separate social contexts means that there is no one group or community that one needs to fit in with.

The overall effect is to allow individuals greater freedom to behave as they please as opposed to conforming with rigid social norms. The socialisation process too has become more heterogeneous. A great variety of role models for behaviour and life style are available through TV and the media in general. In 1950s Ireland, behavioural norms in Los Angeles or even London were distant and largely irrelevant. Today every child is confronted on a daily basis with those norms through the medium of TV.

EVALUATION OF INDIVIDUALISM

Whether the move from collectivism to individualism is a good or a bad thing is a matter of opinion. If material wealth is what we desire and an individualistic culture is part and parcel of economic progress in the global capitalist world in which we operate, then it seems foolish to complain about it. On the other hand the Irish do not seem to be particularly materialistic in value terms. The 1990 European Values survey found that 76 per cent of the Irish sample would like 'less emphasis on money and material possession', a proportion that was well above the European average (Turley, 1995). That we may have some doubts about the value of material wealth, the most obvious benefit of the kind of society evolving in Ireland, does prompt a consideration of possible down-sides to this kind of society.

The bonds between the individual and the community are weaker. The Catholic Church and its teachings are much less influential. The effect is to allow individuals to behave more as they please. The question immediately arises as to how they respond to that freedom. Some of the evidence is certainly negative, though there is no certain way of establishing the causal chain of the behaviours involved. Two disturbing trends have been a rise in anti-social and in self-destructive behaviour.

Anti-social behaviour and individualism

Crime patterns have risen steadily since the mid-1960s, the point at which modern Irish society began to evolve. The annual number of murders (including manslaughters) never rose above 20 between the 1940s and 1973. Thereafter it dipped below 20 in only one year and is currently running at around 50 (Redmond, 2000). Other serious indictable offences have shown an enormous increase over the same period, though there has been a reduction in recent years, which is possibly associated with the improved economic conditions and an end to armed robberies perpetrated to fund the Republican campaign in Northern Ireland.

Self destructive behaviour and individualism

The other unfortunate trend seemingly associated with individualism is self-destructive behaviour. This has taken on two striking manifestations in Ireland: abuse of recreational drugs and suicide.

Use of illegal narcotics such as heroin is a phenomenon particularly (but by no means uniquely) associated with the poorer urban areas of modern industrial countries. In Ireland since the 1970s it has caused a great deal of death and misery largely in working class neighbourhoods of Dublin. It is also accepted as the source of much of our street crime and contributes to the spread of AIDS through the sharing of infected hypodermic needles.

While there is broad societal acceptance of the self-destructive nature of the abuse of illegal drugs, particularly hard drugs such as heroin and cocaine, there is a much more ambivalent attitude to the abuse of alcohol which is used on a far greater scale throughout the country. The Irish have long had a reputation as a hard drinking people, a stereotype which for a long time was not altogether warranted when international statistics were examined. Up until very recently we were well down from the top of the European league table in terms of alcohol per capita consumed. As recently as 1996 on this criterion we were behind Luxembourg, Portugal, France, Germany, the Czech Republic, Hungary and Denmark. Recent figures however show an alarming rise in our per capita consumption. In 1999 we had leaped into the number two position with only Luxembourg ahead of us (World Drink Trends, 2000). In terms of litres of pure alcohol (drank in the form of beer, wine and spirits) our overall consumption in 1999 was the equivalent of 11.6 litres per head. Throughout the 1980s the average was 6.6 litres and in 1961 the average was only 3.4 litres.

Survey data from sources such as the ESPAD 2001 study reveal a number of disturbing findings for Ireland particularly with respect to young people. Among those findings are a very early age of drinking commencement, a low percentage of non-drinkers among younger adults and a marked tendency to drink excessively. Of all children aged 9–17, 29 per cent are current drinkers. The typical age for beginning to drink is now as low as 14–15. Only 7 per cent of females and 5 per cent of males aged 18-34 do not drink. There is a sharp contrast here with older females where in the over 55 age group 36 per cent do not drink. Irish 16-year-olds are top of the European league in terms of binge drinking, with 50 per cent and 60 per cent respectively of girls and boys in the 15–17 age group reporting having been 'really drunk'. In the 18–34 age group a third of males and a quarter of females drink more per week than the amount regarded as safe by medical authorities.

As a nation we may not have deserved our 'hard-drinking' reputation before but clearly we do now. There is a wealth of evidence associating excessive drinking with self-destructive and anti-social outcomes. Alcohol abuse has been found to relate to physical and mental ill-health, car accidents (a contributory factor in 40 per cent of road traffic accidents according to Garda estimates), domestic and street violence, suicide, and work absenteeism (Department of Health, 1996). The recent rapid increase in alcohol consumption in Ireland will inevitably be followed by a marked increase in health and social problems.

Suicide is the other category of self-destructive behaviour we identified above. There has been a marked trend of increase in suicide rates in Ireland since the early seventies, a trend that is tied up to some degree with the pattern of drugs and alcohol abuse we have just discussed. Between 1950 and the early seventies suicides accounted for 2–3 deaths out of every 1000. In 1975–77 period this figure reached 5 and has been climbing since and now stands at around 12 per 1000 deaths (Redmond, 2000). Even allowing for underreporting in the earlier periods (since 1967 the Central Statistics Office has drawn on confidential Garda reports, which should ensure relative accuracy) the rise in suicide rates is very considerable.

The increase has been most dramatic among males aged 15 to 24, a trend that is true of some other countries in Europe as well. Based on World Health Organisation figures for the period 1970–85 quoted by Diekstra (1992) Ireland had the highest rate of increase in Europe for the three age cohorts, 15–19, 20–24 and 25–29. Irish rates of increase dwarfed those for most countries. When absolute rates were examined Ireland was much lower than most other countries. Ireland has been showing a steep increase in suicide rates from a remarkably low baseline (some of which may be down to false reporting in the past.) Based on analysis of correlational data and peaks in suicide in other European countries earlier in the 20th century, Diekstra (1992) suggests that such increases are related to periods of rapid social change involving industrialisation, changes in family structure (increased breakdown), secularisation and increased consumption of alcohol. All of these have been features of Irish society in the last few decades.

Suicide is a very individualist act and is more likely to be adopted as an option when individuals perceive that they have the right to act as they see fit. Formerly, many individuals may have been discouraged from this action by the strong community taboo associated with it and the teaching of the Catholic Church that it was a mortal sin, which could lead to eternal damnation. It may be that the pressure to commit suicide is no greater but the pressure in society not to do so is much less.

The lowering of pressure not to behave in a particular way may be accountable for the higher rates of drug abuse, suicide and crime. In a more collectivist culture, where relations with others are more personal and encompass more of one's life, the pressure to conform to the values of society are greater. One fears to transgress because there is more to lose in terms of one's standing in the community. As an individual with looser bonds to any group, one is freer to behave as one pleases. This inevitably results in a greater level of anti-social and self-destructive behaviour among those who have not internalised strong values opposing such behaviour. A society where the community and authority figures policed the actions of the individual has to a significant extent been replaced by one where the individual must police his or her own actions. The transitional phase may be especially traumatic.

Positive aspects of individualism

It is important not to overly emphasise the negative aspect of individualist societies and romanticise the collectivist alternative. Conformity, a
product of collectivism, can admittedly result in seemingly much lower
crime rates and in less self-destructive behaviour. It can also result in the
cover up of serious wrongdoing and compliance in the abuse of others,
especially those without power in society.

Evidence has emerged in the 1990s of widespread physical and sexual
abuse of children in care – most disturbingly, in the care of religious
orders. In addition, many cases of sexual abuse of children who were not
in care, by individuals in positions of respect and authority, have also
come before the courts. Many of these cases relate back to the 1950s,
1960s and 1970s. Why were these abuses not revealed at the time? The
evidence is that the abused, and in certain cases those who sought to
represent them, were simply unable to gain a hearing, or, worse still, were
faced with reproach for making such allegations. Collectivist societies
are not well equipped to deal with anything that casts doubt on their
virtues, particularly if those being questioned are influential members.
The individualist stance necessary for questioning those in authority is
not facilitated.

It should be remembered that the physical abuse of children in
schools and to a lesser extent in the home (all of it masquerading as the
necessary imposition of discipline) was institutionalised in Ireland up to
recent decades. Is it less or more of a crime for a teacher in a school to
assault a small child than for a mugger to assault a passer-by on the street?
Any objective dispassionate analysis would suggest that the captive and
entirely vulnerable child is the greater victim. Yet this form of crime was
a daily event in the lives of many children, and, since society defined it
in a different way, there was nothing they could do about it. What was
deemed inhuman and degrading treatment of prisoners of war was
deemed acceptable to mete out to small children. Again, the collectivist
nature of society perpetuated this abuse because it was sanctioned by
those in authority.

A further type of abuse is now coming to light through the plethora of public tribunals and investigations launched by the Government into corruption and fraud in industry, banking and public life. While several of the tribunals are ongoing the evidence presented to those to date and the outcomes of completed investigations presents a general picture of financial dishonesty by many rich, influential individuals and institutions. That their activities were not revealed before is again a comment on the nature of society in previous times and that there is a rush of such investigations now says something about how society has changed. In an individualist society the powerful can not assure themselves of the kind of unquestioning loyalty that guaranteed their wrongdoings in the past went unnoticed.

Collectivism means loyalty and conformity. This is a double-edged sword. It can result in adherence to good community values. On the other hand, it can mean that a blind eye is turned to corruption and abuse, and it is those with power who are better placed to capitalise on this.

WORK IN THE EMERGENT SOCIETY

Apart from the obvious reality that it is the change in the amount and nature of work available that has been the main engine behind change in Irish society, the question arises as to how the nature of work is changing the individual and the individual's attitude to work.

The workplace is itself an agent of socialisation. Organisations naturally try to encourage attitudes and behaviours in their employees that will enable work to be carried out more efficiently. Furthermore, the demands of work influence other agents of socialisation such as the educational system and the family. The relationship between the demands of the workplace and the structure of the family has been discussed above. A further influence of the workplace on family and also on education is that schools and parents try to encourage attitudes and behaviours that enable individuals to be successful in the workplace. What can we expect the nature of this influence to be?

Sociologists and social psychologists have attempted to identify the cultural values that flow from the kind of work and organisational systems prevalent in modern developed economies such as we have evolved in

Ireland. Yang (1988) has attempted to synthesise the results of various such studies into a profile of the modern person – the person suited to this kind of society. He identifies the following points:

1. a sense of personal efficacy;
2. low social integration with relatives;
3. egalitarian attitude towards others;
4. an openness to innovation and change;
5. a belief in sex equality;
6. high achievement motivation;
7. independence or self reliance;
8. active participation in social organisations;
9. tolerance of, and respect for, others;
10. cognitive and behavioural flexibility;
11. strong future orientation;
12. empathetic capacity;
13. a high need for information;
14. the propensity to take risks in life;
15. secularization in religious belief;
16. a preference for urban life;
17. an individualistic orientation towards others;
18. psychological differentiation;
19. a non-local orientation.

Much of this profile reflects the individualistic culture discussed above. One or two issues deserve special attention in the Irish context. Several of the points listed may together be encompassed within the idea of an open, rational approach to reality, in opposition to a closed-minded, prejudiced, emotional response. Up to now, Ireland and its workplaces have been largely mono-cultural. Virtually everyone shared the same Irish cultural background. It is very probable that there will be an increase in the future in the proportion of other nationalities resident and working in Ireland. This trend is already underway. An open rational approach is essential to cope constructively with this development to whatever extent it occurs. Prejudice leads to racism, which naturally results in defensiveness and negative reactions that are then taken as evidence to support the prejudice. This spiral is only avoidable by an open attitude in the first place. Some, but by no means all, of the response to asylum seekers witnessed in Ireland to date suggests that a significant proportion of the population are not ready to cope with the demands of a multi-cultural society.

SOCIALISATION IN EMERGENT IRISH SOCIETY

As discussed above, socialisation is the vehicle by which the culture (values and norms) of society are transmitted from one generation to another. The primary role is played by the family, secondary roles by school, workplace and any other circumstances in which individuals interact with others. Each socialising agent is capable of influencing each other.

The role of fear in the socialisation process in traditional Irish society cannot be underestimated. Coercion of one kind or another was part and parcel of life. For children, much of this was of a raw physical nature. If they did not act as their elders demanded, they were likely to be beaten. Corporal punishment with little or no restraining framework was lawful and the norm in schools. Much the same applied in the home. Fear also guided the behaviour of adults: fear of authority and fear of community disapproval.

Apart from all the human rights issues raised, the problem with fear as the primary agent of socialisation is that its effectiveness depends on behaviour being closely policed. It does not encourage any real internalisation of values, and where transgressions can be perpetrated in secret there is little motivation to keep the rules.

It is no accident that our more individualist society has been accompanied by a radical change in approaches to socialisation. Longitudinal studies carried out by Diana Baumrind in California found a strong association between the manner in which children are socialised and how they behave as nine-year olds (Baumrind, 1991). The authoritarian pattern typical of traditional Ireland was not found to be associated with the most positive outcomes. A pattern described as 'authoritative', where parents engage in a great deal of explanation and dialogue with children as to why they should behave in certain ways, was found to be associated with the best outcomes in terms of social competence, achievement orientation, ability to plan and general intellectual ability.

The key difference between socialisation relying heavily on punishment and socialisation emphasising dialogue is the capacity of the latter to get children to take responsibility for their own actions. It is more likely to result in the internalisation of values. This is essential in a society where individuals are expected to make decisions for themselves and where the policing of behaviour by community is weak or absent.

A great deal of the problem of anti-social and self-destructive behaviour, which seems to be associated with our conversion to an individualist society, may be down to inappropriate socialisation. In addition to the issues of crime and drug abuse, Ireland has a major problem with other aspects of civic behaviour such as tax compliance, driving behaviour and littering. To a great extent the rule seems to be that if one can get away with it and one personally benefits, then it is acceptable. A socialisation process where the motive to behave comes from the fear of being caught and punished is not likely to be effective if the chances of being caught are negligible. The authoritative approach, which inculcates personal responsibility and internalisation of rules, is much more effective in such circumstances.

The reality of a move from authoritarian (fear-based) socialisation to an authoritative (rational argument-based) approach can be found in a move from McGregor's Theory X to his Theory Y approach to motivation as discussed in Chapter 8. A general shift in this direction has prompted a re-evaluation in recent decades of the whole practice of personnel management. This has resulted in the emergence of a coherent set of principles for people management sometimes referred to as *human resources management* (see Gunnigle, Heraty and Morley, 1997, pp. 43-48). The emphasis is on greater trust and individualism in employee relations, based on an assumption of common cause between employees and employers. This trend has also been discussed in Chapter 10 in the context of organisational design.

A similar shift from authoritarian to authoritative socialisation has permeated the educational system, resulting in the outlawing of corporal punishment within the whole school system. While corporal punishment of children in the home has still not been outlawed it is likely to be only a matter of time before we follow the lead of other European countries such as Sweden in this respect.

The overall lesson on socialisation is that society functions as an integrated unit. Developments in one sphere will inevitably have a knock-on effect in all others. Socialisation processes in the home influence those in school and work and vice versa. Socialisation is in content and method an expression of culture and culture applies to society as a whole.

As discussed in Chapter 10, the organisations to which we belong, in education, work and so on, each have their own unique cultures. They are not, however, cut off from society at large. The norms and values of the overall culture in Irish society will always have a major influence. Since the effect of culture through the socialisation process is to cause all those who share it to think and act alike to a certain extent whatever their individual personalities or attitudes, Irish individuals inevitably bring common influences to bear on organisations throughout society. So long as we retain any kind of distinctive culture, Irish institutions associated with work, education, pleasure or whatever, will retain their own distinctive characteristics that differ from the institutions of other countries. To the degree that we share norms, values and a way of understanding the world with other nations, life in Irish society throughout all its institutions will feel just like life elsewhere. There is no doubt that, for better or worse, we have gone a great distance in that direction over the last 40 years. 'Emergent' Irish society is a great deal more like that of its European neighbours than was 'traditional' Irish society in its own time.

SUMMARY

Society is *'the system of interrelationships which connects together the individuals who share a common culture'* (Giddens, 1989, p. 32). The system of interrelationships takes place within family, educational, economic, governmental and religious institutions.

Culture may be taken to refer to the *shared values, norms, beliefs and ways of thinking that characterise the members of a society.*

'Socialisation is the process through which children acquire the behaviour, skills, motives, values, beliefs and standards that are characteristic, appropriate and desirable in their culture'

(Newcombe, 1996, p. 346).

Socialisation is the vehicle through which culture is transmitted from generation to generation and by which society replicates itself across generations. It occurs primarily in the family but also in education and wherever individuals interact with each other. The media also have a major role.

Irish society throughout the 20th century may be divided into two phases: the 'traditional' phase which prevailed up to the 1960s and the 'emergent' phase which has been evolving since.

Traditional Irish society had its cultural origins in historical developments towards the end of the 19th century and early in the 20th century. It was primarily a rural society of small landholders and business people involved in providing local services largely deriving from the settlement of the land ownership question after the land war of the early 1880s. There was little industrialisation to promote the growth of urban areas and few sources of employment outside of inheritance of a farm or business. Very high levels of emigration resulted, with a consequent ageing and declining population up to 1961. Ownership and power lay disproportionately in the hands of the elderly, favouring a marked conservatism in attitudes. The Catholic Church had a very high status among a population that was overwhelmingly Catholic in denomination. It wielded enormous influence, controlling the educational system almost in its entirety. Its teachings were unquestioned. State institutions, reflected in the law, mirrored the Catholic ethos unfailingly. The place of women in society was viewed in terms of child rearing and home making, though they made a considerable direct economic contribution to family farms and businesses.

The culture of traditional Ireland was strikingly conservative and emphasised security over advancement. It was dominated by the teachings of the Catholic Church, which was largely anti-materialist and did little to prompt an entrepreneurial spirit. There was a marked insularity and a suspicion of all outside influences. The virtues of things deemed intrinsically Irish, such as Gaelic sports, music, language and historic tradition, were exaggerated, as were the supposed vices of all things foreign. The desire was to foster and maintain a uniquely Gaelic culture even if the consequences were isolation from the outside world and material poverty. Traditional Irish culture, being largely based in small intimate rural communities, was collectivist in nature. Relationships were essentially personal and strong bonds of obligation tied the individual to the community.

The attempt to foster a uniquely Gaelic society unadulterated by outside influences could not be sustained because of its lack of economic viability. It was simply unable to support its own people. In the 1950s the level of emigration was such that those in power came to realise that the future of Ireland as a nation State could not be assured unless it achieved greater economic success. The tariff-protected, closed economy was scrapped in favour of openness to global markets and capital. Attendant on this was an inevitable opening of Irish society to cultural influences of all kinds from abroad.

The 1960s saw the genesis of what is described here as 'emergent Irish society', based on a technologically advanced industrialised economy relying heavily on investment by multi-national corporations from abroad. Today, industry and the services are the main source of wealth and employment. The population is predominantly urban-based, though not nearly as much as other industrialised economies. We are full members of the European Union and have swapped our currency for a common European one. Instead of a closed economy we have one of the most open in the world.

The population has increased; inwards migration has replaced emigration and we have all but caught up on the UK and the average of the EU in terms of national income. Our level of education matches that of other advanced nations, a key feature in our economic success. There is a strong commitment to equality for women, matching European norms. The Catholic Church has experienced a huge decline in vocations and a very considerable weakening in its influence. On important social issues both the law and norms of behaviour have diverged from Catholic teaching, particularly in the area of sexual morality. Delayed procreation, few children and nuclear families are the norm. A high and growing proportion of children are born outside of wedlock, a trend associated with a tendency for unmarried couples to cohabit. There is a marked decline in religious observation measured through weekly attendance at mass. Ireland, however, still retains a distinctive spiritual dimension with a high level of belief in God, though not necessarily the God of organised religion.

The presence of alternative agents of socialisation, scandals undermining the teaching authority of the Church, the demands of the evolving economic system and the rise of 'feminist' consciousness have all contributed to the decline in the relevance and status of the Catholic Church in Ireland.

Irish culture has grown much more individualist. In urban and also in rural areas the bonds tying the individual to the community have weakened considerably. Relationships tend to be of a more instrumental kind. Different individuals are dealt with in different contexts and for different purposes such as at work, in receiving services, as neighbours or as friends or family members. Social relations have become compartmentalised. The overall effect of individualism is to leave the burden of responsibility on individuals for their own behaviour. A possible negative consequence has been a marked increase in both self-destructive and anti-social behaviour. On the positive side, it seems to have allowed for the exposure of abuses perpetrated in secret by people in authority when Ireland had a more conforming collectivist culture.

The profound changes in the nature of work in Irish society are bound to have significant effects on Irish culture. Essentially, a very different kind of person with a different profile of skills, attitudes and values is needed to function effectively in our urban, industrialised economy than was required by the previous economy based on small farms and local service businesses. Yang (1988), based on studies within and across various cultures, has concluded that modern societies such as ours require individuals who are independent and believe in themselves, are interested in achievement, are open-minded, willing to learn and well-equipped to get on with a variety of types of people.

The socialisation process in traditional Irish society relied heavily on fear. It was authoritarian in approach. An authoritative approach which inculcates a greater internalisation of values and behavioural norms based on understanding is more appropriate to an individualist society where there is a much looser external policing of behaviour. External pressure to conform must be replaced by an internal will to behave in accordance with the common good. Failure of adjustment towards the appropriate socialisation process may account for much of the self-destructive and anti-social behaviour that has been attendant on Ireland's conversion from a collectivist to an individualist society.

General societal norms and values penetrate all institutions in society. The move in favour of authoritative socialisation processes is evident in human resource management trends in workplaces and in approaches to discipline in Irish schools.

To the degree that Ireland retains a distinctive culture, the institutions of which its society consists will have their own uniquely Irish feel. To the extent that our culture is shared by other nations, life here will be just like life elsewhere. For better or worse, in the last 40 years we have travelled a long way towards sharing a common culture with our European neighbours.

REVIEW QUESTIONS

1. With particular reference to the issue of work, describe the defining characteristics of Irish society prior to the 1960s.
2. Explain what is implied by the term 'culture' and explain the main cultural changes that Ireland has witnessed over the last four decades.
3. Contrast the characteristics of collectivist and individualist cultures.
4. Discuss the impact of economic development in Ireland on population, wealth, family and community.
5. Contrast the nature of modern or 'emergent' Irish society with that which prevailed before the commencement of industrialisation in the 1960s.

REFERENCES

Arensberg, C.A. and Kimball, S.T., (1940), *Family and Community in Ireland*, Cambridge, Mass: Harvard University Press.

Barrett, A., Callan, T., (ed.), Doris, A., O'Neill, D., Russell, H., Sweetman, O. and McBride, J., (2000) *How unequal? Men and Women in the Irish Labour Market*, Dublin: Oaktree Press in association with the ESRI.

Baumrind, D., (1991), 'Effective Parenting During the Early Adolescent Transition', in P.A. Cowan and E.M. Hetherington (eds), *Family Transitions: Advances in Family Research Transition* (p. 111-163), Hillsdale, New Jersey: LEA.

Bottomore, T., (1987), *Sociology: A Guide to Problems and Literature*, (3rd Edn), London: Allen and Unwin.

Breen, R., Hannan, D.F., Rottman, D.B. and Whelan, C.T., (1990), *Understanding Contemporary Ireland: State, Class and Development in the Republic of Ireland*, London: Macmillan.

Brown, T., (1985), *Ireland: A Social and Cultural History*, London: Fontana Press.

Bunreacht na hÉireann (The Irish Constitution) (1937), Dublin: Government Publications Office.

Commission on the Points System, (1999), *Final Report and Recommendations*, Dublin: Stationery Office.

Diekstra, R.F.W., (1992), 'Epidemiology of Suicide: Aspects of Definition, Classification and Preventive Policies', in P. Creppet, G. Ferrari, S. Platt and M. Bellini, (eds), *Suicidal Behaviour in Europe: Recent Research Findings*, Rome: John Libby CIC srl.

Department of Health (1996), *National Alcohol Policy*, Dublin: Government Publications Office.

ESPAD (2001 In press), *European Schools Project on Alcohol and Other Drugs*, Stockholm: Council of Europe and the Swedish Centre for Information on Alcohol.

EUROSTAT, DG VI, *Agricultural Statistics*.

Foster, R.F., (1989), *Modern Ireland: 1600-1972*, London: Penguin.

Giddens, A., (1989), *Sociology*, Cambridge: Polity Press.

Giddens, A., (1993), *Sociology*, (2nd Edn), Cambridge: Polity Press.

Gunnigle, P., Heraty, N. and Morley, M., (1997), *Personnel and Human Resource Management: Theory and Practice in Ireland*, Dublin: Gill & Macmillan.

Hall, E.T., (1983), *The Dance of Life*, New York: Doubleday.

Hanley, A., (1998a), 'Major Religious Confidence Survey', *Intercom*, March.

Hanley, A., (1998b), *Attitudes to the Catholic Church: The RTE Prime Time/MRBI Survey*, unpublished paper, Maynooth, Ireland: St. Patrick's College, Council for Research and Development, February.

Hanley, A., (2000), *Religious Belief and Practice: A New Survey*, unpublished paper, Maynooth, Ireland: St. Patrick's College, Council for Research and Development.

Hofstede, G., (1980), *Culture's Consequences: International Differences in Work Related Values*, Beverly Hills, CA: Sage.

Hofstede, G., (1983), 'Dimensions of National Cultures in Fifty Countries and Three Regions', in J.B. Deregowski, (ed.), *Expiscations (sic.) in Cross-Cultural Psychology*, pp. 335-355, Lisse: Swets and Zeitlinger.

Hofstede, G., (1991), *Cultures and Organisations: Software of the Mind*, London: McGraw Hill.

Huczynski, A. and Buchanan, D., (1991), *Organizational Behaviour: An Introductory Text*, (2nd Edn), UK: Prentice Hall.

Inglis, T., (1987), *Moral Monopoly: The Catholic Church in Modern Irish Society*, Dublin: Gill & Macmillan.

Kevin, N., (1944), *I Remember Karrigeen*, London and Dublin: Burns, Oates and Washborne Ltd.

Levine, R.V. and Bartlett, C., (1984), 'Pace of Life, Punctuality and Coronary Heart Disease in Six Countries', *Journal of Cross Cultural Psychology*, 15, 233-55.

Lynch, K., Brannick, T., Clancy, P. and Drudy, S., (1999), *Commission on the Points System Research Paper No. 4, Points and Performance in Higher Education: A Study of the Predictive Validity of the Points System.*, Dublin: Stationery Office.

Lyons, F.S.L., (1986), *Ireland Since the Famine*, London: Fontana Press.

MacGréil, M., (1977), *Prejudice and Tolerance in Ireland*, Dublin: College of Industrial Relations. World Drink Trends (2000), Henley-on-Thames: NTC Publications in association with Produktschap voor Gedistilleerde Dranken.

MacGréil, M., (1996), *Prejudice in Ireland Revisited*, Maynooth, Ireland: St Patrick's College.

Mahon, Conlon and Dillon, (1998), *Women and Crisis Pregnancy: A Report to the Department of Health*, Dublin: Stationery Office.

Newcomb, N., (1996), *Child Development: Change Over Time*, (8th Edn), New York: Harper Collins.

O'Connor, P., (2000), 'Ireland: A Man's World', *Economic and Social Review*, 31, 1, 81-102.

OECD1, (2000), *National Accounts of OECD Countries, Main Aggregates*, Vol. 1, Paris: OECD, March.

OECD2, (1999), *Labour Force Statistics 1977-1997*, Paris: OECD.

OECD3, (1998), *Education at a Glance–OECD Indicators 1998*, Paris: OECD.

Population Division of the UN Secretariat, (1998), *United Nations, World Urbanization Prospects: The 1998 Revision*, New York: UN.

Redmond (ed.), (2000), *That was Then, This is Now: Change in Ireland, 1949-99*, Dublin: Stationery Office.

Ruane, F.P., and Sutherland, J.M., (1999), *Women in the Labour Force*, Dublin: Employment Equality Agency.

Smith, P.B. and Bond, M.H., (1993), *Social Psychology Across Cultures*, Hemel Hempstead, England: Harvester Wheatsheaf.

Tonnies, F., (1887), 'Gemeinschaft und Gesellschaft', Leipzig, translated in C.P. Loomis, (1940), *Fundamental Concepts of Sociology*, New York.

Turley, D., (1995), 'The Irish Consumer Through Irish Eyes: European Values Survey 1990', *Irish Marketing Review*, Vol. 8, 91-96.

UN Committee on the Elimination of Discrimination Against Women (1999), *Examination of Ireland's Second and Third Combined Periodic Reports under the UN Convention on the Elimination of Discrimination Against Women: Background and Concluding Comments, Unedited Version*, New York: UN.

Wirth, L., (1938), 'Urbanism as a Way of Life', *American Journal of Sociology*, XLIV, 1-24.

Yang, K. S., (1988), 'Will Societal Modernisation Eventually Eliminate Cross-Cultural Psychological Differences?' in M.H. Bond (ed.), *The Cross-Cultural Challenge to Social Psychology*, Newbury Park, CA: Sage.

Index

Page numbers in italics refer to illustrations.

the role of perception, 146
Levine and Bartlett (1984), 399
Likert scale, 239–41, 271
linguistics, 26
Locke, John, 15
Locurto (1991), 164, 178
Lyons, F.S.L., 394–7, 402

MacGréil, Mícheál, 244–5, 390–91,
    421–2
Maier and Seligman (1976), 141
Mandela, Nelson, 344
Marshall, Barry, 21
Maslow, Abraham, 224
Maslow's Hierarchy of Needs theory,
    282–6, 295, 305, 307, 347
McClelland (1961) — Acquired
    Needs Theory, 288–90, 307
McGregor (1961) — Theory X,
    Theory Y, 288, 290–93, 307–8,
    364, 437
    Higher level needs — can they
        make us work harder?, 291–2
McGregor, Douglas, 356
McHenry, Robert, 291
McKay, D. G., 80–81
measurement of intelligence, 162, 166
measurement of variables, 51–2,
    70–71
    accuracy of measures, 55–7
    temperature scales and the
        absence of a true zero, 56
    interval measurement, 54, 70
    nominal measurement, 52, 70
    ordinal measurement, 52–3, 53, 70
    ratio measurement, 54–5, 70
        measuring wind speed and the
            strength of earthquakes, 55

validity of measurement, 58, 59
reliability of measurement, 56
internal reliability, 57
test-retest reliability, 56–7
measuring personality, 205–8
memory, 6
memory in learning, 146–9, 152
memory tests, 147
Milgram (1963), 257–9
*Minnesota Study of Twins Reared
    Apart*, 213–4
Mitchell (1982), 280, 306
Monochronic time, 399
motivation
    decisional process theories, 295–6
        Equity theory, 299–303
        Expectancy theory, 296–9
        Reinforcement theory, 303–5
    drives and motives, 281–2
    universal needs in Irish society,
        286–7
    universal needs theories, 282, 286
        Alderfer's ERG theory, 285–6
        Maslow's Hierarchy of Needs
            theory, 283–5
    work related needs theories, 288, 295
        Herzberg's Dual Factor theory,
            294
        McClelland (1961) — Acquired
            Needs theory, 288–90
        McGregor (1961) — Theory X,
            Theory Y, 290–93
Muller-Lye illusion, 90, 90, 112–13
Murphy and Zajonc (1993), 82
Murray, Henry, 22

Napier and Gershenfeld (1999), 338,
    343

cknowledgments

The publishers are grateful to the following for permission to reproduce material used in the book:

Bord Failte (pages 232 and 233); Camera Press for pictures of bathroom scales (page 59), Jill Dando (page 75), Halfpenny Bridge Dublin (page 80), B.F. Skinner (page 128), Babe the Pig (page 135), Richard Nixon (page 171), Auschwitz victims (page 184), twin children (page 211), Sigmund Freud (page 217), classroom scene (page 288), family in rural setting (page 360), army on parade (page 369); MacDonagh J. and Weldridge R. for the Figure Ground Illusion (page 91); the Psychological Corporation for simulated items similar to those used in the Wechsler Adult Intelligence Scale (page 157); Sony UK for 'A Seven Person Task Group' (page 323).